# PERSONALITY

## RESEARCH AND THEORY

# PERSONALITY

## RESEARCH AND THEORY

*Nathan Brody*

*The New School for Social Research*

ACADEMIC PRESS  *New York and London*

ACADEMIC PRESS, INC.
111 Fifth Avenue, New York, New York 10003

United Kingdom Edition published by
ACADEMIC PRESS, INC. (LONDON) LTD.
24/28 Oval Road, London NW1

LIBRARY OF CONGRESS CATALOG CARD NUMBER: 78-182632

PRINTED IN THE UNITED STATES OF AMERICA

*To the memory of my father, Abraham Brody*

# CONTENTS

## A CONCLUSION FOR PART ONE

## PART TWO

### Chapter 8  Clinical and Statistical Prediction and Description of Personality

### Chapter 9  Principles of Social Learning

### Chapter 10  The Unconscious

# PREFACE

In writing this book I have attempted to emphasize a number of things which are not traditional in general treatments of the psychology of personality. First, I have emphasized theories and issues which have developed out of empirical research efforts. The theories are those which are subject to disconfirmation and change on the basis of empirical research, and the issues are those which are capable of being resolved by future research or have been resolved (perhaps tentatively) on the basis of available research.

Second, despite my belief that no psychologist has had a greater impact on the study of personality than Freud, I have not attempted a systematic exposition of psychoanalytic theory—although some understanding of this theory would be helpful in dealing with the "paradigm clash" between social learning theory and psychoanalytic theory, which is dealt with in Chapters 9–11. I have chosen to treat psychoanalytic theory in passing for a number of reasons. My sympathies (biases?) lie elsewhere and I feel that the exposition of the theory can be best made by individuals who find its conceptual style congenial. Also a number of books devoted to the systematic exposition of the theory exist (for example, Blum, 1953), and the writings of Freud are widely available and should be read by the student of personality.

Third, I have discussed some studies in great detail and occasionally in juxtaposition with studies apparently leading to opposite conclusions. I have done this in order to give the student some insight into the hazards of the attempt to reach proper conclusions by inferences from empirical work.

This emphasis is compatible with a fourth emphasis—the attempt to indicate the limitations of our knowledge in the area of personality while at the same time indicating promising directions for the future development of a scientifically viable conception of personality which does not now exist.

I hope that this book will be of value to advanced undergraduate and graduate students of personality. It is written at a somewhat more advanced level than is usual. This stems from my attempt to deal critically with existing theory and research. However, I believe the difficulty level of the book does not exceed the difficulty level of books widely used on the undergraduate level in such empirically oriented fields as learning and perception. I hope the book will also be useful to psychologists interested in the area of personality inasmuch as it deals with some material which is not available in other books on personality (for example, an emphasis on the importance of genotypes and constitutional characteristics as sources of individual differences).

# ACKNOWLEDGMENTS

I am deeply grateful to the New School for Social Research. Its generous sabbatical plan provided me with a sabbatical year in London, during which most of this book was written. I am also grateful to the students in my graduate courses in personality who have criticized, improved, and suggested many of the concepts in the book. In particular I would like to mention the contributions of Eugene Beyers, Howard Erlichman, and Roger Zimmerman. My wife, Erness, read large parts of the manuscript and made a number of suggestions for its improvement in matters of style and substance. Finally, it is a pleasure for me to acknowledge a debt to a friend and collaborator from whom I have learned much, Paul Oppenheim.

Tables 2.8, 6.10–6.12 are from *Risk Taking: A Study in Cognition and Personality* by Nathan Kogan and Michael A. Wallach. Copyright (c) 1964 by Holt, Rinehart and Winston, Inc. Reproduced by permission of Holt, Rinehart and Winston, Inc.

Tables 6.6–6.9 are from *The Talented Student:* A Validation of the Creativity–Intelligence Distinction by Michael A. Wallach and Cliff W. Wing, Jr. Copyright (c) 1969 by Holt, Rinehart and Winston, Inc. Reprinted by permission of Holt, Rinehart and Winston, Inc.

The extract appearing on pp. 245–247 is from "Conflict and defense" by George F. Mahl in *Personality: Dynamics, Development and Assessment,* edited by Janis, Mahl, Kagan, and Holt. © 1969 by Harcourt Brace Jovanovich, Inc. and reprinted with their permission.

Extracts appearing on pp. 247 and 248 are from *Social Learning and Personality Development* by Albert Bandura and Richard H. Walters. Copyright (c) 1963 by Holt, Rinehart and Winston, Inc. Reprinted by permission of Holt, Rinehart and Winston, Inc.

Figures 11.1, 11.3; Table 11.5; and the extracts appearing on pp. 249, 252, and 272 are from *Principles of Behavior Modification* by Albert Bandura. Copyright (c) 1969 by Holt, Rinehart and Winston, Inc. Reprinted by permission of Holt, Rinehart and Winston, Inc.

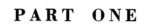

# PART ONE

# CHAPTER 1

# INTRODUCTION

---

## The Study of Personality

The study of personality rests ultimately on the fact of individual differences. Individuals will differ on almost any characteristic which a psychologist chooses to investigate. When these differences form the basis of investigation, we approach the study of personality. Thus, from the point of view expressed in this book, there is no task more fundamental in the study of personality than the attempt to develop a descriptive system which deals with those characteristics of persons which are most essential for the purpose of understanding and predicting their idiosyncratic behavior. This task is logically prior to the study of personality development and change. Before one can ask how persons develop the characteristics which they have, it is necessary to be able to describe those characteristics whose development is being investigated. Similarly, before one can deal with the question of personality change one must be able to describe the characteristics of persons prior to and after the occurrence of a change.

The psychologist interested in the description of personality may use any of a bewildering variety of methods and procedures, each of which can be considered as providing the most fundamental basis of information. One might start with self-report measures in which a person is asked to describe himself either informally or by the use of rating scales. It is possible to assign primacy to such measures on the ground that individuals are the best judges of their own personality. On the other hand, there is a tradition in the psychology of personality, represented by psychoanalytically oriented psychologists, among others, which asserts that individuals may not be aware of the characteristics of their personality which are most fundamental. Such psychologists might wish to supplement self reports by the use of projective techniques such as the Rorschach which allegedly reveal characteristics of persons of which they are only dimly aware. Alternatively, one might attempt to develop dimensions for the description of personality by the use of judgments of a person by other persons who observe him. Reliance on such methods may be suspect in that such judgments may not be impartial or objective, but may be influenced by the characteristics of the person who is the judge. Finally, one might attempt to discover the characteristics of persons by observing their behavior in various situations. One difficulty with this approach stems from the fact that behavior may change fundamentally in different situations. Hence, the attempt to observe behavior in one or more situations may yield a biased and unrepresentative sample of the characteristic behaviors of an individual.

Obviously, the preceding paragraph does not present all of the different kinds of methods or sources of data about persons and does not deal in a comprehensive way with their merits and defects. However, the paragraph should provide sufficient information to support a methodological principle which should circumvent arguments for the primacy of any source of data about personality. That is, in evaluating research on personality we shall put emphasis on the attempt to discover relationships and consistencies among different sources of data. This methodological principle, implicitly and explicitly, forms a leitmotif in several different sections of this book. For example, in evaluating factor analytic approaches to personality, we shall be concerned with the relationship between factors derived from rating scale data and from self-report questionnaires. In discussing projective tests, we shall be concerned with the accuracy of prediction to behavior in other situations which can be achieved on the basis of the analysis of projective test data. Underlying this methodological principle is a kind of skepticism which refuses to accept assertions, either those made by persons about themselves or assertions made by others (including psychologists) about them. Let us examine the meaning of this kind of skepticism. Suppose a psychologist develops a paper-and-pencil test of a characteristic he call altruism. Rather than the acceptance of this label at face value we would be concerned with the network of relationships which relate scores on this alleged test of altruism to other measures and behavior. For example, how do people who differ in altruism behave on various experimental tasks, how do they describe themselves, and how are they described by others? Only subsequent to the examination of such relationships among different sources of data can we begin to refine and develop our conceptions of what is in fact measured by any source of data about personality.

## Plan of This Book

This book is divided into two parts. The first part deals with various attempts to develop dimensions for the description of personality by the use of various kinds of objective tests and measurement procedures. Chapter 2 deals principally with the use of the statistical procedure called factor analysis in order to clarify the relationships which exist among different measures of personality. Chapters 3, 4, and 5 deal with theories which have developed in an attempt to understand what is being measured by personality tests. Chapter 3 deals in general with Eysenck's theory of personality and, in particular, with the relationship between scores on measures of introversion—extraversion and neuroticism developed by him and other behaviors. Chapter 4 deals in general with Spence's theory of anxiety and in particular with the relationship between scores on a measure of anxiety and behavior in a wide variety of experimental tasks. Chapter 5 also deals with the study of the relationship between scores on a test of personality (in this case a projective measure of need achievement) and other behaviors. It emphasizes a theory of risk-taking developed to explain some of these relationships.

Chapter 6 deals with two dimensions of personality which are derived from measurements made of behavior in tasks relating to perceptual and cognitive functioning. In particular, it deals with Witkin's theory of differentiation which is based on an attempt to understand relationships between measures of perceptual behavior and other characteristics. The chapter also deals with research on creativity, emphasizing the relationship between scores on tests of "divergent thinking" ability and other behavior and characteristics of persons. Note that Chapters 2–6 each deal with the study of relationships which obtain among different objective measures of personality. They differ in the measures which they take as their initial focus of investigation: all paper-and-pencil tests and rating scales, etc., tests of introversion–extraversion and neuroticism, a test of anxiety, a test of need achievement, and tests of cognitive abilities.

Chapter 7 ends the first part of the book with a discussion of the sources of the individual differences which have been dealt with in the earlier chapters.

Part 2 deals with a variety of topics which all relate to the validity of clinical psychology and certain procedures for the study of individuals which derive from practices in clinical psychology. The material dealt with in Part 1 presupposes a commitment to the use of various objective procedures for the assignment of characteristics to persons. Such procedures aim to minimize the role of human judgment and attempt to detail scoring procedures which permit the assignment of characteristics to persons by following objective rules. However, it may be the case that our best attempt to understand personality derives from the clinical skills of the trained psychologist, who relies on subjective judgment, intuition and appeal to psychodynamic principles to form a conception of the individual. Chapter 8 deals with this question directly and examines research dealing with clinical prediction and description of personality as well as research which deals with the contrast of clinical and statistical prediction and description. Chapter 9 deals with a theoretical challenge to psychoanalytically oriented personality theories which have developed out of clinical practice posed by social learning theory. Chapters 10 and 11 deal with issues which are central to the evaluation of the "paradigm clash" between traditional psychodynamic theories and social learning theory. Chapter 10 deals with the unconscious and evaluates research purporting to demonstrate unconscious influences on behavior. Chapter 11 deals with the therapeutic procedures which are suggested by social learning theory and contrasts these procedures with psychotherapy. Finally, Chapter 12 presents a conclusion and some suggestions about promising directions for future research.

# CHAPTER 2

# TRAIT THEORY AND FACTOR ANALYSIS

---

## The Discovery of Traits

Traits are consistencies in the characteristic modes of behavior exhibited by an individual in diverse settings. An individual's personality may be described as a collection of traits. In this chapter we shall examine the efforts of psychologists to develop a trait conception of personality.

Traits are usually conceived of as dispositions. A person who has a trait need not invariably exhibit the characteristic mode of behavior described by the trait. When a person is assigned a dispositional trait, one or both of two different meanings is implied—the person exhibits the characteristic mode of behavior described by the trait in a relatively wide variety of situations and/or the person exhibits that behavior in an extreme degree when he does exhibit it. For example, when a person is assigned the disposition to be gregarious, this implies either that the person is usually gregarious and that he tends to be gregarious in many more situations than other people, or that the person is extremely gregarious on those occasions when he is gregarious.

Allport and Odbert (1936) estimated that there are 18,000 words in the English language which designate distinctive forms of personal behavior. Faced with this embarrassment of riches, the psychologist interested in the development of a trait theory of personality has attempted to abstract from this collection of possible trait names a limited number from which he could develop quantitatively varying dimensions which would be applicable to all persons. Each person could then be exhaustively described by indicating his position on each of the trait dimensions.

The development of an adequate trait theory of personality reduces to the discovery of the appropriate set of traits and the development of measures of these traits. For this purpose, psychologists have used a statistical technique called factor analysis.[1] Factor analysis is used by some personality theorists, most notably Cattell (1957, 1965, and Hundleby, Pawlik, and Cattell, 1965) as the foundation for the scientific study of personality.

The factor analytic approach to personality begins with a systematic survey of all devices which are useful for the measurement of any aspect of personality. This would include objective tests, ratings of personality by others, self-report measures of introspective states, measurement of characteristics of physique, physiological measurements such as heart rate and BMR, and objective measurements of characteristic modes of behavior such as length of time a person persists on an insoluble task, etc. Having obtained a population of measures of personality, the factor analyst may then sample in some systematic way some subset of these measures for more intensive investigation. Such an investigation would involve, initially, the administration of this sample or battery of measures to a group of subjects. The data obtained from such an investigation would include a score on each measure for each subject. Initially, the factor analyst would seek to determine the relationship between each pair of measures. This relationship is summarized by a coefficient of correlation.[2] The value of this coefficient can vary between $-1.00$ and $+1.00$. High negative values indicate an inverse relationship between a pair of measures such that persons with high scores on one measure are likely to have low scores on the other; high positive values indicate an opposite pattern of association such that persons with high scores on one measure are likely to have high scores on the other and persons with low scores on one measure are likely to have low scores on the other; a value of correlation close to .00 indicates little or no association between the measures such that knowledge of a person's score on one measure does not indicate a person's score on the other measure. It is possible to obtain, usually with the aid of a computer, the correlation between all possible pairs of measures used in the investigation. In a typical investigation, a factor analyst might have a battery of 100 measures. Such a battery would yield $\binom{100}{2}$ or 4950 correlations between all possible pairs of measures. These correlations

[1] A brief, nontechnical discussion of the method of factor analysis may be found in Cattell (1957). More thorough presentations can be found in Cattell (1952), Fruchter (1954), and Harman (1960).

[2] The reader who is not familiar with the concept of correlation should consult any basic statistics textbook.

TABLE 2.1

*A Correlation Matrix for 100 Measures*

| Tests | 1 | 2 | ... | 99 | 100 |
|---|---|---|---|---|---|
| 1 | | $r_{12}$ | | $r_{1,99}$ | $r_{1,100}$ |
| 2 | | | | $r_{2,99}$ | $r_{2,100}$ |
| . | | | | | |
| . | | | | | |
| . | | | | | |
| 99 | | | | | $r_{99,100}$ |
| 100 | | | | | |

(symbolized by $r$) can be arranged in a correlation matrix as in Table 2.1. The columns and rows of the matrix indicate the different measures or tests used in the investigation. The values in the cells of the matrix would represent the correlations between each pair of tests. Thus, $r_{2,99}$ would indicate the correlation between tests 2 and 99 and in practice would be specified by some value between $-1.00$ and $+1.00$. The factor analysis proper proceeds from this point.

The factor analyst would attempt to discover the minimal number of dimensions or hypothetical factors which need to be postulated in order to account for the correlations in the matrix. An intuitive notion of what is involved in this procedure can be given by considering some hypothetical idealized correlation matrices. Consider a matrix in which all correlations are either $+1.00$ or $-1.00$. Clearly, such a matrix would represent a single factor since knowledge of a person's score on one test would be sufficient to predict scores on all other tests. Consider a matrix in which the values of the correlations between all tests numbered 1–50 were either $+1.00$ or $-1.00$, and the values of the correlations between all tests numbered 51–100 were $+1.00$ or $-1.00$, and finally, the value of all correlations between tests numbered 1–50 and tests numbered 51–100 was .00. In such a case there would be two factors represented in the correlation matrix. One factor would be defined by tests 1–50 and the other factor would be defined by tests 51–100. It would be necessary to know a person's score on each of these factors in order to effectively predict a person's score on each of the tests. A factor may be defined in terms of the tests that are said to "load" on it. The loading of a test on a factor is represented by a hypothetical correlation between a test and the factor. Tests which load or correlate significantly with a factor can serve as "marker" variables for that factor. In the example presented above, tests 1–50 would each correlate $\pm 1.00$ with a factor and would serve as marker variables for that factor; tests 51–100 would each correlate ±1.00 with a different factor and would serve as marker variables for that factor.

It is obvious that obtained correlation matrices would not have the clear structure of the examples used here. Factor analysis permits one to deal with the typical matrix in which the underlying statistical structure is not obvious. The factor analytic technique attempts to find the minimum number of factors which would maximize the loading of a test on one factor and minimize its loading on other factors. Unless the tests have been specially constructed to be pure measures of a factor, the typical test will load on several factors, indicating that it is a measure of several independent things.

By repeating the type of study outlined here many times the factor analyst eventually hopes to investigate the entire domain of personality measures. Hopefully, through the process of repeated investigation some set of common factors will emerge. Factor analysts may use the same or a similar battery of measures with different subjects in order to study the generality of the factor structure. Also, new batteries of tests are studied with the addition of a few marker variables from previous factor analytic investigations in order to study the relationship between new factors and previously discovered factors. A marker variable for a factor which loads highly on that factor may be taken as a relatively pure measure of the factor. If such a marker variable loads highly on a new factor derived from a different investigation, this permits one to infer that the new factor is related to or identical with the previously discovered factor.

The principal factors which emerge from these repeated investigations will represent what Cattell calls the source traits for personality. The meaning of the traits is inductively arrived at by examining the tests which serve as marker variables for the factors and by studying the relationships between scores on the factors and other variables such as success in school. There is at least an initial circularity in the discovery of the meaning of source traits. A trait's meaning is defined principally by the tests which load on the factor which defines the trait. But the meaning of the test, or, more precisely, what the test measures is, in part, known only subsequent to discovery of the factors on which the test loads. As we shall see, the meaning of any personality test is by no means transparent. Personality tests may measure things other than what they appear to measure on casual inspection. The process of discovering the meaning of a source trait is a gradual one subject to repeated refinement. On the basis of the initial studies the factor analyst arrives at some relatively intuitive notion of what is measured by the factor. On the basis of this notion, he may select several measures in a new investigation to study their relationship with the factor. The results of the new investigation serve to refine the intuitive notion of the meaning of the factor. Subsequent to the development of a relatively clear conception of the meaning of a factor, the factor analyst will attempt to develop new tests which are pure measures of the factor. One of the most widely used tests of this type is Cattell's 16 PF, which is a test which is presumed to measure 16 primary factors.

Source traits need not be considered as the ultimate basis for the description of personality. A source trait typically represents an observed covariance or correlation among several different types of measures. For example, the trait UI 16 (UI stands for universal index in Cattell's numbering system) is called unbound, assertive ego versus bound disciplined ego, and it is defined by the following different types of measures: (a) fast speed and tempo which includes rapid physical movement, fast tapping behavior, etc.; (b) high self-assertion; (c) less impairment of performance by frustration; (d) strong physique (Hundleby *et al.*, 1965). Just as a source trait represents something which several diverse things share in common, it is possible to develop still more abstract dimensions which represent observed covariance or correlations among several source traits. In order to develop this idea, it is necessary to distinguish between orthogonal and oblique factor analyses. An orthogonal factor analysis is one in which each factor is statistically independent of every other factor such that the hypothetical correlation among all possible pairs of factors is not significantly different from .00. An oblique factor analysis is one in which factors need not be statistically independent of each other such that the hypothetical correlation between the factors need not be .00. Those psychologists who insist on orthogonal rotations do so, in part, because they find them more mathematically elegant and also because they feel that orthogonal factors are more compatible with the logic of factor analysis in that they represent truly independent dimensions. Cattell has always argued for the necessity of oblique rotation (see Cattell, 1957, Chapter 8). He feels that such rotations are empirically correct and are in fact "forced" upon him by his data. Those theorists who insist on orthogonal rotation are seen by Cattell as refusing to deal with facts because of a commitment to an irrelevant ideal of aesthetic purity.

An oblique factor analysis will result in the discovery of a series of factors which are correlated with each other. The correlations among all possible pairs of such factors may be arranged in a correlation matrix. This correlation matrix may be factor analyzed. The factors which are discovered by this procedure are called second order factors. Personality may be described in terms of source traits based on first order factors, or in terms of a smaller, more abstract set of dimensions based on second order factors. These second-order factors may be called types to distinguish them from traits. A type theory and a trait theory are not antagonistic conceptions of personality. A preference for a trait or type theory represents a preference for a different set of dimensions for the description of personality. The dimensions in a trait description will be more numerous and less abstract than the dimensions in the type description. It is possible to combine both the trait and type approaches into a single descriptive system. This combination leads to a hierarchically structured model of personality represented by several sets of dimensions in which each successive set in the hierarchy contains a decreasing number of dimensions of increasing generality. Figure 2.1 illustrates such a model.

Trait theory may be extended in another direction. Implicit in the factor analytic conception of personality is the assumption that the traits or dimensions which are used to describe personality are the same for all persons. Individuals may differ with respect to their position on the dimensions but the same dimensions are to be used for each person. This is a rather strong assumption. It fails to capture what is at least an intuitively reasonable assumption that certain traits or dimensions are of central importance in the description of a particular personality but only of peripheral importance in the description of someone else's personality. This notion can be built into the trait theory model by adding an additional number to each ordered pair of numbers representing the score for a particular person on a particular trait. This new number would represent the degree to which a particular dimension is relevant for the description of a particular person. "Central" traits for a person would receive higher values than "peripheral" traits. In the limiting case a trait would be as-

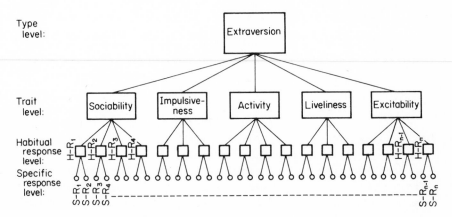

Fig. 2.1. Hierarchial model of personality. Types are supraordinate concepts built up on the observed intercorrelations between traits. (From H. J. Eysenck, *The biological basis of personality*, Figure 14, p. 36, 1967. Courtesy of Charles C. Thomas, Publisher, Springfield, Illinois.)

signed the value zero indicating that it was not relevant for the description of that person. In this way it would be possible to extend the factor analytic model to deal with a situation in which all persons could be described in terms of their position on a limited number of dimensions but the dimensions relevant to the description of any given person need not be exactly the same as the dimensions relevant to the description of another person.

## A Critique of Factor Analytically Derived Trait Theory

For many psychologists, most notably Cattell, the use of factor analysis is a *sine qua non* for the development of a scientific theory of personality. This methodological commitment can be sustained with an argument of compelling clarity. In brief, Cattell would argue that it is necessary to discover the fundamental dimensions of personality before one can discover the laws governing the combination and interrelationships which exist among them. The discovery of the "elements" of a field logically precedes the discovery of laws of their combination. The psychology of personality is in need of some analog of the periodic table of elements in chemistry. Given such a commitment the task for the scientific study of personality, though arduous, is clear—at least in its outlines. Work may now proceed in filling in the details of a system whose basic structure is already manifest. There are a group of psychologists who are either associated with or influenced by Cattell who are energetically engaged in developing this structure. Their articles are frequently concerned with technical problems involved in the use of factor analysis. Such articles deal with the subtleties of the use of an extremely complicated statistical method. Other articles are concerned with refinements of the descriptive system. These publications have acquired an increasingly recondite character. Most psychologists in the area of personality simply do not follow the developments in Cattell's system and fail to be convinced of the logic of his intellectual commitments. It is necessary for the student of personality to clarify his own view as to the legitimacy of Cattell's approach to personality. In what follows we shall examine various criticisms of this approach.

### The Uniqueness Argument

Gordon Allport is the psychologist who has most consistently rejected factor analytically derived traits on the grounds that they fail to do justice to the uniqueness of each person. Allport (1961) objects to the use of traits as the fundamental unit of personality because he argues that traits are, by definition, characteristics which people share in common and by means of which they may be compared. As such they lend themselves to a nomothetic point of view—that is, the discovery of laws whose range of application includes all persons. Allport favors an idiographic point of view—that is, the discovery of laws whose range of applications is limited to an individual person. As a result, Allport prefers as a fundamental unit for the description of personality, personal dispositions. A personal disposition, unlike a trait, is a unique characteristic of a particular person. Allport gives examples of personal dispositions in the following passage: "It would be absurd to compare all people or any large number of them—on a scale designed to measure the peculiar *fastidious exhibitionism* of a Beau Brummel, or the *sexual cruelty* of a Marquis de Sade" (Allport, 1961, pp. 357–358).

The factor analyst would reply to Allport's criticism by asserting that the *fact* of uniqueness is in no way denied by a system based on common traits. If one postulates the existence of several traits and permits an individual to have one of several positions on each trait, it is clear that a vast number of different possible distributions of scores can exist. In fact, given a sufficient number of traits it is easily possible to describe uniquely any individual. Further, it is not clear that personality is unique in any radical sense. Almost everything that is studied by any scientist is unique. The desk on which I am writing is surely unique—if not in design, then by virtue of the idiosyncratic graining of its wood.

Allport replies to the argument that uniqueness is a question of a unique pattern of positions on several common traits as follows: "Personality exists only at a postelementary state; it exists only when the common features of human nature have already interacted with one another and produced a unique, self-continuing or evolving system. . . . I insist only that if we are interested in *personality* we must go beyond the elementarist and reach into the morphogenic realm" (Allport, 1961).

The term "morphogenic" appearing in the quotation from Allport is not clearly defined in his writing (but see Sinnott, 1955). Apparently it refers to a science which deals with the principles which account for the unique combinations which determine the structure or form of something.

Allport's argument is obscure. It is not clear what a postelementary state could be. Is a particular desk in a postelementary state? It is the product, in some sense, of many unique forces which have interacted together to produce it. Therefore, it is not clear why personality is exclusively to be considered postelementary. Further, it is not clear whether Allport wishes to argue that the dimensions of personality are unique to each person and/or that the combination of dimensions is unique for each person. If he wishes to argue that the fundamental dimensions are unique to each person, then his examples apparently contradict his argument. The Marquis de Sade may in fact have had a unique sexual cruelty but the mere fact that his personal disposition can be described by the common terms "sexual" and "cruelty" suggests that the elements which are involved in that personal disposition share much more in common with elements characteristic of many or all men. And if sexuality and cruelty were each unique to the Marquis de Sade then they are not properly called sexuality and cruelty. If the elements which constituted personal dispositions were truly unique, one would have to develop a unique language for the description of the elements which interact to form the unique personality. This does not appear to be feasible.

Alternatively, Allport may mean that the elements combine in unique ways. Subsequent to the discovering of the common dimensions one would have to investigate separately, for each individual, the rules which describe the way in which these elements are combined for him. His latter position is compatible with a factor analytic viewpoint since factor analysts recognize the necessity of discovering combination laws subsequent to the discovery of common elements. However, even here there is room for argument. Combination rules need not be unique. The laws which determine the combination of common dimensions might be valid for groups of individuals who share a common position on two or more common traits. For example, Eysenck (1957) has argued that individuals who are high on both neuroticism and introversion tend to be classified as obsessive compulsive neurotics. A commitment to the view that the discovery of the laws of combination of common characteristics which are valid for a given individual are not valid for any other individual is, at bottom, a commitment to a rather radical indeterminacy. And indeterminacy is rarely, if ever, a useful position for a scientist.

We can conclude that the uniqueness argument against trait theory is without foundation.

## ARE FACTORS INVARIANT?

A minimal condition for the adequacy of a factor analytically derived set of traits is that the hypothetical factors which define the traits must be replicable, or invariant. Just as the discovery of a scientific law rests on the possibility of demonstrating the assumed lawlike relationship in different investigations, so too, the factor analyst must be able to rediscover the fundamental factors in separate investigation. If this condition were not met then each set of factors derived from a particular investigation would be limited in its relevance to that particular investigation. Such a limitation would preclude the possibility of developing a universally valid descriptive system.

The demonstration of factor invariance or replicability is not a simple matter. One should expect the pattern of relations among tests to change

as a result of differences in types of subjects, the composition of the battery of tests, and the conditions of the administration of the tests. Nevertheless, the validity of a set of factors is ultimately dependent on their
replicability. In the older studies, factor invariance was determined by
intuition. Each investigator would examine the set of factors arrived at
and then come to some intuitive judgment as to whether or not the factors
were identical or similar to those found in previous research. This judgment was not completely arbitrary but was based on an examination of
the tests which loaded on the factor. If the pattern of loadings of a set of
tests on a factor appeared similar to the pattern of loadings of the same
or similar tests on a factor previously discovered, the new factor was
judged to be similar to or identical with the previously discovered factor.
This procedure is unsatisfactory since it does not permit an objective
measure of replicability. The possibility exists that the factor analyst is
merely replicating his intuitive interpretations of the factors.

The newer studies dealing with this question have relied on objective
analytical techniques—although there is no completely satisfactory solution to the determination of factor invariance (see Hundleby *et al.*, 1965,
Chapter 3 for a discussion of the technical problems involved).

Peterson (1965) has reported the results of a series of studies of factor
invariance. Factor invariance is determined as follows: Each factor is defined in terms of a series of marker variables—that is, a variable whose
loading on the factor is above some minimum value—usually $\pm.10$. A
second study is conducted using a similar or identical set of variables but
a different population of subjects. Subsequent to the factor analysis of
the data of the second study some attempt is made to see if, on the basis
of an intuitive judgment, the factors derived from the second study are
the same as those derived from the first study. A factor derived from the
second study may be considered the same as a factor derived from the first
study if both factors are defined by the same marker variables and if the
marker variables load the same for both factors. Thus, if variables numbered 3, 17, and 49 have loadings on a particular factor from the initial
investigation of .70, $-.43$, and $+.19$ respectively, these tests ought to
exhibit the same loadings on a factor derived from the second study which
is allegedly identical with the factor derived from the first study. The
degree to which the loadings are in fact similar can be measured by a
correlation between the respective loadings of the marker variables on the
allegedly invariant factors. Further, the degree of similarity of any factor
derived from the first study with any factor from the second study can be
determined by the correlation between the loadings of the marker variables of the first factor with those variables on the second factor. Factors
which are invariant should have high positive correlations, those which

TABLE 2.2

*A Hypothetical Matrix of Correlations between Loadings of Marker Variables for Factors Derived from Two Studies*

|  |  | Study 2 | | | | |
|---|---|---|---|---|---|---|
|  |  | $F_{2,1}$ | $F_{2,2}$ | $F_{2,3}$ | $\cdots$ | $F_{2,N}$ |
| | $F_{1,1}$ | 1.00 | .20 | .20 | | .20 |
| *Study 1* | $F_{1,2}$ | | 1.00 | .20 | | .20 |
| | $F_{1,3}$ | | | 1.00 | | .20 |
| | . | | | | | |
| | . | | | | | |
| | $F_{1,N}$ | | | | | 1.00 |

are not should have substantially lower correlations. A matrix of correlations between marker variables can be constructed as in Table 2.2.

The rows of the matrix in Table 2.2 represent the factors derived from the first study. For example, $F_{1,3}$ is to be understood as the third factor derived from the first study. The columns represent the allegedly invariant factors derived from the second study. Thus $F_{2,3}$ represents that factor derived from the second study which is allegedly invariant with Factor 3 of the first study. The "on diagonal" correlations of 1.00 indicate factor invariance. The lower "off diagonal" correlations indicate that factors which are not judged to be invariant are not in fact invariant.

Table 2.3 presents an actual matrix of such correlations obtained by Peterson in an investigation in which he compared two sets of factors derived from ratings of young adults with a set of factors derived from ratings of seven-year-old children (Cattell and Coan, 1957).

The basis for deciding which factors were invariant were the judgments of Cattell and Coan. The matrix does not offer impressive evidence for invariance. If we start with the factors derived from ratings by adults and examine the correlations of the loadings of their marker variables with those variables for the factor derived from the ratings of the children by looking at the correlations within each column, we find that in five of the nine cases there are allegedly noninvariant factors from the children's study which have higher relationships with the factor derived from the adults' study than the allegedly invariant factor. In most of the cases the "on diagonal" correlations are not substantially higher than the "off diagonal" correlations. Peterson (1965) points out that these data clearly contradict the argument for factor invariance for these two sets of factors.

TABLE 2.3

*A Matrix of Correlations Measuring Factor Invariance Based on Judgments Made by Cattell and Coan*

|            |   | Adults | | | | | | | | |
|------------|---|----|----|----|----|----|----|----|----|----|
|            |   | A  | E  | F  | G  | H  | I  | J  | L  | M  |
|            | A | *08* | 06 | 32 | 03 | 32 | 20 | 05 | 18 | 51 |
|            | E | 49 | *32* | 33 | 21 | 29 | 10 | 14 | 07 | 24 |
|            | F | 21 | 03 | *49* | 02 | 13 | 12 | 41 | 02 | 28 |
|            | G | 35 | 32 | 19 | *61* | 24 | 04 | 28 | 24 | 20 |
| *7-year-olds* | H | 01 | 07 | 29 | 25 | *70* | 08 | 18 | 14 | 04 |
|            | I | 23 | 07 | 06 | 32 | 16 | *41* | 13 | 45 | 01 |
|            | J | 56 | 07 | 01 | 22 | 01 | 06 | *37* | 17 | 07 |
|            | L | 18 | 11 | 11 | 18 | 13 | 19 | 17 | *40* | 03 |
|            | M | 14 | 00 | 28 | 21 | 22 | 07 | 01 | 23 | *14* |

From D. R. Peterson, Scope and generality of verbally defined personality factors. *Psychological Review*, 1965, **72,** 48–59.

Further, these data are typical of the usual matrix of correlations which is obtained in the examination of factor invariance.

Hundleby *et al.* (1965) have summarized a good deal of the evidence dealing with factor replicability for factors derived from objective tests. One of the methods they use to measure factor replicability is derived from an analysis of variance technique.[3] This method involves the comparison of a factor repeatedly discovered in a series of studies involving a series of common measures. One can arrange the loadings of a group of common tests on an allegedly invariant factor in the form of a matrix as in Table 2.4.

In Table 2.4 there are $n$ tests and $N$ studies. $L_{2,3}$ would represent the loading of Test 2 in Study 3 on a particular factor and $L_{3,N}$ would represent the loading of Test 3 on the $N$th study on the allegedly invariant factor. If the matched factor discovered in several independent studies is in fact invariant, then the values within a row should be identical and the variability within a row should be minimal. However, the values within a column should be different from each other since different tests should not, in general, have the same loadings on the same factor. Thus the variability between the rows should be relatively large. That is, the average

---

[3] Elementary discussions of the analysis of variance technique may be found in many basic statistics textbooks. A simple and clear presentation may be found in Spence, Underwood, Duncan, and Cotton (1968). A more comprehensive presentation can be found in Winer (1962).

TABLE 2.4

*A Matrix Representing the Loadings of the Same Tests on an Allegedly Invariant Factor Derived from Several Different Studies*

| | Studies | | | | |
|---|---|---|---|---|---|
| *Tests* | 1 | 2 | 3 | $\cdots$ | N |
| 1 | $L_{1,1}$ | $L_{1,2}$ | $L_{1,3}$ | | $L_{1,N}$ |
| 2 | $L_{2,1}$ | $L_{2,2}$ | $L_{2,3}$ | | $L_{2,N}$ |
| 3 | $L_{3,1}$ | $L_{3,2}$ | $L_{3,3}$ | | $L_{3,N}$ |
| . | | | | | |
| . | | | | | |
| . | | | | | |
| $n$ | $L_{n,1}$ | $L_{n,2}$ | $L_{n,3}$ | | $L_{n,N}$ |

loadings of each of the tests should be different. The ratio of between row variability to within row variability permits a statistical test of the significance of the judgments of factor invariance. Of the eleven factors for which Hundleby *et al.* (1965) provide data of this type, the $F$ ratio formed in this way is not significant for three of the factors. This result can be taken to imply that, for these factors, the loading of the same test on an allegedly invariant factor in different studies is no more similar than the loading of different tests on the same factor in a particular study. Thus, for these three factors, there is no evidence of factor invariance at all. For the remaining factors, the $F$ values are statistically significant, although not very impressive in magnitude. These values range from 1.55 to 3.99 with a median value of about 2.00. These data for the factors which are significantly matched indicate that, on the average, a test's loading on an allegedly matched factor will show more similarity in different investigations than the loadings of different tests on the same factor. However, these data do not show whether other factors derived in a particular investigation are more similar to a particular factor than the factor judged to be invariant. That is, this method provides no basis for the comparison of matched allegedly invariant factors with those which are not matched and thus not allegedly invariant. Further, the rather low $F$ values might be higher if the matchings were made on a different basis. In any case the low $F$ values even for those factors for which the $F$ is significant suggests that the factors are not clearly invariant. All that these values indicate is there is some basis for the matching and some similarity among the matched factors for eight of the eleven factors.

The results of our brief survey of some of the data on factor invariance for Cattell's first-order oblique factors is not encouraging. These data indicate very little basis for assuming that there is a neat factor structure which is replicable in investigations using the same tests with different kinds of subjects.

There is an additional type of factor invariance in which one uses different types of tests involving different methods of measurement with the same subjects. For example, one could derive an introversion–extraversion factor based on self report measurements and an introversion–extraversion factor based on ratings of another person. If the introversion–extraversion factors discovered by these two different methods of measurement are in fact the same factor, a person's score on each of the factors should be the same. If, however, the correlation between a person's scores on the two factors with the same name derived from different methods of measurement is low, then the factors cannot be considered to represent the same trait. If factor analysis is to be used to define the basic traits of personality, then measures based on grossly different methods of measurement should coalesce into a common factor structure. Cattell (1957) has in fact argued that many of the factors derived from self-report methods of measurement are invariant with factors derived from behavior ratings. In order to test for this invariance it is necessary to present a battery of measures containing self-report measures to a group of subjects. These same subjects should also be rated by appropriate individuals on a battery of behavior rating measures. Each set of measures must then be factor analyzed separately. Then, on the basis of an examination of the factors, an attempt should be made to match the factors derived from the two separate methods of measurement. If the factors are invariant, a person's score on matched factors should be identical. Thus, the correlation between scores on matched factors should be close to +1.00 and the correlation between scores on nonmatched factors derived from different methods of measurement should be substantially lower than 1.00. Becker (1960) has summarized the results of several investigations of this problem and has concluded that Cattell's first-order factors derived from self-report data are *not* invariant with those derived from behavior ratings. For example, he reports the results of a study of Meeland (as cited in Becker, 1960) in which the average correlation between matched factors is .37 and the average correlation between nonmatched factors is .32. Peterson (1965) has reported similar data from a study by Wetzel (cited in Peterson, 1965) who administered Cattell's 16 P.F. test to a group of college subjects and obtained behavior ratings for these *S*s on the traits measured by 16 P.F. The correlations between scores on the traits with the same name were not substantially higher than the correlations between scores on traits with different names. Peterson (1965) concludes that Cattell's first-order oblique factors are not invariant over different methods of measurement. Taken with the evidence for the replicability of factors derived from the same tests given to different kinds of subjects, these data provide little evidence for the descriptive adequacy of Cattell's first order factors.

Factor invariance is more easily demonstrated for second-order factors. Peterson (1965) reports that second-order factors tend to be relatively invariant when based on the same tests given to different types of subjects. For example, he reports that the second-order factors derived from the studies of behavior ratings of adults and seven-year-old children reported in Table 2.4 tend to be invariant. In each study two second-order factors were derived. The factors were labeled Adjustment and Extraversion–Introversion. The correlations between the loadings of the marker variables for the second-order factors for the two studies are presented in Table 2.5.

The results presented in Table 2.5 provide clear evidence for the existence of replicable second-order factors. That is, there are high positive "on-diagonal" correlations and substantially lower "off-diagonal" correlations. Further, Peterson reports some correlations between second-order factors derived from self-report and behavior ratings which indicate that the second-order factors correlate reasonably well with behavior ratings of the characteristics measured by the second-order factor. These results indicate that, at present, a descriptive system based on a small number of highly general second-order factors would appear to be the only type of factor analytically derived system for which there is empirical evidence of invariance over different types of subjects and different methods of measurement. These results would favor a type theory rather than a trait theory. In the next chapter we shall discuss Eysenck's descriptive system.

TABLE 2.5

*A Matrix of Correlations Measuring Factor Invariance for Second-Order Factors Obtained from a Study by Cattell and Coan*

|  |  | 7-year-olds | |
| --- | --- | --- | --- |
|  |  | *Adjustment* | *Extraversion–Introversion* |
| | *Adjustment* | .42 | .27 |
| *Adults* | *Extraversion–Introversion* | .10 | .83 |

From D. R. Peterson, Scope and generality of verbally defined personality factors. *Psychological Review*, 1965, **72**, 48–59.

Eysenck's theory employs a factor analytically derived descriptive system based on four trait dimensions which would be, in Cattell's system, second-order factors.

There are a number of possible reasons for the difficulty of replicating first order oblique factors. Peterson (1965) points out that factors are typically extracted in terms of their importance in accounting for the obtained pattern of correlation. The second factor extracted typically accounts for less than half the variance of the first. The factors extracted after the third or fourth factor typically account for very little of the variance and as a result are difficult to replicate. Hundleby *et al.* (1965) discuss a number of reasons why factors are difficult to replicate. These include the possibility that factor structures may differ among different populations of subjects, the possibility that different tests may be required to measure the same characteristics in different types of subjects, and the fact that the marker variables which define a factor change in successive studies leading to the refinement of the factor. All of the above considerations help explain why it is difficult to demonstrate clear replicability for factors. But until such replicability is demonstrated the use of factor analytically derived traits based on first order factors as a descriptive system for personality rests on faith rather than fact.

## SITUATIONS AND TRAITS

In a presidential address given to the American Psychological Association in 1955, Lee J. Cronbach (Cronbach, 1957) argued that psychology had been pursued from two radically different perspectives—individual differences and experimental psychology. The individual difference psychologist takes as his point of departure the naturally occurring differences among individuals. He attempts to find those characteristics of individuals which will be useful in predicting their behavior in as diverse a set of situations as possible. Any variations in a consistent mode of behavior exhibited by an individual as a result of variation in the situation in which he finds himself are treated as errors and are not the subject of investigation in their own right. The experimental psychologist takes as his point of departure his ability to manipulate the environment and studies the effects of this manipulation on the behavior of his subjects. Individual differences in reaction to the environmental manipulation are treated as error and are indicative of the failure of the experimental psychologist to obtain control over the behavior he is investigating. Such individual differences are not the subject of investigation in their own right. Consequently, each type of approach to psychology investigates that which the other type ignores or treats as error.

A neat illustration of these two contrasting approaches can be seen in the differences between two types of industrial psychologists, the human engineer and the personnel psychologist. The human engineer attempts to manipulate working conditions in order to create an environment in which any ordinary individual can function effectively. He ignores individual differences and concentrates on environmental manipulations. The personnel psychologist typically accepts the working conditions of a particular job as fixed. He focuses on individual differences in ability to perform the job.

Cronbach (1957) argues for the necessity of combining these two approaches to psychology. Trait theory is clearly allied to the individual difference approach. Nevertheless Cattell has recognized the importance of considering the contribution of the situation to the determination of behavior. Cattell (1957, 1965) points out that even with a complete knowledge of all of the traits of an individual, it would not be possible to predict his behavior without knowledge of the characteristics of the situation in which a person finds himself. Since a trait is really a dispositional characteristic, it will determine behavior in some situations and not in others. Cattell has attempted to develop a multivariate descriptive system for situations which is derivative from his multivariate descriptive system for traits. This descriptive system is obtained as follows: A response measure is obtained for a group of individuals in a particular situation. For example, grades in high school might be obtained. Each of the individuals in the group is given a battery of measures in order to ascertain their position on a set of source traits. Then, correlations are obtained, separately, between scores on each of the traits and the response measure from the situation. This procedure permits one to discover which traits make a contribution to performance in a particular situation. Furthermore, by examining the direction and magnitude of the correlations one can determine the extent to which each of the traits is involved. A situation may then be described in terms of the traits which contribute to performance in that situation, combined with an indication of the direction and magnitude of the contribution of each of these traits. For example, Cattell states that "classroom performance is an intelligence demanding, introvert favoring, emotional stability testing, docility-rewarding situation" (Cattell, 1965, p. 249).

Does this conception of the relation between situations and source traits represent an appropriate approach to the problem of combining individual difference psychology and experimental psychology? Cattell's multivariate description of a situation is obtained by assuming that situations uniformly engage a trait in all individuals who have that trait. Consider the trait of anxiety. Cattell's approach involves the assumption that each situation will elicit a uniform amount of anxiety in all individuals who have a common position on the anxiety dimension. This seems counterintuitive. For example, some persons might become anxious in intellectual testing situations but not in athletic situations and other persons might become anxious in athletic situations but not in intellectual testing situations. This example suggests that persons might show a common position on a trait but the situation required to elicit the trait disposition might be different for different persons.

There are data relevant to this issue. Consider an experiment by Feather (1961). By use of a theory which we will describe in detail in another chapter, Feather was able to derive the following prediction: individuals high in need for achievement would persist longer on an insoluble task which they were led to believe was easy than individuals low in need achievement; individuals low in need for achievement would persist longer on an insoluble task which they were led to believe was difficult than individuals high in need for achievement. Feather (1961) obtained results which supported his predictions.

How would Feather's results be treated in Cattell's system? First, if persistence is treated as a trait then these results would appear to contradict Cattell's assumption that the situations which elicit a particular trait are the same for all individuals who have that trait. Feather's results permit us to view a trait disposition as being expressed differently in different individuals. Alternatively, one could argue that there are two separate independent traits involved in Feather's experiment, the tendency to persist in insoluble situations which are initially assumed to be difficult and the tendency to persist in insoluble situations which are initially assumed to be easy. This latter conception requires one to define a trait with reference to the situations in which the trait would be elicited. Such a procedure would be at variance with Cattell's attempt to discover source traits which determine an individual's reactions in the widest possible set of situations. Further, the effect of such a situational specification of traits would be to significantly increase the number of traits which would be required to describe personality. And this latter requirement is apparently contraindicated by what is known of the replicability of narrowly defined factors.

The above argument implies that Cattell's approach to specifying the interrelationship of personality and situation is inadequate. What is at issue here is the choice of a starting point for the development of a theory of personality. Cattell demonstrates a fundamental commitment to an individual difference point of view by beginning his investigation with the search for those characteristics of the individual which are of general importance in the widest variety of situations. Situational differences are only dealt with in a limited and derivative fashion subsequent to the development of a descriptive system for individual differences in personality.

An alternative starting point for the development of personality theory is exemplified in the research of Endler and Hunt (1966). They report the results of a series of statistical analyses of the S-R Inventory of Anxiousness (Endler, Hunt, & Rosenstein, 1962). This inventory samples 14 different modes of anxiety responses in each of 11 situations. Thus, there are 154 items. For example, a subject is asked to indicate on a 5-point scale ranging from not at all to much faster whether his heart beats faster when he is starting off on a long automobile trip. Each of the items is written such that a higher score indicates a more anxious response. Scores on this inventory may be attributable to three major sources of variance and their combinations. First, subjects may differ among themselves. That is, certain individuals may report that they are consistently anxious in all situations and other individuals may state that they rarely are anxious. Second, situations may differ such that certain situations characteristically elicit reports of more anxious responding than other situations. Third, responses may differ such that certain modes of response may occur quite often in anxiety producing situations and other modes of response may occur rarely in anxiety producing situations. Finally, any possible combination of these sources may contribute to scores on the inventory. For example, a particular person may report many anxiety responses in a particular situation but not in another. Or, a particular person may respond in terms of certain types of anxiety responses in one situation but with other types of responses in other situations. Endler and Hunt (1966) report the results of statistical analysis of three administrations of this inventory to three samples of college students. By the use of an analysis of variance procedure they were able to estimate the percent of the total variation in scores attributable to the various components which determine the score. Table 2.6 presents the results of their analysis. An examination of Table 2.6 indicates that for this self-report measure of anxiety, differences among individuals are not the major source of variance. Differences in response modes seem to be the major single source of variance. A considerable portion of the variance is contained in the various interactions found by combining two of the three sources of variance. Endler and Hunt (1966) point out that a more comprehensive and adequate description of personality traits may be developed by considering the possibility that a particular individual has a preferred mode of expressing a trait in a particular situation. In any case, their results indicate that the attempt to describe personality in terms of traits without reference to modes of response and situations may not be warranted

TABLE 2.6

*Estimated Variance Components and Percentages for Each Component Derived from a Three-Way Analysis of Variance (Random-Effects Model) of Reported Responses to Situations in the S–R Inventory of Anxiousness from Illinois, Penn State, and York Samples*

| Source | Illinois (N = 67) | | Penn State (N = 169) | | York (N = 53) | |
|---|---|---|---|---|---|---|
| | Variance component | Percent | Variance component | Percent | Variance component | Percent |
| Subject (S) (p) | .213 | 10.42 | .103 | 5.75 | .124 | 6.88 |
| Situation (Sit) (i) | .149 | 7.29 | .094 | 5.25 | .109 | 6.05 |
| Mode of Response (M-R) (j) | .399 | 19.53 | .438 | 24.44 | .425 | 23.57 |
| S × Sit (pi) | .202 | 9.89 | .179 | 9.99 | .181 | 10.04 |
| S × M-R (pj) | .349 | 17.08 | .200 | 11.16 | .201 | 11.15 |
| Sit × M-R (ij) | .131 | 6.41 | .118 | 6.58 | .123 | 6.82 |
| Residual (r) | .600 | 29.37 | .660 | 36.83 | .640 | 35.50 |
| Total variation (components sum) | 2.043 | 99.99 | 1.792 | 100.00 | 1.803 | 100.01 |

From N. S. Endler & J. McV. Hunt, Sources of behavioral variance as measured by the S-R inventory of anxiousness. *Psychological Bulletin*, 1966, **65,** 336–346.

since individual differences *per se* may not be a major determinant of the reaction of an individual to a particular situation.

## ORGANIZATION AND RELATIONSHIP AMONG TRAITS

In order to predict the specific response made by an individual in a particular situation it is necessary to know the relationship among the several traits which enter into the determination of the response to be predicted. For this purpose, Cattell refers to what is called a specification equation of the form, $R = S_1T_1 + S_2T_2 + S_3T_3$. The equation indicates the weights $(S_1S_2\cdots)$ to be applied to each relevant trait score of an individual inorder to predict the response of that individual to a particular situation. The equation represents the simplest possible prediction formula—a weighted linear, additive model. Cattell has indicated that this type of equation is only a first approximation and may not take account of some of the complexities of the relationship among traits and between traits and the response to be predicted. Traits may be curvilinearly related to the response to be predicted. For example, high or low scores on a trait may be indicative of good performance in a situation and intermediate scores may be indicative of poor performance. Such a possibility would be precluded by the form of the specification equation used by Cattell. In addition, the relations among traits may be poorly approximated by the additive relation used by Cattell. Cattell (1965) points out that the relation between a predicted response and a scores on a trait may be modified by position on some other trait. For example, Cattell (1965, p. 251) indicates that the source trait surgency versus desurgency (high surgency is associated with cheerful, sociable, energetic, humorous, talkative, and placid characteristics) acts as a catalyst on sociometric popularity. If a person has a pattern of trait scores which would dispose him to be sociometricaly popular (for example, warm, dependable, etc.) then his popularity is mangified if he is high in surgency. If such a person is low on surgency or desurgent then his sociometric popularity score is lowered. Conversely, if a person has a pattern of trait scores which would dispose him to be sociometrically unpopular, high scores on surgency will magnify this effect and low scores will dampen it. The effect of surgency on sociometric popularity cannot be represented in Cattell's specification equation. The surgency example indicates that the relationship between scores on a source trait and some response cannot be stated independent of knowledge of position with respect to another trait, in this case surgency–desurgency.

In the example given above, surgency acts as a moderator variable. A moderator variable is a variable which influences the magnitude and/or direction of the relationship between two other variables. Consider the following extreme example of a moderator variable. The correlation between variables 1 and 2 is $+1.00$ for individuals above the median on variable 3. The correlation between variables 1 and 2 is $-1.00$ for individuals below the median on variable 3. In this case variable 3 acts as a moderator variable for the relationship between variables 1 and 2. Clearly, one cannot predict the relation between variables 1 and 2 without knowledge of position with respect to variable 3. Cattell clearly recognizes the possibility that source traits may act as moderator variables as our discussion of the role of surgency indicates. Presumably, the problems created by the existence of moderator variables are to be dealt with by introducing changes in the form of the specification equation. For example, one could write separate weighted linear additive equations for individuals with different surgency scores when predicting popularity. In Cattell's descriptive system, moderator variables are dealt with only subsequent to the discovery of the source traits. However, moderator variables can exist not only with respect to the relationship among source traits but also with respect to the measures which serve to define the traits. However, factor analysis ignores the existence of such moderator variables and assumes, in effect, that they do not exist. For the purpose of a factor analysis the relationship between any pair of measures is exhaustively described by a correlation between them without reference to any other variable. This position represents an extreme view of the patterning of relationships among measures of personality. The other extreme would be represented by an assumption that measures of personality are completely configurated such that knowledge of position with respect to all remaining measures is necessary to define the relationship between any pair of measures. The meaning of this continuum can be clarified by extending the notion of moderator variables. Just as a single variable may act as a moderator variable, any pair of variables may act as joint moderator variables. In this case knowledge of position with respect to a pair of variables is necessary to predict the relationship between two other variables. Table 2.7 illustrates a hypothetical example of a double moderator effect. The hypothetical correlations in Table 2.7 indicate that the relationship between variables 1 and 2 cannot be defined independent of knowledge with respect to position on both variables 3 and 4. In this instance variables 3 and 4 act as joint moderator variables for the relation between variables 1 and 2. A minimum of four separate correlations would be required to adequately summarize the relationship between variables 1 and 2. It should be obvious that moderator variables can exist at any level of complexity—single, double, triple, quadruple, etc. The hypothetical case of a completely configurated set of $N$ measures would be represented by the situation in which the relationship between any pair of measures in the set can only be defined by knowledge of position with respect to the $N - 2$ remaining measures which act jointly as moderator variables. Thus, if there was a set of ten completely configurated measures of personality, the relationship between any pair of them would be subject to moderator variables of the 8th degree. As a result it would require (assuming a median split for each variable) $2^8$ or 256 correlations to represent the relationship between each pair of variables.

TABLE 2.7

*A Hypothetical Example of a Double Moderator Effect*

|  |  | Variable 3 | |
|  |  | --- | --- |
|  |  | *High* | *Low* |
| *Variable 4* | *High* | $r_{12} = +1.00$ | $r_{12} = -1.00$ |
|  | *Low* | $r_{12} = -1.00$ | $r_{12} = +1.00$ |

TABLE 2.8

*Correlations for Males between Choice of a Risky Strategy and Verbal Aptitude as Measured by the College Board Tests*

|              |      | Defensiveness | |
|--------------|------|------|------|
|              |      | *Low* | *High* |
| *Test anxiety* | *Low*  | .45   | .28   |
|              | *High* | − .39 | .33   |

Based on Kogan & Wallach, 1964.

Kogan and Wallach (1964) have used moderator variables in their research on risk-taking. In their study they used triple moderator variables. They studied the relationship between pairs of risk-taking measures moderated by sex, test anxiety, and defensiveness. Table 2.8 is adapted from one of the tables published by them. The table represents correlations between a tendency to adopt a risky strategy in a betting task and scores on the verbal test of the College Entrance Examination Board for male subjects. Table 2.8 indicates that the relationship between these two variables is subject to moderator variable effects. For male subjects in their study who were high in Text Anxiety and low in Defensiveness, the correlation is negative whereas it is positive for the other male subgroups.

The existence of moderator variables, as illustrated in the work of Kogan and Wallach, poses great difficulties for factor analysis. As we have seen, the factor analyst assumes, in effect, that there are no moderator variables—a clearly untenable assumption. Using a large battery of measures, it is not possible to systematically search for all possible moderator variable effects. For example, if we started with 100 measures it would be necessary to compute 4950 correlations in order to perform a conventional factor analysis. If one considers the possibility that any variable may act as a moderator variable for any pair of variables one would have to compute 196 correlations to examine the relationship between each pair of variables (this assumes that the potential moderator variables may be dealt with dichotomously). This procedure deals only with the possibility of single moderator effects. In order to consider double moderator variables the relationship between each of the 4950 different pairs of variables would have to be examined separately for individuals who differed with respect to position on any pair of remaining variables. This would involve the computation of 19,012 separate correlations for each pair of variables $\left[ \binom{98}{2} \times 4 \right]$. It should be obvious that it is impossible to systematically search for all possible moderator variables in a large battery of measures. Further, if measures of personality are completely configured, that is, subject to moderation by combinations of all remaining variables, this possibility can never be empirically demonstrated. (It could, however, be taken as a postulate.) The impossibility of empirically establishing the existence of completely configured sets of measures follows first, from the impossibility of examining all of the necessary correlations and, second, from the fact that each consideration of a higher-order moderator variable decreases the number of subjects for whom each of the possible correlations of measures is obtained. For example, if one wishes to search for a tenth-order moderator variable, it would be necessary to divide the sample of subjects into 1024 subgroups. If one assumes that a minimum of 30 subjects are required for each correlation, then one would require something in excess of 30,000 subjects.

Our discussion of moderator variables may be taken as having established two things. First, any approach which assumes that they do not exist cannot adequately represent the pattern of relationships which may exist among measures of personality. Second, any approach which assumes that moderator variables exist at the highest level of complexity excludes all empirical attempts to demonstrate their existence. In the face of these extremes, some compromise is required. One possible compromise would involve the more complete investigation of smaller sets of measures—perhaps chosen for their theoretical relevance—in order to study more thoroughly the pattern of relationships which exist among the variables. Such a position would represent a withdrawal from Cattell's insistence on a multivariate approach to the discovery of traits involving the simultaneous examination of a large battery of measures. However, Cattell's approach is, as we have seen, viable only at the price of a superficial examination of the possible relationships among variables. This criticism of Cattell is analogous to our previous criticism of Cattell's treatment of the relationship between traits and situations. In both instances Cattell wishes to deal with the complexities created by the influence of situations and by the relationship among variables on an *a posteriori* basis—subsequent to the discovery of traits. And in both of these cases, we have argued that these complexities interfere with the discovery and definition of the traits themselves.

METHOD VARIANCE AND THE INTERPRETATION OF FACTORS

In order to arrive at a proper conception of the meaning of a factor, it is necessary to have some conception of what is being measured by the tests which define the factor. Tests which are assumed to measure the same trait in different ways may not correlate highly with each other, and, as a result, cannot be considered as measures of the same trait. Differences in measures as a result of the use of different methods of measurement are attributable to what is called method variance. Where method variance is present, the results of any measurement procedure are, in fact, attributable to the idiosyncrasies of the method of measurement, independent of the nature of what is measured.

A neat illustration of method variance comes from the results of a study by Cartwright, Kirtner, and Fiske (1963). They measured changes between pre- and posttherapy scores for a group of students given psychotherapy at a University Counseling Center. They factor-analyzed these change scores and derived five interpretable factors. The first factor was defined as change in the client's perception of his adjustment. Only self report measures loaded significantly on this factor. The second factor was based on change scores derived from judgments of clinical psychologists other than the therapist using the Thematic Apperception Test. The third factor was based exclusively on judgments made by the client's therapist. The fourth factor was defined by change scores on the Minnesota Multiphasic Personality Inventory (MMPI), an objective paper and pencil test of personality. The fifth factor dealt with length of time in psychotherapy. The factors were orthogonal. None of the factors may be taken as representing an adequate measure of change or improvement as a result of psychotherapy. Rather, each of the first four factors is representative of changes as a result of psychotherapy when a particular method of measurement is used to assess change.

The existence of method variance in measures of personality points to the difficulty of interpreting what is being measured by any personality test. If it is difficult to interpret what is being measured by any personality test, then the interpretation of factors derived from these tests is made difficult. In fact, tests may correlate with each other due to shared method variance and an interpretation of such a correlation based on the content of the test may accordingly be erroneous.

There has been a considerable amount of controversy about the role of method variance in self report measures of personality. One reason for this controversy stems from the fact that a response to any item in a personality test is ambiguous with respect to its basis. Consider the response, "No" to the item, "Do you go to the movies frequently?" The response may indicate at least three fundamentally different kinds of things. First, the response may be based on the manifest content of the item, and may therefore be accepted at face value as indicative of the fact that the individual does not believe that he attends the movies frequently. Second, the response may be based on the latent rather than the manifest content of the item. For example, the person may wish to answer each item in such a way that his response will portray him in a favorable light to the psychologist. Further, the subject might believe that a "Yes" response to this item might indicate he was frivolous. Therefore, he chooses to answer "No." His answer in this case is in response to the content of the item but is not a response to what would appear to be the obvious or manifest content of the item. In such a case the response is to the latent content on the item and is dependent on what may be called a *response set*. Third, the response may be independent of the manifest or latent content of the item—in which case the response is determined by a *response style* (see Rorer, 1965). For example, the person may have a tendency to respond in the negative direction irrespective of the content of the item. If response styles and response sets are present in measures of personality, then interpretations of the meaning of measures based on their manifest content will be erroneous.

Are response sets and response styles important determinants of the response to self report personality measures? Let us begin with the evidence for response styles. The response style which has been most systematically investigated is acquiescence—the tendency to respond consistently true or "Yes" versus the tendency to respond consistently false or "No" to items irrespective of the content of the item. There are three kinds of studies which have traditionally been used to indicate the presence of acquiescence—reliability studies, item reversal studies, and factor analytic studies. Reliability studies require the administration of the same test to the same subject on two different occasions. Two test scores are assigned to each subject. Each test score represents his score on the test when the test is scored for the number of acquiescent (Yes or True or Agree) responses made by the subject. High positive correlation between the acquiescence scores is taken as evidence for acquiescence response style. However, as Rorer (1965) points out this finding is not critical since the individuals may be responding to the content of the items. If each person responded to each item in the two administrations of the test in the same way, then the test–retest correlation of acquiescence scores would be 1.00 even if each person responded solely to the manifest content of the item. Only if we interpret the responses to the items as due to acquiescence response style can we interpret these correlations as supporting the existence of acquiescence response style. But this is precisely what is at issue.

The item reversal studies have provided somewhat more dramatic evidence for acquiescence. These studies are principally concerned with a measure of authoritarianism called the California F scale (Adorno *et al.*, 1950). Items which are indicative of authoritarianism tend to be keyed in the direction of agreement. This then clearly raises the possibility that high scores on the $F$ scale may be due to acquiescence response style rather than true authoritarian tendencies. In order to demonstrate this, psychologists have tried to write "item reversals" for the items keyed in the positive direction such that a response in the negative direction (No, Disagree, etc.) would have the same meaning as a positive response. If the individual responds to both items in the same way—that is, he either agrees with both or disagrees with both, then his responses are taken to be psychologically and/or logically inconsistent and the basis for the response similarity is taken to be the response style of acquiescence. If his responses to the item and its reversal are different, then the individual is presumably responding to the content of the item. The usual procedure in an item reversal study involves the presentation of an $F$ test consisting of items keyed in the positive direction and item reversals keyed in the negative direction. Separate scores are obtained for the original and the reversed items. If the individual is responding consistently to the content of the item, he should respond differently to the original and reversed items, and, accordingly, the correlation between the scores should be high and negative. If, on the other hand, the individual is responding on the basis of acquiescence response style the correlations between the original and the reversed scores should be high and positive. The correlations reported in such studies have varied considerably but have consistently been lower than the maximum possible negative value and have even, on occasion, been positive (see Christie, Havel, & Seidenberg, 1958). These studies have usually been taken as indicating that part of the score, perhaps even the largest part, on the $F$ scale is attributable to response acquiescence. The adequacy of this interpretation rests on the assumption that consistent responses to both the original item and its reversal are somehow inconsistent. For example, if an item reads, "Do you go to the movies one or more times per week?" and its reversal reads, "Do you go to the movies less than once per week?", endorsement or rejection of both the item and its reversal would be clearly logically inconsistent. However, the item reversals used in the $F$ scale studies do not have this unambiguous character. Most of the consistent responses have been double negatives. Many of these double negative response, contrary to the assumption of the writers of item reversals, could be logically consistent. Rorer (1965) gives the following item used in a reversal study and its reversal as an example of an item permitting a consistent double negation: "Every person should have complete faith in some supernatural power whose decisions he obeys without question." The reversal reads: "No person should have complete faith in some supernatural power whose decisions he obeys without question." An individual who disagrees with both responses is not logically inconsistent. He might believe that such faith is desirable for some persons but not for all persons. Such a belief would require him to reject both alternatives. In addition there are items and their reversals which permit consistent double endorsements. The following example is also taken from Rorer (1965). The original *F* scale items reads: "Nowadays more and more people are prying into matters that should remain personal and private." Its reversal reads: "There are times when it is necessary to probe into even the most personal and private matters." Rorer (1965) points out that "one may either endorse or reject both of these statements without in any way contradicting himself. A statement about the necessity of probing is not logically related to a statement about the incidence of probing" (Rorer, 1965, p. 137). Since it is possible to respond to both an item and its reversal in the same way without being inconsistent, the item reversal studies do not provide unambiguous evidence for the existence of acquiescence response style.

The third type of evidence which has been taken as indicative of acquiescence response style comes from factor analytic studies. For example, factor analysis of MMPI scales usually yields two factors. One of these factors has often been interpreted as an acquiescence factor since for the scales loading on the factors their loading is in part a function of their balance with respect to acquiescence. That is, scales for which high scores are obtained by subjects who agree with the items have tended to correlate positively with this factor (see Jackson and Messick, 1961). However, this interpretation of the factor, though plausible, is not unambiguous. The mere fact that these scales have this relationship to the factor does not indicate that the *reason* for the correlation is their imbalance with respect to acquiescence. Block (1965) has come close to rendering this interpretation of the MMPI derived factor untenable. Block took MMPI scales which were unbalanced with respect to acquiescence tendency and randomly deleted items keyed in the dominant direction until all the scales were balanced with respect to acquiescence—that is, each new scale had an equal number of items keyed in the positive and negative direction. He then factor analyzed these new scales and found the usual two factors. However, these factors cannot be interpreted in terms of acquiescence, since the scales are balanced. This finding, in turn, suggests that the original interpretation of one of the factors in terms of acquiescence response style was incorrect.

Our brief survey of the research evidence traditionally offered for the existence of acquiescence response style indicates that none of the evidence may be taken as clearly indicative of its presence. However, an ingenious set of data analyses reported by Campbell, Siegman, and Rees (1967) seem to offer unambiguous evidence of the existence of acquiescence response style. They investigated the relationship between the original $F$ scale and a reversed version of the $F$ scale and "pro" and "con" versions of several other measures. One of the measures they studied was the Taylor Manifest Anxiety Scale. They constructed two versions of this test. One version was worded in the pro direction such that high scores were obtained by subjects who agreed with the items, all of which were taken as indicative of the presence of anxiety. On the "con" version of the Taylor scale a person would get a high score for anxiety only by disagreeing with the items which were taken as indicative of the absence of anxiety. The item reversals were quite successful since the correlation between the two forms when corrected for attenuation was .98. Thus, for the Taylor scale it is clearly possible to construct substantially equivalent tests which are oppositely biased for acquiescence. The correlation between the $F$ scale and each of the forms of the Taylor scale ought to be the same if acquiescence is not involved in the $F$ scale. If acquiescence response style does, in part, determine scores on the original $F$ scale, then the correlation between the $F$ scale and "pro" version of the Taylor scale should be higher than its correlation with the "con" version since the $F$ scale is biased in the pro direction. The correlation between the $F$ scale and the pro-Taylor scale, corrected for attenuation, is .41 and for the $F$ scale and the "con" version the correlation, corrected for attenuation, is .27. The difference between the correlations is significant. Further, the differences, although small, do account for an important part of the relationship. In several analyses Campbell *et al.* (1967) note that scores on the original $F$ scale tend to correlate more highly with pro rather than con versions of tests even where the reversals are completely successful. They estimate, that in the largest effect present in their data, the effect of acquiescence is equal to shared content in determining the relationship between two measures. We can conclude that acquiescence response style does exist although it may not, in and of itself, be the major determinant of relationships among most measures of personality.

The evidence for the existence of response sets—that is, responses to latent rather than manifest content—is not as disputed as the evidence for response styles. The response set which has been most extensively studied is that of social desirability—the tendency to respond to items with that response which is most socially approved or accepted. The original evidence for the existence of social desirability came from a series of studies of Edwards (1953, 1957). He gave a group of subjects a battery of items from standard personality tests and asked the subjects to rate each item as to whether or not its endorsement would be indicative of a socially desirable response. From these ratings of the item he derived a social desirability score. He then submitted these items to another group of subjects and asked them to respond to them in the usual way. Then, for each item he obtained the number of subjects in the second group who endorsed the item. The correlation between the social desirability ratings and the frequency of endorsement of the items was .87. These results have been replicated a number of times (see Edwards, 1957). They indicate that knowledge of position of an item with respect to social desirability is highly predictive of the frequency with which it will be endorsed. These data do not, by themselves, support the existence of the response set, social desirability. By definition, a response set is a response to a latent content of an item. These data are perfectly compatible with the possibility that most subjects truthfully respond to the manifest content of the items. Because we have been exposed to a common socialization most people probably do the socially desirable thing most of the time. Few of us beat our mothers or run nude in the streets.

What would constitute evidence for the existence of the response set of social desirability? Crowne and Marlowe (1964) addressed themselves to this problem by constructing a test in which the only way a subject could respond in a socially desirable way was to lie. The following items from the Marlowe–Crowne scale are characteristic: "Before voting I thoroughly investigate the qualifications of all the candidates." "On occasion I have had doubts about my ability to succeed in life." Marlowe and Crowne assume that the person who responds True to the first item and False to the second is lying in order to give a socially desirable response.

Crowne and Marlowe (1964) developed the hypothesis that socially desirable responses on their test are indicative of a need for social approval. Further, they argue that these responses are an important determiner of behavior in settings other than test taking. In order to develop support for these concepts Crowne and Marlowe and their associates have conducted a series of investigations which are summarized in their book, *The Approval Motive* (Crowne & Marlowe, 1964). The principal hypothesis they investigated was that individuals who score high in their social desirability scale would exhibit more approval seeking behavior. In one of their studies they presented a group of subjects with a boring task. After the task was completed the experimenter asked the subjects a series of questions about the task. Subjects high in need approval (as measured by the Marlowe–Crowne scale) tended to say the task was more interesting than subjects low in need for approval.

In another study, a group of girls was asked to judge the number of knocks they heard on a tape recording. Before stating her response, each girl was exposed to a series of three obviously incorrect judgments by what she thought were fellow participants in the experiment. Then the girls were required to state their judgments. An inaccurate response in this situation is assumed to be indicative of conformity. Such a response is given by the girl who modifies her normal judgment in order to agree with the judgments of others. High need for approval subjects showed more conformity behavior than low need for approval subjects. In both of these studies subjects high in need for approval may be interpreted as responding in a way which attempts to gain the approval of others even if they have to modify their own judgments.

Another study reported by Crowne and Marlowe (1964) dealt with "perceptual defense." In this experimental situation subjects are presented with "taboo" and "nontaboo" words in a tachistoscope—a device permitting a rapid exposure of a stimulus. Each stimulus is presented initially at a rate of exposure which does not permit correct recognition. The stimuli are then exposed for successively longer durations until correct recognition results. Perceptual defense refers to the usual finding that taboo words require longer exposures for correct identification than nontaboo words. In their study, Barthel and Crowne (as reported in Crowne and Marlowe, 1964) conducted a standard perceptual defense experiment. In addition, after the experiment they interviewed each subject about their reaction to the experiment. On the basis of the interview subjects were placed in one of two groups, those subjects who believed the experiment dealt with "speed of perception" and those who believed the experiment dealt with their responses to socially disapproved words. The data obtained in their experiment are presented in Table 2.9 The data in Table

TABLE 2.9

*Mean Differences in Taboo-Neutral-Word Recognition Thresholds between the Experimental Groups*

| | Task categorization | | | | | | |
|---|---|---|---|---|---|---|---|
| | Perceptual | | | Disapproval | | | |
| | N | M | SD | N | M | SD | t |
| High need for approval | 24 | 14.31 | 2.62 | 24 | 22.34 | 6.19 | $5.82^a$ |
| Low need for approval | 24 | 14.26 | 4.17 | 24 | 14.58 | 3.68 | 0.28 |
| | | 0.05 | | | $5.28^a$ | | |

From D. P. Crowne & D. Marlowe, The approval motive, Table 2, p. 103. New York, Wiley, 1964. Reprinted by permission of John Wiley & Sons, Inc.

[a] $p < .001$ two-tailed test.

2.9 indicate that each of the four groups of subjects in the experiment exhibit the perceptual defense effect. However, the group that shows the effect most dramatically is composed of the subjects high in need for approval who indicate that the experiment dealt with their reaction to the taboo words. Apparently, these subjects interpret the experiment as involving a social situation in which they can exhibit socially approved behavior by not responding rapidly to the taboo words.

These experiments (as well as others reported by Crowne and Marlowe) indicate that the responses to the social desirability scale are predictive of a wide variety of nontest behaviors. Consequently, social desirability response set may be considered an important personality characteristic.

We can draw some tentative conclusions about the role of method variance in paper and pencil tests of personality. There is evidence for the existence of both response styles and response sets. The existence of both response styles and response sets means that correlations among tests cannot be invariably attributable to the manifest content of the tests. The ambiguity in the determination of the basis of the relationship between tests extends to the interpretation of the meaning of the factors derived from these correlations.

## THE HIERARCHICAL MODEL

A trait theory based on factor analysis implies the existence of a hierarchical model of the organization of personality. Is the hierarchical model correct? Surprisingly, no answer exists to this question. Although factor analysis inevitably leads to such a representation of personality structure, the evidence is not decisive since this result is a necessary consequence of the method used. Any attempt to develop a taxonomic system based on observed commonalities inevitably leads to the observation of further commonalities. Similar taxonomic systems exist in biology. There are individual animals, which share in common certain properties and are called cows; cows share in common properties with other types of animals and are as a result, mammals, etc. This type of hierarchical organization is taken as being representative of an Aristotelian mode of thought (see Cassirer, 1953; Lewin, 1935). The Aristotelian mode of thought has been criticized by both Cassirer and Lewin. Cassirer states his principal objection as follows:

> In the same way that we ascend from the species to the higher genus by abandoning a certain characteristic, thereby drawing a larger range of objects into the circle, so by a reverse process, the specification of the genus takes place through the progressive addition of new elements of content. Hence, if we call the number of properties of a concept the magnitude of its *content*, this magnitude increases as we descend from the higher concepts to the lower, and thus diminishes the number of species, subordinate to the concept; while, when we ascend to the higher genus, this content will diminish as the

number of species is increased. This increasing extension of the concept corresponds to a progressive diminution of the content; so that, finally, the most general concepts we can reach no longer possess any definite content. The conceptual pyramid, which we form in this way, reaches its summit in the abstract representation of "something" under the all-inclusive being of which every possible intellectual content falls, but which at the same time is devoid of specific meaning.

If the final goal of the method of forming concepts is entirely empty, the whole process leading to it must arouse suspicion. . . . What we demand and expect of a scientific concept, first of all, is this: that, in the place of original indefiniteness and ambiguity of ideas, it shall institute a sharp and unambiguous determination; while, in this case, on the contrary, the sharp lines of distinction seem the more effaced, the further we pursue the logical process. . . . If all construction of concepts consists in selecting from a plurality of objects before us only the similar properties, while we neglect the rest, it is clear that through this sort of reduction what is merely a *part* has taken the place of the original sensuous *whole*. . . . The concept would lose all value if it meant merely the neglect of the particular cases from which it starts, and the annihilation of their peculiarity.

(From E. Cassirer, *Substance and function and Einstein's theory of relativity*, pp. 5 and 6. New York: Dover Publications, Inc., 1953.)

Cassirer's objections to this mode of concept formation readily carry over to the sphere of personality. A source trait is itself an abstraction over several diverse elements. Individuals can arrive at a common position on a source trait by different combinations of the elements (measures) which define it. Similarly, individuals could have the same position on some second-order trait but have a different combination of scores on the source traits from which the second-order trait is derived. Knowledge of a person's position on the second-order trait necessarily involves some loss of information about his position on its constituent elements.

It is probably the case that many psychologists object to Cattell's entire program of research on the basis of what is an objection, in principle, to the Aristotelian taxonomic basis of his research. These psychologists would prefer some type of hypothetico-deductive approach to personality. Using a hypothetico-deductive approach it is possible to deduce specific consequences from abstract representation of a situation, and, as a result, abstraction is not incompatible with what Cassirer calls, "the neglect of the particular." In the next chapter we shall deal with some examples of such an approach.

# EYSENCK'S THEORY OF PERSONALITY

In the next three chapters we shall consider a different approach to the problem of establishing dimensions for the description of individual differences in personality. In the previous chapter we examined the attempt to develop dimensions of personality using an inductive approach which required a minimum of explicit theoretical commitment. In the chapters which follow we shall consider three theories which attempt to develop dimensions for the description of personality by the use of hypothetico-deductive procedures.

Implicit in the evaluation of these theories will be three criteria. First the theory should have a degree of precision and explicitness which permits unambiguous deduction such that it should be possible to derive predictions about what would occur under specified conditions. In order to test such a theory it is necessary to know unambiguously what consequences or predictions may be assumed to follow from the theory.

Second, the conditions specified in the theory for the purpose of deriving consequences from its central assumptions must be empirically realizable. That is, it should be possible to experimentally create the conditions necessary to test the theory. A theory may make precise predictions as to what should occur under certain specified conditions, but the attempt to experimentally create the conditions may tax or overwhelm the ingenuity of the experimenter. We can make this latter point more concrete by considering an example based on one of the theories we shall discuss in Chapter 5, Atkinson's risk-taking model. According to this theory certain kinds of behaviors should result in a situation in which individuals are confronted with a task which they believe to be easy but which they repeatedly fail. The predictions to be made in this situation are relatively unambiguous. However, a problem results if one attempts to set up an experiment to test these predictions. Any experimentally created task which a person assumes is easy for him and which he repeatedly fails creates a credibility problem. If the task is really easy, the person should not fail. As a result the psychologist is usually forced to use deception to create such a situation. But if a subject repeatedly fails the task, he may begin to believe that the psychologist is deceiving him either about the difficulty of the task or about the quality of his performance on the task. If this happens the subject may lose interest in the task and perform it in a perfunctory way. When this behavior occurs the experimental situation is no longer suitable to test the implications of the theory since a confounding variable not explicitly dealt with by the theory has been introduced—that is, the effect of the subject's belief about the deception that has occurred.

Third, the theory should permit one to make deductions which are nonobvious. If a theory permits only the deduction of the obvious, then it is usually the case that there are many alternative theories or assumptions which could also explain the result. On the other hand if a theory permits one to make nonobvious or subtle predictions and if these predictions are confirmed, one gains confidence in the validity of the assumptions which led to the prediction. Consider an example. A prediction which follows from another theory discussed in Chapter 4—Spence's theory of anxiety—is that in a certain type of serial learning task highly anxious individuals exhibit more rapid learning than nonanxious individuals on "easy" items in the list. But highly anxious subjects at the *beginning* of the task should exhibit poorer performance than nonanxious subjects on "hard" items. Further highly anxious subjects should exhibit better performance on hard items during the end of the task than nonanxious subjects. Such a detailed prediction is difficult to arrive at without recourse to the assumptions from which it was derived.

If, then, a theory satisfies each of the conditions listed above, its validity and usefulness depends on the range of predictive consequences which have been tested and confirmed. Ideally, every theory should be evaluated by testing many subtle and nonobvious predictions derived from it.

In order to evaluate hypothetico-deductive theories with reference to the three criteria listed above, it is necessary to become involved with many of the technical details surrounding the theories. In order to know whether a particular deduction unambiguously follows from the assumptions of a particular theory it is necessary to follow the deduction in detail. Mathematics and formal language are sometimes used in this connection in order to facilitate the deductive process.

The attempt to test theories frequently leads scientists to set up artificial and controlled laboratory situations. This may lead students and layment to believe that the theories are limited in their validity to these situations. However, this is not completely correct. Presumably, most theories in use have very extensive ranges of application. Consider, for example, Eysenck's inhibition–excitation theory. If the theory is correct the inhibitory and excitatory processes which Eysenck refers to are invariably present in the nervous system and are fundamental to the acquisition and extinction of all responses even though the theory can be tested most precisely in the laboratory. One of the experiments we shall discuss in this chapter deals with differences in the rate of conditioning of introverts and extraverts under conditions where the unconditioned stimulus (UCS) has low or high intensity. The student encountering such an experiment may feel that the issue is trivial. Indeed psychologists who conduct such experiments may not be interested in these results *per se.* What is of significance is not the differences in rate of conditioning among introverts and extraverts as a function of the intensity of the UCS but what these differences permit us to infer about certain hypothetical processes. These differences are theoretically assumed to be involved in conditioning and in all situations which human beings encounter.

In order to develop the hypothetico-deductive method psychologists concerned with developing dimensions of personality have typically assumed that some measure of individual differences in personality actually is a measure of a hypothetical variable contained in some theory. For example, Spence (1958) has assumed that the Taylor scale (a measure of individual differences in anxiety) is actually a measure of individual differences in anxiety) is actually a measure of individual differences in the hypothetical variable called drive ($D$) in Hullian theory. Given this kind of assumption it is possible to derive predictions about the expected behaviors in particular situations of individuals who score differently on the individual difference measure of personality. If the predictions are consistently confirmed it is possible to infer that the individual difference measure is in fact a measure of the hypothetical variable. If the predictions are not confirmed two kinds of inferences may be made:

1. The theory is wrong.
2. The theory is right but the individual difference measure does not measure the hypothetical variable specified in the theory.

Because of the ambiguity in the inferences to be drawn from disconfirming evidence in this type of research, some psychologists have criticized this approach to the development of dimensions of personality. In my view, their criticism is incorrect. It is usually the case that there is an asymmetry in the consequences of confirmation and disconfirmation of any theory in science. Confirmation always adds confidence in the correctness of the entire theory. Disconfirmation leaves one with the option of either challenging the adequacy of the empirical test—that is, one assumes that the experimental conditions required to test the theory have not been realized—or of questioning any one of several aspects of the theory which are used to arrive at the prediction. Most theories are relatively invulnerable to disproof by any single experimental result since it is possible to rationalize the results of a single test by making *ad hoc* assumptions resulting in the change of one or another details of the theory. (Of course, if a theory *consistently* fails to make adequate predictions, it may be considered disconfirmed and will be abandoned.)

The use of the hypothetico-deductive method for the development of personality dimensions has advantages and disadvantages. Since the test of such theories tends to require the use of the experimental method to establish the conditions specified in the theory, the method results in an unusually coherent integration of the individual differences and experimental approaches to psychology. This, in turn, permits one to make predictions about the behavior of a particular kind of individual in a particular situation. Thus, situational variables are dealt with as an integral part of the meaning of individual difference dimensions rather than being considered incidentally, subsequent to the development of individual difference dimensions. On the other hand, this approach restricts the search for dimensions of personality to those theoretical variables which are dealt with in various general theories of behavior. Since these theories have been developed without special attention to the problem of describing personality there is no *a priori* reason to assume that the variables contained in the theory are well chosen for this purpose. Further, the commitment to the hypothetico-deductive approach leads, at least in its present stage of development in the area of personality, to the development of an independent series of measures of personality, each of which be assumed to measure some hypothetical variable in a different theory. As a result, research on each individual difference measure tends to proceed in isolation of research on every other individual difference measure and these separate research efforts do not lend themselves readily to a systematic integration. By contrast, the factor analytic approach to personality description commits itself unequivocally to the development of a systematic taxonomy. The one personality theorist who has done most to integrate these diverse approaches is Eysenck and we shall begin with a discussion of his theory.

Eysenck's theory presents a natural transition in our presentation, since he, like Cattell, is committed to the use of factor analysis as a basis for the discovery of the principal dimensions of personality. Unlike Cattell, Eysenck is a type theorist, dealing with a small number of allegedly orthogonal second-order factors. Eysenck transcends this descriptive theory by developing a conception of the processes which are the basis of the obtained dimensions of personality. These processes are ultimately rooted in a conception of genetically based differences in the functioning of the nervous system. As a result, Eysenck's theory has a distinctly biological flavor. However, his theory is not exclusively biological since he attempts to show how these individual differences in physiological structure influence the socialization process. This, in turn, permits him to deal with the social and political behavior of individuals with different personality characteristics. As a result, for Eysenck, personality study serves as a bridge between the biological and sociological aspects of psychology.

## The Descriptive System

In addition to a preference for a type rather than a trait theory, Eysenck's use of factor analysis is different from Cattell's in one other aspect. Eysenck has supplemented traditional factor analysis methodology by the use of criterion analysis. In this method, one begins with groups of individuals who share some significant, typically socially defined characteristic. Eysenck has used the method by studying groups of individuals who share a common psychiatric diagnosis—for example, neurotics and psychotics. One then administers batteries of tests to these groups in an attempt to discover which measures serve to differentiate the groups. In this way it is possible to derive factorlike dimensions. This use of criterion analysis serves to eliminate some of the ambiguities inherent in the process of naming and interpreting factors. The criterion groups serve to define the derived dimensions. Eysenck's descriptive system includes the following four dimensions: introversion–extraversion, stability–neuroticism, stability–psychoticism, and intelligence. For the purpose of Eysenck's hypothetico-deductive theory, only the first two dimensions are relevant.

Eysenck contrasts his views of the relationship between neuroticism and psychoticism with a unidimensional theory according to which normals, neurotics, and psychotics represent groups of individuals who differ with respect to position on a unidimensional continuum of psychopathology. Psychotics would represent the most extreme form of psychopathology and neurotics would occupy an intermediate position on this dimension. Eysenck argues that neuroticism and psychoticism represent two orthogonal dimensions, implying that position on one dimension is statistically independent of position on the other. Eysenck argues for the independence of these two dimensions on the basis of two different types of studies.

TABLE 3.1

*Characteristics of Introverts and Extraverts According to Eysenck*

| Dimensions | Introverts | Extraverts |
|---|---|---|
| Neurotic syndrome | Dysthymia | Hysteria |
| Body build | Leptomorph | Eurymorph |
| Intellectual function | Low I.Q./ vocabulary ratio | High I.Q./ vocabulary ratio |
| Persistence | High | Low |
| Speed | Low | High |
| Speed/accuracy ratio | Low | High |
| Level of aspiration | High | Low |
| Intrapersonal variability | Low | High |
| Sense of humor | Cognitive | Orectic |
| Social attitude | Tender-minded | Tough-minded |
| Conditioning | Quick | Slow |
| Reminiscence | Low | High |
| Figural aftereffect | Small | Large |
| Stress reactions | Overactive | Inert |
| Sedation threshold | High | Low |

Based on Eysenck, 1957.

First, factor analysis of ratings of symptoms by psychiatrists indicates the presence of two orthogonal factors (see Trouton and Maxwell, 1956). Eysenck (1957, p. 15) indicates that most of the psychiatrists who participated in the study held views favoring the unidimensional theory. Despite this bias, their latent conceptions, as indicated by the statistical structure of their ratings, apparently were more compatible with a two-dimensional theory. Perhaps, more convincing in support of the two dimensional theory is the application of discriminant function analysis[1] to this problem by S.B.G. Eysenck (as cited in Eysenck, 1957, pp. 17–26). She gave six objective tests to a group of normal, neurotic, and psychotic subjects. By the application of discriminant function analysis she was able to show that there were two underlying dimensions present among these tests. By this technique it was possible to arrive at optimal sets of weights to be applied to the scores which could be used to discriminate among normals, neurotics, and psychotics. Using this procedure she was able to correctly classify 71% of the subjects. These results indicate that, at least with respect to the battery of tests used in her study, normals, neurotics, and psychotics do not fall on a unidimensional continuum.

[1] A discussion of discriminant function analysis may be found in Cooley and Lohnes (1962).

However, it should be noted that these results are not conclusive since, strictly speaking, they are limited in their validity to the tests used. It is possible that there are other batteries of tests which would be equally capable of discriminating between normals and neurotics on the one hand, and between normals and psychotics on the other hand, and which would exhibit a unidimensional structure. However, until such batteries are discovered, Eysenck's two dimensional theory should be preferred on the grounds that independent evidence exists for its validity.

The most important dimension dealt with in Eysenck's theory is introversion–extraversion. Some conception of the range of measures and variables which are included in this dimension by Eysenck can be obtained by examining Table 3.1. Each of the differences between introverts and extraverts reported in Table 3.1 is based on an empirical study. However, the reader should not assume that each difference has been unequivocally supported by a large body of research. We shall examine the empirical basis for some of the assumed differences between introverts and extraverts in what follows.

Eysenck describes the dimensions of extraversion and neuroticism as measured by the Eysenck Personality Inventory as follows:

### EXTRAVERSION–INTROVERSION

High $E$ scores are indicative of extraversion. High scoring individuals tend to be outgoing, impulsive, and uninhibited, having many social contacts and frequently taking part in group activities.

The typical extravert is sociable, likes parties, has many friends, needs to have people to talk to, and does not like reading or studying by himself. He craves excitement, takes chances, often sticks his neck out, acts on the spur of the moment and is generally an impulsive individual. He is fond of practical jokes, always has a ready answer, and generally likes change. He is carefree, easygoing, optimistic, and likes to "laugh and be merry." He prefers to keep moving and doing things, tends to be aggressive and to lose his temper quickly. His feelings are not kept under tight control, and he is not always a reliable person.

The typical introvert is a quiet, retiring sort of person, introspective, found of books rather than people; he is reserved and distant except to intimate friends. He tends to plan ahead, "looks before he leaps," and distrusts the impulse of the moment. He does not like excitement, takes matters of everyday life with proper seriousness, and likes a well-ordered mode of life. He keeps his feelings under close control, seldom behaves in an aggressive manner, and does not lose his temper easily. He is reliable, somewhat pessimistic, and places great value on ethical standards.

### NEUROTICISM

High $N$ scores are indicative of emotional lability and overreactivity. High scoring individuals tend to be emotionally overresponsive and to have difficulties in returning to a normal state after emotional experiences. Such individuals frequently complain of vague somatic upsets of a minor kind, such as headaches, digestive troubles, insomnia, backaches, etc., and also report many worries, anxieties, and other disagreeable emotional feelings. Such individuals are predisposed to develop neurotic disorders under stress, but such predispositions should not be confused with actual neurotic breakdown; a person may have high scores on $N$ while yet functioning adequately in work, sex, family, and society spheres.

(Eysenck & Eysenck, 1968, p. 627)

The relationship between the stabile–neuroticism dimension and the introversion–extraversion dimension is of central importance for Eysenck's theory and serves as the dimensional background for much of his experimental work. Eysenck originally assumed that these two dimensions were orthogonal. Differences in introversion–extraversion serve to distinguish between two fundamentally different types of neurotics. Introverted neurotics are called dysthymics and this rubric is intended to include neurotics classified as anxiety neurotics and obsessive–compulsive neurotics. Extraverted neurotics, on the other hand, include various types of hysterics and psychopaths. The Maudsley Personality Inventory (MPI) developed by Eysenck (1959) was assumed to provide an adequate measure of each of the two principal personality dimensions. These assumptions provide two different methods of studying individual differences in introversion–extraversion. Among neurotic subjects, a comparison of subjects classified as dysthymic with subjects classified as hysteric should be a comparison between subjects who differ in introversion–extraversion. Among normal subjects the extraversion ($E$) scale of the MPI provides the basis for the investigation of the introversion-extraversion dimension.

Subsequent research has led to some modification in this conception (Bartholomew, 1959; Eysenck, 1958; McGuire *et al.*, 1963; Sigal, Star, & Franks 1958a, b). It has been found that hysterics have not, in general, scored high on extraversion. They have usually been found to score relatively close to normals. In addition, hysterics have usually been found to score lower on neuroticism than dysthymics. Consequently, a comparison between dysthymics and hysterics involves a comparison between highly introverted subjects with subjects about average on the introversion–extraversion dimension. In addition, any differences obtained between these groups are confounded with differences in neuroticism since these two groups differ almost as much in neuroticism as they do in introversion-extraversion. Even among normal subjects the $E$ scale and the neuroticism scale ($N$) of the MPI are slightly negatively correlated. This negative correlation between measures of allegedly orthogonal dimensions has led Eysenck to construct a revised version of the MPI called the Eysenck Personality Inventory (EPI) (Eysenck and Eysenck, 1968). In this revised test, the $E$ and $N$ scales are said to be uncorrelated. Unfortunately, much of the research we shall review involves comparisons between groups who differ on the MPI $E$ scale or comparisons between hysterics and dysthymics. Such comparisons cannot be unambiguously interpreted as comparisons between introverts and extraverts.

Psychopaths and criminals have generally been found to score high on both $N$ and $E$ scales. Therefore, differences between dysthymics and psychopaths would provide a more adequate basis for the investigation of differences between neurotics who differ on the introversion–extraversion dimension. Alternatively, Eysenck (1967) has advocated using measures of both $E$ and $N$ in investigations in order to study their interrelationship and joint effect in experimental situations. This is particularly important because, as we shall see, Eysenck (1967) argues that the physiological basis of these two dimensions is not independent.

## The Excitation–Inhibition Theory

Eysenck (1957) has attempted to relate individual differences in introversion–extraversion to hypothetical inherited differences in the functioning of the nervous system. For this purpose, Eysenck refers to the Pavlovian concepts of excitation and inhibition (Pavlov, 1927). He states his fundamental assumptions as follows:

Individuals in whom excitatory potentials is generated slowly and in whom excitatory potentials so generated are relatively weak, are thereby predisposed to develop extraverted patterns of behaviors and to develop hysterical-psychopathic disorders in the case of neurotic breakdown; individuals in whom excitatory potential is generated quickly and in whom excitatory potentials so generated are strong, are thereby predisposed to develop introverted patterns of behavior and to develop dysthmic disorders in the case of neurotic breakdown. Similarly, individuals in whom reactive inhibition is developed quickly, in whom strong reactive inhibitions are generated, and in whom reactive inhibition is dissipated slowly, are thereby predisposed to develop extraverted patterns of behavior and to develop hysterical-psychopathic disorders in case of neurotic breakdown; conversely, individuals in whom reactive inhibition is developed slowly, in whom weak reactive inhibitions are generated, and in whom reactive inhibition is dissipated quickly, are thereby predisposed to develop introverted patterns of behavior and to develop dysthmic disorders in case of neurotic breakdown.

(Eysenck, 1957, p. 114)

Although it is not explicitly stated in the above quotation, Eysenck postulates the existence of a ratio of inhibition to excitation $(I/E)$. The value of this ratio is relatively low for introverts and relatively high for extraverts. In order to understand the implications of Eysenck's assumptions it is necessary to understand the meaning of "excitation" and "inhibitions." Excitation is a relatively straightforward concept. It refers to the neural processes upon which the development of learned associations between stimuli and responses depend. Thus, all other things being equal, individuals with strong excitation potentials would be more able to form learned connections between stimuli and responses than individuals in whom excitatory potentials are weak. Inhibition is a rather more complicated concept. The term reactive inhibition comes from Hull (1943). Eysenck's conception of inhibition involves a modification of views held by both Hull and Pavlov. Reactive inhibition, as the term is used by Eysenck, is very close in meaning to Pavlov's concept of internal inhibition. Eysenck's version of internal inhibition is stated in his "law of temporal inhibition" as follows:

Wherever a stimulus-response connection is made in the central nervous system, both positive (excitatory, facilitative) and negative (inhibitory, obstructive) changes occur in the neural media responsible for the transmission of the impulse. The former type of change is responsible for conditioning and learning and makes easier the passage of the neural impulse linking stimulus and response; the latter type of change is responsible for unlearning and extinction and makes more difficult the passage of the neural impulse linking stimulus and response. Excitatory and inhibitory changes obey different laws; thus inhibition quickly dissipates with time, whereas excitation does not.

(Eysenck, 1957, p. 46)

Thus Eysenck's theory essentially asserts that introverts have inherited a nervous system which permits them to form learned connections between stimuli and responses more rapidly than extraverts. Introverts are more able to respond continually in the same way than extraverts and tend to persist in a particular pattern of response longer than extraverts.

Eysenck has tried to derive most of the known differences between introverts and extraverts by the use of the excitation–inhibition theory. For this purpose, he uses a modified version of Hull's theory of inhibition.

Reactive inhibitions may be conceived of as a fatiguelike neural state which occurs as an inevitable consequence of any excitatory process. In addition to this type of momentary inhibition Eysenck also uses Hull's concept of conditioned inhibition. Whenever an organism ceases to respond in a situation in which reactive inhibition is present, the reactive inhibition is reduced. The response of rest or cessation or responding is rewarded or reinforced by the dissipation of the reactive inhibition. Accordingly, there occurs in such a situation a learned response or response cessation which is called conditioned inhibition. The Hullian theory of inhibition has been subject to considerable criticism on both logical and empirical grounds (see Gleitman, Nachmias, & Neisser, 1954). These criticisms led Eysenck to use a modified version of Hull's theory of inhibition. The theory is expressed in the following equation:

$$s\bar{E}r = f(D_+ \times sHr) + f(D_+ \times sIr) + f(D_- \times sHr) + f(D_- \times sIr)$$

where $s\bar{E}r$ is a measure of the tendency to make a particular response, $D_+$ a drive or the motivation to perform a response, $sHr$ habit, $D_-$ reactive inhibition, and $sIr$ conditioned inhibition.

Eysenck assumes that $D_+$ and $sHr$ always have positive signs and $D_-$ and $sIr$ always have negative signs since they represent tendencies to cease responding. Further, Eysenck assumes that $D_+$ and $D_-$ both being drive states should both multiply $sIr$ and $sHr$ which are habits, on the Hullian assumption that drives multiply habits.

Eysenck's assumptions about differences in $E/I$ ratios combined with his theory of the determinants of performance in simple situations is taken by him to imply that introverts will condition more rapidly than extraverts. As we shall see, the prediction may not clearly follow from Eysenck's theory. Since the prediction is central to his theory, we should examine it in some detail.

Eysenck's theory implies that $D_-$ will develop more rapidly in extraverts than introverts. As a result of the more rapid buildup of $D_-$ and the greater opportunity thus permitted for the reinforcement of $sIr$, extraverts should develop $sIr$ more rapidly than introverts. Introverts, however, should develop $sHr$ more rapidly than extraverts because of their greater excitatory potential. These two groups should not, in general, differ in $D_+$. We can examine the effects of these deductions on $s\bar{E}r$ by examining each of the summed components of $s\bar{E}r$ separately:

$D_+ \times sHr$: Since introverts will develop higher $sHr$ values than extraverts, the product of $D_+$ and $sHr$ should yield higher positive values for introverts than extraverts.

$D_+ \times sIr$: Since extraverts will develop higher $sIr$ values than introverts, the product of the positively signed $D_+$ with the negatively signed $sIr$ should yield algebraically lower values for extraverts than introverts.

$D_- \times sHr$: Extraverts may be expected to develop higher $D_-$ values than introverts. Introverts may be expected to develop higher $sHr$ values than extraverts. Accordingly, no general statement may be made about the relative relationship of the product of these two components for individuals who differ with respect to their position on the introversion–extraversion dimension.

$D_- \times sIr$: Both $D_-$ and $sIr$ may be expected to develop more rapidly in extraverts than introverts. Since $D_-$ and $sIr$ are both negatively signed, their product will be positive. Therefore, extraverts will have higher positive values for this component than introverts.

When we examine each of the determinants of $s\bar{E}r$ we see that the first two components should contribute to more rapid development of reaction potential for introverts than extraverts; one component is indeterminate in this respect, and one component should contribute to more rapid development of reaction potential for extraverts than for introverts. Therefore, this detailed examination of Eysenck's theory suggests that no simple prediction can be made about the relative rate of conditioning of introverts and extraverts without consideration of specific parametric values associated with these theoretical terms. One general prediction should follow. Under conditions where $D_-$ is close to zero, introverts should condition more rapidly than extraverts since only the first two components of $s\bar{E}r$ would be relevant. This can be accomplished by conducting experiments where the interval between conditioning trials is long, permitting the dissipation of reactive inhibition. The difference between rate of conditioning of introverts and extraverts should be magnified under conditions where $D_+$ is high since higher $D_+$ will result in greater differences of the product of $D_+$ and $sHr$ and $D_+$ and $sIr$ in favor of introverts over extraverts. Paradoxically, these predictions are exactly opposite of those subsequently suggested by Eysenck (1965, 1966, 1967) who suggests that introverts should condition more rapidly than extraverts under conditions where $D_+$ is low and under conditions which maximize the possibility for the development of inhibition.

In summary, the discussion of Eysenck's original theory of conditioning in introverts and extraverts suggests that the theory contains some ambiguities and inconsistencies when considered in detail. Alternatively, one can say that the equation determining $s\bar{E}r$ can be abandoned. Such a position would leave one without the specification of a detailed formulation of the laws governing the theoretical combination of variables relating to excitation and inhibition. This is probably not a great loss since such a formulation is not essential for considering the relationship between the introversion–extraversion dimension and conditioning.

Most of the research dealing with Eysenck's theory of individual differences in conditioning has used eyeblink conditioning. In this type of classical conditioning experiment the conditioned stimulus (CS) is usually a tone. It is followed by the presentation of an unconditioned stimulus (UCS) which is a puff of air delivered to the eye. The unconditioned response (UCR) to the UCS is an eyeblink. Conditioning is demonstrated when the CS, in the absence of the UCS, elicits the conditioned response (CR) of an eyeblink. Franks (1956) obtained the results shown in Figure 3.1 in a study of eyeblink conditioning comparing dysthymics (D), normals (N), and hysterics (H). Examination of Figure 3.1 indicates that dysthymics conditioned more rapidly than normals and hysterics. The normal

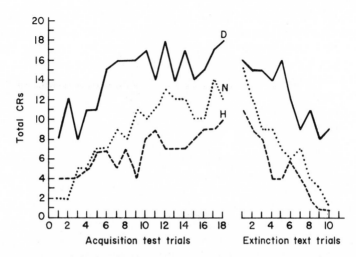

FIG. 3.1. Total number of eyeblink CR's given by each group at each test trial ($N = 20$ in each group). (From C. M. Franks, Conditioning and personality; a study of normal and neurotic subjects. *Journal of Abnormal and Social Psychology*, 1956, **52**, 143–150.)

subjects were not significantly different from the hysterics. If we assume that the relevant individual difference dimension involved when comparing dysthymics to hysterics is introversion–extraversion (rather than neuroticism), then these data indicate that introverts develop classical conditioned responses more rapidly than extraverts. In a follow-up study of normal subjects, Franks (1957b) compared individuals who scored at the extremes of the $E$ scale on the MPI. He found a significant correlation of $-.46$ between scores on the $E$ scale of the MPI and a measure of rate of conditioning. This indicates that, among normal subjects, introverts condition more rapidly than extraverts.

Subsequent to the publication of the book in which Eysenck presented his theory of inhibition and excitation in relation to the introversion–extraversion dimension (Eysenck, 1957) a number of investigators performed studies dealing with the relationship between this individual difference dimension and conditioning. Several investigators have reported that they were not able to replicate Franks's findings. Eysenck (1965) has summarized the experimental literature dealing with this problem. He concluded that those investigators who followed Franks's original procedures replicated his findings and those investigators who did not failed to replicate his results. In particular, the relevant parameter, according to Eysenck, was the use of a partial reinforcement schedule. In partial reinforcement the CS is not invariably followed by the UCS during the acquisition phase of the experiment and is omitted on some trials. Eysenck's review of the literature indicated that those experimenters who, like Franks, had used partial reinforcement tended to find that introverts conditioned more rapidly than extraverts. The one conspicuous exception to this generalization was a reported failure by Franks (1963) to replicate his own findings. Eysenck (1965) argued that his theory predicts more rapid conditioning for introverts only under partial reinforcement conditions and hence the failure to find more rapid conditioning for introverts under total reinforcement conditions is in no way contradictory to his theory. The basis for this assertion is a brief parenthetical statement in his book which reads, "Inhibitory potential is expected to be generated during the unreinforced trials interspersed with the reinforced trials . . ." (Eysenck, 1957, p. 125). However, the statement is not clearly consistent with his own theory. For, according to the law of temporal inhibition, inhibition is developed as an inevitable consequence of the occurrence of any central neural excitatory process. Excitatory processes are present on each reinforced trial and serve to increase the value of $sHr$. As a result, inhibition must be generated on trials where the UCS is present. Further, even if inhibition was not present, differences in excitatory potential should favor more rapid conditioning in introverts than extraverts. As a matter of fact, Eysenck conjectured that differences in inhibitory potentials might not be the most relevant factor (see Eysenck, 1957, p. 125). This conjecture is probably based on the assumption that in the usual classical conditioning experiment the intertrial interval is sufficiently long to permit the dissipation of reactive inhibition. As a result, according to Eysenck's theory, $D_-$ would be zero and the last two determinants of $s\bar{E}r$ may be neglected. Therefore, differences in excitatory potential may be assumed to be more relevant in determining rates of conditioning in introverts and extraverts than differences in inhibitory potential.

. It should be noted that Eysenck's 1965 review of the literature does not provide conclusive evidence that introverts condition more rapidly than extraverts only under partial reinforcement conditions. Rather, this is a conjecture about the relevant difference between studies which have replicated Franks's findings and those which have not. More conclusive evidence on this point would be obtained by comparing partial and total reinforcement conditions in a single experiment. Eysenck (1966) reports the results of such a study conducted by Levey in Eysenck's Maudsley laboratory. In this study the eyeblink conditioning performance of subjects who differed on MPI scales was compared under partial (67%) and total (100%) reinforcement conditions. Levey found that introverts showed more rapid conditioning than extraverts under partial reinforcement conditions, extraverts showed more rapid conditioning than introverts under total (100%) reinforcement conditions. However, this difference was not statistically significant. Therefore, in the only study which deals directly with Eysenck's central argument, the results are not statistically significant.

Levey dealt with two other variables in his study (1) the CS–UCS interval and (2) the intensity of the UCS. He compared an experimental situation in which the onset of the CS was followed by the onset of the UCS by 400 msec. with a situation in which this difference was 800 msec., and he compared an experimental situation in which the intensity of the UCS was 3 lb. per square inch with one in which the intensity was 6 lb. per square inch. Levey found that under both short CS–UCS interval and low UCS intensity, introverts conditioned more rapidly than extraverts, whereas under both long CS–UCS interval and high UCS intensity, extraverts conditioned more rapidly than introverts. These differences were statistically significant. Eysenck (1966, 1967) argues that these findings are predicted by his theory.

The variable which had the greatest effect on differential rate of conditioning in introverts and extraverts in the Levey study was intensity of the UCS (see Figures 3.2a and 3.2b). There are other eyeblink conditioning studies in which introverts have conditioned more rapidly than extraverts where UCS intensity is low. For example, Brebner and Symon (as reported in Eysenck, 1966) have both reported more rapid eyeblink conditioning for introverts using a UCS intensity of .68 lb. per square inch. However, there are published studies in which there is no significant relationship between introversion–extraversion and eyeblink conditioning where UCS intensity has been low. For example, Spence and Spence (1964) found a nonsignificant $r$ of $-.08$ between scores on the $E$ scale of the MPI and eyeblink conditioning using a UCS intensity of 1 lb. per square inch. Therefore, Levey's results are not in agreement on this point with all other studies.

Is the relationship between UCS intensity and rate of conditioning obtained in Levey's study derivable from Eysenck's $E/I$ theory? In this type of experimental situation UCS intensity influences the level of $D_+$. The higher the level of UCS, all other things being equal, the higher the value of $D_+$. As we have seen, under conditions where the intertrial interval is sufficiently large to permit the dissipation of $D_-$, larger values of $D_+$ should imply that the differences between rate of conditioning between introverts and extraverts should increase with introverts showing even more rapid conditioning than extraverts. Therefore Levey's findings with respect to UCS intensity are *not* derivable from Eysenck's original theory.

However, this deduction is more closely related to Eysenck's new theory (Eysenck, 1967)—although this point is not explicitly stated by Eysenck

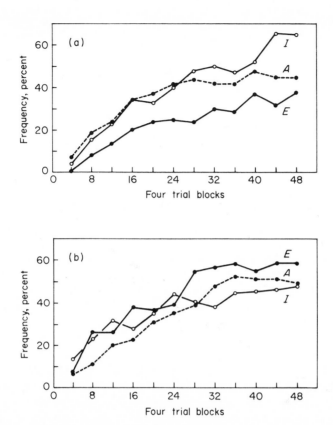

Fig. 3.2. Conditioning curves for conditions which favor introverts (a) and extraverts (b). (Based on Eysenck, 1966.)

in his discussion of Levey's results. Eysenck has attempted to relate differences in the introversion–extraversion dimension to a more explicit physiological theory. The physiological basis of introversion is now assumed to be differences in the threshold of arousal of the reticular activating system. Introverts are assumed to have lower thresholds of reticular arousal than extraverts. This system is widely assumed to be the physiological basis of a continuum of behavioral activation extending from sleep to manic states (see Hebb, 1955; Malmo, 1959; Magoun, 1963). The reticular system serves as a relatively nonspecific projection system for the cortex and serves to create cortical tonus. Various sensory projection systems have direct projection systems to the cortex and also have collaterals leading to the ascending reticular system. Activation of this reticular system is believed to lead to the disappearance of alpha waves in the EEG (or alpha blockage). This is presumably an index of a state of alertness. Reticular arousal also is assumed to be the physiological basis of the orientation reflex which indicates a behavioral state of attention usually produced by novel or intense stimulation.

The level of activity in the reticular system is assumed to be subject to inhibition by the cortex. Eysenck (1967, Chapter V) believes that a theory resembling that held by the Russian psychologist Sokolov (1963) for the orienting reflex provides an adequate model. Sokolov (1963) assumes that the cortex retains traces of previous stimuli. New stimuli are compared with the neural models present in the cortex. If there is a close match between the new stimulus and the neural traces of a previous stimulus, inhibitory impulses are sent from the cortex to the reticular system. If there is no match and the stimulus is novel, then the reticular system is aroused by impulse from the cortex and this in turn arouses the cortex.

Reticular arousal is also produced by strong emotional responses. Emotionality is thought by Eysenck to be dependent upon the activity of a second quasiindependent physiological system called the visceral brain including the hippocampus, amygdala, cingulum, and hypothalamus. Differences in the threshold of activation of the visceral brain are presumed to be the physiological basis of individual differences in the neuroticism-stability dimension. Neurotics are assumed to have low thresholds of such activation. Arousal of the visceral brain system is assumed to lead to arousal of the reticular activating system—but not the converse. As a result, on the physiological level, there should be a dependence between these two systems such that individuals with extremely low thresholds for emotional arousal who are, as a result, high on neuroticism, also tend to be introverted because high levels of arousal of the visceral brain system should lead to arousal of the reticular activating system. According to Eysenck this would account for the negative correlations on the MPI between the *E* and *N* scales and would explain why hysterics tend to be lower on neuroticism than dysthymics.

There is one other important feature of Eysenck's new physiological theory. Eysenck relates his conception of the physiological differences between introverts and extraverts to a distinction used by Russian researchers of organisms with "weak" nervous systems and organisms with "strong" nervous systems (see Gray, 1965). Introverts are assumed to have a weak nervous system and extraverts a strong nervous system. Organisms with weak nervous systems are assumed to respond at lower levels to stimulation and are assumed to respond with greater intensity to stimuli than organisms with strong nervous systems. However, the weak nervous system as a result of its extreme reactivity is more subject to protective or transmarginal inhibition than the strong nervous system. The concept of protective or transmarginal inhibition implies that when levels of excitation are reached which are above some optimal value, inhibition occurs which serves to dampen or decrease such excitation. Eysenck assumes that introverts are more subject to transmarginal inhibition than extraverts. Eysenck's theory thus implicitly assumes some upper level of arousal which is reached at a lower level of stimulus intensity by introverts than extraverts. Once this level is reached, new inhibitory processes occur which reduce excitation. Figure 3.3 presents a hypothetical representation of this theory. Examination of Figure 3.3 indicates that at low levels of stimulus intensity, introverts will be more aroused than extraverts. However, introverts will reach a level of arousal which produces transmarginal inhibition more rapidly than extraverts. As a result of the operation of this form of inhibition, it is possible that at high levels of stimulus intensity cortical arousal should be lower for introverts than for extraverts.

We are now in a position to understand the basis for Eysenck's assumption that introverts will condition more rapidly than extraverts under conditions where UCS intensity is low and extraverts will condition more rapidly than introverts under conditions where UCS intensity is high. Under conditions of low UCS intensity introverts are more cortically

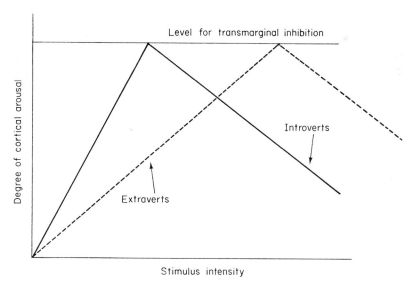

Fig. 3.3. The relationship between stimulus intensity and excitatory processes in introverts and extraverts.

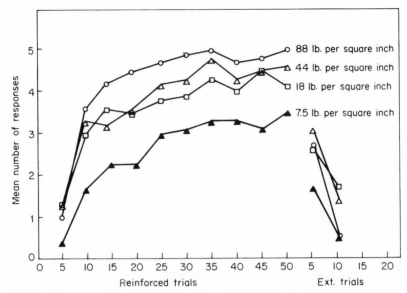

FIG. 3.4. Mean number anticipatory responses for each group of five trials during 50 reinforced and 10 unreinforced trials. (From G. E. Passey, The influence of intensity of unconditioned stimulus upon acquisition of a conditioned response. *Journal of Experimental Psychology*, 1948, **38**, 420–428.)

aroused than extraverts and thus may be assumed to have a higher level of performance. On the other hand, under high levels of UCS intensity, introverts, as a result of transmarginal inhibition, will have a lower level of cortical arousal than extraverts and will, as a result, exhibit less optimal performance.

This deduction is based on the expectation that there is an optimal level of UCS intensity for eyeblink conditioning. This expectation is based on a law, accepted by Eysenck, called the Yerkes–Dodson law (Yerkes & Dodson, 1908). The Yerkes–Dodson law asserts that the relationship between motivation and performance is an inverted U function such that intermediate levels of motivation lead to optimal levels of performance. In addition, the law asserts that the optimal level of motivation in a task is inversely related to task complexity. Therefore, in simple tasks, such as eyeblink conditioning, the relationship between motivation or drive and performance should be a positive one until high levels of motivation are reached at which time performance should decrease. The level of motivation in an eyeblink conditioning situation depends, in part, on UCS intensity. As UCS intensity increases, motivation, represented by $D_+$ in Eysenck's theory, should increase. Eysenck's theory, therefore, would appear to imply that the relationship between UCS intensity and conditioning in a simple classical conditioning situation is an inverted U function with high levels of UCS intensity leading to poorer performance due to the operation of transmarginal inhibition. However, studies dealing with the relationship between UCS intensity and eyeblink conditioning have not found a decrease in rate of conditioning even under extremely high levels of UCS intensity. For example, Passey (1948) found that UCS intensities up to 88 lb. per square inch facilitated eyeblink conditioning (see Figure 3.4). Consequently, there is no direct evidence in the general effect of UCS intensity on rate of conditioning of the operation of transmarginal inhibition—particularly at the highest level of UCS intensity used by Levey (6 lb. per square inch). Therefore, the appeal to transmarginal inhibition to explain Levey's findings of the relationship between UCS intensity and rate of conditioning in introverts and extraverts appears to lack a firm foundation in what is generally known about eyeblink conditioning.

Levey also found in his study that introverts condition more rapidly than extraverts when the CS–UCS interval is short (400 msec.). Extraverts were found to condition more rapidly than introverts when the CS–UCS interval was relatively long (800 msec.). It is known that the optimal CS–UCS interval is approximately 500 msec. (see Kimble, 1961). Shorter or longer intervals generally retard the rate of conditioning. Pavlov (1927) argued that this interval was optimal for the creation of temporally contiguous neural events and argued that this neural contiguity would produce optimal conditioning. Eysenck in referring to the Levey finding explains the results by referring to the short latency of response to stimulation of the introvert. This would presumably imply that the neural processes associated with the onset of the CS should occur more rapidly in introverts than extraverts. However, this should also imply that the neural processes associated with the onset of the UCS should occur more rapidly for introverts than for extraverts. Therefore, the hypothetical neural latency between the onset of the neural processes associated with the CS and the onset of the neural processes associated wtih the UCS should be roughly comparable for both introverts and extraverts. Consequently, it is hard to see why introverts should condition more rapidly than extraverts only under short CS–UCS intervals.

There is one other variable which Eysenck suggests is relevant to the relationship between introversion–extraversion and conditioning. Eysenck (1965) suggests that introverts will not condition more rapidly than extraverts under experimental conditions in which anxiety is aroused. Sweetbaum (1963) failed to find a significant relationship between introversion–extraversion and conditioning in an experimental situation in which the experimenter tried to arouse anxiety. Also, Eysenck (1965) has suggested that the lack of relationship between scores on the $E$ scale of the MPI and eyeblink conditioning reported by Spence and Spence (1964) may be explained by noting that conditioning is conducted in the Iowa laboratory under anxiety arousal conditions. This statement is slightly misleading. The anxiety arousing conditions referred to are those created by the experimental setting itself. No special effort is taken to create anxiety. Ominsky and Kimble (1966) conjecture that failures to replicate relationships between individual differences in anxiety and eyeblink conditioning obtained in the Iowa laboratory may have been due to the rather makeshift appearance of the Duke laboratory in which they worked. When they conducted their experiments in a new elaborate laboratory at Duke they were able to replicate the Iowa results. This reasoning implies that no special procedures are needed to arouse anxiety in an eyeblink conditioning experiment but special procedures are required to reduce anxiety if introverts are to condition more rapidly than extraverts. The alleged effect of anxiety on rate of conditioning of introverts is not a deductive consequence of Eysenck's original theory. Anxiety should, according to Eysenck's theory, increase $D_+$, and, as we have seen, increases in $D_+$ should lead to greater advantage in conditioning for introverts. In terms of Eysenck's new theory, introverts could be expected to condition relatively slowly under anxiety arousing conditions because of the operation of transmarginal inhibition. Alternatively, Eysenck could attempt to explain this relationship by appeal to the interrelationship of his two hypothetical physiological systems. Anxiety arousal should activate the visceral brain system. This in turn should activate the reticular activating system. Therefore, differences in the arousability by external stimuli of the reticular system between introverts and extraverts might disappear under conditions in which the reticular system is aroused by activation of the visceral brain system.

In summary, several tentative conclusions can be drawn about Eysenck's discussion of the relationship between introversion–extraversion and conditioning. Eysenck has said that those investigators who failed to find a relationship between the introversion–extraversion dimension and conditioning failed to pay attention to the details of his theory which specified that this relationship would be obtained only under certain specified conditions. A careful reading of the 1957 theory suggests that, at a minimum, Eysenck failed to specify these conditions in the original statement of his theory, and implied that introverts would invariably condition more rapidly than extraverts. An examination of his theory, further suggests, that the conditions do not in point of fact follow from his theory and are inconsistent with the theory. Further, these conditions are not clearly implied by Eysenck's new theory, although they are for the most part compatible with the theory provided certain additional assumptions are made—for example, the existence of transmarginal inhibition. Finally, there is some inconsistency in the empirical literature and some failure to replicate experiments. In view of these inconsistencies it might be reasonable to suggest that the relationship between introversion and extraversion and conditioning is not clearly understood nor clearly predictable on the basis of Eysenck's theory.

Our discussion of Eysenck's theory as applied to the conditioning situation has left us with some potentially valuable concepts about the introversion–extraversion dimension. These include some ideas about physiological differences between introverts and extraverts and the suggestion that introverts perform best, at least in a simple task, under relaxed conditions. There is little direct evidence of the physiological differences between introverts and extraverts postulated by Eysenck. There are, however, several relevant physiologically oriented studies. One group of studies deals with individual differences in "sedation thresholds." Eysenck (1967, Chapter VI) assumes that introverts being subject to a comparatively high state of cortical arousal would require relatively large doses of a depressant drug to reach certain behavioral levels of inhibition. Introverts should therefore have higher thresholds of sedation than extraverts. Shagass and his collaborators (Shagass, 1956; Shagass & Jones, 1958;

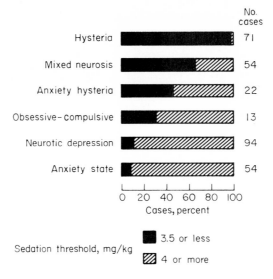

Fig. 3.5. Relative proportions of sedation thresholds above 3.5 and below 4 mg/kg in various psychoneurotic groups. Hysteria includes conversion hysteria and hysterical personality. (Based on Shagass & Jones, 1958.)

Shagass & Kerenyi, 1958; Shagass & Naiman, 1955) have reported several studies of sedation threshold using as a combined index of this threshold changes in the EEG and the occurrence of slurred speech. Shagass and Jones (1958) have reported clear differences in the sedation thresholds for various neurotic groups. Figure 3.5 presents their data. It is clear that neurotic groups which Eysenck assumes to be extraverted (hysterics) have lower sedation thresholds than neurotic groups which Eysenck assumes are introverted (anxiety states, depressions, and obsessive compulsive neurotics). These data as well as other supporting research by Shagass and his collaborators may be taken as indicating that introverted neurotics have characteristically higher levels of arousal than extraverted neurotics and accordingly have higher sedation thresholds.

There are two difficulties involved in the interpretation of these results. First, some investigators have reported difficulty in using the technique of the Shagass group to determine the sedation threshold and felt that the criterion was subjective and difficult to use (see Ackner & Pampiglione, 1958; Boudreau, 1958). Claridge and Herrington (1960) used a behavioral rather than a physiological measure of sedation threshold. In their study they investigated the effects of continuous intravenous injections of amylobarbitone sodium on a digit doubling task in which subjects were required to double randomly presented digits. Sedation threshold was defined as an interpolated point at which there was 50% error in a block of five responses. Their data are presented in Table 3.2. Table 3.2 indicates that those subjects who would be classified by Eysenck as extraverted neurotics

TABLE 3.2

*Sedation Threshold in Various Groups Tested by Claridge and Herrington*

| Group | Mean sedation threshold, mg/kg |
|---|---|
| Civilian dysthymics | |
| Chronic anxiety states | 11.00 |
| Obsessional neurotics | 10.26 |
| Reactive depression | 9.10 |
| Total group | 10.14 |
| Military dysthymics | |
| Total group | 9.34 |
| Hysterico-psychopathy | |
| Conversion hysterics | 6.73 |
| Hysterical personalities | 6.81 |
| Psychopaths | 5.69 |

tend to have lower sedation thresholds than those groups classified by Eysenck as introverted neurotics. Thus, the results of the Claridge and Herrington experiment, using a different method of assessing the sedation threshold of a barbiturate drug agree with those reported by Shagass and his collaborators.

A basic problem in interpreting these results stems from the lack of dimensional purity of the dysthymic-hysterical distinction. As we have indicated dysthymics are *both* more introverted and more neurotic than hysterics. Therefore, it is not clear that these differences in sedation thresholds should be attributable to the introversion–extraversion dimension. Claridge (1967) has reported that the relationship between scores on the *E* and *N* scales of the MPI and various physiological and behavioral indices of arousal tends to be nonsignificant. Claridge has also reported the results of a factor analysis of a number of physiological and behavioral measures as well as the *E* and *N* scales of the MPI. The first factor derived was principally defined by scores on the sedation threshold measure which correlated with the factor .74. The correlations of the *E* and *N* scale scores with this factor were .08 and .00, respectively. This finding suggests that neither neuroticism nor introversion–extraversion as measured by the MPI are, when considered by themselves, significantly related to sedation threshold.

Claridge obtained a second factor in his study. Several measures based on the EEG loaded on this factor. These measures included alpha index—percentage of time alpha rhythm was present whose loading on this factor was −.60; and alpha blocking time—the time for alpha rhythm to return to a resting level after inspection of a rotating spiral whose loading on this factor was .51. Low alpha index and long alpha blocking time could both be taken as indices of a high level of cortical arousal. The loading of the *E* and *N* scales on this factor were, respectively, −.68 and .69. Thus EEG indices of cortical arousal were associated with introversion and neuroticism. Since the sample of subjects from whom the data for the factor analysis were obtained were principally neurotic (the sample included 27 neurotic and 10 normals), the loadings of the *E* and *N* scales on this factor may be taken to represent principally the differences between dysthymics and hysterics. That is, introversion and neuroticism as measured by the MPI are associated with each other and with EEG derived indices of cortical arousal—apparently reflecting in part what may be taken as the results of activation of the reticular activating system. Claridge also reports the results of a second-order factor analysis of these data. He obtained a second-order factor which apparently represents a general factor of arousability. Sedation threshold, alpha blocking time and alpha index load on this second-order factor, respectively, .58, .61,

−.52. The loadings of the $E$ and $N$ scales of the MPI on this factor are, respectively, −.44 and .51. The results of these statistical analyses do indicate that the introversion–extraversion dimension, at least among neurotics, is in fact related to dimensions of arousal which might plausibly be related to the activity of the reticular system. However, the pattern of this relationship does not appear to be precisely what would be predicted on the basis of Eysenck's theory. The introversion–extraversion dimension, *per se*, does not appear to be related to a dimension of arousability. It is only the joint effects of the introversion–extraversion and neuroticism dimensions which appear to be related to this dimension. What Eysenck takes to be the physiological basis of introversion–extraversion appears to be more closely related to the difference between dysthymics and hysterics. But this difference is the result of the joint action of both the neuroticism and introversion–extraversion dimensions. However this dimension cannot precisely be aligned with either of the two principal dimensions of personality. Thus there would appear to be some discrepancy between the causal physiological level of analysis and the descriptive level of analysis. It should be noted that Eysenck's physiological theory does postulate the partial interdependence of the visceral brain and the reticular system. What is not clear to this writer is how Eysenck's physiological theory may be aligned with or used to deduce the taxonomic system developed by Eysenck.

Eysenck and his associates have attempted to extend his $I/E$ and physiological theories to a wide variety of experimental situations. It would be beyond the scope of this book to review all of this research in detail. There is one further type of experimental situation which is central to Eysenck's theory—vigilance. A vigilance task is one in which a subject must respond over an extended period of time to a specified small change in stimulation which occurs sporadically at random intervals. Typical of this type of task is the jump-clock test used by Mackworth (1961). In this task a clock-hand travels around a blank face at a rate of one jump per second—each jump covering a standard distance. The subject is required to respond to a sporadically occurring double jump. Introverts may be expected on theoretical ground to show better vigilance performance than extraverts. There are at least two reasons for this expectation. First, it is generally believed that high levels of arousal produce better performance in vigilance tasks. For example, amphetamine, which is thought to maintain the level of arousal of the reticular system (Elkes, 1961), is known to increase performance in vigilance tasks (Mackworth, 1965; Loeb, Hawkes, Evans, & Alluisi, 1965). Also, Eysenck (1967) has argued that states of inhibition build up during a vigilance task. Since the task is continuous, there is no opportunity for the reactive inhibition which develops to dissipate. As a result, reactive inhibition builds up to the point where it produces an involuntary rest period. If a stimulus coincides with the occurrence of an involuntary rest pause, the subject will fail to respond to it (also see Mackworth, 1968). If extraverts develop inhibition more rapidly than introverts, their performance should be poorer in a vigilance task.

Bakan, Belton, and Toth (1963) reported better performance for introverts than extraverts in an auditory vigilance task in which subjects had to listen to random digits and respond to signals consisting of three consecutive digits forming an odd, even, odd sequence. Claridge (1967) has reported the results of an experiment in which he compared the performance of dysthymics, hysterics, and normal subjects on a similar auditory vigilance task. The results clearly indicate that dysthymics show better vigilance performance than hysterics. Also, hysterics show a greater decline in performance during the course of the experiment than dysthymics. Figure 3.6 shows the results obtained by Claridge. Claridge also obtained measures of arousal during the course of the experiment. He found dysthymics had higher heart rate and skin conductance than hysterics during

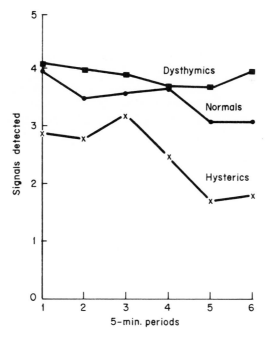

Fig. 3.6. Auditory vigilance curves for dysthymics, hysterics, and normal subjects. (Based on Claridge, 1967.)

the experiment. These results may be taken as clearly supporting and extending the findings of Bakan. However, this interpretation depends on the assumption that the relevant difference between hysterics and dysthymics is their position on the introversion–extraversion dimension. Claridge reports that neither overall vigilance behavior, decline in vigilance, heart rate level in the vigilance experiment, nor skin conductance level in the vigilance experiment are significantly correlated with either the *E* or *N* scales of the MPI in neurotic or normal subjects. These results therefore do not support the findings of Bakan *et al.* (1963). Rather, they suggest that there is some relationship between physiological arousal (at least autonomic arousal) and performance in a vigilance task as suggested by Eysenck, but the underlying physiological dimension is related to the differences between a dimension defined by high neuroticism and introversion which leads to dysthymia versus moderate neuroticism and moderate introversion which leads to hysteria. Thus Claridge's results for vigilance parallel his findings for sedation threshold.

## Eysenck's Theory of Socialization

Our discussion of Eysenck's theory has dealt principally with the biological aspects of his theory. We have not discussed Eysenck's attempt to relate his biological theory to social behavior. Much of Eysenck's work in recent years has been focused on a program of experimental research closely related to his biologically based theories. He has done relatively little recent work on the extension of his biological concepts to the social domain. In his first book dealing with the excitation–inhibition theory, Eysenck (1957) included a chapter on socialization and personality. In this chapter Eysenck accepted the Freudian thesis (although he does not mention Freud in this connection) that socialization, in our culture at least, stresses the inhibition of overt aggressive and sexual responses. Eysenck believes with Mowrer (1950) that this type of socialization is accomplished principally by a conditioning process mediated by the autonomic nervous system and involving anxiety. We shall discuss this view of socialization in greater detail in a later chapter. Briefly, what is involved here is the notion that in the process of socialization anxiety is conditioned to previously neutral stimuli. These include stimuli associated with sexual and agressive tendencies. Any learned response which will remove the anxiety will be rewarded. This process may be illustrated as follows: Suppose an individual, as a result of a conditioning process, becomes anxious whenever he finds himself in a state of sexual or aggressive arousal. This anxiety might be eliminated if the individual learned to inhibit states of sexual and aggressive arousal.

If socialization is primarily a process of inhibiting sexual and aggressive impulses and if this process is principally mediated by conditioning, then individuals who condition rapidly should be "oversocialized" and individuals who condition slowly should be "undersocialized." Over- and under-socialization in this context evidently refers to the degree to which there is a learned inhibition of sexual and aggressive impulses. Eysenck relates his notion of socialization to his personality theory by arguing that introverts, by virtue of their greater capacity to form conditioned responses than extraverts, will be oversocialized and extraverts, as a result of their relatively poor capacity to form conditioned responses, will be undersocialized. Introverted neurotics suffer from an excessive inhibition of sexual and agressive responses, extraverted neurotics from a lack of control of such responses.

The most direct evidence that could be offered in support of Eysenck's views of the relationship between introversion–extraversion and socialization would be a study of the relationship between scores on the $E$ scale and direct, preferably behavioral, measures of sexual and aggressive inhibitions. Such a study has not been done. Rather, Eysenck has related scores on measures of the introversion–extraversion dimension to a factor analytically derived attitude dimension called tender versus toughminded (see James, 1907 for the origins of the concepts). This attitude dimension is assumed by Eysenck to be related to differences in socialization. Toughmindedness involves a constellation of attitudes which are derived from undersocialization. Toughmindedness involves favorable attitudes toward the overt expression of sexual and aggressive impulses. These attitudes, according to Eysenck, include attitudes favorable to flogging, companionate marriage, the death penalty, easier divorce laws, harsh treatment of criminals, abolishment of abortion laws, and capital punishment. Tenderminded attitudes stem from oversocialization and, as a result, are favorable to the inhibition of sexual and aggressive impulses. They include making birth control illegal, pacifism, etc. (see Eysenck, 1957, p. 219). Introverts are assumed to be tenderminded and extraverts are assumed to be toughminded.

The evidence for the relationship between the introversion–extraversion and the tender–tough-minded attitude dimensions is contained in Eysenck's book, *The Psychology of Politics* (see Eysenck, 1954). The principal study reported in the book in support of Eysenck's theory of attitudes involves the factor analysis of the responses of 750 middle class subjects to an attitude questionnaire. Two factors were derived from the study, one of them being the tender–tough-minded factor. Eysenck points out that other factor analytic investigations of the attitude domain have resulted in a somewhat different rotation of factors and are not in complete accord with Eysenck's factor solution (see Ferguson, 1941). The 10 items which load most highly on the tender–tough-minded factor are, in decreasing order of

TABLE 3.3

*Loadings of Items on the Tender–Tough-Minded Factor*

| Item | Loading |
|------|---------|
| Only by going back to religion can civilization hope to survive | $-.65$ |
| Men and women have the right to find out whether they are sexually suited before marriage (for example, by companionate marriage) | .56 |
| Sunday observance is old-fashioned and should cease to govern our behavior | $-.49$ |
| Divorce laws should be altered to make divorce easier | .47 |
| Birth control, except when medically indicated, should be made illegal | $-.42$ |
| Conscientious objectors are traitors to their country, and should be treated accordingly | .39 |
| Our present difficulties are due rather to moral than to economic causes | $-.38$ |
| It is right and proper that religious education should be compulsory | $-.34$ |
| Colored people are innately inferior to white people | .32 |
| War is inherent in human nature | .32 |

Based on Eysenck, 1954.

their absolute loadings on the factor, given in Table 3.3. An examination of Table 3.3 suggests that there is an alternative and perhaps more compelling interpretation of this factor—viz., pro- or antireligious attitudes. Almost all of the items which load positively on the factor involve antireligious attitudes or attitudes which are contrary to church doctrine. Similarly, items which load negatively on the factor tend to be proreligious.

Eysenck reports that these results were replicated in a doctoral dissertation done under his supervision by Melvin. Melvin's study provided the basis for the construction of an improved measure of the tender–tough-minded dimension. The scale based on Melvin's research is reproduced in Eysenck's book (Eysenck, 1954, pp. 277–280). However, Eysenck does not report the loadings of the various items on the factor. Of the 32 items on the scale at least 7 items deal directly with pro- and antireligious attitudes. For example, "Christ was divine, wholly or partly in a sense different from other men," or "The idea of God is an invention of the human mind." A number of of other items on the scale indirectly deal with religious attitudes, since they involve matters of church doctrine. For example, "Sex relations except in marriage are always wrong," "There is no survival of any kind after death." It is apparent that the tender–tough-minded dimension does, at least in part, measure pro- or antireligious attitudes. A number of other items are less directly related to religious belief. Two such items which also were used in Eysenck's original study were, "Crimes of violence should be punished by flogging," and "The death penalty is barbaric and should be abolished." These latter items are perhaps more closely related to Eysenck's conception of this dimension as involving inhibition of aggressive actions. It is, however, interesting to note that the loadings of these items in the original study were .28 and .20 respectively. These items, therefore, had lower loadings than those which were more closely related to religion. We can summarize the import of this discussion by suggesting that it is not clear that the tender–toughminded scale measures attitudes related to inhibition of sexual and aggressive impulses. It is at least equally plausible to suggest that the scale is primarily a measure of religious attitudes and deals with attitudes about the expression of sexual and aggressive impulses only indirectly. This indirect influence stems directly from church doctrine or indirectly from views held by religious leaders.

The principal evidence for the relationship between the introversion–extraversion dimension and the tender–toughminded dimension comes from a study by George (as quoted in Eysenck, 1954). George used Guilford's scales as a measure of introversion–extraversion. He found that the two scales most closely related to the introversion–extraversion dimension, rhathymia and social shyness, correlated with the tender–toughminded dimension +.41 and −.24 respectively. Although the correlations are not high, they do indicate that there is some relationship between these dimensions.

In addition to the lack of clarity of what is in fact measured by the tender–toughminded scale, there are a number of other difficulties in Eysenck's attempted synthesis of the biological and sociological aspects of his theory. It is possible to take issue with his conception of socialization as involving the inhibition of sexual and aggressive impulses by associating them with anxiety. In a later chapter we shall discuss a learning approach to socialization developed by Bandura and Walters which places great emphasis on the role of models and the use of rewards in the development of control over the expression of sexual and aggressive behaviors. From this perspective, Eysenck overemphasizes the role of anxiety and classical conditioning. The issue can be put in nontechnical terms as follows: Eysenck argues that socialization involves becoming afraid of exhibiting sexual and aggressive responses. Bandura and Walters would supplement this view by suggesting  that, in addition, socialization involves learning when and in what form to express such behavior. And this latter form of learning is not essentially a matter of classical conditioning. Thus, one could argue that the degree to which there is inhibition of expression of sexual and aggressive impulses is not solely a matter of potential for the development of classically conditioned responses but is dependent upon the vagaries of the social environment and the kinds of behaviors for which a person is rewarded or punished.

There is one final difficulty with Eysenck's integration. The integration is dependent on the assertion that introverts will invariably condition more rapidly than extraverts. This assertion is rather tenuous. As we have seen, Eysenck himself no longer holds that introverts invariably condition more rapidly than extraverts. Differences in the rate of conditioning are dependent upon a number of parameters associated with the conditioning process. If one cannot assert that introverts will in general condition more rapidly than extraverts, then there is no basis for making sweeping assertions about the socialization process and there is no basis for deriving the social behavior of introverts and extraverts from their alleged physiological foundation.

After this brief review of several aspects of Eysenck's theory, some general appraisal of his work can be offered. It seems to this writer that no other personality theorist has come closer to understanding the form of a generally satisfactory theory of personality. I believe that the fully adequate scientific theory of personality which we do not as yet have will be similar in many respects to Eysenck's theory. That is, it will start with a limited number of dimensions (although not necessarily factorially derived dimensions) which are related to differences in physiological processes. These individual differences should interact with and influence the socialization process. Finally, the theory should be hypothetico-deductive in form—permitting one to predict how a particular kind of individual will behave in a particular kind of situation. Although Eysenck's theory satisfies these desiderata with respect to format, it falls down in several other respects. First, and perhaps most critically, the theory is not invariably in accord with empirical findings. Second, deductions from the theory often involve *ad hoc* assumptions and do not invariably rigorously follow from the central assumptions of the theory. Finally, the theory appears to deal most precisely and extensively with biologically relevant behaviors. However, there is insufficient attention to the social aspects of behavior and there is a failure to deal in an equally thorough and sophisticated way with the socialization process.

# CHAPTER 4

# SPENCE'S THEORY OF ANXIETY AS DRIVE

## Background Research

The next theory we shall consider, Spence's theory of anxiety, is related to Eysenck's theory in several ways. Spence's theory, like Eysenck's, deals with individual differences in classical eyeblink conditioning. Both theories attempt to deal with the relationship between individual differences and performance in a variety of experimental tasks. Both theories use concepts developed by Hull (1943) as part of his comprehensive theory of behavior. There is, however, one principal difference between these theories. Eysenck's theory is a comprehensive theory of personality, while Spence has consistently stressed that his theory is to be understood as a treatment of certain relationships between individual differences in anxiety and behavior in a limited variety of experience situations. He has consistently rejected tests of his theory which deal with extensions of his theory to situations which he believes are outside the boundary conditions of experimental tasks for which relatively precise predictions can be made.

The impetus to Spence's work was the development of a measure of individual differences in anxiety by Taylor (1951, 1953) which is called the Taylor Manifest Anxiety Scale (MAS). In order to develop her measure of anxiety she took approximately 200 items from the Minnesota Multi-Phasic Personality Inventory (MMPI) and gave them to 5 clinical psychologists with instructions to choose those items which were indicative of anxiety. There were 65 items which 4 out of 5 or all 5 clinical psychologists

TABLE 4.1    *Taylor's MAS*

1. I do not tire quickly.    (F)
2. I am troubled by attacks of nausea.    (T)
3. I believe I am no more nervous than most others.    (F)
4. I have very few headaches. (F)
5. I work under a great deal of tension.    (T)
6. I cannot keep my mind on one thing.    (T)
7. I worry over money and business.    (T)
8. I frequently notice my hand shakes when I try to do something.    (T)
9. I blush no more often than others.    (F)
10. I have diarrhea once a month or more.    (T)
11. I worry quite a bit over possible misfortunes.    (T)
12. I practically never blush.    (F)
13. I am often afraid that I am going to blush.    (T)
14. I have nightmares every few nights.    (T)
15. My hands and feet are usually warm enough.    (F)
16. I sweat very easily even on cool days.    (T)
17. Sometimes when embarrassed, I break out in a sweat which annoys me greatly. (T)
18. I hardly ever notice my heart pounding and I am seldom short of breath.    (F)
19. I feel hungry almost all the time.    (T)
20. I am very seldom troubled by constipation.    (F)
21. I have a great deal of stomach trouble.    (T)
22. I have had periods in which I lost sleep over worry.    (T)
23. My sleep is fitful and disturbed.    (T)
24. I dream frequently about things that are best kept to myself.    (T)
25. I am easily embarrassed.    (T)
26. I am more sensitive than most other people.    (T)
27. I frequently find myself worrying about something.    (T)
28. I wish I could be as happy as others seem to be.    (T)
29. I am usually calm and not easily upset.    (F)
30. I cry easily.    (T)
31. I feel anxiety about something or someone almost all the time.    (T)
32. I am happy most of the time.    (F)
33. It makes me nervous to have to wait.    (T)
34. I have periods of such great restlessness that I cannot sit long in a chair.    (T)
35. Sometimes I become so excited that I find it hard to get to sleep.    (T)
36. I have sometimes felt that difficulties were piling up so high that I could not overcome them.    (T)
37. I must admit that I have at times been worried beyond reason over something that really did not matter.    (T)
38. I have very few fears compared to my friends.    (F)
39. I have been afraid of things or people that I know could not hurt me.    (T)
40. I certainly feel useless at times.    (T)
41. I find it hard to keep my mind on a task or job.    (T)
42. I am usually self-conscious.    (T)
43. I am inclined to take things hard.    (T)
44. I am a highly strung person.    (T)
45. Life is a strain for me much of the time.    (T)
46. At times I think I am no good at all.    (T)
47. I am certainly lacking in self-confidence.    (T)
48. I sometimes feel that I am about to go to pieces.    (T)
49. I shrink from facing a crisis or difficulty.    (T)
50. I am entirely self-confident.    (F)

chose as indicative of anxiety. Subsequently, this list was reduced to 50 items. Table 4.1 presents the 50-item MAS and indicates the procedures involved in scoring the items.

Two general questions have been raised about the Taylor scale. The first question was raised by the critics of Spence's work: Is the Taylor scale a measure of anxiety? The second question is one which Spence considers more relevant: Are individual differences in the Taylor scale indicative of individual differences in Hull's construct, drive (D)?

Research dealing with the first question has tended to support the view of the Taylor scale as a measure of anxiety. There have been a variety of studies which have dealt with the validity of the Taylor scale as a measure of anxiety. It has been found that the MAS correlates positively with other paper and pencil measures of anxiety. For example, Raphelson (1957) has reported a correlation of .53 between the MAS and a paper and pencil measure of the tendency to become anxious in testing situations developed by Mandler and Sarason (1952). Also, scores on the Taylor scale have been found to be positively related to behavior ratings of anxiety by psychologists. Typical of these studies is one by Buss, Wiener, Durkee, and Baer (1955) who reported a correlation of .60 between MAS scores and pooled ratings of anxiety of neuropsychiatric patients made by four clinical psychologists. These studies, as well as many others, indicate that scores on the MAS are related to clinical judgments of anxiety and other paper and pencil measures of anxiety.

## The MAS as a Measure of Drive

The Taylor scale was designed as a measure of drive in the Hullian sense. There are several lines of thought which converge in this conception. Many learning theorists in the Hullian tradition have thought of anxiety as a drive. Most of the research dealing with Hull's theory of drive had used animals. In order to extend this research to the human level it became necessary to develop a measure of drive in humans. Taylor turned to anxiety as an important drive and assumed that individual differences in anxiety would be indicative of individual differences in drive level. It was assumed that individuals who were high in anxiety tended to be chronically or constantly anxious and thus would be higher in drive level in any particular situation than individuals who were low in anxiety. Subsequent research has tended to support a conception of the MAS as an acute measure of anxiety. That is, as a measure of the tendency to become anxious in certain situations.

The original research attempting to validate the MAS as a measure of drive in the Hullian sense dealt with eyeblink conditioning. The relationship between differences in drive level and eyeblink-conditioning is derived as follows: The basic equation in Spence's theory is

$$E = f(D \times sHr).$$

This equation states that excitatory potential is a function of drive level multiplied by habit. It follows from this conception that, in a simple learning situation in which a single habit is acquired, higher drive should lead to higher levels of excitatory potential than low drive and this in turn should be reflected in higher levels of performance for the habit which is acquired. Accordingly, individuals who score high on the MAS should condition more rapidly than individuals who score low on the MAS. In addition, the assumption of a multiplicative relationship between drive and habit implies that conditioning curves for individuals who differ in drive level should show progressively larger divergence as conditioning proceeds. This follows from the fact that as $H$ increases over conditioning trials, the product of $D \times H$ will show greater divergence for constant differences in drive level. Spence (1964) has surveyed the eyeblink conditioning literature dealing with this problem. He found that in 21 of 26 studies subjects who scored high on the MAS showed significantly higher levels of performance than subjects who scored low on the MAS. Representative results from two of these studies are presented in Figure 4.1. Note that an examination of Figure 4.1 indicates that the curves diverge over trials in accordance with the multiplicative assumption. Note also that conditioning occurs more rapidly when the unconditioned stimulus is higher. In Spence's theory, the magnitude of the unconditioned stimulus which is assumed to be a noxious stimulus, determines the level of a hypothetical emotional response, $r_e$. The higher the level of $r_e$, the higher the level of drive. Thus, differences in the magnitude of the unconditioned stimulus should have a similar effect on eyeblink-conditioning performance as differences in scores on the MAS, since these differences each lead to differences in $r_e$ which, in turn, lead to differences in drive level.

Spence's review of the literature seems to indicate that the interpretation of the MAS as a measure of drive is supported by the eyeblink conditioning studies. However, there are a number of qualifications which may be suggested. Scores on the MAS are not a major determinant of performance in this type of task. In order to obtain significant results it is necessary to use a large number of subjects whose scores are at the extremes of the distribution of MAS scores. Typically, only those subjects whose scores fall in the upper and lower 20 percent of the distribution of scores on the MAS are included in the study. Actually, the question of the magnitude of the relationship between MAS scores and performance in an eyeblink conditioning task is not crucial. In order to validate the

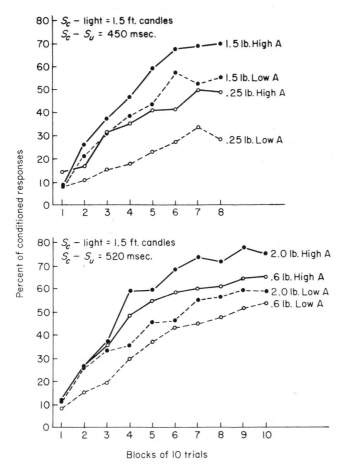

Fig. 4.1. Performance in eyelid conditioning as function of A-score and intensity of US. (From K. W. Spence, A theory of emotionally based drive (D) and its relation to performance in simple learning situations. *American Psychologist*, 1958, **13**, 131–141.)

theoretical assumption that scores on the MAS are related to drive, it is sufficient to find that the predicted relationship is obtained. There are more critical issues to be considered, however, in discussing the relationship between scores on the MAS and drive. If the MAS is a measure of drive then the same reasoning which leads to the prediction of superior performance for high scores on the MAS in eyeblink conditioning should suggest that individuals who score high on the MAS ought to exhibit superior performance in any classical conditioning situation in which the acquisition of a single habit is under investigation. Bindra, Paterson, and

Strzelecki (1955) have reported that differences on the MAS are unrelated to performance in a salivary conditioning task. In this type of classical conditioning situation, the unconditioned stimulus is not noxious but is rewarding. Spence and Spence (1966) interpret these results as indicating that the MAS measures acute anxiety. That is, conditions of threat are required to arouse anxiety. Hence, the MAS may be viewed as measuring the tendency to become anxious in threatening situations. Spence has suggested on the basis of his review of the literature that relationships between MAS and eyeblink conditioning are maximized under conditions where subjects are made to be fearful and uneasy (for example, isolation of subjects, use of dimly lit rooms with complicated apparatus, etc.). Also, in support of the acute hypothesis is a study by Mednick (1957) who found no significant relationship between scores on the MAS and stimulus generalization for subjects who had served in several previous experiments. However, a significant relationship was found for subjects who were experimentally naive. Mednick's results are interpreted by Spence and Spence (1966) as indicating that subjects lose some of their potential to become anxious while participating in psychological experiments after repeatedly serving as subjects. These results suggest that the interpretations of the MAS as a measure of drive is valid only in threatening situations. Spence (1956) has suggested that different rates of eyeblink conditioning as a function of UCS intensity might be attributable to differences in the rate of habit formation rather than drive. The reasoning involved here is as follows: An eyeblink response serves to remove a noxious stimulus—the puff of air to the eye—and therefore is a response which is reinforced or rewarded. Under conditions of high puff intensity the magnitude of the reinforcement is increased since the unconditioned stimulus produces more anxiety. If the growth of habit strength is a function of the magnitude of reinforcement, then the more rapid eyeblink conditioning which occurs when the UCS is high would be attributable to differences in the rate of development of habit strength rather than differences in drive. Subjects who score high on the MAS apparently have a greater capacity to become fearful than subjects who score low on the UCS. Therefore, the former subjects should receive greater amounts of reinforcement whenever they close their eye on the assumption that the puff of air is more noxious to them than to the latter subjects. Accordingly, the more rapid development of eyeblink conditioning among the subjects who score high on the MAS may be attributable to their more rapid development of habit strength.

An alternative explanation which does not refer to drive has been advanced by Hilgard, Jones, and Kaplan (1951). They suggested that subjects who score high on the MAS are worried defensive individuals who come into the conditioning situation with strong response tendencies to blink, and to wince. Since these responses are similar or identical to those which the experimenter wishes to condition, they should show more rapid conditioning. This interpretation implies that the more rapid conditioning of the subjects who score high on the MAS is due to their initial advantage in habit strength. However, Spence (1964) has found that the differences in performance in eyeblink conditioning between subjects who score high and those who score low on the MAS increase over trials. Since the differences are larger at the end of conditioning than at the beginning, it does not seem reasonable to attribute these differences to differences in initial level of habit strength.

This review of the research relating scores on the MAS to eyeblink conditioning indicates that the research has for the most part supported the interpretation of the MAS as a measure of drive in the Hullian sense. However, other interpretations which do not involve the drive concept can be developed to explain the relationship between scores on the MAS and eyeblink conditioning.

In addition to relating MAS to eyeblink conditioning, research has dealt with the relationship between the MAS and performance in a variety of other types of complex learning tasks. The term "complex" as used in this context involves a situation in which several habits are examined rather than a single habit as in the classical conditioning situation. Predictions may be derived relating drive to performance on several types of tasks. The simplest extension of the Spence theory to a complex task involves a task in which several discrete habits are acquired and the various habits are acquired in isolation from each other. One type of task of this type is a noncompetitional paired associate learning task. In this task subjects must learn a list of paired associates—that is, the subject must learn to give the correct response each time a stimulus is presented to him. If the lists fulfill three criteria, unambiguous predictions to the effect that subjects who score high on the Taylor scale will learn the list more rapidly than subjects who score low on the Taylor scale can be made. The criteria are the following:

1. The similarity among the stimuli must be minimal.
2. The similarity among responses must be minimal.
3. The intrapair relationship between stimulus and response must be minimal.

These criteria theoretically imply a situation in which the learning of each stimulus and response may be treated as the acquisition of a discrete habit which minimally interferes with or affects the acquisition of any other response pair. Further, the third criterion creates a situation in which the initial habit strength for any stimulus–response connection is close to zero. Under these conditions, subjects who score high on the MAS (and who are therefore high in drive) should learn the list more rapidly than subjects who score low on the MAS. This follows from the assumption that the probability of making the correct response to any stimulus is a function of the level of excitatory potential which can be expected to be higher under high drive conditions than under low drive conditions. Therefore, there should be little or no difference in performance at the start of the task when habit strength is close to zero. As the task progresses the difference between groups of high and low scorers on the MAS should increase with the group of high scorers on the MAS showing increasingly superior performance. Results in this type of learning task have generally supported these predictions. (See Spence, 1958; Taylor, 1958; Taylor & Chapman, 1955). At least one study has failed to support this prediction (Kamin & Fedorchak, 1957).

It is also possible to design paired associate tasks in which high drive should produce poorer performance than low drive. One such task involves a list in which some of the stimulus items are similar in meaning to other stimulus items. In addition some stimulus response pairs have high initial associative connections (for example, tranquil–placid) while other pairs use stimuli which are related to stimuli in the high associative pairs but use response members which have low associative relationship to these stimuli (for example, serene–headstrong). For these latter stimulus–response pairs, Spence assumes that on the beginning trials of the learning situation there will be a competition of response between the response acquired to similar stimuli on the high associative pairs and the correct response. A subject may be expected to acquire the correct responses for the high associative pairs more rapidly than the correct responses for the low associative pairs. This follows from the expectation that the initial habit strength for the latter responses is lower. Thus, for example, a subject ought to learn the responses placid to the stimulus tranquil more rapidly than the response headstrong to the stimulus serene. During the early trials of the learning situation these differential learning rates should create a situation of response competition. That is, the subject confronted with the stimulus for a low associative pair should have a tendency to make one of two responses—the correct response and an incorrect response which is the response acquired to the similar stimulus in a high associative pair. Thus, for example, the subject presented with the stimulus serene should have both a tendency to respond by saying "placid"—the response acquired to the stimulus tranquil which should generalize to the stimulus serene by virtue of their shared meaning and by saying "headstrong." In the early trials of learning the habit strength associated with the incorrect response (for example, "placid") could be higher than the habit strength associated with the correct response, "headstrong." What would be the effect of differences in drive on the probability of saying the correct response? According to the Hull–Spence theory, drive multiplies all habits which are present in a particular situation. Therefore, in this situation the excitatory potential for both the correct and incorrect response would be higher under high drive conditions than under low drive conditions. However, the algebraic difference between the excitatory potentials increases as drive increases. That is, under high drive conditions the differences between the excitatory potentials for habits which differ in their strength will be greater than under low drive conditions. It follows from Spence's theory (see Spence, 1956, 1958) that the respective probabilities of making different responses are a function of the differences between their excitatory potential. If two responses have unequal habit strengths, then the probability of making the response whose habit strength is greater is increased when the difference between the excitatory potential for that response and its competitor is increased. Therefore, under high drive conditions the probability of making that response whose habit strength is highest is greater than under low drive conditions. These considerations enable us to make predictions about the performance of subjects who differ in scores on the MAS in the paired associate learning task we are considering. Subjects who score high on the MAS (and are therefore high in drive) should make more incorrect responses than subjects low on the MAS during the early trials on the low associative stimulus–response pairs. During the later trials, as learning progresses, the habit strength for the correct response for the low associative pairs should become higher than the habit strength for the competing incorrect response. During these later trials the probability of a correct response for the high MAS subjects on the low associative pairs should be higher than the probability of a correct response for the low MAS subjects. Therefore, restricting the analysis to the low associative pairs we should expect superior performance on the early trials for the low MAS subjects and superior performance on the later trials for the high MAS subjects. There is some evidence supporting the first part of this prediction (Spence, Farber, & McFann, 1956; Spence, Taylor, & Ketchel, 1956) and there is also some negative evidence (Lovass, 1960).

Goulet (1968) has presented a cogent analysis of the relationship between drive and verbal learning. He argues that many of the studies dealing with this problem have failed to adequately consider some of the variables which may influence performance on these tasks. He points out that psychologists interested in paired associate learning have treated this type of situation as one in which there are two functionally different learning tasks or stages—response-learning and associative learning. The response stage involves the learning of the list of response units and the associative stage involves the learning of the "hook up" of each response to its appropriate stimulus (Underwood & Schulz, 1960). This analysis implies that Spence's deduction that more incorrect responses would be given to low associative pairs early in learning by high MAS subjects does not necessarily follow. High drive should facilitate the response learning stage. That is, under high drive conditions subjects should have better learning of the separate responses. Competitional effects among responses would be restricted to the associative stage of learning. Thus, on the early trials of a paired associate learning task high drive should on the one hand facilitate the learning of the appropriate response units and then lead to poorer performance during the associative stage for the stimuli eliciting incorrect competitional responses with dominant response strength. Since differences in drive have opposite effects, no unambiguous prediction may be derived for this task.

A similar confounding exists with respect to some transfer learning situations which have been used to test Spence's theory. One type of transfer experiment deals with the A–B–A–C paradigm. In this situation the subject learns a list of paired associates and is then presented with a second list consisting of the same stimuli but different responses. In one experiment designed to test Spence's theory, Standish and Champion (1960) gave subjects an A–B list consisting of pairs of high association value. The A–C list consisted of pairs of low association value. In this situation one would expect that during the initial trials of learning on the A–C list the habit strengths for incorrect B responses would be higher than the habit strengths for correct C responses. This implies that subjects high in drive should show poorer performance during the learning of the A–C list on the early trials than subjects low in drive because increasing drive should increase the probability of occurrence of the dominant but incorrect responses. As learning progress on the A–C list, the correct or C response should eventually develop greater habit strength than the incorrect B response and this should lead to superior performance for the high drive group later in learning. Using the MAS as a measure of drive, Standish and Champion (1960) obtained data supporting these predictions. However, Goulet (1968) has pointed out that this deduction fails to consider the two-stage analysis of paired associate learning which implies that high drive should facilitate the learning of the response units during the learning of the A–C list and this factor should lead to superior learning for the high drive subjects early in learning. Thus, the deduction is in part confounded. Fortunately, Goulet presents several paradigms which permit more refined tests of the relationship between drive and verbal learning. Unfortunately, few of the studies dealing with this problem have dealt with these refinements. Consequently, much of the research dealing with the relationship between MAS scores and performance in complex tasks has not been sufficiently precise to permit a truly adequate test of Spence's theory. The appearance of Goulet's (1968) article should remedy this situation.

There is, however, at least one published study which provides a very sophisticated test of the Spence theory. Spielberger and Smith (1966) studied behavior in a serial learning task. Subjects were presented with a list of 12 nonsense syllables of low intralist similarity. Subjects were required to anticipate the next syllable in the list and were given 26 trials in which to learn the list of 12 nonsense syllables. Spielberger and Smith (1966) analyzed the results separately for different trial blocks and for different syllables. They designated nonsense syllables in position 1, 2, 3, and 12 as easy words since these syllables elicited the smallest number of errors. Nonsense syllables in serial positions 6, 7, 8, and 9 were designated hard words since they elicited the greatest number of errors. Note that the hard words are in the middle of the list. This agrees well with the usual results for serial learning tasks in which items in the middle of the list are more difficult to learn than items at the beginning or end of the list. This finding is usually explained by assuming that items in the middle of the list are subject to greater competition than items at the beginning and end of the list. In this situation the following predictions can be made. For easy words, that is, for words where response competition is at a minimum, there should be little difference between subjects who differ in drive during the early stages of the experiment since habit strength would be close to zero. As learning progresses and habit strength increases, subjects high in drive should exhibit increasingly superior performance relative to subjects low in drive. For hard words, subjects high in drive should show inferior performance early in learning. This follows from the assumption that response competition exists and that for these words incorrect competing responses are likely to be dominant (that is, have higher habit strength) early in learning. As learning progresses the habit strength for the correct responses should become dominant and subjects high in drive should eventually exhibit superior performance on the hard words. Figure 4.2 presents the results obtained by Spielberger and Smith (1966). An examination of Figure 4.2 indicates that their results for subjects who differ on the MAS are in complete accord with the predictions.

There have been a number of attempts to explain the relationship between scores on the MAS and performance in complex tasks without reference to differences in drive level. Child (1954) has suggested that dif-

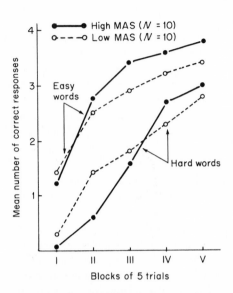

Fig. 4.2. Mean number of correct responses given by HA and LA *S*s on successive trial blocks for easy and hard words. The easy words appeared in serial positions 1, 2, 3, and 12; the hard words appeared in serial positions 6, 7, 8. (From C. S. Spielberger and L. H. Smith, Anxiety (Drive), stress, and serial-position effects in serial-verbal learning. *Journal of Experimental Psychology*, 1966, **72**, 589–595.)

ferences in behavior between subjects who differ on the MAS are to be explained not in terms of the effects of drive *per se* but in terms of differences in what is called, in Hullian theory, drive stimuli. That is, the characteristic stimuli which are associated with any drive state. Child argues that states of high anxiety have associated with them heightened autonomic responses and various covert verbalizations unrelated to the task. These drive stimuli detract from the subject's attention to the task and are considered task-irrelevant. Accordingly, high anxiety subjects may be expected to perform more poorly in complex tasks requiring attention and concentration. This type of hypothesis explains the poorer performance of high anxiety subjects in complex tasks but it does not, in any simple fashion, explain the superior performance of high anxiety subjects in complex tasks. Let us consider, as a concrete example, the findings of the Spielberger and Smith (1966) study. One could explain the initial superiority of the low anxiety subjects on the hard words by arguing that they were unable to adequately concentrate on these difficult items. Similarly, one could argue that the relative lack of difference in performance on the easy words at the beginning of the experiment could be explained by arguing that the distracting effects of the task-irrelevant responses had relatively little effect on the acquisition of easy words which did not require considerable concentration. Also, the relatively greater improvement in performance for the high anxiety subjects over trials might be explained by assuming that high anxiety subjects become less anxious as the task progresses and therefore they are able to pay greater attention to the relevant aspects of the experimental situation. What *cannot* be explained by appeal to the drive stimulus theory is the superior performance of the subjects high in anxiety on both easy and hard words towards the latter part of the experiment. Task-irrelevant responses can detract from performance but they cannot improve performance. Spence has always accepted the possibility that differences in the MAS may reflect both differences in drive level and differences in drive stimuli. What has been at issue in the discussion of the literature relating differences in the MAS to performance is the possibility of dispensing with the drive construct completely. The review of the literature presented here suggests that appeal to the drive concept does provide a more parsimonious explanation of this total body of literature. However, the final decision depends upon the use of more sophisticated research paradigms permitting more precise predictions of the facilitating and debilitating effects of individual differences in anxiety on various tasks.

## Criticisms and Questions Related to Spence's Theory

Spence's research using the MAS may be criticized on a number of grounds. First, it has been suggested that the MAS is not really a measure of anxiety. O'Connor, Lorr, and Stafford (1956) have reported the results of a factor analysis of the Taylor scale in which they found five separate factors. However, this finding does not necessarily indicate that the Taylor scale is not a measure of anxiety since anxiety may be a second-order trait consisting of several distinct first-order traits. Edwards (1957) has reported data which is perhaps more critical of the interpretation of the MAS as a measure of anxiety. As part of his research on social desirability, Edwards developed a 39 item test of social desirability. Edwards found a correlation of −.84 between scores on the MAS and scores on his social desirability scale. A correlation of this magnitude indicates that the MAS may be considered a measure of social desirability. Thus, individuals who obtain high scores on the MAS may be described as individuals who tend to respond to items on personality tests in socially undesirable ways. The magnitude of the correlation between the Edwards social desirability scale and the MAS raises the issue of whether high scores on the MAS are to be taken as indicative of high anxiety or as indicative of low social desirability. Clearly, the connotations, predictions, and implications which follow from these alternative interpretations are not the same. Most of the research dealing with the Taylor scale has dealt with it as a measure of anxiety. Therefore, the interpretation of the MAS as a measure of anxiety may be preferred, if only on heuristic grounds.

Saltz (1970) has also questioned the interpretation of the MAS as a measure of anxiety. Saltz has reviewed a number of studies relating scores on the MAS to performance which he states indicate that individuals who score differently on the MAS may not differ with respect to anxiety but differ rather with respect to the kind of stress to which individuals are sensitive. Subjects who score high on the MAS are assumed to be sensitive to stress induced by failure and the fear of failure. [Note: This interpretation of the MAS is related to one which we shall discuss in Chapter 5 in which measures of anxiety are assumed to be related to a hypothetical motive tendency to avoid failure.] Subjects who score low on the MAS are assumed to be sensitive to stress induced by pain. Each of these groups exhibits disruption of learning under conditions in which the appropriate stress is present. Thus, subjects low in anxiety show poor performance in eyeblink conditioning because the pain elicited by the UCS disrupts their performance.

Saltz's suggestion is a useful one in that it calls attention to the conditions under which individuals with different scores on the MAS are likely to exhibit optimal performance. However, it is difficult to see how Saltz's notion can account for the detailed predictions in a study such as Spielberger's and Smith's which involves predictions of differential performance on different components of the same task at different times.

A second major criticism has been leveled against the research dealing with the MAS as a measure of drive. Kausler and Trapp (1959) noted in an early critique of this work that there was no attempt to show that other drive variables would influence performance on these tasks in the same way as scores on the MAS. The argument that the MAS is a measure of drive would be strengthened if it could be shown that more conventional drive manipulations, for example, hunger, produced differences in performance comparable to those produced by individual differences in the scores on the MAS. Ideally we should have a large body of established empirical findings which indicate the effect of manipulating different sources of drive on a variety of experimental tasks. Since this evidence does not exist, experiments involving the MAS have simultaneously sought to establish what the effect of differences in drive would be in any given task and that the MAS was in fact a measure of drive. Since the effect of differences in drive on performance in any given task is not unambiguously known, it is not clear that the differences in performance of individuals who differ on the MAS invariably reflect differences in drive level.

One of the few studies relevant to this issue has been performed by Franks (1957a). Franks found that subjects who had been deprived of food, water, and tobacco for 24 hours did not show more rapid eyeblink conditioning than subjects who were not deprived. These results suggest that traditional measures of drive (or at least those which are traditional in animal psychology, viz., deprivation) do not relate to eyeblink conditioning. This implies either that drive is not related to eyeblink conditioning or that deprivation is not related to drive. In either case there is an ambiguity and a difficulty in the interpretation of anxiety as a drive.

The failure to include other measures of drive in the usual study involving the MAS leads to a third inadequacy in this body of research. Central to the Hull–Spence theory of drive is the assumption that different sources of drive combine additively. That is, the level of drive present in any given situation is not determined solely by any single source of drive but rather by the combined effect of all sources of drive. As a result of this view of drive, it follows that individuals who are, for example, both anxious and hungry will have higher drive levels than individuals who are either equally anxious and not hungry, or equally hungry and not anxious. This view of drive as a composite of several sources of drive has not been extensively dealt with in research involving the MAS. As a result, one major implication of the theory of anxiety as drive has not been explored.

Finally, it should be noted that Spence's theory does not deal at all with a large number of issues relating to anxiety which have been of central concern to many personality theorists. For example, Spence does not deal with defense mechanisms such as repression, displacement, etc., which are conceived of within psychoanalytic theory as ways of dealing with anxiety. Spence's theory represents an attempt to deal in a relatively rigorous fashion with a limited aspect of a concept which has many ramifications. In effect, theories such as Spence's sacrifice comprehensiveness for rigor. Regrettably, such a sacrifice seems necessary in many cases in our present state of knowledge.

# CHAPTER 5

# ATKINSON'S THEORY OF ACHIEVEMENT MOTIVATION

## Background Research on Achievement Motivation

Atkinson's theory of achievement motivation grows out of research initiated by McClelland and his co-workers in 1948 on the development of measures of human motives. This research grew out of earlier efforts by Murray (1936) dealing with the development of the Thematic Apperception Test (TAT). In this test, subjects are presented with somewhat ambiguous pictures and are asked to write stories to the pictures answering such questions as, What is happening?; Who are the persons?; What has led up to the situation, that is, what has happened in the past?, etc. Murray and his co-workers at the Harvard Psychological Clinic believed that individual motives and needs would be projected into the stories. As a result, by analysis of the content of the TAT, the psychologist would be able to discover a person's motives. McClelland and his co-workers attempted to develop more objective methods of scoring TAT protocols and undertook a program of research to demonstrate the validity of their measures of human motivation. Much of this early research dealt with the need for achievement and is summarized in *The Achievement Motive* (McClelland, Atkinson, Clark, & Lowell, 1953).

The McClelland group began their investigation of need achievement with a study designed to develop an objective scoring system for TAT protocols. The investigation attempted to create experimental conditions which would differentially arouse achievement motivation. In their initial studies they contrasted TAT stories written by subjects in the following conditions: a relaxed condition in which subjects were asked to work on some tasks that were in a developmental stage and then take tests of creative imagination; a neutral condition; and an achievement oriented condition in which subjects were informed that the tasks they were working on were tests of ability prior to taking the TAT. When the TAT protocols written under these various conditions were examined, McClelland and his co-workers noticed that the stories written under achievement-oriented conditions contained more imagery dealing with the need for achievement— defined as concern over performing well in relation to a standard of excellence. By examining the protocols they were able to develop a scoring system for the presence of achievement imagery. The scoring system which evolved from this research consisted in scoring each TAT story (typically a subject is asked to write four stories) for presence or absence of a series of "symptoms" of the presence of achievement motivation. These include:

1. Achievement imagery: defined as a reference to a goal involving competition with a standard of excellence.
2. Need: a stated desire to reach an achievement goal.
3. Instrumental activity: reference to specific activities which are instrumental to the goal.
4. Positive anticipatory goal state: the anticipation of goal attainment.
5. Negative anticipatory goal state: the anticipation of failure to reach the achievement goal.
6. Personal obstacle or block: a reference to an inability to achieve the goal.
7. Environmental obstacle: a reference to some obstacle in the environment which makes attainment of the achievement goal more difficult.
8. Positive affective state: a reference to a positive feeling associated with goal attainment.
9. Negative affective state: a reference to unpleasant affects associated with failure to attain an achievement goal.
10. Nurturant press: a reference to persons who assist someone in attaining an achievement goal.
11. Achievement theme: this is scored when achievement imagery is assumed to be the dominant theme of the story.

These symptoms of need achievement deal with thoughts about the struggles and desires to do well in competition with a standard of excellence. Subjects who were exposed to achievement-oriented instructions tended to write stories which had higher need achievement scores than subjects exposed to relaxed conditions. This finding provided the initial basis for the measurement of need achievement.

Several questions can be raised about the adequacy of this measure. One aspect in which this research represented a major improvement over the earlier attempts by Murray to measure human motives was in the development of an objective and detailed scoring system. Research has established that individuals can be taught to score stories for need achievement and reach high levels of agreement among themselves (see Smith & Feld, 1958). Having established that TAT protocols may be objectively scored the question of the stability of the score over time (reliability) can be raised. Correlations between scores on need achievement tests given to the same subjects at two different times have tended to be low. For example, Lowell (1950) reported a test–retest correlation of .22 in a study in which a single week intervened between the two test administrations. Such results suggest that need achievement is not a measure of a stable characteristic of an individual. However, a measure of correlation treats a person's need achievement score as a quantitative measure. Most research on need achievement has tended to classify individuals as being either high or low on the need achievement measure. Consequently, a more adequate measure of the stability of need for achievement can be obtained by seeing whether individuals classified as high or low in need achievement retain the same classification when retested. Perhaps the most dramatic evidence for stability of need achievement in this latter sense comes from a study by Feld (1967). In conjunction with a longitudinal study of the development of achievement motivation she administered a need achievement test to a group of 14 male adolescents aged 14–16 who had been tested 6 years earlier by Winterbottom (1958). She found that 11 of the 14 boys were assigned the same position (high or low) on the need achievement test that they had received earlier. Other investigators have reported relatively high stability with respect to high or low position for need achievement scores over shorter time periods (see Atkinson, 1950; Haber & Alpert, 1958; Lowell, 1950).

Having established that need achievement scores are stable over time and may as a result be conceived of as indicating some persistent characteristic of an individual we can ask, is the measure valid? That is, is an individual's need achievement score indicative of his need to achieve? The first study to deal with this question was reported by Lowell (1952). Lowell found that subjects who scored high on need achievement had a higher level of performance than subjects who scored low on need achievement on an arithmetic and on a verbal task (see Figure 5.1). Lowell's results indicate that subjects high in need for achievement not only tell stories expressing achievement themes but, when given an opportunity to exhibit their achievement motivation on a task, will in fact work harder than low-need achievement subjects.

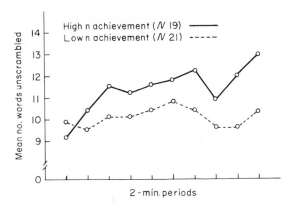

Fig. 5.1. Performance of high and low need achievement groups on scrambled word task. (Based on Lowell, 1952.)

The Lowell finding is not conclusive. One might argue that individuals who score high on need for achievement will work harder in a laboratory task but this does not indicate that such individuals are really high in need for achievement in situations outside the laboratory. In fact, Lazarus (1961) has expressed the belief that scores on need for achievement can be inversely related to actual achievement motivation. That is, the fantasy expression of need achievement is not a direct index of a person's achievement motivation but is rather a compensatory response for the failure to exhibit achievement motivation in everyday life. Results such as Lowell's do not really contradict Lazarus' contention since the laboratory expression of need achievement is not evidence of its expression outside the laboratory. However, there is some evidence that need achievement as measured by the TAT is related to a tendency to express achievement motivation in extra-laboratory contexts. Crockett (1962) using a subset of 597 males selected from a larger random sample of males living in private homes in the United States found a relationship between need achievement scores and upward social mobility. He found that sons who were high in need achievement and whose fathers were in low or middle prestige occupations, had greater occupational mobility than sons who were low in need achievement. However, no differences were obtained in intergenerational occupational mobility for sons differing in need achievement whose fathers were in the upper middle or high prestige occupations. Crockett attributes the lack of relationship between need achievement and occupational mobility for sons of fathers in the upper middle and high occupational prestige categories to the increased importance of education as a basis for upward mobility among these groups. (See also Crockett, 1964; Littig & Yeracaris, 1965.)

The results obtained by Crockett do not unequivocally establish the validity of the need-achievement test as a measure of the tendency to express need achievement in extra-laboratory contexts. Crockett's results tell us very little above the direction of influence of the social mobility and need-achievement variables. If one assumes that children who are high in need-achievement work harder as adults and are as a result more likely to be upwardly mobile, then Crockett's results do provide evidence for the validity of the need-achievement measure. However, there is another interpretation of Crockett's finding. Namely, when upward mobility occurs need-achievement scores increase. Changes in mobility could lead to changes in the characteristic thoughts and preoccupations of an individual. The need achievement score could reflect these changes.

The most ambitious attempt to relate need achievement to extra laboratory changes is contained in McClelland's research. McClelland developed the hypothesis that achievement motivation is in part responsible for the economic growth of societies. The development of this hypothesis is described by McClelland as follows:

### FORMING THE KEY HYPOTHESIS: THE EFFECTS OF THE PROTESTANT REFORMATION ON *n* ACHIEVEMENT

... it was actually a study by Winterbottom (1953) which first pointed to a possible link between achievement motivation and economic development. She was interested in trying to discover how parents, or more particularly mothers, produced a strong interest in achievement in their sons. She first obtained *n* Achievement in their sons. She first obtained *n* Achievement scores on a group of 29 eight-year-old boys and then conducted interviews to determine if the mothers if the "high" had different attitudes toward bringing up children. What she found was that mothers of the "highs" expected their sons to master earlier such activities as the following... :

> Know his way around the city
> Be active and energetic
> Try hard for things for himself
> Make his own friends
> Do well in competition

Furthermore, the mothers of the "lows" reported more restrictions: they did not want their sons to play with children not approved by the parents, nor did they want them to make important decision by themselves. The picture here is reasonably clear. The mothers of the sons with high *n* Achievement have set higher standards for their sons: they expect self-reliance and mastery at an earlier age.

(Winterbottom, 1958, pp. 468–472)

An interesting historical parallel suggested itself. As we have seen, the German sociologist Max Weber (1904) described in convincing detail how the Protestant Reformation produced a new character type which infused a more vigorous spirit into the attitude of both workers and entrepreneurs and which ultimately resulted in the development of modern industrial capitalism. If the Protestant Reformation represented a shift toward self-reliance training and the new "capitalistic spirit" and increased $n$ Achievement, then the relationship found by Winterbottom may have been duplicated at a societal level in the history of Western Europe. The following diagram shows the parallel.

*Weber's hypothesis*

A ————————————————————— D

Protestantism (self-reliance values, etc.)     Spirit of modern capitalism

*Winterbottom's study*

B————————————————— C

Independence and mastery training by parents     $n$ Achievement in sons

That is, the Winterbottom study suggests a psychological means by which the historical development described by Weber may have come about. The Protestant Reformation might have led to earlier independence and mastery training, which led to greater $n$ Achievement, which in turn led to the rise of modern capitalism.

(From D. C. McClelland, *The achieving society*, pp. 46–47. Copyright © 1961 by Litton Educational Publishing, Inc. Reprinted by permission of Van Nostrand Reinhold Company.)

McClelland then proceeded to extend this hypothesis. He argued that differences in need achievement were responsible in part for the economic growth and decline of all societies.

McClelland (1961) has reported a number of studies designed to test his central hypothesis about the relationship of need achievement and economic growth. We shall briefly describe two of these studies to indicate the scope and style of this major research effort.

In order to obtain a test of his hypothesis for countries in the modern world, McClelland needed a measure of achievement motivation and a measure of economic growth for a number of modern nations. McClelland decided to use children's readers as a basis for the measurement of need achievement levels in a particular country. McClelland assumed that the themes of the readers would reflect the motives and values of their cultures. He obtained a sample of stories from children's readers for the period from 1920–1929 from 23 countries and a sample of stories from children's readers for the 1946–1955 period from 40 countries. McClelland then obtained a measure of economic growth for these countries. McClelland used three measures of economic growth over the period from 1925–1950 for the countries in his study. The first measure was based on Clark's measure, international units (i.u.) (Clark, 1957)—a measure of the income per capita expressed in terms of a common reference. McClelland also used a measure of electrical output—electricity produced in kilowatt hours per capita. And finally, McClelland obtained an index combining both of these measures. He obtained these measures for the year 1925 and the year 1950. For each of these measures, there was a relationship between 1925 levels and 1950 levels.

TABLE 5.1

*Correlations of Reader n Achievement Scores with Deviations from Expected Economic Gains*

| Achievement level by year, n | I.U./cap 1925–1959, $N = 22$ | Kwh/cap 1929–1950, $N = 22$ | Both combined, $N = 21$ |
|---|---|---|---|
| 1925 | .25 | .53, $p < .01$ $pd^a$ | .46, $p < .02$ $pd^a$ |
| 1950 | − .10 | .03 | − .08 |

From D. C. McClelland, *The achieving society*, Table 3.5, p. 92. Copyright © 1961 by Litton Education Publishing, Inc. Reprinted by permission of Van Nostrand Reinhold Company.

$^a$ pd = predicted direction.

That is, countries with relatively high rates of economic development in 1925 tended to have high rates in 1950. McClelland, therefore, correlated these scores and then defined economic growth as the deviation from the regression line predicting the expected growth. This measure indicates the degree to which a country had economic growth for the 1925–1950 period which exceeded or fell behind what would be expected on the basis of its 1925 level of economic development. These economic deviation scores were correlated with need achievement scores derived from the 1925 and 1950 readers. Table 5.1 presents these results. Need achievement levels in children's readers in 1925 predicts economic growth for the 1925–1950 period. However, need achievement levels in 1950 are not postdictive of previous economic growth. The fact that high levels of need achievement predict future growth is taken by McClelland to indicate that need achievement influences economic growth and not the converse.

McClelland has also attempted to test his hypothesis using historical data. In a study conducted by one of his students, Berlew, he attempted to relate changes in need achievement to the economic growth and decline of Ancient Greece. McClelland obtained indices of need-achievement levels by scoring samples of Greek literature from three periods, 900–475 B.C., 475–362 B.C., and 362–100 B.C. for need achievement. In order to obtain measures of economic development, Berlew, using considerable ingenuity, derived measures of trading area in square miles. These were obtained by studying the places where Greek earthenware jars (the container used for much of their trade) of different periods were obtained. Figure 5.2 summarizes Berlew's findings. These data confirmed McClelland's expectation. Note that high levels of achievement motivation precede economic growth and low levels of achievement motivation precede economic decline.

*The Achieving Society* contains a number of other studies which, for the most part, provide support for his central thesis.

McClelland's data are correlational rather than experimental. He does not measure need achievement levels in a society and study the resultant changes in economic development. It is a truism of statistics that correlation is not causation. One cannot infer the direction of causality from correlational data. If *a* and *b* are correlated this could imply that *a* influences *b*, *b* influences *a*, or both are influenced by a third variable. McClelland attempts to overcome this difficulty by noting the "time lag" in the relationship. Since changes in need achievement precede by an unspecified period changes in economic levels, then the changes in need achievement must be responsible for the changes in economic growth and not the converse. There is a possible criticism of this argument. The economic indices used by McClelland may have a certain "time lag" built into them. Consider, for example, electrical consumption. Electrical consumption should to some unknown degree reflect economic growth which has preceded the consumption. Prior to any change in consumption, decisions would have to be made to expand production in many industries and to engage in entrepreneurial activities which would at some future date result in increases in electrical consumption. Therefore, it is at least theoretically possible that need-achievement levels in children's readers may reflect entrepreneurial activities which are simultaneously occurring. It is even possible that these entrepreneurial activities may occur prior to the occurrence of changes in the need-achievement content of children's readers. Such changes in the activities of members of a society might well be reflected in changes in the thematic content of the readers. This analysis suggests that,

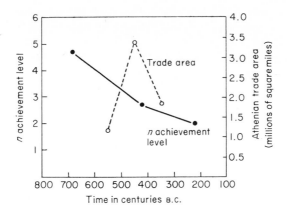

Fig. 5.2. Average *n* achievement level plotted at midpoints of periods of growth, climax, and decline of Athenian civilization as reflected in the extent of her trade area. (From D. C. McClelland, *The achieving society*, Figure 4.1, p. 120. Copyright © 1961 by Litton Publishing, Inc. Reprinted by permission of Van Nostrand Reinhold Company.)

at least on this one central point, McClelland's data may not clearly indicate the direction of causality.

McClelland (1965; McClelland and Winter, 1969) has, in his characteristically ambitious and bold manner, attempted to develop an experimental test of his hypothesis. In order to accomplish this, he has developed a training program which purports to increase the need achievement levels of adults. One version of McClelland's training program is described in an article by Kolb (1965) in which he studied the effects of this training on the school performance of underachieving high school boys. Kolb describes the program as follows:

EXPERIMENTAL CONDITION: THE ACHIEVEMENT MOTIVATION TRAINING PROGRAM

The experimenter lived in the dormitory with the AMTP boys and served as their counselor. The experimenter behaved in a manner consistent with the behavior of a person with high *n* Achievement, so that the subjects would have a visible high *n*-Achievement role model to imitate....

*First session.* The first session was concerned with negotiating a contract. The role relationship emulated was that of a team doing collaborative research on the problem of underachieving. The aim was to involve the students in the hypothesis that the course would improve academic performance and achievement motivation thereby creating in them the expectation that the course would work... .

After negotiating the contract, the characteristics of a person with high-achievement motivation were described. Subjects were told that the person with high *n* Achievement has three major characteristics: he likes and chooses to take personal responsibility for his actions; he takes moderate risks; and he likes and attempts to obtain knowledge of the results of his actions (Atkinson, 1958; McClelland, 1961; McClelland *et al.*, 1953). The remainder of the session was spent describing the racing car game the subjects would play in the next session and suggesting how the characteristics of the achievement motivation would be valuable to a racing driver.

*Second session.* The entire second session was spent playing the race game. The consisted of a miniature race track around which small electric cars could be driven... . As they raced the boys were asked to keep in mind the characteristics of the achieving personality in relation to the race, for example, (a) personal responsibility—How involved am I in the race? Do I care if I win or not? (b) moderate risk taking—How much of the time did I take too much of a risk? How often was I too cautious? (c) using knowledge of results—How well did I use my practice trials to judge my ability?

*Third session.* This session began with an introduction to the process of assessing motivation by analysis of thought (Atkinson, 1958). The boys were then shown how their *n*-Achievement scores related to their performance in the racing game (boys with low *n* Achievement tended to be disqualified).

The discussion then turned to time orientation. During the previous evening the boys had estimated a 30-sec. interval on a stopwatch. Subjects with high *n* Achievement tended to see time as passing more quickly than subjects with low *n* Achievement. Further discussion centered around future orientation, delay of gratification, and ability to control impulses.

*Fourth session.* This session marked the beginning of the shift from structured lecture meetings to a program oriented more toward the individual. In essence the session was a renegotiation of the contract. The group's commitment to the "research team" model was reaffirmed, emphasizing the boy's role in determining the nature of the course. The follow-up and the experimenter's interest in knowing the boys' future grades were discussed.

The last half of the session was spent discussing how thought influences action. The think–talk–act model was explained: if you think and talk in a certain way you will act that way. In particular the direct relationship of achievement thinking to achievement behaviors was discussed. At the end of this session the boys were given $n$ Achievement scoring manuals.

*Fifth session.* This session was devoted to a group discussion on the analysis of Test of Insight stories. Example stories from the protocols of control students were read to the class and discussed. Following this discussion the students were given their own Insight test protocols. They were offered help in scoring their protocols for $n$ Achievement. The expert scoring was given to them upon request. The remainder of the hour was spent in teaching the $n$ Achievement scoring system.

*Sixth session.* A major theme that occurs over and over in the Insight tests is a conflict between achievement and affiliation goals (see Parsons, 1959). One of these stories is quoted below. (Written to Test of Insight, Form A, Story 4, "Bill may not be the best student in his class, but he is the friendliest and the best-liked."

> He fools around a lot to make friends and doesn't do his school work the best he can. He didn't take school seriously and just had a lot of fun. He thinks more about making friends than about getting his homework done. He probably wants to be a mechanic. His marks will keep slipping down and he won't get a good job when he gets out of school.

The session was focused on this conflict and on learning to take realistic risks. An article on how to assess risks was given to the class members. The group discussed risk taking in terms of planning goals and strategies in life situations, making conscious decisions, taking action to attain desired goals, and knowing one's own ability. The Litwin–Ciarlo Business Game (discussed below) which they would all play later that week was described... .

*Litwin–Ciarlo business game.* This training device was perhaps the most popular aspect of the whole project. It is designed to train a person to take moderate risks and use knowledge of results, and to assess his capacity to do so. The subject in this game plays the role of a manufacturer and actually builds the products he contracts for with tinker-toys. He is told that he is the head of a company just starting to manufacture three new products—a missle, an atomic cannon, and an airplane. He must order sufficient parts to build each of these products and actually try to assemble them in three separate 5-min. production periods. Only completed units are purchased, so if he orders too many he loses what is invested in the leftover parts, and if he orders too few his profit is lower than it should have been. The subject makes his decisions and assesses risks using two types of information: printed statistics giving prices, profits, and average construction times for each product and his own timed practice construction times for each product. The game takes an hour to play and gives scores on risk taking and use of past performance as an indicator of future performance. A couple of boys learned to run the game and did a large part of the administration for the other boys.

(Kolb, 1965, pp. 785–786)

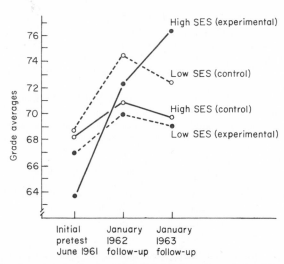

F
IG
. 5.3. School grade average in pretest and follow-up periods. (From D. C. Kolb, Achievement motivation training for underachieving high school boys. *Journal of Personality and Social Psychology*, 1965, **2,** pp. 763–792.)

If the achievement training program is successful, and if McClelland's hypothesis is correct, then the individuals who have been exposed to such programs should engage in activities which affect the economic development of their society. Kolb's (1965) paper presents detailed information about an attempt to use this procedure to help underachieving high school boys improve their grades. Kolb started with a group of 57 boys who were placed in a summer school program. Of the boys, 20 of the 57 received achievement motivation training. He found that the boys who participated in this training had greater improvement in their grade-point average 1 and 2 years later than did the boys in the control group. However, further analysis indicated that the improvement in grade-point average was restricted to boys in the achievement training group who were relatively high in socioeconomic status. (See Figure 5.3.)

Kolb's results raise some questions about the efficacy of achievement motivation training. The finding that this training is seen to have significant impact on individuals with relatively high socioeconomic status suggests that the training may be efficacious only for individuals who have had early achievement training of some sort and/or individuals who return to a social situation which provides support and encouragement for achievement oriented activities.

McClelland and Winter (1969) have reported the results of a series of studies designed to create achievement motivation in businessmen in India. They found that achievement motivation training produced a number of changes in the entrepreneurial behavior of the businessmen. Relative to a control group who did not receive the training, the businessmen who received the training were more likely to start a new business or to be involved in a major expansion of their firm. Also, the businessmen given this training showed significant increases in the number of hours they worked, in the number of people in their employ, and in the amount of money they invested in their businesses.

The research reported by McClelland and Winter indicates that changes in achievement motivation produce the kinds of changes in entrepreneurial behavior which could lead to economic change and development. In addition, these studies establish that changes in achievement motivation do have significant consequences for behavior in extra-laboratory settings.

## Atkinson's Risk-Taking Model

Atkinson's model treats need achievement as a theoretical variable which combines in specified ways with other theoretical variables. This relatively precise and formal representation of what is measured by the need achievement test permits one to derive predictions of the expected behaviors of individuals who differ in achievement related motives. This model grows out of a synthesis of several "expectancy" theories (see Feather, 1959). Perhaps the most relevant theories are Tolman's expectancy theory (Tolman, 1955) and an analysis of the determinants of level of aspiration developed by Lewin and his collaborators (Lewin, Dembo, Festinger, & Sears, 1944). In Tolman's theory, the tendency to perform a particular act is a multiplicative function of three kinds of variables. A motivational variable representing the need or desire for some particular goal object, an expectancy variable which may be conceived of as a quantitatively varying belief that some particular act in a particular situation will lead to the goal object, and the incentive or the value of the goal object to the individual. Lewin's analysis of level of aspiration behavior also deals with variables which are conceptually similar to those used by Tolman. For Lewin the choice of a particular task with a particular level of difficulty associated with it is a multiplicative function of the valence or value associated with success at the task and the subjective probability of success at the task. The valence of success corresponds to Tolman's incentive variable and the subjective probability of success corresponds to Tolman's expectancy variable. In addition, Lewin discusses two motives which influence level of aspiration behavior, the hope of success and the fear of failure. In summary, in theories developed by both Lewin and his collaborators and by Tolman, emphasis is placed on multiplicative relationships among motive, expectancy, and incentive variables.

Atkinson developed his risk taking model, initially, to deal with level of aspiration or choice behavior. He assumed, as did Lewin in his analysis, that an individual in an achievement-oriented situation who must choose a task of a particular level of difficulty is in a conflict situation in which both a tendency to seek success $(T_s)$ and a tendency to avoid failure $(T_{af})$ were involved. Each of these tendencies was assumed to be determined by a multiplicative relationship among motive, expectancy, and incentive variables. Thus, $T_s$ associated with a particular task is defined by the following equation:

$$T_s = M_s \times P_s \times I_s$$

where $M_s$ refers to the motive to achieve success, $P_s$ to the subjective probability of success—that is, to the subject's expectancy that his performance on a particular task will be successful, and $I_s$ refers to the incentive value of success—that is, the value of success on a particular task to the individual.

Atkinson (1957), following an earlier assumption of Lewin *et al.*, assumes that in achievement related tasks—that is, in tasks in which success is related to a feeling of pride in competition with some standard of excellence—there is a special relationship between $I_s$ and $P_s$. $I_s$ is assumed to equal $1 - P_s$. This assumption implies that the incentive value of success at a task is related to the subjectively defined difficulty of the task. Thus, success at an easy task is assumed to have a lower incentive value than success at a difficult task.

Atkinson defines $T_{af}$ in a conceptually parallel manner as follows:

$$T_{af} = M_{af} \times P_f \times I_f$$

where $M_{af}$ refers to the motive to avoid failure, $P_f$ to the subjective probability of failure, and $I_f$ to the incentive value of failure. Atkinson assumes, again in agreement with the Lewin *et al.* analysis, that there is a special relationship between $P_f$ and $I_f$ in an achievement related task. The incentive value of failure is assumed to equal $-(1 - P_f)$. The negative sign in front of the parenthesis indicates that failure is a noxious event which is unpleasant for an individual and which he should attempt to avoid. The degree to which failure at a particular task is noxious or unpleasant is dependent upon the difficulty of the task. If the task is easy and $P_f$ is as a result relatively low, then $1 - P_f$ will be relatively high and $-(1 - P_f)$ will be a high negative number. On the other hand, if the task is difficult, $P_f$ will be high, $1 - P_f$ will be relatively low, and $-(1 - P_f)$ will be a relatively low negative number. This simple algebra indicates the psychological basis of the assumption relating $I_f$ and $P_f$. Namely, failure at an easy task is more unpleasant or noxious than failure at a difficult task.

It should be noted that Atkinson assumes that $P_s + P_f = 1.00$. Therefore $P_f = 1 - P_s$. Substituting in the equation defining the relationship between

TABLE 5.2

*The Product of $P_s$ and $I_s$ and $P_f$ and $I_f$ for Different $P_s$ Values According to the Atkinson Model*

| $P_s$ | $P_s \times I_s$ | $P_f \times I_f$ |
|---|---|---|
| .1 | .09 | $-.09$ |
| .3 | .21 | $-.21$ |
| .5 | .25 | $-.25$ |
| .7 | .21 | $-.21$ |
| .9 | .09 | $-.09$ |

From J. W. Atkinson, *An introduction to motivation*, Table 9.3. Copyright © 1964 by Litton Educational Publishing, Inc. Reprinted by permission of Van Nostrand Reinhold Company.

Note: $I_s = 1 - P_s$; $P_f = 1 - P_s$; $I_f = -P_s$.

$P_f$ and $I_f$, we find that $I_f$ is equal to $-P_s$. Thus on an easy task when $P_s$ is high, $I_f$ is high and negative and on a difficult task where $P_s$ is low, $I_f$ is low and negative.

Atkinson's equations defining $T_s$ and $T_{af}$ imply that $P_s$ and $P_f$ respectively multiply $I_s$ and $I_f$. The resulting products of this multiplication for different levels of $P_s$ are presented in Table 5.2.

An examination of Table 5.2 indicates that the products of both $P_s$ and $I_s$ and $P_f$ and $I_f$ reach their maximum absolute values when $P_s$ is equal to .5, and the absolute value of the products decreases if $P_s$ is increased or decreased. The product of $P_s$ and $I_s$ is positive whereas the product of $P_f$ and $I_f$ is negative.

Atkinson assumes that all persons have both $M_s$ and $M_{af}$. Thus, for any achievement related task both $T_s$ and $T_{af}$ are assumed to be present. The total motivational tendency or resultant tendency is assumed to equal the combined effects of $T_s$ and $T_{af}$. Resultant tendency equals $T_s + T_{af}$. The resultant motivation associated with any task is dependent upon the relationship between $M_s$ and $M_{af}$ in a particular person. Table 5.3 illustrates resultant tendencies for tasks differing in $P_s$ for different values of $M_s$ and $M_{af}$.

An examination of Table 5.3 indicates the major implication of this model. Individuals in whom $M_s > M_{af}$ should have their highest positive resultant tendency associated with tasks for which $P_s$ is at an intermediate level $-.5$. Individuals in whom $M_{af} > M_s$ should have negative resultant tendency associated with all achievement related tasks but their negative resultant tendency should be highest for tasks where $P_s$ is equal to .5. For these individuals, tasks which are very easy (high $P_s$) or very difficult (low $P_s$) should have lower negative resultant tendencies and should be

TABLE 5.3

*Resultant Achievement Motivation $(T_s + T_{af})$ in 4 Hypothetical Persons Who Differ in Strength of Motive to Achieve $(M_s)$ and Motive to Avoid Failure $(M_{af})$*

|  | Task | $P_s$ | $I_s$ | $T_s$ | $P_f$ | $I_f$ | $T_{af}$ | $T_s + T_{af}$ |
|---|---|---|---|---|---|---|---|---|
| | A | .90 | .10 | .27 | .10 | $-.90$ | $-.09$ | .18 |
| When $M_s = 3$ and | B | .70 | .30 | .63 | .30 | $-.70$ | $-.21$ | .42 |
| $M_{af} = 1$ | C | .50 | .50 | .75 | .50 | $-.50$ | $-.25$ | .50 |
| | D | .30 | .70 | .63 | .70 | $-.30$ | $-.21$ | .42 |
| | E | .10 | .90 | .27 | .90 | $-.10$ | $-.09$ | .18 |
| | A | .90 | .10 | .27 | .10 | $-.90$ | $-.18$ | .09 |
| When $M_s = 3$ and | B | .70 | .30 | .63 | .30 | $-.70$ | $-.42$ | .21 |
| $M_{af} = 2$ | C | .50 | .50 | .75 | .50 | $-.50$ | $-.50$ | .25 |
| | D | .30 | .70 | .63 | .70 | $-.30$ | $-.42$ | .21 |
| | E | .10 | .90 | .27 | .90 | $-.10$ | $-.18$ | .09 |
| | A | .90 | .10 | .27 | .10 | $-.90$ | $-.27$ | 0 |
| When $M_s = 3$ and | B | .70 | .30 | .63 | .30 | $-.70$ | $-.63$ | 0 |
| $M_{af} = 3$ | C | .50 | .50 | .75 | .50 | $-.50$ | $-.75$ | 0 |
| | D | .30 | .70 | .63 | .70 | $-.30$ | $-.63$ | 0 |
| | E | .10 | .90 | .27 | .90 | $-.10$ | $-.27$ | 0 |
| | A | .90 | .10 | .09 | .10 | $-.90$ | $-.27$ | $-.18$ |
| When $M_s = 1$ and | B | .70 | .30 | .21 | .30 | $-.70$ | $-.63$ | $-.42$ |
| $M_{af} = 3$ | C | .50 | .50 | .25 | .50 | $-.50$ | $-.75$ | $-.50$ |
| | D | .30 | .70 | .21 | .70 | $-.30$ | $-.63$ | $-.42$ |
| | E | .10 | .90 | .09 | .90 | $-.10$ | $-.27$ | $-.18$ |

preferred to tasks of intermediate difficulty. However, individuals in whom $M_s > M_{af}$ should prefer tasks of intermediate difficulty.

It is obvious that any empirical investigation of the implications of this theory requires a determination of the relationship between $M_s$ and $M_{af}$ for groups of individuals. Atkinson assumes that the projective measure of need achievement is a measure of the variable $M_s$ in his theory, and that the Mandler–Sarason Test of Test Anxiety (Mandler & Sarason, 1952) is a measure of the variable $M_{af}$. These assumptions have usually led to a decision to assume that individuals who score high on need achievement (above the median) and low on the Mandler–Sarason scale are individuals in whom $M_s > M_{af}$. Similarly, individuals who score low on need achievement and high on the Mandler–Sarason are assumed to be individuals in whom $M_{af} > M_s$. These empirical identifications have permitted the test of several implications of the Atkinson model. These tests invariably rest on the simultaneous acceptance of two different kinds of assumptions. First, that the individual difference measures are in fact measures of the hypothetical variables $M_s$ and $M_{af}$ as defined in the theory. Second, that the theory contains a correct analysis of the determinants of behavior in achievement related situations.

The earliest tests of the model concerned level of aspiration behavior. McClelland (1958) had obtained preliminary evidence that children who scored high in need achievement (as measured by Aronson's graphic procedure, see Aronson, 1958) tended to toss rings in a ring-toss game from intermediate distances whereas children low in need for achievement tended to avoid the intermediate distances. Atkinson and Litwin (1960) conducted an investigation of ring-toss behavior in subjects with different patterns of scores on the projective test of need achievement and on the Mandler–Sarason test. They assumed that individuals in whom $M_s > M_{af}$ should choose tasks of intermediate difficulty and should therefore tend to toss rings from intermediate distances. Individuals in whom $M_{af} > M_s$ should choose easy or difficult tasks and as a result in the ring toss game should elect to toss rings from long or short distances. Figure 5.4 presents their

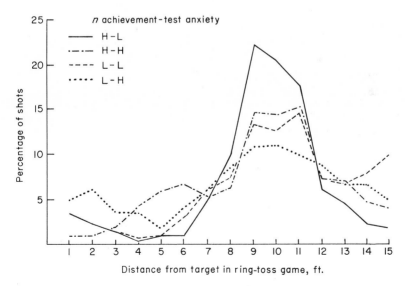

FIG. 5.4. Percentage of shots taken from each distance by college men in a ring-toss game. Graph is smoothed according to the method of running averages, for *Ss* classified as High or Low simultaneously in *n* achievement and test anxiety, H–L (N = 13), H–H (*N* = 10), L–L (*N* = 9), L–H (*N* = 13). (Based on Atkinson & Litwin, 1960.)

results. An examination of Figure 5.4 indicates that the results were in agreement with predictions.

Mahone (1960) extended this analysis of level of aspiration to occupational choice among college students. Mahone began his investigation by asking college students to estimate the percentage of college students who had the ability to succeed in various occupations. These estimates were highly correlated with sociological estimates of the prestige associated with various occupations. Certain occupational goals are more difficult to achieve than others. Accordingly, the choice of an occupation involves, in part at least, a choice among goals differing in the $P_s$ values associated with them. The Atkinson theory thus implies that individuals in whom $M_s > M_{af}$ should choose occupations of intermediate difficulty and individuals in whom $M_{af} > M_s$ should choose occupations in which success was easy or difficult. Mahone (1960) argued that these predictions should be refined by a consideration of the subjective difficulty of the occupational choice. That is, an individual may choose a difficult occupation (for example, physician) which he believes, given his estimate of his ability, is easy for him. Mahone computed a subjective goal discrepancy score defined as the difference in the subject's estimate of his own ability relative to other college students and his estimate of his ability required to achieve success at his chosen occupation. This distribution of goal discrepancy scores was divided into thirds. Mahone found (see Table 5.4) that subjects who scored high in need achievement and low in text anxiety tended to have goal discrepancy scores in the middle third of the distribution. Subjects with an opposite pattern

TABLE 5.4

*Effect of Individual Differences in n Achievement and Anxiety on Subjective Goal Discrepancy of Vocational Aspirations of Male College Students*

| n achievement | Anxiety | N | Absolute goal discrepancy score | |
| --- | --- | --- | --- | --- |
| | | | *Mid–third* | *Highest or lowest third* |
| High | Low | 36 | 50%[a] | 50% |
| High | High | 30 | 30% | 70% |
| Low | Low | 40 | 38% | 62% |
| Low | High | 28 | 18%[a] | 82% |

Based on Mahone, 1960. The distribution of goal discrepancy scores was divided into thirds.

[a] $p < .01$.

of scores on the individual difference measures tended to have goal discrepancy scores in the upper or lower thirds of the distribution. These results imply that subjects in whom $M_s > M_{af}$ tend to have relatively realistic occupational levels of aspiration. They choose occupations which are of intermediate difficulty for their assumed ability. Subjects in whom $M_{af} > M_s$ apparently choose occupations which are either relatively difficult or relatively easy for them, given their assumed level of ability.

In these two studies intermediate difficulty is defined in terms of the distribution of goal-setting behaviors. There is no direct evidence that intermediate ability coincides with a $P_s$ value of .5. The precise prediction derived from the Atkinson model is that individuals in whom $M_s > M_{af}$ should prefer tasks at which the $P_s$ value is .5. Therefore these studies provide evidence for the model only if tasks of intermediate difficulty coincide with $P_s$ values of .5. Brody (1963) attempted to obtain evidence relevant to this issue. In his study, subjects were presented with a sequential decision task in which they were required to make a decision about the number of circles in a deck of cards. Subjects were permitted to look at the cards one at a time. Subjects were required to choose the card at which they were willing to make their decision. The longer they delayed their decision the greater their probability of success. In addition, the subjects were required to state their confidence in their decision if they were to make it at that trial each time they looked at a card. Brody obtained the confidence level of the subjects at the trial in which they made their decision. The prediction derived from the Atkinson model is that individuals in whom $M_s > M_{af}$ should make their decision at the trial at which their $P_s$ is .5. Individuals in whom $M_{af} > M_s$ should make their decision either where $P_s$ is low or high. Brody found no evidence for this prediction. Brody then divided the distribution of confidence levels at the trial of decision into quartiles. He found that subjects for whom $M_s$ may be assumed to be higher than $M_{af}$ tended to make their decisions in the intermediate quartiles of the distribution and subjects for whom $M_{af}$ may be assumed to be greater than $M_s$ tended to make their decisions in the lower or highest quartiles. However, the intermediate quartiles included confidence values ranging from 65–95 (see Table 5.5). Although the $M_s > M_{af}$ subjects tended to choose a task of intermediate difficulty, this chosen level of difficulty did not coincide with the value of .5 which would be expected on the basis of Atkinson's model. Atkinson and Feather (1966) have noted that Brody's results do not clearly contradict Atkinson's model unless one assumes that the subject's stated level of confidence is a direct measure of $P_s$. They prefer to consider a subject's $P_s$ as a "complexly determined instrumental act" whose relationship to the hypothetical $P_s$ contained in the theory is not necessarily 1:1. However, the relationship between stated

TABLE 5.5

*Number of Subjects in First, Second, Third, and Fourth Quartiles of
the Distribution of Reported Confidence at the Trial of Decision*

| $n$ achievement | Test anxiety | $Q_2$ (100) | $Q_4$ (<65) | $Q_{2 \text{ and } 3}$ (65–95) |
|---|---|---|---|---|
| High | High | 7 | 1 | 3 |
| High | Low | 2 | 0 | 11 |
| Low | High | 3 | 4 | 4 |
| Low | Low | 0 | 4 | 5 |

From N. Brody, Achievement, test anxiety and subjective
probability of success in risk taking behavior. *Journal of Abnormal and Social Psychology*, 1963, **66,** 413–418.

$P_s$ and the hypothetical value of $P_s$ is at present unspecified. This creates a
source of ambiguity in the test of the model.

The studies described above represent tests of relatively direct predictions
derived from Atkinson's model. In what follows we shall consider tests of
somewhat more indirect implications derived from the model. These
implications deal, respectively, with level of aspiration behavior, persistence, and performance.

Moulton (1965) was interested in the phenomena of atypical shift in level
of aspiration. An atypical shift is the choice of a more difficult task following
failure at an easier task or the choice of an easier task following success at a
more difficult task. Moulton set up a level of aspiration situation in which
subjects were required to work on a task of intermediate difficulty whose $P_s$
value was assumed to be .5. The experiment was designed in such a way
that the experimenter could manipulate success or failure at the task. One
half the subjects succeeded at the original task, and one half of the subjects
failed. Subjects were then required to choose a task which was either easier
or more difficult than the initial task chosen by the subject. Moulton quite
reasonably assumed that success on the intermediate task would lead to an
increase in the $P_s$ values of all the tasks and failure would lead to a decrease
in $P_s$ values for all the tasks. The $P_s$ values assigned by the experimenter to
the easy and difficult tasks prior to the subjects success or failure at the
task of intermediate difficulty were equidistant from .5, .25, and .75,
respectively. Following success on the intermediate task the $P_s$ value for
the difficult task should be closer to .5 than the $P_s$ value for the easy task.
Therefore, subjects in whom $M_s > M_{af}$ should tend to choose the difficult
task rather than the easy task. This choice would represent a typical
shift—the choice of a more difficult task following success at an easier task.
Subjects in whom $M_{af} > M_s$ should tend to choose the easy task rather

than the difficult task. This choice would represent an atypical shift—the choice of an easier task following success at a more difficult task. Subjects in whom $M_{af} > M_s$ should tend to choose the easier task since the $P_s$ for this task is further from .5 than the $P_s$ for the difficult task. This choice represents an atypical shift in level of aspiration. Following failure the $P_s$ values on the easy task should be closer to .5 than the $P_s$ values on the difficult task. Therefore, Moulton reasoned that subjects in whom $M_s > M_{af}$ should have a typical shift in this task—the choice of the easier task following failure. Subjects in whom $M_{af} > M_s$ should have an atypical shift—the choice of a more difficult task following failure. Table 5.6 presents Moulton's results. Examination of Table 5.6 indicates that only the avoidance-oriented subjects (subjects in whom $M_{af}$ is assumed to be greater than $M_s$) show any substantial number of atypical shifts.

Perhaps the most elegant test of the Atkinson model to date deals with persistence. Feather (1961) derived hypotheses from the model about individual differences in persistence at tasks which were thought to be easy or difficult. Persistence is usually defined in psychological research as the length of time a person continues to work on a task on which he fails to find an acceptable solution. Feather used insoluble puzzles in his study. He investigated persistence on these puzzles when the subjects were told that the task was easy and when the subjects were led to believe the task was difficult. Feather assumed that continued failure on the task tended to

TABLE 5.6

*Type of Shift in Level of Aspiration as Related to Resultant Motivation*

| | Type of shift | | |
|---|---|---|---|
| *Resultant motivation* | *Atypical* | *Typical* | *N* |
| Avoidance-oriented | 11 | 20 | 31 |
| Ambivalent | 3 | 28 | 31 |
| Approach-oriented | 1 | 30 | 31 |
| Total | 15 | 78 | 93 |

Avoidance-oriented versus approach-oriented, $\chi^2 = 8.37$[a]
Avoidance-oriented versus ambivalent, $\chi^2 = 4.52$[b]

Based on Moulton, 1965.
[a] $p < .01$.
[b] $p < .05$.

decrease $P_s$. If the subject begins the task believing that it is difficult ($P_s < .5$), failure on the task leads to a situation in which $P_s$ changes are moving away from .5. In this situation Atkinson's model implies that individuals in whom $M_s$ is assumed to be greater than $M_{af}$ should find themselves in a situation in which their resultant motivational tendency becomes less positive the longer they stay in the task. Individuals in whom $M_{af} > M_s$ should find their resulting motivational tendency becoming less negative the longer they persist on the task. If the subject begins the task with the expectation that it is easy ($P_s > .5$) and meets failure, changes in $P_s$ should, at least initially, lead him to a $P_s$ of .5. Under these conditions subjects in whom $M_s > M_{af}$ should initially find the task one in which their resultant motivational tendency is becoming increasingly positive. On the other hand, subjects in whom $M_{af} > M_s$ should find themselves in a task in which, at least initially, their resultant motivation becomes more negative as they persist on the task. Given this analysis, Feather was able to derive predictions indicating that subjects in whom $M_s > M_{af}$ would tend to persist more on easy than on difficult tasks and subjects in whom $M_{af} > M_s$ would tend to persist more on tasks defined as difficult than on easy tasks. Table 5.7 presents Feather's results. Examination of Table 5.7 indicates that Feather obtained clear-cut support for his predictions.

The last topic we shall deal with is the relationship between need achievement and performance using Atkinson's model as a basis for prediction. In our previous discussion of performance differences between individuals high or low in achievement motivation little emphasis was placed on the situational determinents or conditions under which individuals who differ in achievement related motives will perform differently. Clearly Atkinson's model implies that optimal performance and effort would be exhibited by individuals in whom $M_s > M_{af}$ in tasks for which $P_s$ is .50. Similarly, less than optimal interest and effort would be expected from individuals in whom $M_{af} > M_s$ when $P_s$ is .5. O'Connor, Atkinson and Horner (1966) tested implications derived from Atkinson's theory about the motivational implications of ability grouping in the schools. They studied the performance of 6th grade children who were either switched from a 5th grade heterogeneous classroom to a homogeneously ability grouped 6th grade or to a heterogeneous 6th grade classroom. In a heterogeneous classroom there should be a large number of children for whom school represents a particularly easy or difficult situation. Children above average in ability should, in comparison to others, find the school situation relatively easy and children below average in ability should find the school situation relatively difficult. Under conditions of ability grouping most of the children in the classroom should find themselves in competition with children of relatively equal ability. Accordingly, the school situation should

TABLE 5.7

*Persistence Following Failure Related to Initial Expectancy of Success and Motivational Disposition of the Individual: Number of Subjects Who Were High and Low in Persistence in Relation to Stated Difficulty of the Initial Task and the Nature of Their Motivation*

| | | | Persistence trials | |
| --- | --- | --- | --- | --- |
| *Achievement, n* | *Test anxiety* | *Stated difficulty of task* | *High (above median)* | *Low (below median)* |
| High | Low | $P_s = .70$ (easy) | 6 | 2 |
| | | $P_s = .05$ (difficult) | 2 | 7 |
| Low | High | $P_s = .70$ (easy) | 3 | 6 |
| | | $P_s = .05$ (difficult) | 6 | 2 |

*Partition of $\chi^2$*

| Source | Value | *df* | *p* |
| --- | --- | --- | --- |
| Motivation $\times$ persistence | .12 | 1 | ns |
| Expectation $\times$ persistence | .12 | 1 | ns |
| Motivation $\times$ expectation $\times$ persistence | 7.65 | 1 | < .01 |
| Total | 7.89 | 3 | < .05 |

Based on Feather, 1961.

tend to be defined as one of moderate difficulty for most of the children. This analysis implies that children in whom $M_s > M_{af}$ should tend to perform better in homogeneously grouped classrooms than in heterogeneous classrooms. Conversely, children in whom $M_{af} > M_s$ should tend to perform better in heterogeneous classrooms than in homogeneous classrooms. O'Connor *et al.* found that children in whom $M_s$ was assumed to be higher than $M_{af}$ did in fact perform better in homogeneous ability grouped classes. They found that 79 percent of these children showed above median gains in arithmetic and reading in homogeneous classes. Only 40 percent of the $M_s > M_{af}$ children showed above average gains in the heterogeneous classrooms. No differences were found in performance among children in whom $M_{af}$ can be assumed to be greater than $M_s$ and who were assigned to homogeneous or heterogeneous classrooms. There was some slight evidence that these latter children showed greater interest in school when placed in heterogeneous rather than homogeneous classes. On the whole, the results of the O'Connor *et al.* study do extend the predictive range of Atkinson's model in that they show some of the conditions under which individuals who differ in achievement related motives may be expected to exhibit optimal performance.

Beyers (1968) has also done research dealing with the performance implications of Atkinson's risk taking model. In his study he dealt with performance on a digit symbol substitution task in which subjects were given what they were told was an easy or difficult goal (do better than 10 percent or 90 percent of the population). Subjects worked on the task for 4 trials. By the use of false feedback, Beyers permitted half the subjects given the easy goal and half the subjects given the difficult goal to fail on each trial. These subjects were told that their performance as of that trial was not adequate to meet the goal assigned to them. The remaining subjects were given success feedback after each trial. Beyers assumed that $M_s > M_{af}$ subjects would perform better under easy-fail and hard-success conditions than they would under easy-success and hard-fail conditions. These predictions follow from Atkinson's theory since under easy-success and hard-fail conditions $P_s$ is moving away from .5. Accordingly, the task should be one in which the subject for whom $M_s > M_{af}$ should lose interest. On the other hand the easy-fail and hard-success conditions ought to, at least initially, lead to a situation in which $P_s$ approaches .5. Then the subject in whom $M_s > M_{af}$ ought to find the task of increasing interest to him. Conversely, Atkinson's theory implies that the subject in whom $M_{af} > M_s$ should show better performance under easy-success and hard-fail conditions than under easy-fail and hard-success conditions. Beyers results failed to support these predictions. However, Beyers went on to make a further more refined data analysis. He had obtained subjective probability of success estimates from each of his subjects at each trial. He then argued that the relationship between individual differences in motivation and performance in different experimental conditions was dependent upon the subject's reaction to the experimental conditions and its effect on subjective probability of success. Accordingly, Beyers attempted to make predictions about the relationship between changes in $P_s$ and changes in performance as the subject worked on the task. Under easy-success conditions subjects begin the task with $P_s$ values above .5. In this condition, $P_s$ increases over trials. For subjects for whom $M_s > M_{af}$ the more rapidly $P_s$ increases the more rapidly they should lose interest in the task. This implies that the relationship between the slope of $P_s$ changes and the slope of performance changes for $M_s > M_{af}$ subjects should be negative. For subjects for whom $M_{af} > M_s$, rapid increases in $P_s$ should be accompanied by rapid reduction

TABLE 5.8

*Predicted and Obtained Signs of Correlation of $P_s$ Slope and Performance Slope on the Digit-Symbol Task in the Easy Success and Hard Difficult Conditions as a Function of Motive Orientation*

|  | Easy success | | Hard failing | |
|---|---|---|---|---|
|  | *Predicted* | *Obtained* | *Predicted* | *Obtained* |
| $M_s > M_{af}$ | − | − .30 | + | + .25 |
| $M_{af} > M_s$ | + | + .02 | − | − .08 |

Based on Beyers, 1968.

Note: Initial $P_s$ and initial performance levels are partialed out.

in negative resultant motivation. Consequently, for these subjects, Beyers predicted that the correlation between the slope of $P_s$ changes and the slope of changes in performance should be positive. Different predictions for the signs of the correlation between $P_s$ slope and performance slope were derived by Beyers for the hard-fail condition. In this condition initial $P_s$ is less than .5 and $P_s$ decreases over trials. The more rapid the decrease in $P_s$ the more rapid is the decrease in positive resultant motivation for $M_s > M_{af}$ subjects and the more rapid is the decrease in the negative value of the resultant motivation for the $M_{af} > M_s$ subjects. If performance reflects resultant motivation, then this analysis implies that there should be a positive correlation between the slope of $P_s$ changes and the slope of performance changes for $M_s > M_{af}$ subjects under this condition. The corresponding correlation for the $M_{af} > M_s$ subjects should be negative. Beyers obtained results in agreement with these predictions (see Table 5.8). Beyers results thus indicate that detailed predictions can be made about the relationship between achievement related motives and performance if one obtains information about the subject's reaction to the task.

## Concluding Comments

At the beginning of Chapter 3 criteria for the evaluation of hypothetico-deductive theories were discussed. Of the theories discussed in Chapters 3, 4, and 5, Atkinson's risk taking model would appear to come closest to satisfying these criteria. Eysenck's theory does not invariably permit rigorous reductions. Spence's theory, at least from the point of view of Goulet's analysis, has not been adequately tested.

On the other hand, from the point of view of personality theory only Eysenck's theory purports to present a comprehensive theory of personality. The deductions from his theory have not been uniformly rigorous but they have covered a great variety of situations.

The three theories which have been discussed in this chapter have each developed a specialized vocabulary. They have been dealt with in a relatively independent fashion. Actually it is possible to discern certain respects in which the dimensions of personality dealt with in these theories may be substantively related to each other. The MAS is assumed by Eysenck (1957) to be a measure of both neuroticism and introversion–extraversion. Individuals who score high on the MAS are thus considered to be introverted neurotics. In terms of Claridge's analysis the MAS may be assumed to be, in part at least, a measure of the physiologically based dimension which combines both neuroticism and introversion–extraversion.

It is also possible to discern certain relationships between the variables dealt with in Spence's theory and in Atkinson's theory. The MAS correlates with the Mandler–Sarason test anxiety scale which Atkinson uses to define $M_{af}$ (the fear of failure motive) in his theory. Individuals who score high on the MAS may, therefore, be considered as high in $M_{af}$.

The empirical and conceptual relations among these variables are not sufficient to provide a basis for integrating what is known about each of them. It is not clear how some of the detailed results of Spence's conditioning studies could be derived from Atkinson's theory of achievement motivation. Or, conversely, how Atkinson's level of aspiration results could be derived from Spence's theory of anxiety. This theoretical isolation of the various personality dimensions dealt with in this chapter illustrate the principle shortcoming of the hypothetico-deductive method as a basis for developing dimensions of personality.

# CHAPTER 6

# COGNITIVE APPROACHES TO THE DEVELOPMENT OF DIMENSIONS OF PERSONALITY

In the past 20 years there has been an increased emphasis on cognitive approaches to personality. There are several current research efforts, stemming from different intellectual traditions, which have attempted to derive dimensions of personality from a consideration of individual differences in cognitive processes.

The consideration of all the current research efforts dealing with cognitively derived dimensions of personality is beyond the scope of this book. We shall focus on two such research efforts, Witkin's research on differentiation and research on creativity, as being more or less representative of all of these research efforts.[1]

Cognitive approaches to personality share several characteristics:

First, and most obviously, cognitive theorists have taken individual differences in styles of thinking as the starting point for their investigations. Although this would appear to be an obvious starting point, it

---

[1] Current research efforts which are relevant include the work of Klein (1954, 1958) and Gardner (1962; Gardner *et al.*, 1959) which derives from psychoanalytic ego psychology; Bieri's (Bieri, Atkins, Brian, Leaman, Miller, & Tripodi, 1966) research on complexity–simplicity, which is based on Kelly's theory of personal constructs (Kelly, 1955); Harvey, Hunt, and Schroder's (1961; and Schroder, Driver, & Streufert, 1967) research in a dimension called "abstract–concrete" which is derived from a conception of sequential stages in psychological development; and Rokeach's (1960) work on the "open" and "closed" mind.

represents a relatively new point of departure for personality theory. Personality theorists have traditionally emphasized motivational, emotional, and biological characteristics of individuals and have tended to underemphasize the importance of thought processes.

Second, cognitive theorists in the area of personality have tended to emphasize style over content. That is, they have emphasized the importance of formal characteristics of thought—the way in which a person thinks about things rather than the actual content of thought.

Third, cognitive theorists have tended to assume that cognitive styles are related to other personality characteristics of individuals. Therefore, it has been assumed that it is possible to predict other important personality characteristics from a knowledge of an individual's cognitive style.

Fourth, cognitive theorists have treated cognitive styles as traits. That is, as characteristics of individuals which tend to be invariant irrespective of the situation with which a person is confronted. Thus, there has been an emphasis on the consistency in stylistic characteristics of thought.

## Witkin's Theory of Differentiation

### THE PERCEPTUAL BASIS

Witkin's theory exemplifies each of the criterion of a cognitive theory listed above. In addition, his theory is based on an extensive body of empirical research.

Witkin's theory grew out of observations of individual differences in a perceptual task called the rod-and-frame test (RFT). In this test a subject is seated in a completely dark room and is required to adjust the position of a luminous rod to the true vertical. The rod is surrounded by a luminous square frame. The experimenter is able to independently tilt the position of the rod and of the frame. The subject is required to adjust the rod to the true vertical under conditions where the rod and the frame are tilted in the same or in opposite directions. In addition, the experimenter is able to tilt the chair in which the subject is sitting. If the chair is not tilted the subject is able to refer to the position of his body as a basis for the judgment of the true vertical. The subject's score on this task is based on the absolute deviation of his settings from the true vertical under several conditions of body, frame, and rod tilt. Witkin found that subjects differed considerably in their scores on the RFT.

After a considerable amount of experimentation, Witkin assumed that the basis for performance on this task was the ability to overcome an "embedding context." This ability is one which permits a subject to ignore or deemphasize irrelevant misleading aspects of a situation in order to concentrate on those aspects which provide the basis for correct performance. In particular, this ability would enable a subject to disregard the misleading influences of the tilted frame or his tilted body in order to concentrate on the rod, thus permitting him to set it at the true vertical.

Witkin has studied the relationship between scores on the RFT and two other perceptual tasks which are assumed to be measures of the ability to overcome an embedding context—the body-adjustment test (BAT) and the embedded-figures test (EFT).[2] In the BAT, a subject is placed in a room which can be tilted. His chair can be tilted independently of the room. The S's task is to set his chair to the true vertical while the room remains tilted under conditions in which the room and chair are initially tilted in the same or opposite directions. The S's score on the test is based on the absolute deviation of his chair settings from the true vertical. Witkin interprets performance on this task as a measure of the ability to overcome an embedding context. In this instance the context which must be overcome is the tilted room. The subject must attend to cues from his body and ignore or discount the misleading visual appearance of the room.

The EFT was studied by Witkin as a means of checking his assumption that individual differences in the RFT and the BAT were attributable to ability to overcome an embedding context. The EFT is based on a series of figures developed by Gottschaldt. A simple figure is invariably hidden

TABLE 6.1

*Coefficients of Stability for Perceptual Test Scores: Children*

| Age of subjects, years | Retest interval, years | N | | BAT | | RFT | | EFT | | Index | |
|---|---|---|---|---|---|---|---|---|---|---|---|
| | | M | F | M | F | M | F | M | F | M | F |
| 10–14 | 4 | 27 | 24 | .58 | .66 | .56 | .57 | .51 | .69 | .64 | .88 |
| 14–17 | 3 | 27 | 24 | .68 | .88 | .82 | .75 | .95 | .95 | .87 | .94 |
| 10–17 | 7 | 27 | 24 | .31 | .63 | .49 | .53 | .48 | .68 | .50 | .79 |
| 8–13 | 5 | 26 | 22 | .14 | .36 | .71 | .61 | —[a] | — | —[a] | — |

Based on Witkin *et al.*, 1962.

[a] The EFT was not given to this group at 8. In the absence of EFT scores, total index scores could not be computed.

[2] Unless otherwise noted, references to Witkin's research refer to research discussed in a book written by Witkin and his collaborators, Witkin, Dyk, Fatterson, Goodenough, & Karp (1962).

TABLE 6.2

*Intercorrelations among Three Perceptual Test Scores for Different Age Groups*

| Test | Age | N | RFT | BAT |
|------|-----|-----|-----|-----|
| EFT | 10 | 60 | .31 | .36 |
|     | 12 | 50 | .51 | .45 |
|     | 13 | 59 | .55 | .42 |
|     | 15 | 50 | .31 | .26 |
|     | 17 | 48 | .42 | .27 |
| RFT | 8  | 53 |     | .30 |
|     | 10 | 60 |     | .30 |
|     | 12 | 50 |     | .25 |
|     | 13 | 59 |     | .45 |
|     | 15 | 50 |     | .41 |
|     | 17 | 48 |     | .40 |

Based on Witkin *et al.*, 1962.

in a complex geometrical figure. The outlines of the simple figure may form the boundaries of several subpatterns in the complex figure. The subject's score on this test is based on the length of time required to find the simple figure on a series of trials based on different figures.

Witkin has conclusively shown that these tests have high test–retest reliability. Witkin reports test–retest correlations over a three-year period of .84 and .66 for the RFT, .77 and .74 for the BAT, and .89 and .89 for the EFT for men and women, respectively (Witkin *et al.*, 1962, p. 40). In addition, Witkin has reported relatively high test–retest correlations for different groups of children for periods of time extending from three to seven years. These data are presented in Table 6.1.

Not only are scores on each of these three perceptual tests relatively stable, but these tests are substantially correlated with each other. Table 6.2 presents the results of a study in which correlations among these tests were obtained for subjects at different ages. Table 6.2 indicates that the tests are substantially related to each other at each of the age levels investigated. The relatively high and consistent correlations among these three perceptual tests provide the empirical justification for Witkin's procedure of obtaining a single score for a subject which combines his score on each of the three tests. This combined score is called the perceptual index.

## DIFFERENTIATION AND PERSONALITY

Up to this point in our discussion of Witkin's theory we have done little to indicate that we are dealing with a theory in the area of personality. Actually, this difference in perceptual functioning provides the basis for Witkin's research into many other characteristics of his subjects. The relationship between scores on the perceptual index and other characteristics of the person is mediated by a more general theoretical understanding of what is being measured by the tests comprising the perceptual index. Witkin uses the theoretical concept of differentiation, previously used in psychology by Lewin (1935; 1951) and Werner (1948) as the most inclusive basis for his theory. Degree of differentiation of a system refers to the complexity of its structure. Highly differentiated systems are composed of many heterogeneous and specialized subsystems. Witkin describes the consequences of differentiation for psychological systems as follows:

Among the major characteristics of the functioning of a highly differentiated system is specialization. The subsystems which are present within the general system are capable of mediating specific functions which, in a relatively undifferentiated state, are not possible or are performed in a more rudimentary way by the system as a whole.

When used to describe an individual's psychological system specialization means a degree of separation of psychological areas, as feeling from perceiving, thinking from acting. It means as well specificity in manner of functioning within an area. Specific reactions are apt to occur in response to specific stimuli as opposed to diffuse reaction to any of a variety of stimuli. Parts of a perceptual field are experienced as discreet rather than fused with their background. Impulses are channelized, contrasting with the easy "spilling over" characteristic of the relatively undifferentiated state.

(Witkin *et al.*, 1962, pp. 9–10)

Psychological development is accompanied by increasing differentiation. At any chronological age individuals will differ with respect to the degree of differentiation they have attained. Witkin assumes that the degree of differentiation attained by an individual is likely to be reflected in a large variety of behaviors. The differentiation hypothesis, which serves as the central guiding concept in Witkin's research, refers to the expectation that indices of differentiation derived from different spheres of behavior will be positively correlated with each other.

The perceptual index is taken by Witkin as a measure of differentiation. This follows from the assumption that the differentiated individual is able to achieve an analytic perception of the environment and to make distinctions which permit him to segregate items from the context in which they are embedded.

Using the differentiation hypothesis as a basis for his predictions, Witkin has dealt with the relationship between the perceptual index and defensive behavior. The concept of psychological defenses is derived from Freudian theory. Defense mechanisms are devices used by the ego in an attempt to deal with unacceptable unconscious impulses typically stemming from the id. Witkin assumes that individuals who are relatively undifferentiated should tend to use primitive defenses such as repression and denial more frequently than relatively differentiated individuals. Repression is a defense mechanism which prohibits an unconscious impulse from entering consciousness by, according to Freud's energy theory, the use of a counterforce. Denial is a defense mechanism which permits the unacceptable impulse some access to consciousness where it is dealt with by the conscious denial of its existence. Witkin's assumption is based on a number of considerations. First, in Freudian theory, repression and denial are developmentally primitive defenses. Individuals who are relatively undifferentiated may be assumed to use those defenses which are characteristic of primitive and early stages of development. Second, Witkin asserts that clinical experience suggests that a person who is highly differentiated is unlikely to use massive repression or primitive denial. Third, repression and denial are, according to psychoanalytic theory, defenses which are used in an undifferentiated way. That is, it is unlikely that a person will separate an item from its context and repress that item. Rather, repression is more likely to be used in an unsubtle way which results in the massive blockage of a whole area of impulses.

Individuals who are relatively differentiated are assumed by Witkin to use more sophisticated defenses such as intellectualization—a defense which involves an artificial separation of the affect or emotional content associated with an impulse from its intellectual content. Obviously, such a separation would involve the ability to differentiate.

Witkin and his associates have performed several studies dealing with this hypothesis. In one study a clinical psychologist analyzed figure drawing, Rorschach, and TAT test data. She assigned ratings to each subject on the basis of these data indicating the extent to which the subjects had, in her judgment, a well-organized defensive structure versus a relatively fluid, diffuse and easily penetrable defensive structure. These ratings correlated .61 with the perceptual index—indicating that relatively undifferentiated individuals are likely to have diffuse and easily penetrable defensive structures. Of course these data are not conclusive since the validity of the clinical judgments by which the defensive structures are inferred is open to question. It is possible that the judgments may, in fact, be based on some characteristic of the individuals tested other than their defensive structures. The question of the validity of judgments based on projective test is a controversial one.

In another study Witkin reports the results of an analysis of the handling of themes of aggression in TAT stories. Stories told in response to a card which elicited themes of aggression were assigned a rating indicating whether the aggression expressed in the story was of a direct and uncontrolled character or of a more modulated and subtle character. This rating correlated .54 with the perceptual index indicating that individuals who are assumed to be relatively undifferentiated express aggression in stories in a direct and uncontrolled form. If one assumes that such a form of expression is indicative of a more primitive defensive structure which alternates between repression and denial on the one hand and direct uncontrolled expression of impulses, then this finding supports Witkin's hypothesis relating differentiation to psychological defenses.

Finally, Witkin reports that there is a relationship between scores on the perceptual index and the recall of dreams. Relatively differentiated individuals tend to recall more dreams than relatively undifferentiated individuals. It is possible to argue that failure to recall dreams is an indication of a tendency to use repression as a defense. Individuals may fail to recall their dreams because the dreams may express unconscious impulses which they would normally repress. Hence, individuals who have low dream recall may be prone to use repression as a psychological defense.

In addition to differences in defensive behavior there have been a number of studies reported which have dealt with the relationship between scores on the perceptual index and social behavior. Witkin reports several studies which seem to indicate that individuals who score low on the perceptual index are more influenced by others and are less able to rely on their own judgments than individuals who score high on the index. Presumably this follows from the differentiation hypothesis in that undifferentiated individuals would be unable to isolate the ideas and suggestions of others from their own and would as a result tend to assimilate them with their own ideas. More differentiated individuals, on the other hand, would be able to isolate (differentiate) their ideas from those of others. In one study a relationship was found between scores on the perceptual index and behavior in an autokinetic experiment. In this type of experiment an individual is confronted with a stationary dot of light in a darkened room. Individuals characteristically report that the dot is moving. This experimental situation is often used to measure social influence. In this type of experiment a confederate of the investigator who is acting as a subject along with the true subject reports various movements in the dot of light. The effects of the confederate's judgments on the subjects judgments are assessed. Individuals who score low on the perceptual index tend to be more influenced by the judgments of the confederate than individuals who score high on the index.

There are related studies which indicate that there are relationships between scores on the perceptual index and indices of independence and self reliance. Witkin reports that subjects who score low on the perceptual index tend to be more unsure of themselves when taking a TAT test than subjects who score high on the perceptual index. The differentiated subject tends to rely on his own conception of the nature of the task and is, as a result, less likely to ask the examiner clarifying questions than the undifferentiated subject.

DIFFERENTIATION AND INTELLIGENCE: THE ZIGLER CRITIQUE

Witkin has also dealt with the relationship between scores on the perceptual index and intelligence. Research has indicated that there are substantial correlations between scores on the perceptual index and measures of intelligence and intellectual ability. Witkin has reported correlations ranging up to .76 between scores on the perceptual index and scores on the Wechsler Intelligence Scale for Children (WISC). The relationship between intelligence and the perceptual index has led Zigler (1963a, b), in a critical review of Witkin's research, to argue that the index is principally a nonverbal measure of intelligence. Before evaluating this criticism in detail we shall examine Witkin's own views of the relationship between intelligence and differentiation. Witkin reports the result of a factor analysis of the WISC and the perceptual tasks which are included in the perceptual index. The factor analysis was undertaken in order to discover if the relationship between the perceptual index and intelligence was "carried" by specific subtests of the WISC. They derived three oblique factors. The first factor was principally defined by verbal scales on the WISC. The WISC vocabulary, information and similarities scales had the highest loading on this factor. The perceptual tests which comprise the perceptual index had positive but nonsignificant loadings on this factor. The third factor was principally defined by high positive loadings (ranging from .61 to .74) of the perceptual tests contained in the perceptual index. The WISC picture completion, block design, and object assembly scales loaded .52, .50, and .33, respectively on this factor. This factor is considered by Witkin as a measure of differentiation. He argues that the three scales from the WISC which load on this factor may be considered, in part, as measures of differentiation. For example, in the block design test a subject is required to use blocks to construct a particular design. Successful performance on this task requires the subject to isolate particular blocks from the conglomerate in which they are found in order to assigne them their proper position.

Witkin's views on the relationship between intelligence and differentiation may be succinctly stated as follows:

1. Indices of differentiation, such as those included in the perceptual index are *not* measures of intelligence. In particular, these indices are not related to verbal measures of intelligence.

2. Some nonverbal measures of intelligence are, in part, measures of differentiation.

3. The concept of differentiation is rather more developed theoretically than the concept of intelligence as it is used in standardized tests of intelligence. Accordingly, to conceive of measures of differentiation as measures of intelligence is to replace a relatively sophisticated theoretical concept with a primitive theoretical concept.

Zigler would not accept this argument. In what follows we shall present a somewhat expanded version of Zigler's views. First, it is not correct to assert that verbal measures of ability are not related to the perceptual index. In almost every study of measures of intelligence there is a positive correlation between verbal and nonverbal measures. Witkin found in his factor analysis of the WISC that the verbal comprehension factor correlated .34 with the factor he interpreted as a measure of differentiation. Similarly, Cohen (1959), in his factor analysis of the WISC, found that verbal comprehension factors were correlated with nonverbal factors. In addition to the positive relationship between verbal ability and differentiation, Bieri, Bradburn and Galinsky (1958) have reported significant positive correlations between scores on the EFT and the college board measures of mathematical ability.

The consistent positive correlations among various measures of intellectual ability form the empirical base for the theory that all measures of intelligence reflect to a greater or lesser degree one fundamental ability called *g* (see Spearman, 1927). Cattell (1963b; Horn & Cattell, 1966) has developed this theory further. He has suggested that *g* has two discernible but related components called fluid and crystallized intelligence, the latter being principally a measure of the effects of tuition and learning and the former representing a relatively fixed capacity which influences the rate of intellectual development and the individual's reaction to his environment. Measures of intelligence measure, in different degrees, both components. The WISC scales which are related to the perceptual index are generally assumed to be predominantly measures of fluid intelligence —particularly the block design test. The WISC scales which define verbal ability in Witkin's factor analytic study are generally assumed to be predominantly measures of crystallized intelligence. Thus, it can be argued that the perceptual index is primarily a measure of nonverbal fluid intelligence.

We now have a theoretical dilemma. We have reasonable grounds for considering the perceptual index either as a measure of intelligence or as a measure of differentiation. The research conducted by Witkin and his associates has been generated by the differentiation theory. Therefore, on heuristic grounds it is that theory which is to be preferred. It is exceedingly unlikely that the body of research we have relating the perceptual index to other behavior would have been generated by conceiving of the index as a measure of intelligence. Nevertheless, now that we have an extensive body of research it is legitimate to question the adequacy of the differentiation interpretation and to seek alternative and possibly superior interpretations to the one arrived at by Witkin.

Zigler rejects the differentiation interpretation of Witkin's research, in part, because it lacks precision. He asserts that its relationship to the various findings is largely "metaphorical." In my view this is a justified criticism. Witkin's theory is not a rigorous hypothetico-deductive theory which permits unambiguous deductions. Theories vary in their rigor. The theories discussed in Chapters 3, 4, and 5 each had algebraic formulations which permitted one to make deductions with the aid of mathematical manipulations. The differentiation concept clearly has not attained this degree of rigor. Most of the deductions mediated by the differentiation concept involve appeal to hidden premises and do not unambiguously follow from the concept *per se*. Consider, for example, the research relating preferences among defense mechanisms and differentiation. It can be argued that repression could be an index of high rather than low differentiation. One could imagine a person whose area of repression is very "narrow." For example, one could imagine that a man represses sexual desires for women who have certain characteristics, for example, women who are between 32 and 35 and who are tall, blonde, and have green eyes. Such a use of repression would presumably depend on highly developed differentiation abilities. Of course, it could be argued that such a repression violates the understanding of repression given in psychoanalytic theory. But in this case Witkin's deduction appeals to concepts which are not explicitly stated in the differentiation concept. Of course this sort of appeal to hidden premises is not a unique feature of Witkin's theory but is in fact present, to some degree, in most theories.

Perhaps the principal difficulty with the differentiation concept is its extensity. The concept is so broad that one can use it to deduce almost any result. Consider Witkin's explanation of the relationship between scores on the block design scale of the WISC and the perceptual index.

Witkin asserts that success on this task requires an individual to isolate the block from its surround and see it in new combinations. But such an argument can clearly be extended to almost any task. For example, a common form of vocabulary test requires a person to select the best definition of a word among several given alternatives. One could argue that successful performance requires the individual to separate and differentiate words which are less relevant in order to select the word which is most precisely defining. Thus, the individual who is not able to distinguish between alternatives which are close to adequate but are incorrect and words which are precisely defining will make errors and hence will have a lower score. Such a vocabulary test may therefore be assumed to be, in part, a measure of differentiation. The point of the above deduction is to suggest that the concept of differentiation is sufficiently vague as to permit its extension, in a trivial way, to a wide variety of tasks. It is difficult to know the boundary condition of such a theory—that is, the situations in which it does or does not apply. Ambiguity as to the predictive consequences of a theory tends to make a theory invulnerable to disproof.

Not only is the concept of differentiation overly extensive in application but there are situations where it apparently should directly apply where it does not. There is evidence that verbal tasks which seem to require the ability to overcome an embedding context do not relate to the perceptual index. For example, Guilford, Frick, Christensen and Merrifield (as cited in Kagan & Kogan, 1970) found that a task in which individuals had to unscramble words was not related to a factor containing perceptual tasks which Karp (1963) has shown is related to the perceptual tasks used by Witkin to measure differentiation. Also Podell and Phillips (1959) found no relationship between performance on a verbal anagrams task in which a subject had to make as many words as possible using the letters contained in a meaningful word and scores on a factor called spatial decontextualization which is similar to Witkin's perceptual index. The apparent lack of relationship between Witkin's perceptual index and verbal tasks which seem to involve the ability to overcome an embedding context has led Zigler to suggest that the perceptual index might be more aptly construed as a measure of spatial decontextualization. The use of the qualifying term "spatial" is an attempt to more carefully specify what is being measured by the perceptual index.

We have discussed the respects in which the differentiation concept is inadequate as the theoretical foundation for Witkin's research. Is intelligence an adequate foundation? The initial attractiveness of the intelligence interpretation stems from Occam's razor—the principle of parsimony. One of the striking findings contained in Witkin's research, which is not extensively discussed by him, is the apparent similarity of the

## TABLE 6.3

*Correlations among Variables Studied by Witkin*

| | 1 | 2 | 3 | 4 | 5 | 6 | 7 | 8 | 9 |
|---|---|---|---|---|---|---|---|---|---|
| 1. Perceptual index | — | .66** | .57** | .33* | .41* | .77** | .18 | .12 | .26 |
| 2. Intellectual index | .66** | — | .54** | .44** | .26 | .53** | .07 | .21 | .28 |
| 3. Sophistication of body concept (figure drawing) | .57** | .54** | — | .42* | .37* | .44* | .11 | .06 | .33 |
| 4. Approach to task (TAT) | .33* | .44** | .42** | — | .52** | .51** | .56** | .54** | .45* |
| 5. Rorschach percept analysis | .41* | .26 | .37* | .52** | — | .46** | .39* | .57** | .46** |
| 6. Cognitive clarity (interview) | .77** | .53** | .44** | .51** | .46** | — | .53** | .37* | .54** |
| 7. Interview general clinical analysis | .18 | .07 | .11 | .56** | .39* | .53** | — | .55** | .61** |
| 8. Organization level "TAT | .12 | .21 | .06 | .54** | .57** | .37* | .55** | — | .37* |
| 9. Verbal index | .26 | .28 | .33 | .45* | .46** | .54** | .61** | .37* | — |

Cluster 1

Cluster 2

Based on Witkin *et al.*, 1962. $N = 30$ for all correlations except those involving variable 7, where $N = 29$. The boxed-in areas represent the two main clusters.

\* Significant at the .05 level (one-tail test used for $r$ between any pair of the following variables: 1, 3, 4, 5, 8; two-tail tests used for all other correlations).

\*\* Significant at the .01 level.

122

pattern of relationships between the perceptual index and other measures and what Witkin calls the verbal index (a measure of verbal ability based on the scales defining Factor 1 in Witkin's analysis of the WISC) and these same measures. Table 6.3 presents a set of correlations obtained by Witkin among a group of measures including the perceptual index and the verbal index. Note that the verbal index and the perceptual index both correlate positively with all the remaining variables. The verbal index correlates positively with each of the five variables with which the perceptual index is significantly correlated (variables 2–6). The correlations of the verbal index with these variables range from .28 to .54. Witkin has placed two boxes around the correlations reported in Table 6.3 in order to indicate that the perceptual and verbal index have somewhat different clusters of relationships. Nevertheless, the fact remains that both of these indices are positively related, albeit to different degrees, to the same set of variables.

According to Witkin, the verbal index is not a measure of differentiation. This leaves unexplained the similarity of the pattern of relationships of the perceptual and verbal index. One obvious explanation is that the perceptual index and the verbal index are each measures of different aspects of general intelligence, *g*, and that the relationship between each of these variables and other variables is mediated by intelligence. Thus the appeal to intelligence as an explanation of Witkin's findings has the initial advantage of explaining the relationships obtained with the verbal index whereas the appeal to differentiation does not.

If intelligence is the critical variable accounting for the relationship between the perceptual index and other variables, then the statistical control for differences in intelligence should reduce or remove these relationships. Since most of the studies done by Witkin have not controlled for intelligence the issue is in some doubt. There are some studies which have controlled for intelligence and found relationships between measures of differentiation and other variables. However, these studies for the most part do not deal with variables which are central to the differentiation hypothesis. There is, however, one study which deals with an issue which is central to Witkin's theory where intelligence is controlled. Minard and Mooney (1969) attempted to test the idea, derived from Witkin's theory, that individuals who were high in differentiation would be less influenced by emotions in their cognitive processes. Such individuals would be able to perceive stimuli which had emotional significance without distortion. In order to test this idea they selected, on the basis of a word association test, words which had emotional significance for an individual. They then presented these words tachistoscopically and compared the subjects' ability to identify these words with their ability to identify words matched for frequency of occurrence in English and physical characteristics which did not have emotional significance for the subjects. They were able to derive a measure of the extent to which the subject's identification of words was influenced by their emotional significance for him. They found that this index correlated .41 with a measure of differentiation based on the tasks defining the perceptual index. In addition, they found that their measure of the effect of emotion on perceptual recognition was unrelated to intelligence.

The Minard and Mooney study represents an important advance in testing a central concept in Witkin's theory. In addition to the demonstration that their central finding is not a function of intelligence, they were able to demonstrate an aspect of the differentiation hypothesis using an objective measure which is probably a purer index than the usual clinical techniques used in this research. If further research testing other aspects of the differentiation concept controlling for intelligence and using objective measures supported the theory, then the argument that intelligence was the central mediating concept in Witkin's research would no longer be viable. However, this body of research does not exist at present.

We have suggested, on empirical grounds, that it is plausible that intelligence may mediate many of the relationships reported by Witkin. Is it possible to argue on theoretical grounds that intelligence is involved in these relationships? We shall argue that this is possible. Consider the relationships between the perceptual index and personality characteristics that we have discussed. It can be argued that the clinical psychologist who judged the TAT and Rorschach for characteristic modes of defense was responding, in part, to intellectual differences. Individuals of high intelligence should be capable of more sophisticated verbal productions and more complex reasoning processes. Protocols of persons with high intelligence might well be judged as indicating more sophisticated defenses than protocols of persons of low intelligence on the basis of the sophistication of verbal material and judgment processes revealed in the protocols. Similarly, the analysis of themes of aggression in the TAT may also be influenced by intellectual differences. A person of high intelligence would presumably be capable of more subtle forms of verbal expression than a person of low intelligence and this difference might in and of itself account for the characteristic difference in the way in which aggression is dealt with in stories. In addition it can be argued that persons of high intelligence might be rewarded more often for indirect expression of aggression than persons of low intelligence. The use of sarcasm and other forms of verbal insult is a frequent alternative to physical assault as a means of expressing aggression. Individuals of high intelligence would probably find forms of verbal aggression more successful than individuals of low intelligence by virtue of their greater verbal facility. Consequently, they would be more likely to persevere in this manner of expressing aggression. A person who used such a form of aggression might very well be judged to express aggression indirectly. Finally, the ability to recall dreams may, in part, be dependent upon verbal ability.

In addition, the relationships between the perceptual index and social behavior might be due to intellectual differences. One could explain the greater self-reliance and independence of the individual who scores high on the perceptual index by arguing that individuals of high intelligence are more likely to be rewarded for independence of judgment than individuals of low intelligence since their judgments are more likely to be considered correct. Individuals of low intelligence, on the other hand, are more likely to be dependent upon others to provide assistance and suggestions.

Differences in intelligence may also be seen as influencing relationships between the perceptual index and other variables which we have not yet considered. Witkin has reported positive relationships between the perceptual index and a measure of the extent of the subject's ability to impose structure on the Rorschach ink blot test. The perceptual index is also positively related to scores on a cognitive clarity index obtained from an interview. These results are taken by Witkin to indicate that individuals who are highly differentiated are more able to impose structure and order in amorphous situations than individuals who are relatively undifferentiated. Alternatively, one could argue that individuals who are high in intelligence would be judged as clearer and more coherent in their ability to deal with these situations by virtue of their superior reasoning and verbal abilities.

Witkin has reported that the perceptual index is positively related to a measure of the sophistication of body concept based on the "draw-a-man" test (see Machover, 1949). Witkin asserts that more differentiated individuals develop a more sophisticated and differentiated concept of their body which is reflected in their drawings of persons. On the other hand, the draw-a-man test is used as a nonverbal measure of intelligence (see Goodenough, 1926). The intelligence scale scores derived from the drawings used by Witkin are highly correlated ($r = .74$) with Witkin's sophistication of body concept measure. Consequently, differences in nonverbal intelligence could easily account for the obtained differences in sophistication of body concept ratings for individuals who differ in their score on the perceptual index.

There are sex differences on the perceptual index. Although there are many complications with respect to this finding (it does not hold at every age level, the effects of other variables such as "ego strength" and masculinity-femininity as opposed to biological sex may influence the finding), most of the research indicates that males score higher on the perceptual index than females. (See Kagan and Kogan, 1970; and Maccoby, 1966, for reviews of this literature). It is well known that males are superior in nonverbal indices of intelligence to females. Females, on the other hand, tend to be superior to males on verbal measures of intelligence (see Tyler, 1965). Consequently, the sex differences in Witkin's indices of differentiation are compatible with the view that the perceptual index is, in fact, a measure of nonverbal intelligence.

If one permits a certain leeway in what constitutes an acceptable explanation it is at least plausible to argue on both empirical and theoretical ground that differences in intelligence mediate the relationship between the perceptual index and other variables. In a limited sense it is possible to simultaneously view the perceptual index as a measure of differentiation and of intelligence. Witkin's research indicates that one component of *g* is spatial decontextualization ability. In this sense, Witkin's research and theorizing serves to clarify and specify more precisely what is measured by tests of general intelligence.

It is not surprising to find that measures of intelligence are so widely related to other behaviors. Intelligence tests measure the kind of abilities which are required for success in our society. Their validity is derived ultimately from their ability to predict success on intellectual tasks which are considered valuable by our society. Much of an individual's social experience, particularly for the kind of middle-class subjects generally used by Witkin in his research, derives from his intellectual ability. Individuals are rewarded, punished, and reacted to on the basis of their intellectual ability. We even have a social role called intellectual. Consequently, differences in intellectual ability may relate to many kinds of behavior.

## Creativity

### APPROACHES BASED ON DIVERGENT ABILITY

Most psychologists agree that I.Q. tests measure an important respect in which individuals differ in ability. Are there any other important intellectual abilities which are not measured by conventional intelligence tests? In this section we shall consider research which deals with this question. In particular, we shall examine research which attempts to show that creativity is an ability of great social significance which is either not measured at all, or not measured to any substantial degree, by conventional tests of intelligence. Most of the research we shall discuss has assumed that individuals who differ in creativity share certain formal or stylistic characteristics of thought. Further, it is assumed that these formal characteristics of thought are related to many other personality characteristics. We shall therefore examine individual differences in creativity as an important cognitive style.

In order to establish that creativity is a cognitive style in the sense indicated above, it is necessary to:

1. Indicate the sorts of behavior which are indicative of creativity;

2. Show that individuals who exhibit these behaviors share certain formal characteristics of thought which are uncorrelated with intelligence; and

3. Show that these characteristics of thought are associated with other personality characteristics.

Although the point is debatable, it seems to me that the nature of the behaviors which are creative is not particularly problematic. Creativity involves the production of something which is novel and which is judged by recognized authorities to be socially significant and valuable. Instances of creativity, such as the choreography of a classic ballet, the assertion of a critical perspective on a writer, the invention of an engineering process, or the discovery of a scientific theory invariably involve the production of something which is, at least marginally, different from anything which has existed before. Novelty is a necessary but not a sufficient condition of creativity. In order for something to be called creative, recognized authorities must judge it to be valuable. With respect to scientific creativity, the authorities are usually a subset of the scientific community concerned with relevant areas of research. Occasionally, a contribution to science is not initially judged to be valuable and significant but is only recognized retrospectively. However, we do not consider a product as creative unless some recognized body has judged it to be valuable. A similar state of affairs obtains with respect to artistic creativity—although in this case there may often be considerably more controversy among authorities and there may also be a clash of opinion between authorities and the "common man." Edgar Guest and Norman Rockwell may be popular but they have little standing in the community of critics professionally concerned with literature and painting.

The use of the judgment of experts has circumvented difficulties involved in the definition and measurement of the kinds of behaviors which are creative. The focus of the research to be reviewed here deals with the characteristic styles of thought of individuals whose productions are judged to be creative.

Much current research on creativity has proceeded from a distinction between divergent and convergent processes of thought. Convergent thought processes are those which end in a single correct response. Standard intelligence tests are measures of convergent thought since each of the items on the test typically has a single correct answer. Divergent thought processes are those which do not culminate in a single correct response but rather diverge over a variety of different types of appropriate responses. For example, a person may be asked to list all the different uses that he can think of for a brick. Excellence in divergent thinking typically is measured by the number of different kinds of responses which an individual can produce and/or the number of statistically unique responses—that is, responses which are given by the individual alone. Conventional intelligence tests do not measure divergent thinking. It has been argued, by Guilford (1957, 1959) among others, that divergent thinking tests are measures of creativity. Further, since conventional intelligence tests do not measure divergent thinking ability they are not measures of creativity.

The research we shall review has more or less assumed without question that divergent thinking tests are measures of creative ability. Two things have been at issue in this research:

1. The relationship between divergent thinking ability and scores on intelligence tests.
2. The personality characteristics of individuals who excel in divergent thinking ability.

A number of studies have reported low positive correlations between measures of divergent thinking ability and measures of intelligence. One of the best known of these studies is one reported by Getzels and Jackson (1962). They gave a series of divergent thinking tests to a group of high school age students attending a private school whose mean intelligence quotient was 132. The divergent thinking tests included a word association test in which subjects were required to give as many definitions as possible to a common stimulus word, an unusual uses test and tests of divergent thinking ability dealing with spatial, mathematical, and verbal materials. Table 6.4 presents the correlations obtained by Getzels and Jackson among their divergent thinking tests and between these tests and intelligence. Note the relatively low correlations between the measures of divergent thinking and intelligence. Wallach and Kogan (1965) have analyzed the data reported in Table 6.4 and have reported that the average correlation between measures of creativity and intelligence in Getzels and Jackson's study is approximately .27. Getzels and Jackson concluded, on the basis of these data, that intelligence and creativity were relatively

TABLE 6.4

*Intercorrelations among Creativity and Intelligence Tests*

| Variable number | Test | 1 | 2 | 3 | 4 | 5 | 6 |
|---|---|---|---|---|---|---|---|
| 1 | Word association | | 369 | 344 | 303 | 420 | 378 |
| 2 | Uses | 371 | | 206 | 222 | 175 | 186 |
| 3 | Hidden shapes | 351 | 197 | | 159 | 414 | 366 |
| 4 | Fables | 320 | 276 | 153 | | 220 | 131 |
| 5 | Make-up problems | 488 | 279 | 525 | 269 | | 246 |
| 6 | Intelligence quotient | 371 | 147 | 303 | 115 | 393 | |

Based on Getzels & Jackson, 1962. Boys (above diagonal) $N = 292$. Girls (below diagonal) $N = 241$.

independent of each other, at least among a high IQ group such as they studied.

Having concluded that intelligence and creativity were independent, Getzels and Jackson formed two groups of subjects—those subjects who excelled on their measures of creativity (had scores in the top 20 percent) but did not excel in intelligence (had scores below the top 20 percent) and those subjects who excelled in their measures of intelligence but not their measures of creativity. They then attempted to ascertain the personality characteristics of these relatively "intelligent" and relatively "creative" students.

The creative subjects tended to have more unconventional values than the intelligent subjects. They did not value personal characteristics which were likely to lead to professional success. The creative subjects had many more, and more unconventional, vocational aspirations than the intelligent subjects. The creative subjects tended to use humor and violence much more in their writings and drawings than the intelligent subjects. Getzels and Jackson (1962) believe their findings are compatible with a Freudian theory of creativity according to which creative individuals are distinguished by their ability to incorporate and integrate into their reality oriented thought processes material which has been repressed and is normally unconscious (see Freud, 1948). This ability is called "regression in the service of the ego" (see Kris, 1953; Schafer, 1958). The greater access to normally repressed material would apparently account for the unconventionality of the creative subjects and their greater use of violence and humor in their fantasy.

Getzels and Jackson's findings are compatible with other studies of individuals who excel in divergent thinking ability.  Torrance (1962) found that primary school children who excelled in divergent thinking tests of creativity developed by him (see Torrance, 1966) tended to produce wild and silly ideas and made drawings which were judged as playful and humorous. Weisberg and Springer (1961) found that children who excelled in Torrance's test of creative ability were rated by a psychiatrist as having a sense of humor more often than children who scored low on Torrance's test of creativity.

Getzels' and Jackson's study has been the subject of considerable controversy principally dealing with the question of whether their findings establish that measures of creativity are independent of measures of intelligence. Wallach and Kogan (1965) report that the average correlation among the measures of creativity used by Getzels and Jackson was .32. Recall that the average correlation between measures of creativity and intelligence was .27. Tests of intelligence have approximately the same relation to the tests of creativity used by Getzels and Jackson as the tests of creativity have to each other. Consequently, we can, on the basis of these data, argue that tests of intelligence are tests of creativity. Further, the correlations between tests of creativity and tests of intelligence reported by Getzels and Jackson is artifically depressed by three factors. First, the tests of intelligence are age corrected. That is, they are scored as intelligence quotients (I.Q.)—mental age/chronological age. Tests of creativity are not age corrected. If they were, the correlation between them and tests of intelligence would probably increase. Second, Getzels and Jackson had a limited range of intelligence in their study—the upper range. A restriction in the range of a variable decreases the magnitude of its correlation with other variables. Third, the tests of creativity they used had relatively low test-retest reliability. Tests which do not correlate highly with themselves cannot correlate highly with other tests. Yamomoto (1965) has reported a study of the relationship of measures of intelligence and divergent thinking ability in which he corrected for range restriction and attenuation(the unreliability of measures) and he reported a correlation of .51 between these two types of measures. Hassan and Butcher (1966) found, in a partial replication of the Getzels and Jackson study using a group of Scottish children whose mean I.Q. was 102, a correlation between an aggregate creativity measure and intelligence of .74. Finally, in a factor analytic study of relations between tests of divergent thinking ability and tests of intelligence, Cropley (1966) found two oblique factors. The first factor was principally defined by Verbal I.Q., academic average, and vocabulary. The second factor was principally defined by measures of divergent thinking ability. However, the correlation between these factors was .51. The results we have discussed up to this point, indicate that measures of divergent thinking ability, although possibly partially distinct from measures of intelligence, are substantially related to them.

Wallach and Kogan (1965) performed the first study in which there was a clear separation between measures of divergent thinking ability and intelligence. The principal innovation in their study was the use of a game-like atmosphere when presenting measures of creativity. In the research we have reviewed, divergent thinking ability has been assessed under testlike conditions. Wallach and Kogan (1965) argue that such conditions may not be optimal for the assessment of creativity. Test conditions typically have some degree of time pressure associated with them. Many instances of creative thinking occur under conditions where time limits are not present. Kepler was said to have taken many years to discover the elliptical orbit of the planets. However, one could argue that many instances of creative work do occur under conditions of time pressure, and in fact that time pressures are becoming a ubiquitous feature of creative work. Wallach and Kogan have a more cogent theoretical reason for arguing that time pressures should be minimized when one is assessing divergent thinking ability. As we have seen, divergent thinking ability is, in part, indicated when an individual makes a unique response. In most situations, initial responses are common and ordinary. It is only as the obvious and common responses are exhausted that unusual and unique responses emerge. Therefore, the person excelling in divergent thinking ability may need time to exhibit the full range of his response repertoire. Also, it can be argued that testlike conditions foster an excessively critical attitude which may inhibit an individual and prevent him from exhibiting the full range of possible responses in his repertoire. For these reasons, Wallach and Kogan used a gamelike relaxed atmosphere when assessing divergent thinking ability. They used 5 tests of divergent thinking ability:

1. Instances: a test in which the subject is required to list as many things as he can which are instances of something—for example, name all the round things you can.

2. Alternate uses: for example, list all the uses of a knife.

3. Similarities: a test requiring an individual to list all the ways two things are similar.

4. Pattern meanings: a test in which the subject is required to list all the different things which various abstract images could represent.

5. Line meanings: a test in which one is asked to name all the things which various line patterns make you think of.

For each of these five tests they derived two measures—number of different responses and the number of unique responses. In addition, they included 10 measures of intelligence in their study. These included various subtests of the WISC and several measures of school achievement. They then proceeded to obtain correlations among these measures. It was found that 43 of the 45 correlations among the measures of divergent thinking ability were statistically significant. The level of correlation required for significance was .16. Similarly, 43 of the 45 correlations among measures of intelligence were statistically significant ($r > .16$, $p < .05$). However, of the 100 correlations between measures of intelligence and measures of divergent thinking only 11 were significant, and none of these correlations exceeded .23 in value. Wallach and Kogan's data clearly establish statistical independence between measures of divergent thinking ability and intelligence. Having established this Wallach and Kogan then proceeded to form separate groups of male and female subjects who scored relatively high on both kinds of measures, low on both kinds of measures, high on divergent thinking ability and low on intelligence, and high on intelligence but low on divergent thinking ability. They collected further data from these various groups of subjects in order to ascertain the personality characteristics associated with various combinations of these two kinds of thinking ability. In presenting this part of the results of the Wallach and Kogan study we shall rely on a reanalysis of their data reported by Cronbach (1968). Cronbach argues that his statistical analysis of the Wallach and Kogan data is superior to the one originally presented by them. Without going into technical details, Cronbach's analysis seems superior on two grounds. First, he does not separate his subjects by sex, whereas Wallach and Kogan do. Cronbach indicates that there is little evidence of sex differences in the Wallach and Kogan data. Consequently a simpler and more powerful analysis is obtained by ignoring them. Second, in the statistical technique used by Wallach and Kogan, analysis of variance, there is no provision for an estimate of the amount of variance in the various measures accounted for by the two independent variables, intelligence and divergent thinking ability. Cronbach used a statistical technique called multiple regression analysis (see Cohen, 1968) which permits one to assess not only whether a particular variable is significantly related to another, but also permits one to assess the magnitude of the relationship. The results obtained in Cronbach's re-analysis of the Wallach and Kogan data are presented in Table 6.5. One of the striking things about the data in Table 6.5 is the indication that differences in divergent thinking ability (called $F$ by Cronbach) are of relatively little importance in accounting for variation in the dependent variables in the Wallach and Kogan investigation. The variables with the closest relationship to divergent thinking ability are "large bandwidth" and "more acceptance of bizarre labels." However, differences in divergent thinking ability account for only 4 percent of the variance in these dependent variables, leaving 96 percent of the variance unaccounted for. By contrast, differences in intelligence, called A for achievement by Cronbach in order to indicate that the tests which measure intelligence in the Wallach and Kogan study have a substantial emphasis on school success and crystallized intelligence, are very substantially related to some of the variables studied by Wallach and Kogan. Note that intelligence is significantly related to ratings of "concentration on school work," "interest in school work," and "does not deprecate work," and determines 56, 44, and 30 percent of the variance in these variables respectively. The pattern of relationship of each of these variables is relatively coherent. High intelligence tends to be related to variables which indicate adjustment to the school situation. Divergent thinking ability tends to be related to variables which indicate impulsivity and lack of inhibition. Attention seeking and not hesitant fit in a reasonably obvious way with this interpretation. Also the relationships with the acceptance of bizarre labels and large bandwidth (that is, large boundaries for class inclusion) indicate that individuals who are high in divergent thinking ability tend not to exercise critical judgment in their thought processes or tend to have wider latitudes of acceptance of responses.

It is also noteworthy that there are some relationships between intelligence and divergent thinking ability considered jointly and the dependent variables studied by Wallach and Kogan. All of these relationships are of the same form. Individuals who are high on both intelligence and divergent thinking ability, or low on both intelligence and divergent thinking ability exceed individuals high on only one of these variables. Children who are high on both variables are more confident and socially accepted than children who are high only in intelligence. This is not surprising. What is somewhat surprising is that children who are low on both of these measures seem more successful in the school setting than children high in divergent thinking ability but low in intelligence: Cronbach suggests that this latter group may be higher in maladjustment than the other three groups studied.

Although Wallach and Kogan have succeeded in showing that it is possible to clearly distinguish intelligence and divergent thinking ability, they have not shown that differences in divergent thinking ability are a particularly important determinant of other personality characteristics.

The results obtained by Wallach and Kogan indicating that measures of intelligence and divergent thinking ability are statistically independent have been supported by Wallach and Wing (1969). They dealt with a group of college freshmen. They used the Scholastic Aptitude Test measures of verbal and mathematical ability as their measures of intelligence and

TABLE 6.5

*Cronbach's Reanalysis of Wallach and Kogan Data*

*Characteristics associated with high A index (15 relations)*

| | |
|---|---|
| Concentrates on schoolwork | 56% |
| Interested in schoolwork[a] | 44% |
| Does not deprecate own work[a] | 30% |
| Confident[a] | 14% |
| Not hesitant[a] | 11% |
| Sought as companion[a] | 6% |
| Object sorting more inferential and less relational | 5% |
| Better story quality | 4% |
| More emotional attribution (paths) | 8% |
| More emotional attribution (sticks) | 3% |
| More correct attributions (abstract) | 7% |
| Less acceptance of bizarre labels | 3% |
| Less test anxiety | 10% |
| Less general anxiety | 5% |
| Less defensiveness | 3% |
| More mature story endings | 7% |

*Characteristics associated with high F index (6 relations)*

| | |
|---|---|
| Not hesitant[a] | 3% |
| Seeks attention[b] | 3% |
| Large "bandwidth"[c] | 4% |
| More emotional attribution (sticks) | 3% |
| More acceptance of bizarre labels | 4% |
| More text anxiety | 3% |

*Characteristics associated with high-high or low-low pattern, over and above main effects (6 relations)*

| | |
|---|---|
| Seeks companionship[b,c] | 8% |
| Sought as companion | 6% |
| Confident | 4% |
| Not hesitant | 4% |
| Does not deprecate own work | 3% |
| Interested in schoolwork | 2% |

Based on Cronbach, 1968.
Percentage indicates dependent variable variance accounted for.

[a] Relation with *AF* affects interpretation.
[b] *AF* effect not accompanied by main effect.
[c] Relation may hold for girls only.

they used number of responses and number of unique responses in four divergent thinking tests administered under relaxed conditions as their measures of divergent thinking ability. The 16 correlations between their measures of intelligence and their measures of divergent thinking abilities ranged in value from −.07 to .09—indicating substantial independence between these two kinds of measures. The correlation between their measures of verbal and mathematical ability was .38 and the correlation among their measures of divergent thinking ability ranged from .36 to .66.

Having established the independence of their measures of intelligence and divergent thinking ability, Wallach and Wing explored the relationship between differences on each of these abilities and accomplishments in a diverse set of extracurricular activities. They formed six groups of subjects—those in the top and bottom third of divergent thinking ability when that ability is measured in terms of *number* of responses, and those in the top and bottom third of divergent thinking ability when that ability is measured in terms of the number of *unique* responses, and those in the top and bottom third of their measures of intelligence. In order to obtain information about accomplishments outside the classroom each subject was asked to fill in a self-report form dealing with his various accomplishments. The areas dealt with are presented in Table 6.6. Tables 6.7, 6.8, and 6.9 present the number of subjects in each of the high and low groups who endorsed each of the items.

The clearest and most dramatic finding which emerges from an examination of Tables 6.7, 6.8, and 6.9 is that differences in divergent thinking ability are positively related to talented accomplishments outside the classroom and differences in intelligence are not. Individuals high in divergent thinking ability as measured by number of responses (productivity) endorse 16 of the 34 items significantly more often than individuals who are low in productivity. By contrast, differences in intelligence are related to only 4 of these accomplishments and in two of these cases individuals who are low in intelligence endorse the items more often than individuals who are high in intelligence. Wallach and Wing (1969) argue, on the basis of these data, that divergent thinking ability is related to creativity and talented accomplishment outside the classroom. Whereas variations in intelligence, at least among a high intelligence sample such as college students, are not.

I have a number of reservations about this conclusion. First, Wallach and Wing did not measure intelligence in the sense of g but rather academic accomplishment. Whether measures of intelligence which emphasize fluid intelligence would exhibit similar results is a moot point. Second, Wallach and Wing used volunteers in their study and report that only 40 percent of the subjects who were approached participated. Although this may be a laudable procedure from an ethical point of view it raises some issues

TABLE 6.6

*Talented Accomplishments Studied by Wallach and Wing*

*Leadership*
a. Participated as an active member of one or more student organizations
b. Nominated for or appointed to office in a student organization
c. Elected president or chairman of a student organization
d. Elected president of student government or class
*Art*
a. Created art work such as painting, drawing, sculpturing, cartooning, photography (not as part of a course)
b. Had art work exhibited or published
c. Entered an artistic competition or contest
d. Won a prize or an award in art competition
*Social Service*
a. Actively participated in programs sponsored by community or religious groups, such as Scouts, 4-H Clubs, YMCA, YWCA, YMHA, CYO
b. Elected or appointed officer of such a group
c. Received an award or prize for work in service group
*Literature*
a. Wrote original poems, plays, stories, articles, essays (not as part of a course), but have not published
b. Published original writings in school paper
c. Had original writings published in public newspaper, magazine, anthology (not school publication)
d. Won a literary prize for creative writing
e. Worked on editorial staff of paper or annual
f. Edited school paper or annual
*Dramatic Arts*
a. Participated in activities of speech, debate or dramatic group
b. Played minor role in cast or crew of plays sponsored by school, community, or religious groups; or entered debate or speech contest
c. Played major role in dramatic production
d. Received an award for acting, playwriting, or other phase of dramatic production
e. Won an award in a state or regional speech or debate contest
*Music*
a. Played a musical instrument
b. Sang as a soloist or member of a group
c. Composed or arranged music
d. Performed music with school or community group
e. Won prize or award in musical competition
f. Participation as a regular professional musician, or had professional performance given of music composed or arranged
*Science*
a. Participated as a member of a science club or reading and discussion group
b. Built a piece of equipment or laboratory apparatus (not as a part of a course)
c. Appointed teaching or laboratory assistant
d. Entered a scientific competition
e. Won first, second, or third prize in a state or regional science contest
f. Attended a summer science program sponsored by the National Science Foundation

Based on Wallach & Wing, 1969.

TABLE 6.7

*Percentage of High and Low Ideational Productivity Groups Endorsing Each Self-Descriptive Item*

| Item | *High productivity,* $N = 167$ | *Low productivity,* $N = 169$ | $\chi^2$ | $p$ |
|---|---|---|---|---|
| *Leadership* | | | | |
| (a) | 98 | 92 | 5.75 | < .02 |
| (b) | 92 | 79 | 11.07 | < .001 |
| (c) | 58 | 39 | 11.43 | < .001 |
| (d) | 16 | 14 | 0.25 | n.s. |
| *Art* | | | | |
| (a) | 43 | 24 | 13.38 | < .001 |
| (b) | 17 | 7 | 8.26 | < .01 |
| (c) | 12 | 5 | 4.71 | < .05 |
| (d) | 7 | 2 | 5.77 | < .02 |
| *Social service* | | | | |
| (a) | 78 | 71 | 2.36 | n.s. |
| (b) | 49 | 46 | 0.35 | n.s. |
| (c) | 27 | 18 | 4.22 | < .05 |
| *Writing* | | | | |
| (a) | 52 | 29 | 18.12 | < .001 |
| (b) | 43 | 31 | 5.19 | < .05 |
| (c) | 13 | 7 | 4.29 | < .05 |
| (d) | 11 | 8 | 0.94 | n.s |
| (e) | 45 | 40 | 0.84 | n.s |
| (f) | 21 | 17 | 0.61 | n.s. |
| *Drama* | | | | |
| (a) | 54 | 47 | 1.32 | n.s. |
| (b) | 61 | 52 | 2.62 | n.s |
| (c) | 24 | 20 | 0.78 | n.s. |
| (d) | 8 | 4 | 2.63 | n.s |
| (e) | 10 | 11 | 0.09 | n.s. |
| Music | | | | |
| (a) | 58 | 53 | 1.00 | n.s. |
| (b) | 40 | 37 | 0.29 | n.s. |
| (c) | 10 | 8 | 0.64 | n.s. |
| (d) | 46 | 45 | 0.01 | n.s. |
| (e) | 14 | 14 | 0.04 | n.s. |
| (f) | 4 | 6 | 1.00 | n.s. |
| *Science* | | | | |
| (a) | 40 | 28 | 5.16 | < .05 |
| (b) | 22 | 12 | 5.72 | < .02 |
| (c) | 20 | 11 | 6.05 | < .02 |
| (d) | 37 | 26 | 4.30 | < .05 |
| (e) | 9 | 1 | 10.63 | < .01 |
| (f) | 10 | 7 | 1.01 | n.s. |

Based on Wallach & Wing, 1969.

TABLE 6.8

*Percentage of High and Low Ideational Uniqueness Groups Endorsing Each Self-Descriptive Item*

| Item | High uniqueness, $N = 166$ | Low uniqueness, $N = 167$ | $\chi^2$ | $p$ |
|---|---|---|---|---|
| Leadership | | | | |
| (a) | 96 | 93 | 2.08 | n.s. |
| (b) | 86 | 80 | 1.65 | n.s. |
| (c) | 52 | 46 | 1.08 | n.s. |
| (d) | 15 | 13 | 0.25 | n.s. |
| Art | | | | |
| (a) | 43 | 23 | 15.02 | < .001 |
| (b) | 18 | 7 | 8.16 | < .01 |
| (c) | 10 | 5 | 3.56 | n.s |
| (d) | 6 | 2 | 2.72 | n.s. |
| Social service | | | | |
| (a) | 74 | 74 | 0.00 | n.s |
| (b) | 48 | 46 | 0.07 | n.s. |
| (c) | 27 | 17 | 5.20 | < .05 |
| Writing | | | | |
| (a) | 52 | 26 | 24.86 | < .001 |
| (b) | 40 | 24 | 9.59 | < .01 |
| (c) | 10 | 5 | 2.16 | n.s. |
| (d) | 12 | 8 | 1.70 | n.s. |
| (e) | 46 | 36 | 3.76 | n.s. |
| (f) | 17 | 16 | 0.03 | n.s. |
| Drama | | | | |
| (a) | 52 | 46 | 1.32 | n.s |
| (b) | 58 | 52 | 1.62 | n.s |
| (c) | 25 | 20 | 1.15 | n.s. |
| (d) | 9 | 4 | 4.17 | < .05 |
| (e) | 7 | 10 | 0.98 | n.s. |
| Music | | | | |
| (a) | 54 | 55 | 0.00 | n.s. |
| (b) | 39 | 38 | 0.02 | n.s. |
| (c) | 10 | 9 | 0.04 | n.s. |
| (d) | 43 | 45 | 0.15 | n.s. |
| (e) | 11 | 15 | 0.90 | n.s. |
| (f) | 3 | 5 | 1.17 | n.s. |
| Science | | | | |
| (a) | 38 | 31 | 2.03 | n.s. |
| (b) | 22 | 15 | 2.51 | n.s. |
| (c) | 22 | 9 | 10.36 | < .01 |
| (d) | 31 | 29 | 0.26 | n.s. |
| (e) | 8 | 4 | 3.46 | n.s. |
| (f) | 8 | 6 | 0.44 | n.s |

Based on Wallach & Wing, 1969.

TABLE 6.9

*Percentage of High and Low Intelligence Groups Endorsing Each Self-Descriptive Item*

| Item | High intelligence, $N = 168$ | Low intelligence, $N = 170$ | $\chi^2$ | $p$ |
|---|---|---|---|---|
| *Leadership* | | | | |
| (a) | 92 | 94 | 0.21 | n.s. |
| (b) | 82 | 84 | 0.23 | n.s. |
| (c) | 44 | 55 | 4.28 | ≈ .05 |
| (d) | 12 | 13 | 0.08 | n.s. |
| *Art* | | | | |
| (a) | 32 | 37 | 1.14 | n.s. |
| (b) | 9 | 12 | 1.04 | n.s. |
| (c) | 5 | 7 | 0.19 | n.s. |
| (d) | 3 | 4 | 0.32 | n.s. |
| *Social service* | | | | |
| (a) | 75 | 71 | 0.68 | n.s. |
| (b) | 51 | 40 | 4.53 | ≈ .05 |
| (c) | 20 | 22 | 0.14 | n.s. |
| *Writing* | | | | |
| (a) | 36 | 36 | 0.01 | n.s. |
| (b) | 37 | 30 | 2.03 | n.s. |
| (c) | 12 | 8 | 1.69 | n.s. |
| (d) | 10 | 8 | 0.16 | n.s. |
| (e) | 36 | 48 | 4.67 | ≈ .05 |
| (f) | 16 | 18 | 0.31 | n.s. |
| *Drama* | | | | |
| (a) | 42 | 48 | 1.34 | n.s. |
| (b) | 57 | 51 | 1.09 | n.s. |
| (c) | 21 | 24 | 0.57 | n.s. |
| (d) | 6 | 4 | 0.58 | n.s. |
| (e) | 8 | 8 | 0.05 | n.s. |
| *Music* | | | | |
| (a) | 54 | 54 | 0.01 | n.s |
| (b) | 39 | 35 | 0.42 | n.s. |
| (c) | 9 | 8 | 0.05 | n.s. |
| (d) | 47 | 49 | 0.11 | n.s |
| (e) | 11 | 14 | 0.60 | n.s. |
| (f) | 4 | 4 | 0.07 | n.s. |
| *Science* | | | | |
| (a) | 30 | 36 | 1.16 | n.s. |
| (b) | 18 | 22 | 0.81 | n.s. |
| (c) | 12 | 15 | 0.83 | n.s. |
| (d) | 34 | 27 | 1.88 | n.s. |
| (e) | 10 | 5 | 2.77 | n.s. |
| (f) | 14 | 5 | 6.95 | < .01 |

Based on Wallach & Wing, 1969.

about the comparability of their findings with other investigations of divergent thinking ability using a nonvolunteer sample. There is some indication in the evidence we have reviewed that individuals who are high on divergent thinking ability may have difficulty in adjusting to the school situation and may be somewhat rebellious. One might speculate that they would be somewhat uncooperative. From this perspective Wallach and Wing might have obtained a nonrepresentative sample of tractable and cooperative individuals who excel in divergent thinking ability. Third, talented accomplishment as defined by Wallach and Wing is not equivalent to "creativity" in the sense in which that term is used here. That is, most of the items in their questionnaire do not indicate that individuals have produced something novel which is judged to be valuable. There are some items which come close to indicating this. Items d in the art, literature, and dramatic categories, and e in the music and science categories would appear to indicate creativity as defined here. Looking at the data for this subset of items we get a somewhat different picture. Differences in productivity are significantly related to 2 of these 5 items—items d in art and e in science. Differences in intelligence are related to none of them. However, in no case do individuals who are high in productivity score higher on these items than individuals who are high in intelligence. It is the low productivity subjects who seem to be lower than the low intelligence subjects. An extreme example is found in item e for the science category—won a prize in a science contest. Of the high productivity subjects, 9 percent endorse this item, whereas only 1 percent of the low productivity subjects and 10 percent of the high intelligence subjects endorse it. The average percentage of endorsement of the items indicative of creativity as defined here in the Wallach and Wing data is 8 percent for the high intelligence group, 10 percent for the high productivity group, and 8 percent for the high uniqueness subjects. These differences are hardly dramatic. They suggest individuals of high intelligence are about as likely to be talented in ways related to creativity as individuals who are high in divergent thinking ability.

## CONVERGENT THINKING AND CREATIVITY

Up to this point in our discussion we have not dealt extensively with an assumption which plays a central role in the research we have reviewed— viz., tests of divergent thinking ability are measures of creativity. There is a lack of directly relevant empirical evidence on this point. It has been more or less taken as self-evident that divergent thinking ability represents an essential or even the essential cognitive ability which distinguishes individuals who are creative. There are both empirical and theoretical grounds for challenging this assumption. MacKinnon (1962, 1964) in a study of creativity among architects which we shall discuss, found no relationship between ratings of creativity and scores on Guilford's tests of divergent thinking ability. Also, Mednick (1962) has developed a test of creativity which appears to be predictive of ratings of creativity which measures convergent thinking. Since Mednick's research is central to the theoretical conception of creativity to be developed here we shall discuss it in some detail.

Mednick (1962) defines creativity as the ability to form new combinations of associative elements which meet specified requirements. Note that Mednick's definition emphasizes that responses which are judged creative must fulfill certain criteria. As it stands, the definition is compatible with either a divergent thinking or a convergent thinking definition of creativity. If an individual is asked to state all the uses he can think of for a brick, all of his responses presumably fit some rather loose criterion of relevance to the question asked. On the other hand, if one demands of a response that it fit an extensive and demanding list of criteria then the number of responses which may be acceptable become limited. A measure of ability to generate responses which fit demanding criteria may very well be a measure of convergent thought processes. It is this latter aspect of creativity which is emphasized in Mednick's test called the Remote Associates Test (RAT). The RAT consists of a series of items of similar structure. Each item requires the subject to produce a verbal associate which "fits" or is an appropriate response to each of three stimulus words included in that item. The subject's score on the test is the number of correct responses which can be given in a fixed period of time. Each item has one or possibly two correct answers. Hence, the RAT is a measure of convergent thinking ability.

Several studies indicate that there is a relationship between scores on the RAT and judgments of creativity. Mednick (1962) found a correlation of .70 between scores of the RAT and ratings of the creativity of students of architecture by their instructors. In another study of the creativity of psychology graduate students, Mednick found a correlation of .55 between ratings of the creativity of these students and scores on the RAT. Finally Mosteller (as cited in Mednick, 1962) found a correlation of .58 between a composite judgment of the creativity of childrens' drawings and their scores on the RAT. This last finding is of some interest in that it indicates a relationship between the RAT which is a verbal measure and a nonverbal measure of creativity.

It is possible to support Mednick's choice of a convergent measure of creativity on theoretical grounds. Instances of creativity would invariably appear to involve the production of a response which satisfies criteria. It is relatively easy to think of scientific creativity in this way. The person who develops a new scientific theory is generally faced with the task of accounting for or explaining a variety of known empirical phenomena. Given any single empirical phenomenon it is rather easy to generate a variety of different explanations. However, as one attempts to account for a range of phenomena the constraints on possible interpretations become formidable. The scientist in such a task is not *essentially* concerned with generating a large number of alternative theories. One would have a very poor, if not an absurd, measure of scientific competence if one measured the number or uniqueness of theories generated by a scientist. Rather, such a scientist is essentially engaged in discovering a theory which most clearly accounts for a wide range of phenomena and which is contradicted by none or by a very limited set of phenomena.

The emphasis on the role of criteria in judging a creative response can be extended to a consideration of artistic and literary creativity. Creativity in the arts always functions under constraints. The constraint may be imposed in a more or less general way by the characteristics of the medium— think of the demanding requirements of the sonnet—in which one is work- ing, or more fundamentally by the logic and structure of the particular creative work one is undertaking. A writer is restricted in what words may be written in a particular work by the words which have come before and by some general conception of the structure and organization involved in the work under creation. And, *mutatis mutandis*, the same is true for a composer or painter. Aesthetic license is not creativity.

In summary, the view expressed here is that creativity essentially in- volves convergent thought processes. Divergent thinking ability may play a role in creativity in that excellence in divergent thinking ability might provide an individual with a wide set of alternatives which to consider. In support of this, Mednick, Mednick, and Jung (1964) have found that individuals who score high on the RAT tend to respond with more words in a continual word association task than individuals who score low on the RAT. On the other hand, there is no obvious or necessary theoretical link between excellence in divergent thinking and creativity as defined here. That is, the ability to produce many different and many unusual responses which satisfy minimal constraints is not necessarily indicative of the ability to produce a single response which fulfills demanding requirements.

We have concluded that divergent thinking ability can be independent of intelligence. However, we have also argued that divergent thinking ability is not necessarily indicative of creative ability. We are then left with the following question, "Is creativity independent of intelligence?" There is one study in which relationships among the RAT, divergent thinking measures, and intelligence measures were investigated. Cropley

(1966) factor analyzed the responses of 320 junior high school students with a mean Thorndike–Lorge I.Q. of 114.3 to these measures. He found that the RAT correlated .39 and .28 with the verbal and performance intelligence scores. Cropley found two oblique factors. The first factor was principally defined by scores on vocabulary, verbal intelligence quotient, and academic average. These variables had loadings of .85, .83, and .80 respectively on this factor. The RAT's loading on this factor was .55. The second factor obtained by Cropley was correlated with the first, $r = .51$. It was principally defined by measures of divergent thinking ability. The loading of the RAT on this factor was .03. On the basis of these data Cropley concluded that the RAT was not a measure of creativity but was rather closely related to traditional measures of verbal intelligence.

From the point of view expressed here, it would be more justifiable to argue that tests of divergent thinking ability do not measure creativity but that the RAT does. This would then imply that creativity *is* related to intelligence. It is possible to supply a theoretical rationale for the relationship of creativity and intelligence. High intelligence is a necessary condition of creative work in many fields. One cannot be creative in many areas of science without the intellectual ability to master the highly complex mathematics of the technical vocabulary in use in that field. Similarly, literary creativity requires a high degree of verbal ability. And, I suspect, that creativity in the visual arts and in music also involves abilities which are related to $g$.

In short, intelligence may be seen as a necessary condition of creativity. It is a sufficient one? There is a fair amount of evidence that it is not. MacKinnon (1962, 1964) has found a nonsignificant negative correlation between ratings of the creativity of architects and their scores on an intelligence test. Similarly, Mednick (1962) reports that the correlation of the Miller Analogies Test, an alleged measure of intelligence among individuals of high intelligence, with creativity ratings of a group of psychology students was .06. Roe (1953) reports that eminent scientists exhibit a wide range of scores on tests of ability and do not uniformly score high on these tests.

The data on ratings cited above would appear to be incompatible with Cropley's data showing a substantial loading of the RAT on a factor of verbal intelligence. That is, if the RAT is a measure of creativity which is substantially related to intelligence one would expect that measures of intelligence would be related to ratings of creativity. Actually the disagreement is apparent rather than real. Cropley's subjects had a mean I.Q. of 114. Subjects with I.Q.s as low as 114 would probably not be admitted into a professional school of architecture or a graduate school to study psychology. All of these data are compatible with what has been called the "threshold theory" of the relation of creativity and intelligence. (See Barron, 1963; Torrance, 1962.) The theory asserts, in effect, that intelligence is a necessary but not a sufficient condition of creativity. Above a certain level of intelligence, a threshold, further variations in intelligence are unrelated to creativity. This theory would imply that measures of creativity and intelligence might be substantially correlated if one considers something close to the full range of permissible variation on the intelligence variable. However, correlations between measures of creativity and intelligence based on data obtained only from individuals who are high in intelligence will tend to approach zero. Yamomoto (1965) has obtained evidence for the threshold theory using divergent thinking measures of creativity. He reports correlations, corrected for attenuation and restriction of range, between measures of divergent thinking ability and I.Q. of .88 for subjects with I.Q.s below 90, .69 for subjects with I.Q.s between 90 and 110, −.30 for subjects with I.Q.s between 110 and 130, and −.09 for subjects with I.Q.s above 130. In another study, Yamomoto and Chimbidis (1966) found a correlation of .5 between a measure of intelligence and scores on the Minnesota Tests of Creativity for subjects with I.Q.s below 120 and a correlation of .2 between these variables for subjects with I.Q.s above 120. On the basis of the evidence reviewed above, it would be reasonable to expect that correlations between the RAT and I.Q. for individuals of different I.Q.s would exhibit a similar pattern to that found by Yamomoto for the relation of divergent thinking measures and I.Q.

If the threshold theory is correct, there must be a distinction between what is measured by tests of intelligence, and measures of creativity. A clue to the nature of this distinction may be contained in Mednick's report of a negative correlation between the RAT and grade point average (see Mednick, 1962). This finding may be taken to indicate that academic success, even at advanced stages of education, is not principally a question of creative ability. Academic success as indicated by grade-point average frequently involves the ability to master a body of existing knowledge. Rarely is there an emphasis, at least in formal course work, on the ability to create new knowledge. Tests of intelligence may be viewed as measuring an individual's capacity to acquire various forms of knowledge. However, this ability although necessary to the ability to produce something novel of value is no guarantee that the individual will possess this latter ability.

The main points of our discussion of creativity can be recapitulated as follows:

1. Divergent thinking measures are not measures of creativity.
2. Creativity can be measured by convergent thinking measures which

require an individual to supply a response which fulfills demanding criteria.

3. Intelligence is a necessary but not a sufficient condition for creativity.

## THE PERSONALITY CORRELATES OF RATINGS OF CREATIVITY

We have discussed personality characteristics associated with variations in divergent thinking ability. However, if tests of divergent thinking ability are not measures of creativity this leaves open the question of the personality characteristics associated with creativity. MacKinnon's investigation of architects deals with this question (MacKinnon 1962, 1964). MacKinnon studied three groups of architects. One group was selected from individuals nominated by professors of architecture as the most creative architects in the country. A second group of architects were less eminent individuals who were associated with the first group. The third group of architects were "ordinary" architects neither selected for eminence nor associated with those who were eminent. The architects in group 1 spent a weekend at the Institute for Personality Assessment and Research at the University of California. The architects in the other groups filled out an extensive battery of tests. MacKinnon reports a number of differences among these three groups. MacKinnon reports that more than 80 percent of the architects in Group 1 and less than 80 percent of the architects in Groups 2 and 3 describe themselves as inventive, determined, independent, individualistic, enthusiastic, and industrious. MacKinnon does not report the actual percentages of architects in each group who described themselves in these ways. Consequently, it is not clear whether these are descriptive differences of major or minor significance. MacKinnon also reports a number of significant differences on scores on the California Personality Inventory. Although there were statistically significant differences among these groups on various scales, the correlation between scores on any of these scales and the ratings of the creativity of all of the architects in his study was relatively low. The highest correlation between these variables was .31. Consequently, scores on the California Personality Inventory would be of little use in predicting the creativity of architects.[3] MacKinnon did however obtain some rather dramatic differences among these architects on some of the other measures he used in his study. He found such differences on the Meyer–Briggs test which is based on Jung's personality typology (Jung,

---

[3] It is possible to object to this conclusion. It would be possible to obtain a very high multiple correlation between scores on several scales and the ratings of creativity even though no scale has a substantial correlation with the ratings. And, MacKinnon does in fact report such multiple correlations. However, such a multiple correlation must be considered very cautiously. It would be exceedingly unlikely to "hold up" in a validation study.

1923). Of the architects in Group 1, 58 percent were assigned to the perception as opposed to the judgment category. Only 17 percent of the architects in group 3 were assigned to the perception category. Perhaps the clearest differences obtained by MacKinnon involved the Strong Interest Inventory (Strong, 1943). Scores on the artist's scale of the Strong correlated .59 with ratings of creativity. Responses on the Strong indicative of interests similar to Bankers were strongly negatively correlated with the creativity ratings, $r = -.66$. Finally, a masculinity–femininity index derived from the Strong was negatively correlated with the judgments of creativity, $r = -.48$, indicating a positive association between creativity and femininity. MacKinnon also found differences among his groups of architects on the Allport–Vernon–Lindzey (1951) study of values. The architects in Group 1 scored high on the aesthetic and theoretical scale and low on the economic scale of this test. The economic scale had the highest correlation with the creativity ratings, $r = -.48$.

The MacKinnon study is one of the most comprehensive studies of the personality characteristics associated with differences in creativity. The most critical issue that can be raised with respect to his findings concerns their generality. That is, are these personality characteristics associated with differences in creativity in other fields or endeavor? This question is rather difficult to answer since other studies with which the MacKinnon investigation could be compared have not, in general, used the same personality measures or have not obtained groups of individuals who differ in creativity using criteria comparable to those used by MacKinnon. There is, however, at least some inferential basis for suggesting that the MacKinnon data must be accepted cautiously. Taylor and Ellison (1964) report that the Meyer–Briggs test was of little use in predicting differences in ratings of creativity among a group of scientists in a large research organization.

The data with the Strong are more difficult to evaluate since the Strong test has rarely been used in connection with studies of creativity. I suspect that the results may, in part, be limited in their generality. Architects do not invariably think of themselves as creators or artists. I suspect that many "ordinary" architects of the type probably included in Group 3 may conceive of their work in terms of performing a technical rather than creative service for financial gain. I would guess that a study comparable to MacKinnon's using groups of painters who differed with respect to their eminence in the field of painting but not with respect to their conception of themselves as creative artists would fail to find dramatic differences on the Strong. As for MacKinnon's data on masculinity–femininity, there is at least some indirect evidence which suggests that responses which are feminine are not invariably associated with creativity in males. Roe (1953) has studied groups of eminent scientists in several fields. One of the respects in which these various groups of scientists differ is in the pattern of their quantitative and verbal abilities. Roe finds that eminent theoretical physicists score very high on tests of verbal and spatial ability. Experimental physicists, on the other hand, are high on tests of spatial ability and low on verbal ability tests. Anthropologists on the other hand tended to be high on verbal ability scales but relatively low on both spatial and mathematical ability. What is of interest in these results is that eminent experimental physicists tend to have a masculine rather than a feminine pattern of ability—nonverbal skills exceeding verbal skills. In addition, the physicists in Roe's study reported early interests in mathematics, chemistry, physics, or gadgeteering and very few had literary or humanistic interests. By contrast, the social scientists in Roe's study, anthropologists and psychologists, frequently had interests in literature and the humanities. The interests characteristic of physicists in Roe's study hardly seem those characteristic of females. On the basis of these data one suspects that the Strong scales associated with differences in the creativity of architects would be of little use in predicting ratings of creativity among physicists— particularly among experimental physicists.

Cattell (1963a; Cattell & Drevdahl, 1955) has also studied the personality characteristics associated with creativity using as a basis for his investigation the Cattell 16 P.F. test. Cattell reports that scientists selected for their creativity differ from the population at large, and from people educated as scientists but who have chosen not to emphasize research and who have achieved eminence as teachers and administrators, in a number of respects on the 16 P.F. test. It should be noted that Cattell's research does not involve comparisons among groups of individuals who are all engaged in the same activity, that is, research, but who differ in their demonstrated capacity for creative work. Rather, Cattell, is comparing individuals who are engaged in different activities. Cattell reports a number of consistent differences in first order factors in his taxonomy of personality factors. He also indicates that the pattern of differences on the 16 P.F. indicated that creative individuals differ from noncreative individuals on a second-order factor. Since we have argued that the second order factors in Cattell's system are more reliable and valid than the first order factors we shall summarize Cattell's findings by indicating that creative scientists are introverted rather than extraverted. Cattell also reports that eminent writers as well as scientists tend to be higher in introversion than the population at large (see Drevdahl & Cattell, 1958). Do Cattell's results accord with other studies of creativity on this point? Again, it is rather hard to say since other investigators have not, in general, used the 16 P.F. as their measure of personality. Again, there is at least some indirect evidence which suggests that Cattell's results must be accepted with caution. MacKinnon (1962, 1964) found the architects in each of the three groups he studied to be classified as introverts with about equal frequency (roughly two-thirds of the time) on the basis of the Meyer–Briggs test. Hence, in his study introversion was not related to creativity. Of course, there is no guarantee that what is called introversion on the Meyer–Briggs test is in any way related to what is called introversion by Cattell. Roe (1951b) does report that the physicists in her study were, particularly as children, very withdrawn and were frequently social isolates. This finding would tend to support Cattell. On the other hand, this pattern was not characteristic of the social scientist in Roe's (1953) study. She reports that half of the social scientists in her study began dating in high school and dated happily and extensively from then on. She reports that occasionally shyness was found among the social scientists but it was nowhere near as extreme and characteristic as it was for the physical scientists.

This brief review of some of the studies of the personality characteristics of individuals who differ in terms of their rated creativity indicates that little progress has been made on this problem. We cannot point to a *replicated* body of findings which indicate that differences on standardized measures of personality are consistently related to ratings of creativity in diverse fields. The lack of consistently replicated results at present may be due simply to the dearth of studies on this problem or, to suggest a somewhat more heretical position, to the possibility that there are very few if any personality characteristics which are consistently associated with creativity in diverse fields. I suspect that the latter possibility is nearer the truth. There is very little intrinsic or theoretical connection between the personality characteristics which have been reported to be associated with creativity and creative ability *per se* Put another way, there is no overarching theory from which one can deduce relationships between creativity and personality. The one possible exception to this may be the Freudian notion of regression in the service of the ego. Although there is some evidence for this notion in the kind of data reported by Getzels and Jackson there is not a great deal of evidence for this notion in research dealing with individuals who differ in creativity rather than divergent thinking ability. And, there is some negative evidence. Roe (1951a) reports that eminent biologists seem very concrete and factual. Their Rorschach protocols are more restricted and better controlled than those of biologists who are not eminent. This finding is exactly the opposite of what one would expect on the basis of Getzels and Jackson's data if one assumed that Getzels and Jackson were in fact studying the personality correlates of creativity rather than divergent thinking ability. Apparently, openness to normally repressed material is not an invariable characteristic of creativity.

If we entertain the hypothesis that there are no personality correlates of creativity, we are then faced with the problem of explaining the substantial findings obtained by such investigators as MacKinnon. Such findings are indicative of creativity in a particular field. The personality differences which are known to exist are probably related to choice of a particular field of endeavor. Individuals who excel in mathematical ability are more likely to enter a scientific than a literary field, etc. Further, the characteristics associated with success in a particular field may not be intrinsic to that success but may merely reflect the social role assigned to individuals engaged in a particular profession. And, this social role may have attracted individuals to engage in this profession in the first place. For example, the social role of artist is, in our society, one which is associated with bohemian and unconventional attitudes. However, in another society such as ancient Greece where the social role of artists was somewhat akin to that of craftsman, these attitudes might not be associated with artists. Or again, consider the socially withdrawn, introverted characteristics which Cattell and Roe have found to be associated with eminence in the physical sciences. We have had, particularly since World War II, the emergence of "big" science. That is, large scale scientific research projects involving the collaboration of many different scientists. It is possible that the change in the setting in which scientific research takes place may involve something of a change in the social definition of the scientifically adept from lonely genius to cooperative colleague. In turn, this change may attract individuals with different personality characteristics to scientific research and this change might lead to different personality characteristics associated with scientific eminence. In short, it is not at all clear that there are personality characteristics which are intrinsically rather than accidentally associated with creativity.

## Concluding Comments

One of the assumptions common to research on divergent thinking ability and to Witkin's research as well as to many other research programs dealing with cognitive approaches to personality is that there are stylistic consistencies in thought which are invariant for particular individuals over situations. The preference for the study of style over content in thought processes is not unrelated to the assumption of stylistic consistency. The content of thought clearly is situation specific. However, styles of thought may in fact be invariant across situations. Therefore, the preference for style over content is an attempt to find relatively abstract dimensions which might be reflected in any particular thought process of an individual.

The invariance assumption is rarely the subject of investigation in its own right. Rather, it is more or less implicitly taken for granted. There is at least one major study in which the consistency of cognitive processes was a specific focus of investigation.

Kogan and Wallach (1964) have studied individual differences in risk-taking. Their investigation focused on the extent to which an individual responded consistently in a conservative or risky fashion in diverse situations. Thus, the assumption of consistency of cognitive processes was the direct subject of investigation. They administered a large battery of tests potentially involving an element of risk-taking to a group of male and female undergraduates. They divided their subjects into eight groups. This was done by considering data from male and female subjects separately. Then within each of these groups they formed four different personality groups based on scores on the Mandler Sarsaon Test of Test Anxiety and on the Marlowe–Crowne scale. Then they obtained correlations separately for each of these groups of subjects between various risk-taking measures. Tables 6.10, 6.11, and 6.12 present representative results from their study. Table 6.10 presents the correlations for male subjects between the tendency to use a risky strategy in a betting situation—maximization of gain which involves the choice of that option in a betting situation which permits the maximum gain under the most favorable outcome—and choice of conservative alternatives in a paper and pencil test called the choice dilemmas test. Note that the highest correlation between these measures is obtained for the subjects who are high on both Test Anxiety and the Marlowe–Crowne scale. Table 6.11 presents similar data indicating the relationship between tendency to pursue a maximization of gain strategy in a task involving skill and choice of conservative responses on the choice dilemmas

TABLE 6.10

*Correlations between Tendency to Choose a Maximization of Gain Strategy in a Betting Task and Scores on the Choice Dilemmas Task for Four Groups of Male Subjects*

|  |  | *Marlowe–Crowne* | |
| --- | --- | --- | --- |
|  |  | *Low* | *High* |
| Test anxiety | Low | − .42 | − .32 |
|  | High | .03 | − .58 |

Based on Kogan & Wallach, 1964.

TABLE 6.11

*Correlations between Tendency to Choose a Maximization of Gain Strategy in a Skill Task and Scores on the Choice Dilemmas Task for Four Groups of Male Subjects*

|  |  | Marlowe–Crowne | |
|---|---|---|---|
|  |  | Low | High |
| Test anxiety | Low | − .24 | − .22 |
|  | High | .05 | − .55 |

Based on Kogan & Wallach, 1964.

task. Note that the subjects who are high on both of the personality tests again have the highest correlation between these measures indicating that for these subjects a preference for risky strategies in the skill task is negatively associated with the tendency to answer conservatively in the choice dilemmas test. Table 6.12 presents correlations for these four groups of male subjects between two other measures of risk-taking, number judgments, and clues. Both of these measures are sequential decision tasks in which an individual chooses the point at which he makes a decision while receiving more and more information. The longer the subject delays his decision the greater the probability of it being correct. Note that Table 6.12 indicates that males who are high on both personality measures exhibit the greatest consistency of performance on these two tasks.

TABLE 6.12

*Correlations between Scores on Number Judgments and Clues for Four Groups of Male Subjects*

|  |  | Marlowe–Crowne | |
|---|---|---|---|
|  |  | Low | High |
| Test anxiety | Low | .17 | .31 |
|  | High | .41 | .56 |

Based on Kogan & Wallach, 1964.

Kogan and Wallach attribute the consistency of risk-taking propensities in the male subjects who are high on both of the personality measures to a combination of two hypothetical variables. They assume that individuals who are high on Test Anxiety have a tendency to perceive various situations in terms of the possibility of success or failure on them. Consequently, they are sensitized to the risk-taking dimension. Individuals who are high on the Marlowe–Crowne are concerned with what Kogan and Wallach call "image maintenance." That is, they tend to have a consistent image of what is a desirable posture or stance *vis à vis* risk and then tend to exhibit behavior compatible with that posture irrespective of the situation in which they find themselves. Thus, the male subjects who are high on both Test Anxiety and on the Marlowe–Crowne Scale are both sensitized to the risk-taking dimension and attempt to adopt a consistent risk-taking posture. This combination accounts for their apparent consistency of behavior in diverse risk-taking situations.

Kogan and Wallach's research shows an exemplary concern for the conditions under which consistency of behavior across diverse situations occurs. As such, their research represents a methodological advance over the usual research in the area of cognitive styles which assumes consistency. The Kogan and Wallach study also points the way to a possible further extension of research on individual differences in cognition. Once the assumption of an overarching consistency in cognitive styles is abandoned it becomes possible to put the study of content in the forefront of research interest. One of the important historical precursors of the current emphasis on cognitive approaches to personality was the research on the Authoritarian Personality (Adorno *et al.*, 1950). These authors attempted to find connections between cognitive content and style. In particular they suggested that authoritarian attitudes were associated with a formal characteristic of thought, rigidity. Research on cognitive dimension of personality could profit from a renewed emphasis on the content of thought, and by a consideration of the possible relations between content and style.

# CHAPTER 7

# SOURCES OF INDIVIDUAL DIFFERENCES IN PERSONALITY

It is a truism that individual differences in personality arise from the influence of genetic and environmental factors and their interaction. However, the methodological and conceptual implications of this obvious statement have not been sufficiently recognized in research dealing with the development of personality.

Much of the research on personality development attempts to correlate environmental variation with variation in personality development. Environmental variations refer to such variables as parental behavior measured by observation, self-report or the current or retrospective reports of children about their parents, and to socialization practices associated with different cultures or social groups. In such investigations it is usually assumed that the relationships which have been found are attributable to the influences of socialization practices on the development of personality. This inference about the direction of causality is warranted on the assumption that, with the exception of extreme constitutional anomalies, there are few, if any, individual differences relevant to personality development which are present at birth which might be responsible for relationships between individual differences in personality and socialization practices.

The presence of a relationship between variations in socialization practices and individual differences in personality can, at least on logical grounds, be explained in one of three ways: individual differences present at birth might influence socialization practices, socialization practices might influence personality, or there might be some complex interaction of these influences. Consider an example. Winterbottom (1958) found a relationship between early independence training and the development of achievement motivation. This finding could imply that:

1. early independence training leads to the development of achievement motivation;

2. there are genetic or constitutional characteristics which lead to the development of achievement motivation. In addition, the constitutional characteristics which lead to the development of achievement motivation lead parents to give children with these characteristics early independence training;

3. there is a complex interaction between genetic or constitutional characteristics and parental behaviors which leads to the development of achievement motivation. For example, both early independence training and genetic characteristics might be necessary but not sufficient conditions for the development of achievement motivation. That is, achievement motivation might require both a genetic capacity and the presence of early independence training for its development.

In this chapter we shall review evidence which suggests that genetic factors are an important determinant of individual differences in personality. We shall also deal with the methodological and conceptual implications of this evidence.

Before reviewing this evidence it will be helpful to make some general remarks about heredity and environment. When we speak of the influence of heredity on behavior we refer to the influence of genes on behavior. The phrase, "behavior X is inherited," is misleading if not incorrect. Genes cannot exert their influence on behavior without the presence of an environment. A child may, at birth, have the genetic capabilities of an intellectual giant, but, unless he is properly nurtured, his genetic capabilities will not be actualized. Similarly, we cannot consider the influence of the environment on behavior without presupposing some organism with various genetic capacities upon whom a particular environment may act. Consequently, heredity and environment presuppose each other. When we speak of genetic influences on behavior we do not refer to influences which are immutable and which will exert their effects in any or all environments. Consequently, the phrase, "behavior X is inherited" should be properly considered an elliptical form of a more accurate phrase, "behavior X is influenced by genetic variations in a particular environment (s) with various characteristics."

The disease phenylketonuria provides a neat example of the influence of the environment on a genetically influenced characteristic. Phenylketonuria is thought to be a disease caused by a single recessive gene.[1] The individual who is homozygous for this gene lacks an enzyme whose action is important in the normal development of the brain. Such individuals are typically mentally defective. However, if this disease is detected early in infancy it can be treated by the use of a phenylalanine restricted diet and the effects of the disease can be substantially mitigated (Berman, Walsman, & Graham, 1966). This example illustrates the influence of the environment on what is called the expressivity of a gene—the intensity of the phenotypical manifestation of the genotype. The expressivity of the genotypes which influence personality are probably influenced by a myriad of environmental factors. We can underscore this point by some speculations about schizophrenia. There is evidence that there are genotypes which predispose an individual to the development of schizophrenia. Whether these genotypes will lead to the development of schizophrenia might well depend on the presence of environmental conditions. Even in the hypothetical case where a particular genotype will lead to the development of schizophrenia 100 percent of the time (providing the individual remains alive past a certain age) in any currently known environment it is entirely possible that biochemical or psychotherapeutic interventions might be discovered which would prevent the development of schizophrenia for individuals with that genotype—thus drastically reducing its influence of the development of schizophrenia. Note that the environmental intervention need not be of a biochemical sort but might well be psychotherapeutic. The establishment of a genetic etiology for a particular disease does not necessarily imply the proper form of treatment for the alleviation of that disease.

## The Inheritance of Personality

THE METHODOLOGY OF TWIN STUDIES

Much of what we know about the influence of genes on personality comes from research on twins. Accordingly, we shall consider the logic of this type of study in some detail. Twin research attempts to capitalize on a fortuitous experiment of nature. There are two types of twins, monozygotic (MZ) twins who derive from the splitting of a single fertilized ovum and dyzygotic (DZ) twins who derive from the fertilization of two

[1] An excellent discussion of principles of genetics for psychologists can be found in Fuller and Thompson (1960).

independently formed ova. MZ twins have identical genetic characteristics; DZ twins are as similar genetically as siblings and have roughly 50 percent genetic overlap. Differences which occur between MZ twins must derive from the influence of the environment. Differences between DZ twins derive from the influence of both genetic and environmental variations. Differences between pairs of DZ twins in excess of differences between pairs of MZ twins are taken as indicative of genetic influences on behavior on the assumption that the intrapair similarity of environment for DZ twins is equal to the intrapair similarity of environment for MZ twins. The assumptions involved in twin studies may be stated slightly more formally as follows: Differences between pairs of MZ twins $(D_{MZ})$ are due only to environmental influences $(E)$. Differences between pairs of DZ twins $(D_{DZ})$ are due to genetic influences $(H)$ and $E$. If $E$ has the same value for both $MZ$ and $DZ$ twins then:

$$D_{DZ} - D_{MZ} = H$$

The central methodological issue in twin research concerns the comparability of the intrapair similarity of environment of MZ and DZ twins. The argument against twin research asserts that MZ twins, by virtue of their similarity of appearance, are treated more alike than DZ twins and hence if they exhibit greater similarity than DZ twins with respect to some characteristic this is attributable in part or totally to the greater similarity of their environment and is not indicative of genetic influences on behavior.

There are a number of caveats which can be added to this criticism in order to properly evaluate it.

First, even if the environments of MZ twins are more similar than the environments of DZ twins this would be indicative of an "indirect" genetic influence. That is, it would be indicative of a gene-environment interaction by means of which genotypes could influence and shape the impact of the environment on the individual. Such an influence would not be independent of, or unrelated to, genetic influences.

Second, there is very little "hard" empirical evidence which indicates that MZ twins are in fact treated more alike than DZ twins—although there is a good deal of speculation on this point. Smith (1965) has done one of the few systematic empirical studies dealing with this issue. He obtained concordance rates (degree of agreement with respect to some response category) for MZ and DZ twins for a variety of environmental factors. Table 7.1 summarizes his results. Table 7.1 indicates that pairs of MZ and DZ twins are often concordant to the same degree for a variety of environmental conditions. However, there are a number of respects in which MZ twins are more concordant than DZ twins.

TABLE 7.1

*Proportions[a] Concordant with Selected Habits for MZ and DZ Twin Pairs, by Sex*

| Habit | Males | | Females | | Both | |
|---|---|---|---|---|---|---|
| | MZ | DZ | MZ | DZ | MZ | DZ |
| Eating between meals | 72.5 | 66.7 | 77.1[b] | 57.5[b] | 75.0[b] | 61.6[b] |
| Snack before bedtime | 50.0 | 66.7 | 60.4 | 62.5 | 55.7 | 64.4 |
| Time usually go to bed | 59.0 | 72.7 | 72.9 | 57.5 | 66.7 | 64.4 |
| Time usually get up | 60.0 | 53.1 | 72.9 | 65.0 | 67.0 | 59.7 |
| Dressing alike | 59.0 | 57.1 | 68.7[b] | 33.3[b] | 64.4[b] | 40.3[b] |
| Study together | 23.1 | 9.1 | 54.2[b] | 20.5[b] | 40.2[b] | 15.3 |

Based on Smith, 1965.

[a] Proportions are based on varied number of pairs depending on response item.

[b] $p \leq .05$.

The bearing of Smith's results on the issue of the similarity of the environment of pairs of MZ and DZ twins is somewhat obscure. High concordance rates for MZ twins with respect to such categories as playing a musical instrument may simply reflect the influence of genetically determined characteristics. That is, musical interest and ability may be genetically influenced. Studying a musical instrument may reflect, in part, the influence of genetic characteristics on the parental decision to provide musical training for the child. Consider another example. Smith found higher concordance rates among pairs of female MZ twins than pairs of female DZ twins for the category of "dressing alike." The decision to dress alike, again, might be influenced by genetic similarities which alter parental behavior and may, in fact, not be indicative of a decision by the parents to dress female MZ twins alike which is made prior to extensive interactions with their twins.

The essential point at issue in the critique of twin studies is the notion that parents and other socializing agents exert greater influences toward similarity in MZ than DZ twins independent of the actual similarities among such twins. Evidence such as that obtained by Smith does not address itself to this issue since such evidence does not indicate the source or reason for the concordance.

There is one type of study which provides evidence of the effect of parents' beliefs about the zygosity of their twins on the tendency to treat them alike. Many parents are mistaken about the zygosity of their twins. Shields (1962) reports that 33 percent of the parents of same-sexed female DZ twins mistakenly believed them to be MZ. Comparisons between

same-sexed DZ twins believed to be identical with DZ twins not believed
to be identical can provide information about the effects of parental beliefs
about similarity and also the presumed tendency to treat twins assumed
to be identical more alike. Scarr (1966) in a study of 6–10-year-old female
MZ and DZ twins, found that true zygosity was a more important determinant of similarity than believed zygosity. She found that the degree
of concordance for such categories as degree of independence and expected
maturity of behavior, parentally perceived similarity, and tendency to
dress alike was dependent upon actual rather than believed zygosity.
Scarr's data suggest that the greater similarity of the environment of MZ
twins as compared to DZ twins is due, in part, to the influence of genetic
characteristics on parental behavior. The similarity is not necessarily the
result of parental attempts to introduce uniform methods of treating
children assumed to be identical.

Third, even if there is evidence that there are respects in which the environment of MZ twins is more similar than the environment of DZ twins,
this finding is irrelevant to an argument that a particular behavior is
genetically influenced unless it can be shown that the respects in which
there are greater environmental similarity for MZ than DZ twins are
critical for the development of the behavior in question. For example,
suppose that there is greater concordance for MZ than DZ twins for the
category, parent uses physical punishment to control child. This finding
is irrelevant to the inference from twin studies that, say, schizophrenia is
a genetically influenced disease. In order for the finding on concordance
for the use of physical punishment to be relevant it must be shown that
the tendency to use physical punishment has etiological significance for
the development of schizophrenia. This crucial step is rarely taken.

Fourth, we have assumed that parents exert unequal pressures creating
greater similarity among MZ than DZ twins. On *a priori* grounds it is
equally plausible to argue the opposite. Parents of MZ twins may attempt
to accentuate differences among MZ twins in order to emphasize their
individuality and separate identities. Such parental behavior might include attempts to dress MZ twins differently, supplying them with different hobbies, placing them in different classes, and even creating different conceptions of their personality which might act as self-fulfilling
prophecies. Similarly, MZ twins might also attempt to emphasize and
exaggerate their individuality.

Fifth, Price (1950) believes that twin studies underestimate the influence
of genetics. He argues that the intra-uterine environment of MZ twins is
more divergent in respects which are of etiological significance for behavior
than the intra-uterine environment of DZ twins. MZ twins are usually,
but not invariably, monochorionic and thus share mutual intra-uterine

circulation. DZ twins are invariably dichorionic. Price points out there are special problems associated with being monochorionic. This condition can result in an unequal distribution of nourishment to the twins. The consequences of this condition could be assessed by doing a study comparing MZ twins who are monochorionic with MZ twins who are dichorionic. If Price's assumptions are correct the latter should be more concordant in many respects than the former. Such a study has not, to my knowledge, been done. There is, however, one study which provides some tentative and indirect evidence for Price's thesis.

Brown, Stafford, and Vandenberg (1967) investigated the effects of differences in birth order and birth weight in MZ and DZ twins. They found greater concordance among 1–6-month-old MZ than DZ twins for such categories as sleeping and feeding problems. Among the MZ twins who were discordant for these categories it was the twin who weighed less and who was first born who tended to have sleeping and feeding problems. No such differences between lighter and heavier, and first- and second-born DZ twins were found. This finding may indicate that inadequacy of nourishment of the lighter and first-born MZ twin, probably associated with being monochorionic, may have consequences for behavior after birth. Divergencies in the adequacy of intra-uterine nourishment of DZ twins may not be as large and consequently such differences may be of negligible importance in subsequent personality development.

There is additional evidence that differences in birth order and birth weight among twins may have consequences for subsequent development. Tienari (1966) studied a sample of twins born in Finland between 1920–1929. He obtained data with respect to 54 variables and performed a factor analysis. His first factor was principally defined by the following variables: more of a leader in a youth with a loading of .78; more dominating in childhood, .68; ratings of psychological disturbance, $-.62$; social position, .52; better at school, .51; achieved higher socioeconomic status, .48; and birth order, .37. These data indicate that the twin who was first born was more likely to be dominant in childhood and socially successful. Factor 5 in Tiernari's study was principally defined by the following: physically stronger, .66; heavier at birth, .53; and left home earlier, .37. These data indicate that the twin who was heavier at birth was more likely to be physically stronger and to be higher on some indices of independence.

Willerman and Churchill (1967; see also Churchill, 1965) have also obtained data on the consequences of differences in birth weight for subsequent development in twins. They found that twins who weighed less at birth tended to have lower performance and verbal I.Q.s at ages 8–10 than their cotwins who were heavier at birth.

The evidence we have briefly reviewed suggests that differences in birth weight and birth order in twins may have consequences for subsequent development. However, there is little evidence that these differences may be of unique importance for MZ twins. Consequently, there is little evidence in support of Price's views.

Sixth, there is one type of study which provides data on the effects of environmental variation on the expressivity of genotypes. Studies which compare MZ twins reared apart with MZ twins reared together give some insights into the consequences of adding divergencies in the intrapair similarity of environment of MZ twins. Fortunately, Shields (1962) has compared the personality characteristics of MZ twins reared apart and reared together with DZ twins. And, as we shall see, being reared apart has little or no influence on the expressivity of the genotypes which influence personality.

Although no definitive statement can be made about the similarity of the environment of MZ and DZ twins, there appears to be little persuasive evidence which supports the argument which criticizes the twin method on grounds that there is greater similarity of environment among MZ twins than DZ twins. Further, where there is greater similarity for MZ twins, the Scarr study suggests it is plausibly attributable to genetic influences of children on parents. Finally, the Shields study provides us with the opportunity of comparing a group of MZ twins who have undoubtedly experienced *greater* environmental differences than a group of DZ twins. This permits an empirical evaluation of the effects of divergencies in environmental similarity.

There are a number of other methodological issues which are associated with twin research. Perhaps the most critical of these concerns the question of zygosity determination. In some of the earlier studies determination of zygosity was not always reliable. In more recent research zygosity determination is usually made with the aid of serological techniques (concordance for various blood types) and is, for all practical purposes, a negligible source of error.

In view of the above discussion of the methodology of twin studies it would appear that there is little persuasive reason to challenge the logic of this method of research. We shall, accordingly, in what follows, assume that evidence of greater similarity among MZ than DZ twins is evidence of genetic influences on behavior.

## CONCORDANCE RATES FOR SOCIALLY RELEVANT CATEGORIES

We shall divide our discussion of twin studies into two parts—those dealing with concordance rates for socially relevant categories of behavior, and those dealing with quantitatively varying personality dimensions. The distinction is, in part, arbitrary, since many characteristics of behavior which are treated as dichotomies may also be treated as continua. For example, it is possible to consider criminality and neuroticism as dichotomies, for example, criminal–not criminal, or as quantitatively varying dimensions.

The typical investigation of concordance rates for some socially relevant category of behavior involves the choice of a category of behavior and the definition of some population of individuals assigned to that category from which all twins will be studied. The procedure involves finding the twins (referred to as cotwins) of all members of the population (referred to as probands), determining the zygosity of all twin pairs, and their concordance or discordance with respect to the category of behavior under investigation. For example, an investigator might choose to study all individuals who are twins and who have a diagnosis of schizophrenia and who are also hospitalized in New York State in 1970. The investigator would have to obtain information on the zygosity and the concordance or discordance of each of the twin pairs in his study.

The category of behavior which has been most intensively investigated is schizophrenia. Several studies have obtained concordance rates for MZ and DZ twins for schizophrenia. There is no single number which best expresses these respective values. Concordance rates for schizophrenia will vary as a function of some of the following variables:

1. *The nature of the sample.* Two main types of samples of probands have been used—consecutive and resident samples. Resident samples involve starting with probands who are in residence at a particular time or over a particular time span in a hospital(s) and who are diagnosed as schizophrenic. Consecutive samples involve the study of probands admitted to a hospital(s) over a period of time who are diagnosed as schizophrenic. Since individuals who have mild cases of schizophrenia are more likely to be released from the hospital than individuals who have severe cases of schizophrenia, resident samples tend to include a disproportionate number of long term chronic cases. There is evidence that severity of schizophrenia in the proband is positively associated with concordance rates (see Gottesman & Shields, 1966). Consequently, resident samples tend to yield higher concordance rates than consecutive samples.

2. *The procedures used to diagnose the cotwins.* There are a number of possible ways of deciding whether the cotwins are concordant or discordant. These vary from the insistence that the cotwin be considered schizophrenic if and only if he has been admitted to a hospital and assigned the diagnosis schizophrenic in the official records of the hospital to a decision

to consider a cotwin schizophrenic if, in the opinion of a clinically trained investigator, he has a "schizophrenic like" personality. Obviously, the more rigorous the definition of what constitutes concordance in the cotwin the lower will be the concordance rate.

3. *Procedures for age-correction.* A number of probands may be young. Their cotwins may be discordant for schizophrenia. However, some of the cotwins may subsequently develop schizoprenia. Various formulae have been used to age-correct raw concordance rates. Concordance rates will vary dependent upon the procedures used in age-correction.

4. *The country in which the research is undertaken.* There is some suggestion that concordance rates for schizophrenia among MZ twins may be lower in the Scandinavian countries than in other parts of the world. There is no accepted explanation for this. It may be due to peculiarities of the environment in Scandinavia, or the result of artifacts in studies of the inheritance of schizophrenia in the Scandinavian studies.

Gottesman and Shields (1966) have reviewed all of the studies comparing concordance rates for schizophrenia in MZ and DZ twins. On the basis of an exhaustive review of the literature they conclude that these separate studies represent replications of each other. That is, each of the studies essentially supports the others in finding the concordance rates are higher for MZ than DZ twins. The quantitative differences in concordance rates which have been reported are, for the most part, explained by reference to the factors listed above. Table 7.2 presents a complete summary of the studies reviewed by Gottesman and Shields (1966). Table 7.2 clearly indicates that concordance rates have been much higher in MZ twins than in DZ twins. The results clearly indicate that there are genotypes which predispose an individual to schizophrenia.

The results of twin studies on the inheritance of schizophrenia are supported by studies of adoption. (See Rosenthal, 1970, for a general discussion of these studies.) Heston (1966) studied a group of children whose mothers were hospitalized for schizophrenia at the time of their birth. The children were separated from their mothers at birth and were raised by someone other than biological mother. Among 47 such children, Heston found 5 who were schizophrenic. The age-corrected risk for schizophrenia in this group was 16.6 percent—a figure which is comparable to or in excess of the risk for the development of schizophrenia which is found among children of schizophrenic mothers who are raised by their biological mother. Evidently, the socialization practices of a schizophrenic mother have little or no influence on the expressivity of the genotypes which are relevant for schizophrenia.

Although the evidence clearly implicates genetic factors in the etiology of schizophrenia there is little or no knowledge of the environmental conditions, if any, which are of etiological significance for the development of the disease. Mednick and McNeil (1968) have argued that much of the research on etiological factors in schizophrenia is of limited value. The typical study involves a comparison of schizophrenics with other individuals who serve as a control group. Differences between the schizophrenics and the control group are then assumed to be of critical importance in understanding the etiology of schizophrenia. There are two principal difficulties with this type of study. Mednick and McNeil indicate the differences which are obtained may often be due to the consequences of the disease and may not have been present prior to the onset of the disease. For example, many of the characteristics of schizophrenia may be due to their relatively long term hospitalization. Consider a second example. Parental reports of the childrearing methods used by the parents of schizophrenics may be influenced by the need of the parents to remove blame from themselves for the development of their child's illness.

More generally, reports that indicate that schizophrenics have experienced certain environmental conditions more often than other groups represent data in which the conditional probabilities are backward. That is, they give us the probability that if a person is schizophrenic he has experienced some particular environmental event. Even where this probability is substantially higher than the probability that the control group has experienced this event it does not provide evidence that the event is of etiological significance. What is required is the probability that if a person has experienced the event he will be schizophrenic. And this latter probability can be substantially different from the former probability.

In order to circumvent these difficulties, Mednick and McNeil recommend the use of "high risk" methods. In this type of study, individuals with a high risk for schizophrenia—in this case the children of schizophrenic mothers—are studied longitudinally prior to the development of the disease. By comparing children of schizophrenic mothers who develop schizophrenia with those who do not, some insight may be obtained into etiological factors which are present *prior* to the onset of the disease and are thus not a result of the consequences of the disease.

There is one other type of data which has been used to suggest that schizophrenia is influenced by environmental factors. A large number of studies have found that the incidence of schizophrenia varies inversely with socioeconomic status (see Dohrenwend & Dohrenwend, 1967). This finding has been taken to indicate that environmental factors associated with low socioeconomic status have etiological significance for the de-

TABLE 7.2

Summary Table of Twin Studies of Schizophrenia

| Investigator | Country | Concordance | | | | | | Sampling | |
|---|---|---|---|---|---|---|---|---|---|
| | | MZ | | DZ SS | | DZ OS | | Resident versus consecutive admissions | Long stay versus short stay |
| | | Pairs | (%) | Pairs | (%) | Pairs | (%) | | |
| Kallmann | | | | | | | | | |
| Preadolescent (1956) | USA | 15/17 | 88 | 8/35[a] | 23 | a | | R + C | L |
| Adult (1946) | USA | 120/174 | 69 | 34/296 | 11 | 13/221 | 6 | R + C | L |
| Slater (1953) | UK | | | | | | | | |
| Resident sample | | 17/26 | 65 | 4/35 | 11 | 0/36 | 0 | R | L |
| Consecutive sample | | 7/11 | 64 | 4/23 | 17 | 2/18 | 11 | C | L |
| Essen-Müller (1941) | Sweden | 7/11[b] | 64 | 4/27[b] | 15 | — | | C | L |
| Rosanoff (1934) | USA | 25/41 | 61 | 7/53 | 13 | 3/48 | 6 | R | L + S? |
| Inouye (1961) | Japan | 33/55 | 60 | 2/11 | 18 | 0/6 | 0 | R + C | L + S |
| Luxenburger (1928) | Germany | 11/19 | 58 | 0/13 | 0 | 0/20 | 0 | R + C | L + S |
| Gottesman & Shields (1966) | UK | 10/24 | 42 | 3/33 | 9 | — | | C | S |
| Harvald & Hauge (1965) | Denmark | 2/7 | 29 | 2/31 | 6 | 1/28 | 4 | Neither | n.a. |
| Kringlen (1964)[c] | Norway | 2/8 | 25 | 2/12 | 17 | — | | R + C | L |
| Tienari (1963)[c] | Finland | 0/16 | 0 | — | | — | | Neither | n.a. |

164

| Investigator | Country | Is severity related to concordance | Sex with higher concordance | Sample sex surplus | Hospital versus author diagnosis | Blood and/or fingerprints in zygosity diagnosis |
|---|---|---|---|---|---|---|
| Kallmann | | | | | | |
| Preadolescent (1956) | USA | ? | ? | M | A | Yes |
| Adult (1946) | USA | Yes | Neither | F | A | No |
| Slater (1953) | UK | | | | | |
| Resident sample | | Yes | F | F | A | Yes |
| Consecutive sample | | Yes | Neither | Neither | A | Yes |
| Essen-Müller (1941) | Sweden | No | Neither | Neither | A | Yes |
| Rosanoff (1934) | USA | ? | F | F | H | No |
| Inouye (1961) | Japan | Yes | Neither | F | A | Yes |
| Luxenburger (1928) | Germany | Yes? | Neither | Neither | A | No |
| Gottesman & Shields (1966) | UK | Yes | Neither | Neither | H | Yes |
| Harvald & Hauge (1965) | Denmark | ? | ? | ? | H | Yes |
| Kringlen (1964)[c] | Norway | No | | | H | Yes |
| Tienari (1963)[c] | Finland | No | | | A | Yes |

Based on Gottesman & Shields, 1966.

[a] DZ pairs not broken down by type and include OS pairs.

[b] Includes psychoses with schizophrenic-like features and Kaij (1960) follow-up. On other criteria MZ concordance ranges from 0%–86% (see text).

[c] Neither Kringlen nor Tienari included female probands.

165

TABLE 7.3

*Heterogeneous Twin Sibship Data on the Expected Incidence of Manic-Depressive Psychosis*

| | Number of cases | | | Partly uncorrected morbidity rates | | | |
|---|---|---|---|---|---|---|---|
| | Siblings half sibs | DZ twin pairs | MZ twin pairs | Half sibs | Siblings | DZ cotwins | MZ cotwins |
| Rosanoff *et al.* | ? | 67 | 23 | | 1.5 | 16.4 | 69.6 |
| Lixenburger *et al.* | 263 | 13(3)[a] | 4(29)[a] | | 12.7 | 0.0–33.3[a] | 75.0–96.6[a] |
| Schulz (Ruedin) | 844 | | | 1.4 | 7.4–23.8 | | |
| | (124) | | | | 11.7 | 23.3 | 66.7 |
| Slater | 171 | 30 | 6 | | | | |
| Kallmann | 206 | 55 | 27 | 12.5 | 18.0 | 23.6 | 92.6 |
| | (16) | | | | | | |

Based on Kallmann, 1954.

[a] Casuistically reported cases.

velopment of schizophrenia. However, this conclusion is not compelling. It is possible that individuals who become schizophrenic may tend to be downwardly mobile. Over a number of generations the tendency to differential downward mobility could lead to a high incidence of genotypes which predispose an individual to the development of schizophrenia among individuals with low socioeconomic status.[2]

We can summarize this brief review of etiological factors in schizophrenia as follows: genetic factors are the only etiological factors for which we have adequate evidence.

There is also evidence that the other major "functional" psychosis, manic depression, is influenced by genetic factors. Kallmann (1954) has summarized the relevant data (see Table 7.3).

Table 7.3 indicates that, in the majority of studies, incidence rates vary as a function of genetic similarity. Note again the high concordance rates among MZ twins and the relatively low concordance rates among DZ twins.

There are a number of twin studies which have established concordance rates for behavior deviances other than the psychoses. Shields (1954) has summarized data on concordance rates for criminal behavior and juvenile

[2] For evidence that schizophrenia leads to downward mobility see Goldberg and Morrison (1965) and Lystad (1957).

TABLE 7.4

*Studies on the Inheritance of Criminality and Delinquency*

| | | | | MZ | | DZ | | | |
| | | | | | | Same sex | | Other sex | |
| Condition studied | Author | Country | Year | Concordant | Discordant | Concordant | Discordant | Concordant | Discordant |
|---|---|---|---|---|---|---|---|---|---|
| Adult crime | Lang | Germany | 1929 | 10 | 3 | 3 | 15 | — | — |
| Adult crime | Stumpfl | Germany | 1936 | 11 | 7 | 7 | 12 | 12 | 26 |
| Adult crime | Kranz | Germany | 1936 | 20 | 11 | 23 | 20 | 7 | 43 |
| Adult crime | Borgström | Finland | 1939 | 3 | 1 | 2 | 3 | 2 | 8 |
| Adult crime | Rosanoff et al. | USA | 1934 | 25 | 12 | 5 | 23 | 1 | 31 |
| Juvenile delinquency | Rosanoff et al. | USA | 1934 | 39 | 3 | 20 | 5 | 8 | 32 |

Based on Shields, 1954.

167

delinquency. The studies indicate that concordance rates are higher for MZ twins than DZ twins. It should be noted that most of these studies were undertaken before the use of serological techniques in twin research was widespread. Kranz (1936) did use serological techniques to determine zygosity and obtained somewhat higher concordance rates for crime among same sex DZ twins than those obtained by other investigators (see Table 7.4). However, all of the studies reviewed by Shields including Kranz's study did find higher concordance rates among MZ than DZ twins for crime and juvenile delinquency. Table 7.4 presents Shield's summary of these data.

Kallmann (1952) has reported a twin study dealing with male homosexuality. In his study Kallmann used an index developed by Kinsey (Kinsey, Pomeroy, & Martin, 1948). A score of 3 or above on this index may be taken as indicative of strong homosexuality. Table 7.5 indicates that Kallmann found 100 percent concordance rates among a group of 37 male MZ homosexuals using a score of 3 or above for the cotwin as being

TABLE 7.5

*Kallmann's Data on Concordance among MZ and DZ Male Homosexuals*

| Proband rating | MZ *cotwin rating* | | | | | |
|---|---|---|---|---|---|---|
|  | 6 | 5 | 4 | 3 | 2,1,0 | Sum |
| 6 | 16 | 3 | 0 | 0 | 0 | 19 |
| 5 | 3 | 3 | 1 | 2 | 0 | 9 |
| 4 | 0 | 1 | 2 | 2 | 0 | 5 |
| 3 | 0 | 2 | 2 | 0 | 0 | 4 |
| Total | 19 | 9 | 5 | 4 | 0 | 37 |

| Proband rating | DZ *cotwin rating* | | | | | |
|---|---|---|---|---|---|---|
|  | 6,5 | 4,3 | 2 | 1 | 0 | Sum |
| 6 | 0 | 1 | 1 | 5 | 5 | 12 |
| 5 | 0 | 0 | 0 | 1 | 5 | 6 |
| 4 | 1 | 1 | 0 | 0 | 2 | 4 |
| 3 | 0 | 0 | 0 | 1 | 3 | 4 |
| Total | 1 | 2 | 1 | 7 | 15 | 26 |

Based on Kallmann, 1952.

indicative of concordance for homosexuality. The concordance rate among 26 male DZ twins was 12 percent. Kallmann reports that his study of the case histories indicates that the twins who were concordant for homosexuality developed their homosexuality independently. In no case was there any indication that a twin was led to the practice of homosexuality by the actions of his cotwin. Kallmann's data indicate that there are genotypes which predispose males to develop homosexuality.

Kallmann's findings must be accepted cautiously. His sample consisted of hard core homosexuals who were frequently reported to him by various agencies dealing with homosexuality. His sample and findings may not be representative of homosexuality where it does not come to the attention of social agencies.

Concordance rates among MZ and DZ twins have been reported for alcoholism and smoking. Kaij (1960) has reported a twin study dealing with alcoholism in Sweden. The population for the study was obtained from individuals whose names were entered in official records of alcohol abuse. Serological methods were used. Kaij established five classes of alcoholism:

1. No entry on official records.
2. One conviction for alcohol abuse or two convictions older than 10 years.
3. Two convictions with one being recent or more than two convictions.
4. An indication that the individual has been reported as alcoholic to the temperance board by a relative.
5. Subject of compulsory proceeding for alcohol abuse or, cirrhosis of the liver.

Kaij found a concordance rate of 36 percent among 25 MZ probands in category 2 with concordance being defined as a cotwin in categories 3, 4, or 5. Among 34 MZ probands in categories 3, 4, or 5 the concordance rate was 89 percent. The concordance rate for 66 DZ probands in category 2 was 22 percent and the concordance rate for 80 DZ probands in categories 3, 4, or 5 was 26 percent. These data indicate that severe and persistent alcoholism among MZ probands is usually associated with severe and persistent alcoholism among their cotwins. The lower concordance rates for DZ probands who are severely alcoholic indicates the importance of genetic influences in the development of alcoholism.

Roe (1945) carried out an adoption study of children of alcoholic fathers who were reared in foster homes. She compared such children to a control group of children who were raised in foster homes whose parents had no history of alcoholism. She found no significant differences in drinking behavior in the two groups.

If we accept the findings of the Kaij and Roe studies at face value, we can infer that a particular genotype combined with a particular environment are both necessary for the development of chronic alcoholism. Neither is sufficient by itself. It is instructive to contrast this pattern of results with those found in studies of schizophrenia where adoption and subsequent rearing in "normal" homes does not appear to decrease the probability that a child whose biological mother is schizophrenic will develop schizophrenia—suggesting that the expressivity of the genotypes for alcoholism are more likely to be influenced by specific environments than the genotypes for schizophrenia.

Friberg, Kaij, Dencker, and Jonsson (1959) and Shields (1962) have both reported concordance rates for smoking among twins. Friberg *et al.* report concordance rates of 86 percent among MZ probands who were smokers or former smokers, with concordance being defined as being or having been a smoker. The concordance rate for DZ probands was 69 percent. Shields has reported concordance rates for smoking for MZ twins raised together, for MZ twins raised apart, as well as for DZ twins. He reports concordance rates of 79 percent for MZ twins raised apart, 71 percent for MZ twins raised together, and 50 percent for DZ twins. Shield's data indicate that the relatively high concordance rates among MZ twins remain high even when a certain divergence in the similarity of their environment exists. The higher concordance rates for MZ twins indicates the influence of genetic variation in smoking behavior.

We have reviewed research dealing with concordance rates for several classes of behaviors. The data has indicated, rather consistently, the importance of genetic influences. There is at least one behavior category for which there is no evidence that genetic effects are involved. Kallmann, Deporte, Deporte, and Feingold (1949) have reported almost complete discordance for suicide among both MZ and DZ twins.

STUDIES DEALING WITH THE INHERITANCE OF QUANTITATIVELY VARYING DIMENSIONS

In this section we shall consider studies dealing with genetic influences on various dimensions of personality. Much of this research concerns relationships between MZ and DZ twins on standardized personality tests. The results of these studies are frequently expressed in terms of Holzinger's heritability coefficient, $H'$, defined as follows:

$$\frac{S^2_{dDZ} - S^2_{dMZ}}{S^2_{dDZ}}$$

Where $S^2_{dDZ}$ represents the variance of the within pair differences among DZ twins and $S^2_{dMZ}$ represents the variance of the differences among MZ twins. $H'$ represents an estimate of the degree to which a particular characteristic is determined by genetic influences. $H'$ represents an underestimate of the influence of genetic factors since DZ twins who share 50 percent genetic overlap are used as the basis for estimating variations in genetic influence in the population.

A number of investigators have used standardized personality tests which yield several scores on each of several scales as a basis for their studies of the inheritance of personality. Vandenberg (1962) used a sample of 45 MZ and 37 same-sex DZ twins in his study. He used the Thurstone Temperament Schedule and one of Cattell's tests as his measures of personality. He found significant $H'$ estimates for 4 of the 7 scales on the Thurstone test: Active $-.67$, Vigorous $-.59$, Impulsive $-.46$, and Sociable $-.47$. Three of the thirteen scales on the Cattell test yielded significant $H'$ scores. These were Nervous Tension $-.52$, Neuroticism $-.69$, and Will Control $-.47$. Vandenberg determined $H'$ values for a number of other types of measurements covering such areas as motor skills, perceptual abilities, and intellectual abilities. Vandenberg found the lowest $H'$ values in the personality area.

Vandenberg included a number of perceptual measures in his study. These included measures related to those which comprise Witkins perceptual index. Vandenberg found a significant $H'$ value of .60 for a block design test similar to that included in the WISC, a significant $H'$ value of .67 for a Gottschaldt embedded figures test, and a nonsignificant $H'$ value of .40 for a perception of the upright test. These data, taken together, indicate that Witkin's perceptual index is influenced by genetic factors.

Gottesman (1962, 1963, 1966) has also obtained $H'$ estimates for scales on standardized personality tests. Gottesman's (1962, 1963) study involved a sample obtained from public schools in Minneapolis-St. Paul. Serological techniques were used. The principal personality tests used were the MMPI and one of Cattell's tests. He found significant H' values for five of the ten MMPI scales: Depression $-.45$, Psychopathic Deviate $-.50$, Psychasthemia $-.37$, Schizophrenia $-.42$, and Social Introversion $-.71$. Some of the data on the Cattell test were puzzling. Gottesman found nonsignificant correlations between MZ twins for 6 of the 14 scales on the Cattell test. However, DZ twins had significant correlations for 4 of these 6 variables. This finding is difficult to explain and led Gottesman to suggest that the test might not be valid.

In a second study using a sample obtained from the Boston area, Gottesman (1966) obtained significant $H'$ values for six of the nineteen scales on the California Personality Inventory. The H' values ranged from

.32 to .49. Gottesman points out that the scales on the California Personality Test for which he obtained significant $H'$ values are related to a more general factor of introversion–extraversion believed to be present in the California Personality Inventory.

The Vandenberg and Gottesman studies have dealt with the inheritance of rather "narrowly" defined personality dimensions. In Chapter 2 we have indicated that such dimensions may not be as valid as more broadly defined personality dimensions. Eysenck (1956; Eysenck & Prell, 1951) has dealt with the inheritance of the more broadly defined dimensions of personality, neuroticism, and introversion.

Eysenck and Prell (1951) studied the inheritance of neuroticism. They investigated a group of MZ and DZ twins who were born in London. The twins were given a battery of 17 tests. A criterion group of neurotic subjects was used in order to define a neuroticism factor with the use of criterion analysis. A neuroticism factor was extracted which correlated with the criterion .76. The factor was defined by three measures, static ataxia (body sway) whose loading on the factor was .66, body sway suggestibility with a loading of .53, and auto kinetic movement with a loading of .45. Note that two of the three tests which define neuroticism are motor tests and the third is a perceptual test. Further, the correlation of each of the three tests with the criterion was low. The highest correlation was .30 for static ataxia and the lowest was .17 for autokinetic movement. The magnitude of the correlation of the test with the criterion suggest that they are, individually, only slightly related to neuroticism. The $H'$ values for the tests were .69 for static ataxia, .70 for body sway suggestibility, and .65 for autokinetic movement. The intraclass correlation[3] for the MZ twins on the neuroticism factor was .85. The corresponding value for the DZ twins was. 22, resulting in an $H'$ value for the neuroticism factor as a whole of .81. Eysenck and Prell's results must be accepted cautiously since the neuroticism factor is defined by only three tests which have relatively low correlations with the critierion. Of course, the neuroticism factor as a whole does correlate highly with the criterion. What is not clear from Eysenck and Prell's data is whether other tests which would correlate with the criterion of neuroticism and which would serve to more broadly define a neuroticism factor would exhibit $H'$ values of this magnitude. If they

---

[3] The intraclass correlation is a measure obtained from the analysis of variance. $H^1$ may also be defined as

$$\frac{\gamma_{MZ} - \gamma_{DZ}}{1 - DZ}$$

where $\gamma_{MZ}$ is the value of the intraclass correlation for MZ twins and $\gamma_{DZ}$ is the value for DZ twins.

would, and in view of the correlation of this factor with the criterion it is at least plausible to expect that they would, this would indicate that neuroticism is very substantially influenced by genetic factors.

Eysenck and Prell's findings on the inheritance of neuroticism are partially supported by the findings of a study by Scarr (1966). She studied MZ and DZ female twins between the ages of six and ten and obtained ratings of their apprehensiveness and anxiety in a play situation. She obtained intraclass correlations for anxiety ratings of .88 for MZ twins and .28 for DZ twins yielding an $H'$ value of .83. On both intuitive and theoretical grounds we would expect that ratings of anxiety are a component of, or are associated with, Eysenck's general neuroticism factor.

Wilde (1964) has also reported a twin study dealing with the inheritance of neurotic tendencies as measured by a biographical questionnaire. Two measures of neurotic tendencies were obtained, a general neurotic instability score, and the score for functional bodily complaints. The intraclass correlations were .55 for MZ twins and .11 for DZ twins on the former measure and .67 and .34 on the latter measure. These findings give added support for the assertion that neurotic tendencies are influenced by genotypes. However, there were some puzzling findings in Wilde's study. He found that DZ twins who had lived apart from their twin for 5 or more years were more similar to each other than pairs of twins who were resident in the same household or who had lived apart for less than 5 years.[4] For example DZ twins who lived apart had intraclass correlations of .28 and .64 on the two measures of neurotic instability, whereas DZ twins living together had intraclass correlations of $-.14$ and $-.05$ on these measures. This suggests that DZ twins who are similar tend to live apart from each other.

Eysenck (1956) has also studied the inheritance of extraversion–introversion. The subjects were those used previously in the Eysenck and Prell (1951) study of neuroticism. Eysenck gave his subjects a battery of tests and extracted three factors, an intelligence factor, a factor based on autonomic nervous system measures and an introversion–extraversion factor which was defined by two indices from the Rorschach, self and teacher ratings of social popularity, and slow and accurate work on a tracking task. The loading of these tests on the factor ranged from $-.38$ for slow and accurate work to $-.63$ for M percent on the Rorschach and .63 for social popularity ratings. The intraclass correlation for MZ twins on the introversion–extraversion factor was .50 and the corresponding correlation for the DZ twins was $-.33$. Eysenck regards this latter cor-

---

[4] The separated twins were not reared apart—they were only living in separate residences.

TABLE 7.6

*Intraclass Correlations and H' Estimates for Rating Scale Measures of Introversion–Extraversion*

| Measure | $r_{MZ}$ | $r_{DZ}$ | $H'$ |
|---|---|---|---|
| Adjective check list of need affiliation | .83 | .56 | .61 |
| Counseling readiness | .56 | .03 | .55 |
| Fels friendliness | .86 | .36 | .78 |
| Fels social apprehension | .88 | .28 | .83 |
| Observer's rating of likeableness | .93 | .83 | .61 |

Based on Scarr, 1969. (Reprinted by permission of The Society for Research in Child Development, Inc.)

relation as a nonsignificant deviation from .00. The $H'$ value obtained for this factor was .62. It must be accepted somewhat cautiously in view of the negative correlation for the DZ twins.

Scarr (1969) has reported the results of a study of the inheritance of introversion–extraversion among a group of girls in the Boston area with a mean age of 97 months. She used adjective checklist data obtained from the girls' mothers and various rating scales filled out by observors including the Fels scales for friendliness and social apprehensiveness. Table 7.6 presents the intraclass correlations and $H'$ estimates for the measures used by Scarr. Note that the $H'$ estimates vary from .55 to .83, indicating that genotypes are important determinants of the variance of scores on the rating scales used by Scarr.

Wilde (1964) has reported one of the few studies of the inheritance of introversion with negative results. He found an intraclass correlation of .37 for MZ twins and .35 for DZ on a measure of introversion derived from a biographical questionnaire. It should be noted that Wilde did not use a measure of this dimension which had been widely used in other research.

Shields (1962) has also studied the inheritance of introversion–extraversion and neuroticism. In addition, Shields included a sample of MZ twins who were reared apart. Shields studied 44 pairs of MZ twins reared together and 44 pairs of MZ twins reared apart. Zygosity determination was made with the aid of serological data. Of the 44 pairs of MZ twins reared apart, 21 were separated at birth or during the first two months of life. Of the 44 pairs, 30 were separated during the first year of life, 6 pairs were separated between one and two years of age, 2 pairs between two and three years, two pairs at four years, one pair at 5 years, one pair at seven, one pair at eight, and one pair at nine. Of the 44 pairs, 10 who were separated were reunited some time before the age of eighteen. The mean number of years which this group of ten twins was separated prior to their eighteenth birthday was 10.9. These data indicate that the 44 pairs of twins reared apart spent a substantial amount of time in different families.

Of the MZ twins reared apart, 14 pairs were brought up by unrelated families and 30 pairs of twins were brought up in different branches of the same family usually by grandparents or aunts and uncles. Few of the separated twins were brought up in homes with large differences in social class. This latter fact is of some interest. In studies of the inheritance of intelligence data on MZ twins reared apart are frequently discounted because it is usually the case that pairs of twins reared apart are placed in homes which do not differ substantially in socioeconomic status. Consequently, the twins reared apart have experienced an environment which is only minimally varied with respect to factors which are allegedly critical for the development of intelligence. However, such an argument loses much of its force in the area of personality if the data on relationships between DZ twins raised together are accepted at face value. DZ twins show minimal relationships on standardized personality tests—the value of the intraclass correlation for DZ twins rarely exceeds .30. Such data indicate that individuals who have 50 percent genetic overlap and who are raised in the same family are not highly similar with respect to the characteristics measured by tests of personality. Consequently, we can argue that individuals raised in different branches of the same family or by individuals from different families with similar socioeconomic status are raised by individuals whose personalities differ substantially. If the variability of personality among socialization agents is monotonically related to variability in the creation of environments which vary significantly for the development of personality, we should expect that the MZ twins reared apart in Shields' study should experience wide divergencies in their environment.

TABLE 7.7

*Intraclass Correlations Obtained by Shields for* MZ *Twins Reared Together,* MZ *Twins Reared Apart, and* DZ *Twins*

|  | MZ *together* | MZ *apart* | DZ |
|---|---|---|---|
| Height | .94 | .82 | .44 |
| Weight | .81 | .37 | .56 |
| Intelligence | .76 | .77 | .51 |
| Extraversion | .42 | .61 | .17 |
| Neuroticism | .38 | .53 | .11 |

Based on Shields, 1962.

Shields used a personality questionnaire developed by Eysenck to assess introversion–extraversion and neuroticism. The intraclass correlations for these variables as well as for height, weight, and intelligence are reported in Table 7.7. Table 7.7 indicates that variations in the environment clearly influence genotypes only in the case of weight. The two personality measures, surprisingly, indicate slightly greater similarity for MZ twins reared separately than for MZ twins reared together. This difference is probably most parsimoniously explained as a chance variation from a "true" difference of zero. We can conclude that being reared apart does not have any effect at all on the expressivity of the genotypes which influence the dimension of neuroticism and introversion–extraversion.

## Conclusion and Implications

One possible inference which may be drawn from twin studies is that variations in the environment are of little or no significance as sources of individual differences in personality. The data in support of this rather extreme assertion are, in the main, of two kinds. First, there are the results of the Shields' study on MZ twins reared apart. Although Shields' data are unequivocal in indicating that variations in the environment do not influence the similarity of MZ twins with respect to the personality dimensions which seem best established (see Chapter 2), it might be prudent to accept his results cautiously in view of the fact that we have only a single study dealing with this problem. However, there is a second type of data which also supports this rather unconventional inference. In most cases, twin studies indicate relatively low degrees of similarity among DZ twins. Twin studies dealing with the inheritance of quantitatively varying personality dimensions rarely report intra-class correlations for DZ twins exceeding .30. In the studies of neuroticism and introversion–extraversion we have reviewed the intraclass correlations for DZ twins were as follows: Eysenck and Prell (1951) report an intraclass correlation for DZ twins on neuroticism of .21, Wilde reported values of .11 and .34, and Shields reported a corresponding intraclass correlation of .11. For introversion–extraversion, Eysenck reported an intraclass correlation for DZ twins of −.33, Scarr found correlations ranging from .03 to .82, and Shields reported a corresponding correlation of .17. If the bulk of these data are accepted at face value, they would appear to indicate that the similarity of environment experienced by DZ twins is not a sufficient condition to produce an extensive degree of similarity on dimensions of personality. Data indicating the DZ twins are highly similar in some characteristic are ambiguous with respect to the influence of heredity and environment since DZ twins not only experience similar environments but also have 50 percent genetic overlap. However, data indicating that DZ twins are *not* similar with respect to some characteristic indicates that similarity of environment is not critical for the development of that characteristic. This latter statement is based on the apparently reasonable assumption that same sex DZ twins reared together do in fact experience a relatively similar environment.

There is a second somewhat different way of interpreting the results of the twin studies we have reviewed. It may be that the values for the intraclass correlation for DZ twins are artificially deflated by errors of measurement. That is, the hypothetical "true" value of the intraclass correlations for DZ twins obtained on perfectly valid and reliable measures of neuroticism and introversion may be significantly higher than the obtained values on the measures of these dimensions actually used. Eysenck and Prell (1951) have discussed the implications of errors of measurement in twin studies. It is apparent that an argument that the intraclass correlation for DZ twins is depressed by errors of measurement is *mutatis mutandis* of equal validity when applied to the values of the intra-class correlations for MZ twins. Eysenck and Prell (1951) indicate that twin studies may underestimate the influence of heredity on personality because measures of personality are rarely factorially pure. That is, a measure of neuroticism may be a measure of neuroticism as well as a measure of many other characteristics—for example, social desirability. If one holds to the view that neuroticism is inherited but social desirability is not, then the value of the intraclass correlation for MZ twins will be depressed. On the whole, it is a reasonable expectation that the values of the intraclass correlations for both MZ and DZ twins are subject to greater depression by errors of measurement in the personality area than in other areas which have been investigated in twin research. This is obviously true with respect to height and weight where errors of measurement are virtually non existent and probably true with respect to such areas as motor behavior, perception and intellectual ability. If the true values of the intraclass correlations for both MZ and DZ twins on measures of personality are higher than the obtained values then the true values of $H'$ in the personality area are higher than the reported values. The highest values obtained for $H'$ are for measures of such physical variables as height. The values of the intraclass correlation for height are typically about .90 for MZ twins and .50 for DZ twins (see Table 7.7 for the values obtained by Shields). It is apparent that substantial increases in the values of the intraclass correlations for both MZ and DZ twins would substantially increase the $H'$ values in the personality area to the point where they begin to approach those obtained for height and weight. The point of this argument is that there really is no way of knowing the relative importance of genetic influences in the personality area as opposed to other areas. Findings such as Vandenberg's that the $H'$ values obtained in the personality area are lower than those obtained in other areas do *not* indicate that genetic influences are less important in this area unless the measurements from which we infer $H'$ values are equally valid—and that is unlikely.

The twin studies taken as a whole indicate that genetic variables are of substantial importance in determining individual differences on the fundamental dimensions of personality. Do we have evidence that environmental events are important in determining personality? I do not believe that we have much, if any, evidence that points in this direction. We indicated in the beginning of this chapter that much of the evidence of this kind indicated a relationship between socialization practices and personality. But the direction of the relationship was ambiguous. Once the possibility of genetic influence on personality is accepted, evidence of relationships between personality and socialization practice become open to the possibility that genetic differences in personality influence socialization practices.

Bell (1968) has argued for just such a reinterpretation of the direction of effects in studies of socialization. Bell speculates that there are several kinds of constitutional differences (that is, differences present at birth which reflect the effects of genes, the intra-uterine environment, and the birth process itself) which might elicit different patterns of behavior from parents. For example, he assumes that children may constitutionally differ in assertiveness. Children who are highly assertive will persist in activities and will be difficult to control. Such behavior might elicit active and aggressive interventions on the part of the parents. Bell suggests that the finding that parents of delinquent children use physical punishment more often than the parents of nondelinquent children may be explained in terms of parental responsiveness to constitutional differences in assertiveness. Consider another example. Lower class parents in our society use physical punishment more often than middle class parents (Bronfenbrenner, 1958). Bell assumes that the use of physical punishment by parents may be a response to hyperactivity. Children who are constitutionally hyperactive may be difficult to control without the use of force. In a study we shall discuss, Waldrop, Pedersen, and Bell (1968) found that congential abnormalities associated with complications of pregnancy during the first trimester are strongly associated with hyperactivity. If lower-class mothers experience greater frequency of such complications than middle-class mothers, then they will have hyperactive children more often and may, as a result, be led to use physical punishment more often than middle class mothers.

Bell's hypotheses are clearly speculative. However, in view of the findings on genetic influences on personality hypotheses of the *form* advanced by Bell appear to be both plausible and even necessary.

Bell's hypotheses and the traditional hypotheses about directions of effects in socialization are both unidirectional. Whereas the traditional hypotheses assert that parents influence children, Bell asserts that children influence parents. It is possible to conceive of a more complex model in which a particular personality characteristic is assumed to reflect the influence of a particular kind of environment on a particular genotype. Schafer (1966) has reported data which provides a neat illustration of this type of interaction. She studied a group of infants who had been hospitalized before the age of 30 weeks. After the infants had recovered but prior to their discharge from the hospital she obtained activity ratings and their Developmental Quotient on the Cattell test (Cattell, 1940). Children who had experienced the relatively unstimulating hospital environment would be expected to suffer some degree of decrement in their Developmental Quotient. After the infants returned home the Cattell test was administered again. Schafer found that the changes in Developmental Quotient were dependent upon activity ratings. For the neonates with the lowest activity rating, the mean gain in Development Quotient as a result of returning home was 17.25. For the neonates with the highest activity ratings the Developmental Quotient had a mean decrease of 4.00. Schafer suggests that these results indicate the effects of constitutional differences in reaction to environmental deprivation. Active neonates are apparently unaffected by the deprivation of stimulation in the environment—perhaps this is due to their ability to supply their own stimulation. Inactive neonates are apparently greatly affected by the deprivation of stimulation in the hospital environment. Schafer's study illustrates the joint effect of environment and constitutional differences in determining behavior.

There is one large scale longitudinal study of personality development in which emphasis has been placed on the interaction of constitutional and environmental events (Thomas, Chess, & Birch, 1968; Thomas, Chess, Birch, Hertzig, & Korn, 1963). Thomas and his collaborators have investigated the characteristic patterns of mood and temperament of neonates (Thomas *et al.*, 1963). They have found a number of consistencies which persist through the first few years of life and which they assume are constitutional. One aspect of their research dealt with a longitudinal study of 136 children with particular emphasis on the emergence of behavior problems (Thomas *et al.*, 1968). Thomas and his collaborators were able to identify a group of 14 of these children whom they classified as temperamentally difficult. These children exhibited irregularity of biological functioning. They had irregular sleeping, feeding, and elimination patterns. In addition, they were easily disturbed by novelty and showed slow adaptability to change. They were irritable and frequently had negative moods. Their temperamental reactions were intense—they would shriek, laugh loudly, and cry loudly. Of the children in the temperamentally difficult group, 70 percent subsequently developed behavior problems. The incidence of behavior problems among this group of children was much higher than that of the other children studied. Thomas and his collaborators argue that the characteristics of temperament associated with a high incidence of behavior problems are constitutional in character. The interviews from which they inferred the temperamental characteristics of the children they studied occurred at a mean age of 3.3 months. The behavior problems occurred much later.

Thomas and his collaborators attempt to trace the environmental consequences of temperamental differences in children. They suggest that temperamentally difficult children tend to influence the behavior of their parents in ways which are harmful to their personality development. Thomas and his collaborators suggest that such children are treated differently from their siblings. Parents allegedly develop unconscious feelings of hostility toward these children. Also, parents tend to unwittingly reward intense crying and extreme reactions. This comes about through an initial tendency of parents to ignore manifestations of extreme distress of temperamentally difficult children. If the child persists in intense crying and screaming the parents eventually lose their capacity to ignore the child. Consequently, this pattern of parental behavior rewards the child persistent and intense reactions, thereby reinforcing the child's constitutional characteristics.

Thomas and his collaborators explicitly adopt an interactionist model. They believe the constitutional characteristics can influence parental behavior and that parental behavior, in turn, can affect and modify the constitutional characteristics of which they are a function. The terms, "consonance" and "dissonance" are introduced to describe some of the respects in which environments may interact with constitutional characteristics. A dissonant environment is one which is unsuited to the constitutional characteristics of a child and a consonant environment is one which is suited to these characteristics. Consider one of their examples. Children may constitutionally differ with respect to their position on an activity dimension. Hyperactive children would probably find a rural or suburban environment more consonant than an urban environment. Such children would tend to find a crowded urban apartment with less access to play areas dissonant.

The research of Thomas and his collaborators provides a model for unraveling the interaction of heredity and environment in the personality area. In order for this type of research to be successful it is necessary to be able to untangle cause and effect. Thomas and his collaborators have had some success in this direction principally because the constitutional characteristics they studied were manifest at a very early age permitting them to study the reactions of parents to these characteristics and the subsequent reactions of the child. However, constitutional characteristics though present, by definition, at birth may not be manifest at an early age. A study by Honzik (1957) provides an illustration of this problem. She studied the relationship between parent's education and the intelligence of foster children. Honzik found that the correlation between children's intelligence and the biological and foster parents educational level at age 2 was .00. At age 13 the correlation between foster children's intelligence and the educational level of their foster father was .00. The correlation between foster children's intelligence and the educational level of their biological father was .42. Honzik's study apparently indicates that the phenotypical manifestations of the genotypes which influence the development of intelligence were not detectable at age two. However, they were detectable at a later age and this apparently accounts for the significant correlation between the biological father and the child. The methodological implications of Honzik's research may be generalized to the personality area. The phenotypical manifestations of the genotypes which influence personality may not be detectable at an early age. If this were true it would be difficult to separate the influence of heredity and environment on behavior even though one is doing a longitudinal study starting at birth. In such a case one might wrongly attribute a phenotypical manifestation of a genotype to socialization practices which had preceded it when these socialization practices might be incidental to the emergence of the behavior in question. This type of problem can be circumvented by discovering ways of identifying genotypes at an early age and then tracing the influence of the environment on their expressivity.

We have argued that most studies of socialization practices do not permit unambiguous inferences about the influence of the environment on personality. In what follows we shall discuss two kinds of studies which may permit such inferences.

A number of studies have been done on differences in personality between first-born and later-born children (see Sampson, 1965) for a general review of this literature). A number of investigators have found that first-born children are over-represented in samples selected for intellectual eminence. (See Altus, 1966; Bradley, 1968; Schachter, 1963; Terman, 1925)

For example, Terman (1925) found many more first-born children than would be expected by chance among his sample of intellectually gifted children. Perhaps of greater relevance to personality, Schachter (1961) found that first-born children are more likely to seek to affiliate with others under conditions of stress than later-born children.

The studies of birth order are particularly relevant to the issues with which this chapter is concerned since such differences are clearly not, in any obvious way, attributable to genetic influences. Therefore, it is natural to attribute these differences to the influence of socialization practices associated with the way in which "experienced" and "inexperienced" parents treat their children. Bell (1965) indicates, however, that these differences may, in part, be attributable to constitutional differences. Weller and Bell (1965) found that first-born and later born-children were different at birth. They studied infants 60–110 hours after birth and found higher skin conductance and respiration rates for later-born than first-born children. These differences may or may not reflect differences which are of importance for subsequent personality development. However, these differences do raise the possibility that differences between first- and later-born children may be constitutional in character.

Further, complications of pregnancy and birth are more common among older mothers than younger mothers. And, obviously, the average age of mothers of later-born children is greater than the average age of mothers of first-born children. There is some evidence that such complications may be of significance for subsequent personality development. Perhaps, the most dramatic evidence of this sort comes from a study by Waldrop *et al.* 1968). They studied relationships between the presence of minor physical anomalies of the type associated with Downs syndrome presumably present at birth and the behavior of two-and-a-half-year-old nursery school children. The anomalies they studies are assumed to be related to the presence of noxious agents in the first trimester of pregnancy or possibly to chromosomal irregularities. The list of anomalies studied are presented in Table 7.8. Waldrop, Pedersen, and Bell also obtained a number of behavior measures based on teacher ratings and observation of the behavior of the children. These data were factor analyzed. A single clear factor emerged for both males and females which appears to be related to hyperactivity. Table 7.9 presents the measures which principally define the factor and the correlation between these measures and a score for the number of anomalies present for each child. Note the consistent and substantial correlations between the scores for what is presumably a measure of a constitutional characteristic and scores for the measures which define the "hyperactivity" factor.

TABLE 7.8

*List of Anomalies and Scoring Weights*

| Anomaly | Weight |
|---|---|
| *Head* | |
| Electric hair: | |
|   Very fine hair that won't comb down | 2 |
|   Fine hair that is soon awry after combing | 1 |
|   Two or more whorls | 0 |
| *Eyes* | |
| Epicanthus: | |
|   Where upper and lower lids join the nose, point of union is: | |
|     Deeply covered | 2 |
|     Partly covered | 1 |
| Hypertelorism: | |
|   Approximate distance between tear ducts: | |
|     $\geq 1.5$ inches | 2 |
|     $> 1.25 < 1.5$ inches | 1 |
| Ears | |
| Low seated: | |
|   Bottom of ears in line with: | |
|     Mouth (or lower) | 2 |
|     Area between mouth and nose | 1 |
| Adherent lobes: | |
|   Lower edges of ears extend: | |
|     Upward and back toward crown of head | 2 |
|     Straight back toward rear of neck | 1 |
| Malformed ears | 1 |
| Asymmetrical ears | 1 |
| Soft and pliable ears | 0 |
| *Mouth* | |
| High palate | |
|   Roof of mouth: | |
|     Definitely steepled | 2 |
|     Flat and narrow at the top | 1 |
|   Furrowed tongue (one with deep ridges) | 1 |
|   Smooth-rough spots on tongue | 0 |
| *Hands* | |
| Fifth finger: | |
|   Markedly curved inward toward other fingers | 2 |
|   Slightly curved inward toward other fingers | 1 |
| Single transverse palmar crease | 1 |
| Index finger longer than middle finger | 0 |
| *Feet* | |
| Third toe: | |
|   Definitely longer than second toe | 2 |
|   Appears equal in length to second toe | 1 |
| Partial syndactylia of two middle toes | 1 |
| Gap between first and second toe (approximately $\geq \frac{1}{4}$ inch) | 1 |

Based on Waldrop *et al.*, 1968. (Reprinted by permission of The Society for Research in Child Development, Inc.)

TABLE 7.9

*Loadings of Measures Used by Waldrop, Pedersen, and Bell on "Hyperactivity" Factor and the Correlations of Physical Anomalies Score with These Measures*

| Males | | | Females | | |
|---|---|---|---|---|---|
| Measure | Loading | Correlation with anomalies | Measure | Loading | Correlation with anomalies |
| Inability to delay gratification | .86 | .50 | Inability to delay gratification | .86 | .76 |
| Nomadic Play | .85 | .38 | Involvement | .78 | .39 |
| Frenetic Play | .84 | .42 | Frenetic play | .77 | .58 |
| | | | Nomadic play | .77 | .41 |
| Spilling and throwing | .83 | .40 | Perseveration | .74 | .60 |
| Emotional aggression | .71 | .31 | Opposes peer | .71 | .32 |
| Squeals | .69 | .41 | Spilling and throwing | .66 | .39 |
| Opposes peer | .67 | .34 | Tractability | − .66 | − .54 |
| Preseveration | .65 | .55 | | | |
| Watching peer | − .68 | − .31 | | | |

Based on Waldrop *et al.*, 1968. (Reprinted by permission of The Society for Research in Child Development, Inc.)

Mednick (S. Mednick, personal communication) has found in his study of children with high risk for schizophrenia that one of the respects in which the children of schizophrenic mothers who become schizophrenic differ from the children of such mothers who do not become schizophrenic is in the frequency with which these children have experienced birth complications. He found significantly more birth traumas among the group of children who became schizophrenic than in the group which did not.

The studies of Mednick and Pedersen, Waldrop and Bell indicate that variables which affect the processes of gestation and birth may influence subsequent personality development. Since these processes may be different in first- and later-born children, these differences, may, in part, be responsible for some of the personality differences which have been found to distinguish first- and later-born children. The point of this argument is not to suggest that constitutional differences are a more plausible source of explanation of the differences between first- and later-born children than those associated with variations in socialization practices. Rather, the argument merely illustrates the difficulty of unambiguously asserting that these differences are attributable to postnatal environmental effects.

Studies of hermaphrodites provide a second possible example of the influence of socialization practices on personality which are independent of constitutional differences. Hermaphrodites are individuals who have a contradiction between the predominant external appearance of their genital organs and their "true" biological sex as determined by chromosomal analysis. This condition may or may not be discovered at birth. Hampson (1965) has studied such individuals. On the basis of his clinical investigations he argues that such individuals can successfully develop the sex-linked behavior patterns of either sex. Their sexual orientation is dependent upon the information provided to their parents at birth which determines the parents belief as to their true sex. As a result, a hermaphrodite whose true genetic sex is female can be successfully raised as either a male or female and will, presumably, develop the sex-linked personality and behavior patterns which are appropriate for the sexual orientation chosen by the parents. Hampson argues, on the basis of these data, that sexual orientation is not a matter of biology but is dependent upon socialization practices. Even if Hampson's conclusions are correct for hermaphrodites it may be difficult to generalize from these data to sex linked behaviors of individuals who are not hermaphrodites. Hermaphrodites may lack some of the hormonal characteristics of their true sex. A hermaphrodite who is chromosomally a male because of the underdeveloped state of his testes may not develop all of the hormones characteristic of males. Such an individual may be more pliable with respect to sex-linked characteristics since his behavior is not as biologically directed as a normal male's behavior. A male who is not a hermaphrodite, who is strongly genetically disposed toward a masculine personality, may not be as pliable and might not be able to develop feminine characteristics even if, for some reason, his parents decided to raise him as a female. Also, the findings on the inheritance of homosexuality suggest that at least one sex-linked behavior-sexual attraction is influenced by genetic variables.

Jessor, Young, Young, & Tesi (1970) have studied the relationship between personality and drinking behavior in young men living in Boston and in two Italian cities, Rome and Palermo. For the Boston sample they found that there is a positive relationship between personality attributes indicating frustration, alienation, and powerlessness and drinking. No such relationship was found for the Italian samples in their study. They concluded, plausibly, that the differences in the relationship they obtained are attributable to differences in the socialization of drinking behavior in Italy and America. Their conclusion is buttressed by the fact that all the subjects in their three samples had four grandparents from southern Italy. This control for ancestry is, however, imperfect with respect to eliminating the possible role of genotypes in the different relationships obtained in the study. It is possible that grandparents of the American youth in the Jessor *et al.* study may have had different personality characteristics associated with the decision to migrate to America than the parents of the Italian youth. These personality differences may have been associated with differences in personality relevant genotypes. Consequently, the possibility exists that the different relationships may be related, in part, to differences in genotypes.

The foregoing examples indicate some of the difficulties in attempting to obtain unambiguous evidence of the influence of socialization practices, independent of genetic characteristics, on personality. Our best opportunity to understand the influence of socialization practices on personality would appear to depend upon attempts to make provision for constitutional differences by adopting an interactionist model. Such a model would attempt to trace the effects of a particular environment on individuals with a particular constitutional set of characteristics. Such an approach would appear to provide a method not only for understanding the impact of the environment on personality but also, for understanding the effect of the environment on the expressivity of the genotypes which influence personality. For the present, however, the best established statement that can be made with respect to the sources of individual differences in personality is that genetic influences are important. Beyond this, little else seems established.

# A CONCLUSION FOR PART ONE

In this brief conclusion for Part 1 we shall indicate a possible direction for future research in personality and we shall attempt to briefly summarize and synthesize some of the material which has been dealt with earlier.

## A Pro-Eysenck Position

It seems to me that much of the material presented earlier (particularly the material in Chapter 7) supports a conception of personality which has greater compatibility with Eysenck's theory of personality than with any other conception of personality. First, there are two general respects in which Eysenck's theory and research seem admirable. His hypothetico-deductive theory is presented with sufficient clarity that one can determine relatively unambiguously which deductions follow from the theory. It may strike the reader that this is a rather backhanded compliment inasmuch as I have attempted to indicate that some of the deductions which have been made from the theory do not rigorously follow from its central assumptions. However, this criticism should be balanced against the view that no other general conception of personality exists which is presented with a degree of rigor which would enable one to determine precisely what sorts of predictions do in fact follow from its assumptions. To be able to state precisely what one assumes is no small achievement. Further, I have argued that, at certain crucial points (for example, Claridge's study indicating a single dimension of arousal related to both neuroticism and introversion–extraversion) the theory is not in complete accord with empirical results. Again, there are few theories in the area of personality for which one can determine whether existing data support or contradict the theory.

In addition, no other researcher in the area of personality has attempted to relate individual difference measures based on paper-and-pencil tests to as wide a variety of behavior as Eysenck has. In Chapter 3 we have presented only a small sample of the set of tasks which Eysenck has studied.

In addition to these rather admirable general characteristics of Eysenck's theory, there are a number of other respects in which the theory appears to be correct or more nearly correct than its competitors. First, our review of factor analytic research supports the view that personality is best described (or at least more validly and reliably described) in terms of a limited number of very general personality dimensions. Further, there does seem to be support for the view that the dimensions of introversion–extraversion and neuroticism seem to be present in all systematic dimensional analyses of personality (see Eysenck & Eysenck, 1969). Finally, the research we have reviewed in Chapter 7, providing evidence that these dimensions are influenced by genotypes, also provides support for the view that the measures of these dimensions of personality developed by Eysenck do in fact get at some very fundamental characteristics of individuals. That is, if the measures were unreliable and meaningless, they would not be as substantially influenced by genotypes as the research indicates. Consequently, we can conclude with Eysenck that at a most fundamental level of personality there exists at least two dimensions of personality which are influenced by genotypes.

The data supporting the importance of genotypical influences in personality is at least compatible, if not strongly supportive of two other general characteristics of Eysenck's theory. First, these data support the attempt to relate individual differences in personality to some kind of biological foundation on the reasonable assumption that genotypical differences result in biological differences. Second, the presence of genotypical influences on personality supports the attempt to understand socialization in terms of the interaction of constitutional characteristics with socialization practices. Eysenck is one of the few personality theorists who has attempted to deal with socialization from this perspective.

There is one final rather general respect in which our review of research in personality supports Eysenck's position. Eysenck deemphasizes cognitive dimensions of personality other than intelligence. Our review of research on cognitive dimensions of personality indicated, at least for the two dimensions considered, that intelligence is substantially related to these dimensions and is an important personality characteristic in its own right. I do not wish to defend the proposition that there are no important cognitive dimensions of personality which are unrelated to intelligence. However, I do believe that individual differences in intelligence are at least as important a personality dimension as any other cognitive dimension and that, as a first approximation, the assertion that individual differences in intelligence are the basic cognitive dimension of personality is not unreasonable.

 The principal limitation in Eysenck's conception of personality stems from the feeling that a dimensional analysis of personality based on four dimensions (and only two of these are the subject of extensive theoretical analysis) provides us with a system which does not do justice to the complexity and richness of the human personality. Eysenck has indicated that his system of personality description might be supplemented by a consideration of position with respect to narrowly defined or first-order factors (see Eysenck & Eysenck, 1969). However, he has also indicated that, at present, descriptive systems based on such dimensions have not proved to be reliable. Hence we are left with a rather limited system for the description of personality. Eysenck has attempted to circumvent this difficulty by the use of the hypothetico-deductive apparatus of his theory in an attempt to derive an extensive set of characteristic social behaviors of individuals who differ on his biologically derived dimensions of personality. However, this is one of the least successful aspects of his theory. In a general sense, the inadequacy of Eysenck's derivations of social behaviors stems from the strain placed on the deductive capacities of his theory (indeed, one is tempted to argue of any biologically based theory) by the attempt to derive social behavior without ever describing the details of the socialization practices to which an individual with a particular genotype is exposed. For example, it is hard to see how one could derive the kind of specific detail of social behavior which is of interest to Bandura and Walters when they argue that some boys have learned to react aggressively outside of the home but not in the home by appeal to genotypically influenced biological characteristics of personality. However, this example does indicate a direction in which Eysenck's theory might be extended in order to provide a more differentiated descriptive system for personality. One might assume, as does Eysenck, that personality can be described in terms of a limited number of biologically based, genotypically influenced personality dimensions. A more complete description of personality might be obtained by then considering the characteristic socialization practices to which individuals with particular genotypes were exposed.

# PART TWO

# CHAPTER 8

## CLINICAL AND STATISTICAL PREDICTION AND DESCRIPTION OF PERSONALITY

Psychologists frequently are required to make predictions about the future behavior of individuals. The predictions might concern success or failure at a job or in a school situation, recidivism among parolees, the possibility of successful response to psychotherapy, and the likelihood of successful adjustment following release from a mental hospital.

The development of an adequate descriptive system for personality should enable psychologists to make more accurate predictions about individuals. Knowledge of position with respect to some of the dimensions of personality we have considered would enable us to make predictions about persons which could be of practical value. For example, Eysenck's theory and research imply that introverts would do better than extraverts in a radar operator's job involving continuous meticulous attention to detail with little opportunity for social interaction.

Despite the fact that there are situations for which predictions may be derived from knowledge of position with respect to the dimensions of personality we have discussed, these dimensions have not figured prominently, if at all, in the situations of greatest practical importance to society. There are a number of reasons for this lacuna between theory and practice. In part, the discrepancy is due to the demonstrable lack of progress in developing a systematic taxonomy of personality. In part, the discrepancy derives from the fact that we do not have theories which would permit us to derive predictions for many of the situations of interest to the applied psychologist. Finally, even in situations in which predictions can be derived from our theoretical knowledge of personality, the predictions may not be of sufficient accuracy to be useful.

## Clinical and Statistical Prediction Compared

DEFINITION

How do psychologists take account of individual differences in personality in order to make predictions about persons? Two broadly contrasting methods have been used, the clinical and the statistical. The clinical method may involve any or all of the following:

1. The collection of a large body of information about a person which might include interview data, data from projective tests, and data from scores on objective tests.

2. Using these data the psychologist forms an impression of the personality of the person. The impression of the personality may, and usually does, include the ascription of genotypical characteristics—that is characteristics which are not based on descriptions of observed behaviors but which are assumed to account for or explain the observed behaviors of persons. Frequently, the clinically derived conception of an individual's personality may be influenced by the theoretical concepts of psychoanalytic psychology.

3. On the basis of the conception of the personality formed by the clinician, a prediction is made stating the probable behavior of the individual in a particular situation. For example, X will improve if given psychotherapy.

The procedure by which the clinician arrives at a conception of the individual including the precise cues used and the rules for combining these cues is not specified nor are the rules which enable the clinician to derive predictions from the conception of the individual specified. Statistical prediction may involve any or all of the following procedures:

1. The use of a limited pool of data or information which is typically in quantitative form. Such data might include rank in high school class, age, scores on paper and pencil tests of personality, and I.Q.

2. A formula is derived from an examination of the relationship between the data and the criterion to be predicted specifying the optimal procedure to be used in combining the data to arrive at a prediction. Frequently the combinatorial rules are derived from the formal use of statistical procedures resulting in a specification equation. Since the rules for combining data to arrive at a prediction are specified, the prediction may be derived by someone with little professional training or may even be done by computer.

In 1954 Meehl wrote a book in which he presented a lucid analysis of clinical and statistical prediction. Meehl began his discussion by noting that it is customary for the adherents of each method to refer to it with honorific terms and to assign pejorative terms to the other method. Thus, the adherents of the clinical method may call it dynamic, global, meaningful, holistic, and subtle, while calling the statistical method mechanical, atomistic, additive, cut and dried, and artificial. Similarly, the adherents of the statistical method are likely to assign such terms as operational, communicable, verifiable, public, and objective to it while characterizing the clinical method as mystical, transcendent, metaphysical, supermundane, and vague. After this semantic purge, Meehl presents his analysis. He begins with a distinction between the kind of data one uses and the method by which the data are combined. The data from which one derives predictions may be clinical, statistical or mixed. The terms, "clinical data" and "statistical data," as used here, will define a continuum representing the degree to which human judgment is involved in the measurement procedures which permit the assignment of a number or a category to a person. At one end of the continuum one might have such data as age, height, weight, and scores on a paper and pencil test where the scoring procedure was sufficiently detailed as to permit machine scoring of the test. At the other extreme one might have judgments about genotypical characteristics on the basis of projective test data and/or interview data. An example would be the judgment of latent homosexuality derived from an interpretation of a Rorschach protocol. An example of data which are intermediate on this continuum might be the score for "good form" responses on the Rorschach. There are scoring rules for this type of response but an element of judgment is involved in the application of the rules. The data from which predictions are derived may be more or less purely statistical, purely clinical, or may contain mixtures of both kinds of data.

The data from which a prediction is derived may be combined by statistical or clinical procedures. Statistical combinations, in rough agreement with our previous usage, refer to combination procedures in which no element of human judgment enter. They may be of two types—formal and informal. The former are those which use formal statistical procedures to derive optimal specification equations, typically multiple regression equations. The latter contain rules which are not derived from formal statistical procedures. An example of such an informal statistical method of combining data might be to obtain the algebraic sum of all positive and negative signs. Clinical methods of combining data are those for which there does not exist a complete specification of the procedures to be followed in arriving at a prediction. Of necessity, human judgment is involved in the process of using data to arrive at a clinical prediction.

The criterion to be predicted usually, if not invariably, involves clinical judgments—although this may not be immediately apparent. Consider some examples. If the criterion is recidivism it is obvious that at some point a judge or a parole officer must decide whether or not a particular action of a parolee constitutes a violation of parole. Improvement in psychotherapy typically is measured in terms of the judgments of the therapist. Grade point average involves averaging a variety of independent judgments by different professors.

We can summarize our discussion up to this point by asserting that the prediction situation with which we are concerned involves the prediction of a clinical criterion by a variety of procedures involving various combinations of clinical and statistical data combined by clinical or statistical procedures.

In addition to the obvious question of the effectiveness (accuracy) of these various kinds of predictions there are a number of other questions which can be raised about them. Meehl (1954) considers whether clinical methods of combining data are, in terms of the underlying process involved, fundamentally different from statistical methods of combining data. It can be argued that clinical methods of combining data simply duplicate statistical methods. When faced with such a task the clinician searches his memory and attempts to assess the predictive value of a number of cues present in the data and then assigns an appropriate weight and arrives at a prediction. Such a view of clinical combinations of data would imply that they are inefficient procedures which, with respect to the process by which a prediction is derived, essentially duplicate formal statistical procedures. There are at least two arguments against such a view of clinical methods of combining data. First, the clinician might take account of a datum that has never occurred before which would lead him to change his prediction. For example, a particular person might always attend the movies on Friday night. A statistical prediction would imply that the probability of that person going to the movies on Firday night is 1.00. A clinician asked to predict whether that person will attend the movies Friday night would predict that he would not if he knew that the person was hospitalized for an illness. No statistical formula could duplicate this prediction because the datum whose occurrence changes the prediction may never have been present before and, as a result, its weighting could not be assigned on the basis of an examination of the predictive relationships which have held in the past. The second respect in which the clinician may not simply duplicate the statistical method of combining data derives from the clinician's ability to form hypotheses. A statistical method of combining data bridges the gap between data and prediction without the intervention of a theory or hypothesis about the personality of the individual to which the prediction refers. The statistical formula merely codifies the past relationships between data and criterion. The process of hypothesis formation in this context is analagous to theory formation in science in that no hypothesis or theory is ever a simple implication of a body of facts. This process, in Jerome Bruner's felicitous phrase, involves going beyond the information given. Meehl gives the following dramatic example of an act of hypothesis formation in clinical work taken from Reik:

> One session at this time took the following course. After a few sentences about the uneventful day, the patient fell into a long silence. She assured me that nothing was in her thoughts. Silence from me. After many minutes she continued about a toothache. She told me that she had been to the dentist yesterday. He had given her an injection and then had pulled a wisdom tooth. The spot was hurting again. New and longer silence. She pointed to my bookcase in the corner and said, "There is a book standing on its head." Without the slightest hesitation and in a reproachful voice I said, "But why did you not tell me you had an abortion."

(From Reik, T., 1948 as cited in Meehl, 1954)

Obviously, no statistical method of combining data could duplicate this dramatic prediction.

## Reviews of Studies Involving Prediction of Socially Relevant Criteria

We have argued that clinical methods of combining data are fundamentally different from statistical methods and further, that clinical methods may, in principle, be superior to statistical means of combining data. However, this tells us nothing about how these methods compare in accuracy of prediction in practice. Meehl was able to find 16–20 studies in which some direct comparison of the accuracy of clinical and statistical prediction was possible. Meehl's analysis of these data indicated that in all but one study (and there were valid reasons to doubt the results of this study) the statistical method of combining data was superior to the clinical method. Consider two of the studies reviewed by Meehl. Sarbin (1942) did a study comparing clinical and statistical methods of predicting grade point average. The statistical procedure used statistical data—rank in high school class and scores on college aptitude tests. The data were combined statistically by use of a two variable regression equation. The clinical predictions were made by individuals working in the college admissions office. They were given the data used in the statistical prediction, and, in addition, they were given an opportunity to interview the individuals, and they were given access to data from psychological tests. The correlations between the predicted scores and the obtained grade point averages for the clinical predictions were .35 for men and .69 for women. The statistical predictions correlated with the obtained grade point averages .45 for women and .70 for men. In addition to the slight superiority of the statistical method there was one other interesting finding in Sarbin's study. He found that the correlation of the statistical data with the clinical prediction was higher than the correlation of that data with the statistical prediction. Apparently, though given an amount of information which exceeded that used by the statistical formula, the clinician relied on the statistical data to a greater and nonoptimal extent than the statistical means of combining the data.

In another study reviewed by Meehl the statistical method of combining data was clearly superior to the clinical method. Wittman (as cited in Meehl, 1954) prepared a scale of 30 variables which were assumed, on the basis of clinical intuition and research, to be related to prognosis for recovery from schizophrenia. The variables ranged from factual data to genotypical judgments—for example, is the patient oral erotic or anal erotic. The statistical means of arriving at a prediction were informal involving the addition of positive signs. The statistical means of combining data in this study represents a rather crude quantification of clinical judgment. The clinical prediction with which it was compared was the pooled judgments of four psychiatrists based on the case history of the patients. The statistical prediction was correct in 81 percent of the cases, the clinical in 44 percent. In a follow-up study, the 30 variable prognosis scale was correct in 68 percent of the cases and the clinical prediction was correct in 41 percent of the cases.

Meehl points out that the majority of studies reviewed by him involve predictions of one of three things, grade point average, recidivism, and recovery from psychosis. On the basis of his review of the available data, Meehl concluded that the statistical method of combining data was superior to the clinical method of combining data when the criterion to be predicted was a rather broad category of behavior. Meehl's analysis generated a considerable amount of controversy and further empirical research. In 1966, Sawyer reviewed 45 studies dealing with this issue. The studies reviewed by Sawyer may be generally characterized as follows: The majority of studies deal with subjects who were either college students, men in the armed services, or patients in mental hospitals. The most frequent criteria predicted were grades, response to therapy, and parole violation. In about one half the studies the clinician making the prediction was a psychologist or a psychiatrist. The statistical method of combining data was usually by means of a multiple regression equation. Sawyer attempts to go beyond Meehl's summary by considering not only the procedures used to combine the data but also the kinds of data which are combined. Sawyer categorizes the studies into eight classes:

1. Clinical data combined clinically.
2. Clinical data combined statistically.

3. Statistical data combined clinically.

4. Statistical data combined statistically.

5. Mixed data (both statistical and clinical) combined clinically.

6. Mixed data combined statistically.

7. Clinical synthesis in which the statistical prediction is given to the clinician.

8. Mechanical synthesis in which the clinical prediction is included as a datum in the statistical prediction.

Table 8.1 presents the results of all the comparisons among these types of predictions. One of the things which emerges from an examination of the data in Table 8.1 is the extreme orderliness of the data. If a particular method of prediction is superior to another in one comparison it is equal or superior to that method in all other comparisons reported in the literature. There is a substantial degree of agreement among diverse studies. Table 8.1 also indicates that for all kinds of data statistical methods of combining data are invariably equal to or superior to clinical methods of combining data. This can be seen rather more clearly in Table 8.2 which provides a summary of the data in Table 8.1. In each of the cells of Table 8.2 are entered the number of times a particular method was superior to any other plus one half the number of times it was equal to any other method. Note that the column representing statistical means of combining data is always clearly higher than the column representing clinical means of combining data. Sawyer notes that there is some slight indication in the data summarizing studies of clinical and statistical prediction that mixed data combined statistically may be superior to statistical data combined statistically. Thus, the clinician may contribute to superior prediction when his contribution is confined to the data acquisition phase of prediction. However, this possibility is merely hinted at in the data and is nowhere near as clear as the data indicating that the clinician is inferior to the statistical formula when combining data.

There are at least two studies which challenge this generalization. Holt (1958; Holt & Luborsky, 1958a,b) has championed the clinician's role in prediction. Holt argues that the studies reviewed by Meehl involve comparisons between statistical prediction and what he calls naive clinical prediction as opposed to "sophisticated" clinical prediction. Sophisticated clinical prediction involves a detailed analysis of the requirements for success on the criterion and includes systematic data on the relationships between the predictor variables and the criterion. Holt and Luborsky (1958a,b) report data on the results of an intensive effort to develop sophisticated clinical predictions of success in psychiatry. Their subjects were physicians who applied for residency training at the Menninger Clinic over a six-year period. The principal criteria they used were ratings

TABLE 8.1

Conclusions from 45 Clinical—Statistical Prediction Studies

| | Number of comparisons in which the row method surpassed, equaled, and was surpassed by the column method | | | | | | | | Number of studies | Number of comparisons | Percentage of comparisons | | |
| Method | 1 | 2 | 3 | 4 | 5 | 6 | 7 | 8 | | | Superior | Equal | Inferior |
|---|---|---|---|---|---|---|---|---|---|---|---|---|---|
| 1. Pure clinical | — | 0-3-1 | 0-0-0 | 0-0-2 | 0-0-0 | 0-1-1 | 0-0-0 | 0-0-2 | 7 | 10 | 0 | 40 | 60 |
| 2. Trait ratings | | — | 0-0-0 | 0-3-1 | 0-3-0 | 0-0-1 | 0-1-0 | 0-0-1 | 9 | 14 | 7 | 72 | 21 |
| 3. Profile interpretation | | | — | 0-7-3 | 0-2-0 | 0-0-0 | 0-1-0 | 0-0-0 | 12 | 13 | 0 | 77 | 23 |
| 4. Pure statistical | | | | — | 5-9-0 | 0-2-0 | 0-2-0 | 0-7-0 | 28 | 41 | 27 | 73 | 0 |
| 5. Clinical composite | | | | | — | 0-1-4 | 0-2-0 | 0-1-7 | 25 | 34 | 0 | 53 | 47 |
| 6. Mechanical composite | | | | | | — | 0-0-0 | 0-2-0 | 8 | 12 | 50 | 50 | 0 |
| 7. Clinical synthesis | | | | | | | — | 0-0-0 | 3 | 6 | 0 | 100 | 0 |
| 8. Mechanical synthesis | | | | | | | | — | 11 | 20 | 50 | 50 | 0 |

From J. Sawyer, Measurement and prediction, clinical and statistical. *Psychological Bulletin*, 1966, **66**, 178–200.

TABLE 8.2

*Summary of Conclusions from 45 Clinical–Statistical Studies*

| Mode of data collection | Mode of data combination | | | |
| --- | --- | --- | --- | --- |
| | Clinical | | Mechanical | |
| Clinical | 1. Pure clinical | 20% | 2. Trait ratings | 43% |
| Mechanical | 3. Profile interpretation | 38% | 4. Pure statistical | 63% |
| Both | 5. Clinical composite | 26% | 6. Mechanical composite | 75% |
| Either or both[a] | 7. Clinical synthesis | 50% | 8. Mechanical synthesis | 75% |

From J. Sawyer, Measurement and prediction, clinical and statistical. *Psychological Bulletin*, 1966, **66**, 178–200.

Note: In each cell is the percentage of the comparisons in which the method surpassed, plus one half the percentage of the comparisons in which it equaled, the other method.

[a] Plus, for the clinical synthesis, the prediction of Method 2, 4, or 6; or, for the mechanical synthesis, the prediction of Method 1, 3, or 5.

by psychiatrists who acted as supervisors of the residents and ratings by their peers in various aspects of psychiatric work. The judgments of peers and supervisors were factor analyzed separately and in each case one clear factor emerged reflecting general competence in psychiatry. The intersubjective agreement among raters was high. In addition, the correlation between peer and supervisors ratings of competence was high, $r = .8$. The principal criteria against which predictions were to be evaluated were supervisor and peer ratings of overall competence.

Holt and Luborsky attempted to develop rules for scoring several kinds of clinical data obtained from such tests as the word association test, the Rorschach, the TAT, and the Wechsler–Bellevue scales. These rules attempted to objectify various signs and indices derived from the test which might be useful in prediction. Although a great deal of effort went into this effort, the results were for the most part disappointing. The rules which seemed promising when developed for the first four classes failed to predict competence among the fifth and sixth classes. Holt and Luborsky built another experiment in to their prediction study. They gave the clinicians who were to make predictions various parts of the data. They found that the clinicians were able to predict most accurately when they were presented with the total data contained in each resident's folder. The claim for the efficacy of sophisticated clinical prediction rests on the use of all of the data available to the clinician. The data included TAT, Rorschach, Wechsler–Bellevue, interview data, and a complete application folder. The results obtained were as follows: Judge 1's predictions correlated with supervisors ratings, $r = .57$ and with peer's ratings $r = .48$. Judge 2's predictions correlated with supervisor ratings .22 and with peer ratings .48.

Holt and Luborsky were committed from the outset of their investigation to the use of sophisticated clinical prediction. Consequently, little effort was placed on the use of statistical data or statistical methods of combination. However, they report some attempts at statistical prediction. They found that a psychologists scale from the Strong Interest Inventory designed to predict success in experimental psychology correlated .21 and .22 with supervisor and peer evaluations of competence. The best single predictor was verbal I.Q. which had a correlation with the criterion of supervisor ratings of .47. The best multiple correlation combining verbal I.Q., the Strong psychology scale, and some Rorschach indices was .56 against the criterion of supervisor ratings. However, Holt and Luborsky point out that the statistical predictions did not cross validate. The statistical predictions were derived from classes five and six. When they were used to postdict the ratings of the first four classes the validity correlations were decreased. The verbal I.Q. correlated .00 with supervisor ratings for class four and .27 for classes one through four. The regression equation yielding a multiple correlation of .56 when cross validated against supervisors ratings for classes one through four shrank to .13. Without the use of the Rorschach which seemed to be the least stable predictor, the multiple regression equation yielded a correlation of .24 against the criterion of supervisors ratings for classes one through three (class four being atypical in some respects was omitted in this test). On the basis of the disappointing results in cross validation Holt and Luborsky argue that sophisticated clinical methods are superior to statistical methods when predicting such complex criteria as success in psychiatry.

Since Holt and Luborsky's study represents one of the very few studies in which clinical prediction was superior to statistical prediction we shall examine it quite carefully to see if their conclusion is warranted. Perhaps the first point to note about the study was that very little effort was expended in the attempt to derive valid statistical predictions. No attempt was made to use standardized personality tests such as the MMPI or the California Personality Inventory. Statistical combinations of rating scale data were not evaluated. Obviously, no advocate of statistical prediction would argue that *any* data will yield superior predictions. The efficacy of statistical procedures is invariably predicated on the attempt to use a sample of relevant data.

Second, Holt and Luborsky report that some of the clinical predictions may have been contaminated by accidental access of the clinical predictors to opinions about the residents by their supervisors. When these doubtful predictions were removed from the data analysis the correlations between Judge 1's predictions and the criteria became .52 and .32 for supervisor and peer ratings, respectively. The correlations of Judge 2's predictions with the criteria were .17 and .36 for supervisor and peer ratings, respectively. Although the point is debatable, if we assume that supervisor's ratings are more valid indices of success in psychiatry than peer ratings we have as our best estimates of the validity of sophisticated clinical prediction in the Holt and Luborsky study correlations of .52 and .17 for the two clinicians involved. This figure should be compared with a validity correlation of .56 for the multiple regression equation and .47 for verbal I.Q. alone. This comparison suggests that statistical predictions were superior or equal to the best clinical prediction and certainly superior to the average clinical prediction. Of course, Holt and Luborsky rest their argument on the demonstrable failure of the statistical procedures to cross validate. There are reasons to question the validity of the cross-validation argument. Holt and Luborsky point out that their prediction situation was rather unusual in that the individuals whose performance was being predicted changed systematically from year to year. The study started after World War II and their first subjects were veterans whose average age was about seven years greater than the average age of their last class. When the characteristics of the new sample to be predicted are significantly different from the original sample used to derive a statistical formula it is not surprising to find a drop in the value of the correlation. A somewhat fairer way of cross validating the statistical predictions in the Holt and Luborsky study would be to randomly divide the sample of class five and six residents into two groups. One group would be used to derive the statistical formula and the second group might be used to cross validate it in a sample which is not significantly different from the sample used to derive the formula. In addition to the possibility that Holt and Luborsky may not have used the most valid method of cross validating the statistical prediction there is a further difficulty with the cross validation argument. Holt and Luborsky do not cross validate their clinician's predictions. They assume that the one clinician who was successful would be successful if he were to predict the ratings of another class. But this is conjecture, not fact. There is at least one reason to believe that Judge 1 would not be able to achieve a validity correlation as high as .52 in a replication. The value of .52 was one of four validity correlations reported and was higher than the other three. According to the law of statistical regression a unit with an extreme value in a distribution on replication would be expected to have a value between the original value and the mean of the distribution. In summary, the alleged superiority of the sophisticated clinical method in the Holt and Luborsky study rests on an assumption which might not be valid.

One of the clearest examples of the superiority of clinical prediction over statistical prediction is contained in a study by Lindzey (1965; see also Meehl, 1965). He reported an attempt to predict homosexuality using the TAT. The subjects were 40 male college students, 20 were admitted homosexuals and 20 subjects had no known history of homosexuality. A clinician experienced in the use of the TAT was able to correctly assign 95 percent of the subjects to the correct category (homosexual versus nonhomosexual) on the basis of their TAT stories. The best statistical prediction obtained from these data was an unweighted sum of TAT signs which was able to achieve correct classification for 85 percent of the protocols. In a follow-up study predicting homosexuality among a sample of 30 male prisoners, two clinicians were able to achieve correct classification of the protocols in 80 and 60 percent of the cases, respectively. The unweighted sum of TAT signs used for the college students achieved correct classification in 57 percent of the cases. This second study is not, strictly speaking, a study of the efficacy of statistical prediction but is rather a study of the generality of the statistical formula from one group to a second group. Ideally, a comparison of the statistical and clinical methods of prediction for the prison group should have been preceded by the development of a statistical formula for that group. However, the first study reported by Lindzey clearly indicates the superiority of the clinical method of combining TAT data to predict homosexuality. In commenting on these results Lindzey refers to the psychometric intractability of the TAT. Apparently, all of the cues contained in the extended verbal material of the TAT cannot easily be classified and used for prediction.

REVIEW OF STUDIES INVOLVING THE PREDICTION
OF PERSONALITY CHARACTERISTICS

It is interesting to note that in the one study in which we have clear evidence of the superiority of the clinician the criterion predicted is a specific personality characteristic. In the studies reviewed by Meehl and Sawyer the criteria were usually outcome variables. That is, the criteria did not require a clinician to predict what a person is like but rather the expected outcome of the individual's performance in some situation— for example, psychotherapy, parole, college, etc. It may very well be that such predictions are clinically meaningless. The clinician might argue that a person's response to therapy would depend on such variables as the personality of the therapist and the methods of therapy which are used (see McArthur, 1966). It is characteristic of the attempt to predict outcome variables that the clinician has incomplete information about the characteristics of the environment which are likely to impinge on an individual and affect the outcome. Consequently, the efficacy of clinical prediction might be more reasonably tested in situations in which the clinician attempts to develop descriptions of personality. We have already noted that the clinician may form an impression or conception of personality as an intermediate step in the attempt to derive predictions of outcome variables. Perhaps the clinician is able to arrive at a satisfactory conception of the individual but this conception may not permit adequate prediction of outcome variables.

When we turn to studies of the prediction of personality characteristics we face an immediate problem. What criteria shall be used. Suppose we want to decide whether a clinician's assertion that, "X is a latent homosexual" is correct or not. Typically our only criterion is the clinical judgment asserting this. Two methods have been used to circumvent this difficulty. The first method derives from the psychometric rule that reliability sets an upper boundary to validity. In this context, reliability refers to the degree of inter-subjective agreement among clinicians. If clinicians do not agree among themselves then the question of the validity of their individual assertions is without object. Of course if the clinicians were to agree among themselves, for example, X is a latent homosexual, this does not imply that the judgment is valid. Hence reliability is necessary but not sufficient for validity. Evidence of lack of reliability becomes evidence of lack of validity. The second attempt to arrive at criteria for personality descriptions involves the use of therapist's judgments as a basis of validating descriptions of a person.

Goldberg and Werts (1966) studied the reliability of clinical judgments of four traits, social adjustment, ego strength, intelligence, and dependency. Their approach was based on Campbell and Fiske's (1959) multitrait–multimethod matrix. Fundamental to this analysis of validity is the attempt to show that different methods of measurement of the same trait agree among themselves to a greater extent than the agreement obtained by measuring different traits by the same method of measurement. If the latter agreement is greater than the former agreement this would imply that the tests are predominantly measures of method variance rather than trait variance (see Chapter 2). In the Goldberg and Werts study each clinical psychologist was given a different source of data for his prediction. The data used were derived from the MMPI, Wechsler–Bellevue, Rorschach, and the vocational history. The degree of agreement among the four clinical psychologists for each of the traits predicted with each using data from a different source was .17 for social adjustment, −.01 for ego strength, .25 for intelligence, and .11 for dependency. The average agreement for all four traits was .11. These data indicate quite clearly that psychologists using different sources of data as a basis for prediction of personality characteristics simply do not agree among themselves. These data, if given the usual interpretation, would imply that each of the measures is method specific and that none of them clearly permits the inference of personality characteristics. The advocate of clinical prediction would, however, have valid grounds for complaint against the study. He might argue that the procedure followed here violates clinical practice in the interest of research design. The clinician would rarely attempt to describe a person using a single data source but would rather attempt to form an impression by integrating all of the data available.

Sines (1966) has argued that clinical descriptions cannot be valid because they are not reliable. He cites his analysis of data from a study by Lewinsohn, Nichols, Pulos, Lamont, Nickel, & Siskind (1963) in support of this conclusion. Lewinsohn *et al.* had psychologists describe patients using data in hospital charts and psychological test data. The descriptions of a common set of traits were categorized into two groups by Sines—the phenotypical and the genotypical. The distinction rests on the degree of inference from observation which is involved in the description. For example, if a psychologist asserts that a person is likely to become angry when threatened his assertion, though involving some interpretation of observations, refers to behaviors which are relatively public and observable. On the other hand when a psychologist asserts that a person has unconscious hostility toward his mother, the assertion does not directly refer to behaviors which are more or less observable. Rather it involves a complex inference from what is observed. Sines' analysis of the Lewinsohn *et al.* data indicated that the intersubjective agreement among clinicians for the genotypical trait descriptions was .17 and for those classified as phenotypical the agreement was .51. Sines argues that clinical judgments of genotypical characteristics are not valid. The clinician should thus be limited to a description of characteristics which are observable. Such an argument, in effect, asserts that the clinician has no special competence to go beyond the kinds of descriptions which any intelligent observer of an individual might make. And, where the clinician does go beyond a description of behavior to attempt to find underlying causes by introducing genotypical characteristics his judgments are likely to be invalid. (See also Mischel, 1968 for a similar view.)

Before evaluating this rather sweeping conclusion we shall review other relevant studies. Two studies have been reported which attempt to validate clinical predictions by using as a criterion descriptions of patients by psychotherapists who, presumably, know the patients well. Silverman

(1959) dealt with the validity of projective tests. His study dealt with an attempt to validate clinical data combined clinically against a criterion of therapists descriptions. The clinicians who participated in the study were given Rorschach, TAT, drawings of house and tree, and a most unpleasant concept test. The choice of instruments was, with the possible exception of omission of data from the Wechsler–Bellevue test of intelligence, a more or less typical battery of diagnostic tests. Therapists were asked to describe their patients by doing a $Q$ sort. In this procedure the therapist is handed a deck of cards containing descriptive statements and he sorts them into two piles—those which are applicable to the patient and those which are not. In order to control for the "Barnum effect," that is, the assignment of trivial descriptions which apply to everyone and which therefore lead to spuriously high agreement, Silverman had each of the therapists do a $Q$ sort for a second patient (control) whose projective test data were not given to the clinicians. The clinical psychologists predicted the $Q$ sorts of the patient whose projective test data they analyzed. The predictions were correlated with the therapists' $Q$ sorts for that patient and for the second control patient. Silverman divided the $Q$ sorts into six areas—motivational needs and affects, character traits, diagnosis and symptoms, interpersonal behavior, and infancy and childhood perceptions. Table 8.3 presents the correlations between the predictions and $Q$ sorts for the patient and the control patient for each of the six areas. With the possible exception of the area of character traits there is little evidence for successful prediction. The overall validity correlation for all areas was .28. The correlation of the predictions with the $Q$ sorts of the control patients was .14, indicating that even the low value of .28 is in fact inflated by the Barnum effect.

In Silverman's study the clinician was not given an opportunity to actually administer the projective tests. He worked from blind protocols

TABLE 8.3

*Validity Coefficients Obtained by Silverman*

| Item | Patients | Controls |
|---|---|---|
| Defenses | .16 | .08 |
| Motivational needs and affects | .23 | .07 |
| Character traits | .44 | .16 |
| Diagnosis and symptoms | .43 | .32 |
| Interpersonal behavior | .14 | .03 |
| Infancy and childhood perceptions | .32 | .18 |

From L. H. Silverman, A $Q$-sort study of the validity of evaluations made from projective techniques. *Psychological Monographs*, 1959, **73** (Whole No. 477).

and as a result he might have missed many cues which would have improved the validity of his predictions. Marks (1961) has reported a study of clinical prediction in a child guidance clinic. In his study the clinicians were given an opportunity to administer tests to patients and to conduct a full diagnostic interview. The clinician used a variety of diagnostic tests (the modal number of tests used by each clinician was three) typically including such tests as the Draw a Person Test, Rorschach test, and the Stanford–Binet test of intelligence. The criterion used was therapists $Q$ sorts of patients. The correlations of the judges' predictions with the therapists' $Q$ sorts ranged from .09 to .32 with an average validity correlation of .22. This value is rather close to that obtained by Silverman. These data suggest that the addition of a diagnostic interview does not appreciably increase the accuracy of clinical descriptions.

There are several studies which bear on the validity of clinical descriptions of personality which have as their central focus the study of differences among clinicians of different degrees of experience. These studies rather uniformly indicate that clinical experience is not related to accuracy of description or prediction.

Sarbin, Taft, and Bailey (1960) reviewed several studies dealing with this question and concluded that there was no clear evidence that psychological training or experience was related to ability to predict and describe personality. More recent studies have supported this conclusion. Goldberg (1959) compared the accuracy of different groups of individuals in predicting organic brain damage from Bender–Gestalt protocols. The choice of task is highly relevant to clinical practice since the Bender–Gestalt is typically used as a screening test to detect patients suffering from organic brain damage. Goldberg used three groups of judges in his study, clinical psychologists with 4–10 years experience, clinical psychology trainees with 1–4 years of clinical experience, and secretaries with no psychological training. The secretaries were told that the Bender–Gestalt test is used to detect organic brain damage and they were asked to predict which protocols were made by individuals who were brain damaged. Some of the protocols were obtained from individuals who had a confirmed neurological diagnosis of brain damage and other protocols came from patients for whom there was no indication of brain damage. Goldberg found that the experienced clinicians were correct in their judgments in 65 percent of the cases, the trainees were correct in 70 percent of the cases, and the secretaries were correct in 67 percent of the cases. Goldberg concludes that the Bender–Gestalt is of some use in detecting organic brain damage. But it is useful in those cases in which the manifestations of the damage in the test protocols are so gross and obvious that they may be detected by individuals with no professional training.

Turner (1966) investigated the effect of professional training on skill in predicting from the Rorschach. Turner used four groups of 25 judges in his study. The groups were composed of individuals who were fellows of the society of projective techniques and who were experts in the use of the Rorschach, recently graduated Ph.D.s in clinical psychology, graduate students in clinical psychology, and a group of undergraduates with no familiarity with the Rorschach. The judges were required to predict statements about patients in a mental hospital made by the hospital staff. Only statements for which there was agreement among the staff were included. Each of the 4 groups of judges achieved approximately 65 percent accuracy of prediction.

The studies we have reviewed dealing with clinically derived predictions and descriptions of personality characteristics suggest that such descriptions have little validity. There is little evidence that experience in the use of clinical data permits psychologists to make inferences about personality which are valid and reliable. The data we have reviewed rather strongly challenges the emphasis on diagnostic skills in the training of clinical psychologists. Such training is generally given in the belief that experience and sophistication in the use of clinical data will permit the psychologist to make valid inferences about the personality characteristics of persons— particularly about the genotypical foundations of personality. The evidence we have reviewed does not support this belief.

We have dealt with clinical predictions of personality characteristics. Is it possible to describe personality by statistical procedures? Halbower (as cited in Meehl, 1956) has reported a study comparing clinical and statistical descriptions of personality. Halbower developed a set of rules which would permit him to classify 58 percent of the MMPI profiles of a group of outpatients in a mental hygiene clinic into four profile types. In order to develop a statistical description of personality he selected at random five patients in each of the four profile groups. The therapists of these patients filled in a 154-item $Q$ sort which contained predominantly phenotypical items. The average response of the five patients sharing a code classification was used as a basis for developing what Meehl (1956) calls a "cookbook" description of personality. These descriptions were cross-validated against therapist $Q$ sorts for additional outpatients of the mental hygiene clinic. The validity correlations for each of the four profile descriptions were .68, .69, .84, and .88. When the descriptions were cross validated with a group of inpatients in an attempt to test the generality of the descriptions the validities were somewhat lower, dropping as low as .36. The median correlation for all eight descriptions was .69. Halbower compared these predictions with clinical predictions based on MMPI profiles. The validities obtained for the clinical predictions using the same sets of profiles ranged from .29 to .63 with a median value of .46. The statistical predictions were clearly superior to the predictions of the clinicians based on statistical data combined by clinical procedures. Note also that the validities obtained in Halbower's study were considerably higher than the validities reported by Marks and Silverman for clinical predictions of clinical data combined by clinical procedures for a similar criterion, therapists' $Q$ sorts. However, such comparisons must be made cautiously. For one thing Halbower's rules for classifying MMPI profiles permit him to make predictions in only 58 percent of the cases. However, in principle, the procedure could be extended to permit classification of a larger number of MMPI profiles. Another important difference between the Halbower study and the Silverman study was that Silverman had a relatively large number of genotypical descriptions in his investigation whereas Halbower did not. And, as we have seen, there is some data indicating that genotypical characteristics may be more difficult to predict than phenotypical descriptions. However, Marks had his clinicians predict predominantly phenotypical characteristics. Despite these qualifications and reservations the results of the Halbower study suggest that statistical descriptions of personality are possible and, that they may be more valid than descriptions derived from clinical or mixed data combined clinically.

Marks and Seeman (1963) have attempted to use the MMPI as a basis for statistical description of abnormal personality. Using their clinical experience they devised rules which would permit the unambiguous classification of MMPI profiles into 16 categories. These rules could be used to classify approximately 80 percent of the profiles of the patients in their sample. They then had patients' therapists, or, if the therapist was not available someone working from the therapist's notes, pick the 12 adjectives which were most descriptive of the patient and the 12 adjectives which were least descriptive from a list of 108 predominantly phenotypical descriptive adjectives. By noting adjectives which were consistently associated as descriptive or not descriptive of individuals sharing a profile classification Marks and Seeman were able to develop a series of 16 personality descriptions which may be used to characterize an individual with any of the 16 MMPI profiles. Marks and Seeman's book represents an attempt to automate the process of personality description in clinical settings.

A similar, but somewhat more radically statistical approach to the development of personality descriptions has been reported by Sines (1966). Sines attempted to develop classifications of MMPI profiles without the use of clinical intuition as a basis for the initial classification. Sines relied on the statistic $D^2$ for this purpose. Given any two profiles of scores on a set of scales their similarity may be assessed by obtaining the squared difference between scores on each of the scales and summing the squared differences. This sum is called $D^2$. By setting a value of $D^2$ which is arbitrarily low, pairs of profiles may be selected which are only minimally different from each other. Sines classifies profiles as belonging to the same type if and only if the value of $D^2$ obtained by comparing a profile to some hypothetical profile—defined by a set of values for each scale—is less than some minimal value. By this procedure it is possible to classify profile types.

Sines then attempted to develop statistical descriptions of personality. For this purpose he took the folders of a group of patients in a mental hospital. The folders contained descriptions of the patients by official hospital personnel, such as social workers, psychologists, psychiatrists, ward personnel, etc. Then Sines recorded *every* descriptive statement made about the patient. He has developed a coding system which contains 2500 descriptors which summarizes the total set of descriptors used by the hospital personnel. Sines then noted that many descriptors were more or less synonymous. He was able to group the descriptors into categories indicating roughly comparable descriptions. Table 8.4 provides an example

TABLE 8.4

*Range of Statements Considered To Be Synonymous with a Coded Descriptor*

---

Descriptor statement
0332035 shows symptoms of anxiety and tension

  Equivalent statements:
    anxiety
    anxiety tension state
    anxious expectation
    became acutely upset shortly after her move to a new town
    complained of feeling nervous
    complained of marked nervousness
    complained of nervous exhaustion
    complains that she has continued to be nervous and upset
    cries uncontrollably, cannot sit down, cannot walk, became so tense that she
      had to run out in the yard
    denied emotional factor in symptoms of tenseness and nervousness
    general nervousness, fears, and physical symptoms of anxiety for 15 years
    nervous
    nervous and upset
    nervous exhaustion
    nervousness
    nervousness for a number of years
    seen originally for nervousness
    shows anxiety
    symptoms of anxiety
    talks about feeling nervous
    tense
    tense feelings
    tension
    unbearable tension prior to treatment

---

Based on Sines, 1966.

TABLE 8.5

*Descriptors Statistically More Frequent among Members of the 4–3 Male Group*

| Code | Statement | Code | Statement |
|------|-----------|------|-----------|
| 0100032 | Close to own children | 0337027 | Chest X-ray negative for TB |
| 0200037 | Quit school before grade 12 | 0338045 | Escaped from hospital one or more times |
| 0303018 | Emotional instability | | |
| 0303054 | Worried | 0501007 | Dependent on father |
| 0312036 | No history of seizures | 0501019 | Father is physically ill |
| 0314007 | Coherent | 0501028 | Father was rejecting |
| 0314017 | General information good | 0501035 | Relationship with father is not close |
| 0314022 | Lack of judgment | | |
| 0314044 | Denies hallucinations | 0502047 | Closer to mother than father |
| 0315035 | Diagnosis: schizophrenic reaction, chronic undifferentiated type | 0502071 | Mother is quite talkative |
| | | 0503009 | Dependent upon parents |
| | | 0503039 | Relates well to parents |
| 0316008 | Some loss of auditory acuity | 0602019 | Feels inferior to siblings |
| 0322053 | Facial scars | 0701002 | Age: 25–29 |
| 0323040 | Height: 6 ft. | 0703015 | Not interested in sports |
| 0325025 | Little if any insight | 0706019 | Planning or has planned to divorce spouse |
| 0325049 | Seclusive | | |
| 0326028 | History of several accidents | 0707008 | Preoccupied with personal appearance |
| 0332009 | Defensive | | |
| 0332010 | Demanding | 0709021 | Did not attend church regularly |
| 0332031 | Seeks attention | 0711006 | History of nomadic behavior |
| 0332039 | Timid | 0713004 | Socializes well |
| 0332058 | Impulsive | 0713009 | Financial irresponsibility |
| 0332059 | Ingratiating manner | 0713012 | Well liked by others |
| 0332064 | Manipulative | 0714005 | Attracted to young girls |
| 0332081 | History of hostile or aggressive behavior | 0716007 | Denies excessive drinking |
| | | 0716017 | Turns to alcohol during periods of stress |
| 0332089 | Said to be a follower | | |
| 0333023 | Immature | 0718008 | History of trouble with the law |
| 0333027 | Lack of sense of responsibility | 0719001 | Enlisted in armed forces |
| 0333043 | Sensitive | 0801036 | Spouse rejects patient |
| 0333066 | Uses projection | 0801071 | Antagonistic and hostile toward spouse |
| 0342006 | Talkative | | |
| 0343000 | Attempted suicide | 0900009 | Occupation is unskilled or semiskilled |
| 0343002 | Does not appear to be suicidal | | |
| 0343004 | Made suicidal threats | 0900031 | Irregular work pattern while in the hospital |
| 0345015 | Previous psychiatric treatment | | |
| 0345017 | Previously treated with EST | | |

Based on Sines, 1966.

TABLE 8.6

*Selected Characteristics of Prisoners Who Generate a 4–3 MMPI Profile*

| Offense | Number | Percent | Offense | Number | Percent |
|---------|--------|---------|---------|--------|---------|
| Murder | 8 | 44 | Total convicted of | | |
| Rape | 6 | 33 | crimes of violence | 14 | 78 |
| Armed robbery | 3 | 17 | Paternal absence | | |
| Burglary | 3 | 17 | or rejection | 10 | 56 |
| Bad checks | 1 | 5.5 | | | |

Based on Sines, 1966.

of the range of descriptors included under the rubric of anxiety and nervous tension.

By coding all of the statements in a patient's record, Sines is able to discover if certain descriptors are frequently associated with certain empirically derived MMPI profiles—thereby developing a statistical description of personality. An example of the type of description which is possible is given in Table 8.5 which presents descriptors associated with a particular MMPI profile in a university hospital population. Note that persons with this MMPI profile seem to be self-centered and nonsocial and to respond with aggressive behavior in threatening situations. This statistically derived prediction was cross-validated in a prison sample. Sines found that approximately 5 percent of the prisoners had this profile as compared with 1 percent of the patients in the university hospital. Table 8.6 presents the descriptors assigned to individuals in the prison sample. Examination of Table 8.6 indicates that individuals in the prison sample with this profile are likely to have committed crimes of violence. Again antisocial and violent behavior seems characteristic of individuals with this profile.

The work we have reviewed in this chapter on the development of statistical descriptions of the total personality has been confined to one test, the MMPI, and there has been relatively little attempt to demonstrate that such statistically derived descriptions have validity for a wide range of subject groups. However, the preliminary data we have suggests that such descriptions are possible and that they may be more valid than the more typical diagnostic descriptions based on clinical data clinically combined.

## The Process of Prediction

### CONFIGURAL VERSUS LINEAR PREDICTION

Our discussion of clinical and statistical prediction has focused on the accuracy of such predictions. In this section we focus on research which attempts to elucidate the process by which predictions are made. One focus of process research in this area deals with the extent to which persons use nonlinear combinations when making predictions. Much of this research initially stemmed from the belief that clinicians might be superior to statistical formulas in their ability to combine data in nonlinear ways. What is involved in this claim stems from a consideration of the standard form of a multiple regression formula. Such a formula is a linear additive combination having the form in the case of a two-variable prediction equation of

$$aX + bY$$

where $a$ and $b$ represent appropriate constants and $X$ and $Y$ represent predictor variables. It is theoretically possible that such a linear additive combination of variables might poorly approximate the true relationship between the predictor variables and the criterion. For example, if variable $Y$ is a moderator variable such that for individuals who score high on $Y$ the correlation between $X$ and the criterion is strong and positive and for individuals who score low on $Y$ the correlation between $X$ and the criterion is strong and negative, the linear additive model will not adequately define the relationship between $X$ and $Y$ and the criterion. If the clinician is in fact able to appropriately deal with such nonlinear configural models he might have an advantage over the statistician using a standard multiple regression formula.

The alleged limitation of the statistical formula is, however, apparent rather than real. In recent years psychologists have become increasingly aware of the use of nonlinear multiple regressions (see Cohen, 1968). There is no reason why one cannot have regression equations of two variables of the form

$$aX + bY + cXY + dX^2Y + eXY^2 + fX^2Y^2 + gX^2 + hY^2$$

By considering the weightings for cross products of predictor variables and the weightings for higher powers of variables, it is possible to capture nonlinear combinations of variables. It would, however, be rather difficult in practice to discover the appropriate weightings for such nonlinear relationships where several variables are included. It would be necessary to have large numbers of subjects in order to discover the appropriate weightings of these variables. Therefore, even though it is possible, in principle, to discover nonlinear relationships using multiple regression procedures, if the relationships are complex involving interactions among several variables it might not be possible in practice to discover them.

Can clinical predictions be represented by a linear formula? Hoffman, Slovic and Rorer (1968) have used analysis of variance techniques in an attempt to gain information about this issue. They studied a prediction situation in which gastroenterologists had to decide whether a given combination of symptoms indicated that an ulcer was benign or malignant. The gastroenterologists were presented with 96 different combinations of symptoms formed by considering all possible combinations of five dichotomous variables and one variable with three values. For each combination each gastroenterologist made a prediction as to the likelihood of those symptoms being associated with a benign or malignant ulcer. By the use of analysis of variance procedures they were able to determine the portion of the variance in prediction which was attributable to main effects and to interactions. The main effects would represent the contribution of linear additive effects and the interaction would refer to nonlinear effects involving combinations or configurations of variables. They point out that 90 percent of the variance in judgments was attributable to main effects. Hence for these subjects, in this prediction situation, a simple regression equation, without the use of cross products or higher powers of variables, would be able to substantially represent the process by which these judgments were made. Of course, it is possible that the use of nonlinear relationships as represented in the 10 percent interaction variance, might occasionally contribute to greater accuracy in this type of prediction. A number of interesting additional findings emerged from this analysis of the process of prediction in gastroenterology. Hoffman, Slovic, and Rorer found that there was substantial disagreement among the predictions made by the nine radiologists in their study—six of whom were practitioners and 3 of whom trainees. The correlations of agreement among their judgments ranged from −.11 to .83 with a median value of .38.

The heavy dependence on linear combinations in the study of Hoffman, Slovic and Rorer is not unusual. Hoffman (1968) reports that, in a series of studies conducted at the Oregon Research Institute, the variance attributable to linear combinations of variables was between 64 and 80 percent. There are however, some studies in which nonlinear combinations of variables have been found. Slovic (1966) had subjects judge intelligence using two artificial cues, scores on an English Effectiveness test and need achievement scores. Both cues were assumed by the subjects to be positively related to intelligence. When a conflict between the cues occurred, for example, high English Effectiveness score and low need achievement score, subjects tended to discount the need achievement score. Thus the relationship between need achievement and intelligence was dependent upon scores on English Effectiveness, indicating that English Effectiveness acted as a moderator variable and that the relationship between these two variables and intelligence was nonlinear.

Hammond and Summers (1965) presented subjects with a concept learning prediction task in which they had to learn to combine two cues to arrive at a correct prediction. The formula that defined correct prediction involved a combination of linear and nonlinear cues. They found that subjects who were told that the relationships between the cues and the criterion as defined by the experimenter was nonlinear were able to learn to rely on the nonlinear cue.

What do these studies tell us about linear and configural prediction? It appears that, in the majority of situations studied, human judgments can generally be represented as a linear combination of several cues. Where there is a conflict between cues they may discount one of the cues thus introducing nonlinearity. Further, the Hammond and Summers study shows that human beings can learn to use nonlinear cues, if it is required by the constraints of the task presented to them. The extent of the reliance on linear cues in prediction situations should not be surprising. Green (1968) points out that as long as each cue is monotonically related to the criterion, a linear additive model will be a substantially adequate representation of the formula for cue combination. It is only when there is a nonmonotonic relationship between the cue and a criterion such that a particular cue will sometimes indicate high values and sometimes low values on the criterion, dependent upon the value of other variables, that linear representations of the process of cue combination will be truly inadequate. We have no truly convincing evidence that human beings do in fact combine cues in actual prediction situations in ways which take account of such non-monotonic relationships. This may, however, be due to the fact that the right situations have not been studied.

Are there criteria which can only be predicted accurately by nonlinear combinations of cues? Goldberg (1965) has done one of the few systematic studies of this question. He used data originally collected by Meehl (1959) in a study which compared clinical and statistical predictions using MMPI profiles of psychotics and neurotics in a sample of 861 patients from seven clinics. Clinical predictions using the MMPI profiles were made by 29 clinicians—13 clinical psychologists with the Ph.D. and 16 graduate students at the University of Minnesota. The graduate students were about as accurate as the clinical psychologists. The validity coefficients for all of the clinical predictions ranged from .14 to .39 with an average coefficient of .28, yielding approximately 62 percent correct classification. A variety of statistical rules were tried in an attempt to discover the optimal procedure for combining MMPI profiles. Goldberg found that a linear combination rule involving 5 MMPI scales was the most accurate predictor of this criterion. The rule

$$(L + Pa + Sc) - (Hy + Pt)$$

had a cross validated validity correlation of .44 and was able to correctly identify 70 percent of the cases. This linear rule was superior to the configural scoring rules devised by Meehl and Dahlstrom (1959) and it was superior to a nonlinear multiple regression equation obtained by investigating eight indices, $X$, $Y$, $X^2$, $Y^2$, $XY$, $X^2Y$, $XY^2$, and $X^2Y^2$, for each of 55 pairs of MMPI scale scores. Goldberg's results apparently indicate that his simple linear formula effectively summarizes much of the significant predictive value of the MMPI for this criterion. It is unlikely that any dramatic improvement of the prediction of neurotic and psychotic profiles on the MMPI will result from the search for more complex nonlinear scoring rules. More accurate prediction will probably be attainable only by the inclusion of new sources of data and cues into the statistical rules of combination. Data comparable to that obtained by Goldberg for other prediction situations do not exist. Although it is reasonable to assume that there are some prediction situations where nonlinear combinations will be superior to linear combinations we do not know what they are.

## Computer Simulation of Prediction

The Hoffman *et al.* (1968) study uses the analysis of variance as an analytic tool to reconstruct a subject's reliance on various cues and their combinations. Kleinmuntz (1963, 1967, 1968) has used computer simulation in an attempt to reconstruct and duplicate the process by which the clinician arrives at a decision. Kleinmuntz studied the prediction of adjustment and maladjustment among college students using the MMPI. The subjects used were college students who arrived at a college counseling center. He asked clinicians to predict to the criterion of counselors judgments of adjustment or maladjustment. He then selected a clinician who was particularly accurate in his predictions and asked him to sort MMPI profiles while speaking into a tape recorder to obtain a transcript of the reasons for various decisions. The clinician generated 60 hours of tape recorded material. Using these data as a basis, Kleinmuntz attempted to codify the rules used by the clinician in arriving at a decision. Some rules were added and the entire set of rules were programmed for a computer. Figure 8.1 presents a flow chart of the sequential series of rules which are applied by the computer. Having developed a procedure for computer simulation of this prediction process, Kleinmuntz attempted to validate the computer predictions. He found, using a variety of samples from different colleges, that computer predictions of judgments of adjustment and maladjustment by college counselors were about as accurate as the best clinical prediction of these judgments and superior to the average clinical prediction using MMPI profiles (see Table 8.7).

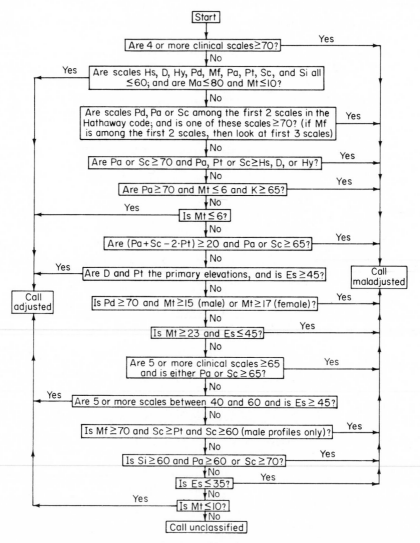

Fig. 8.1. Flow chart of MMPI decision rules. (Based on Kleinmuntz, 1968.)

Kleinmuntz's work with the MMPI indicates a general procedure for the automation of clinical judgment. It is probably the case that for any prediction situation in which the data are in quantified form, or can be fitted into a limited set of discrete categories, or are some combination of the above, that a computer simulation of clinical judgment can be developed following procedures analogous to those used by Kleinmuntz.

TABLE 8.7

*Percents Hits and Misses of Computer Programmed Rules and Clinicians with Five* MMPI *Samples*

| Sample | Computer | | Best clinician | | Average clinician | |
|---|---|---|---|---|---|---|
| | *Hits* | *Misses* | *Hits* | *Misses* | *Hits* | *Misses* |
| Brigham Young (N = 100) | 72 | 28 | 68 | 32 | 63 | 37 |
| Nebraska (N = 116) | 86 | 14 | 78 | 22 | 74 | 26 |
| Iowa (U = 155) | 65 | 35 | 65 | 35 | 61 | 39 |
| Missouri (N = 198) | 71 | 29 | 75 | 25 | 70 | 30 |
| Bucknell (N = 151) | 62 | 38 | 65 | 35 | 60 | 40 |

Based on Kleinmuntz, 1968.

Where the data from which the predictions are made are verbal materials which cannot be adequately categorized, computer simulation of prediction would be prohibited. There are two possible advantages which follow from computer simulation of clinical methods of combing data. By studying those clinicians who excel in prediction it is possible to develop a set of rules which will codify optimal prediction procedures and may even surpass them since the computer is likely to be more consistent in the application of rules. Second, once the process of codification of rules is ended, a significant economy in the cost of prediction is achieved.

## Conclusions and Implications

The research we have reviewed would appear to have practical implications. We shall consider first the implications of studies which have attempted clinical and statistical descriptions of personality characteristics. The research we have reviewed suggests that personality descriptions arrived at by clinicians on the basis of the usual diagnostic interview and projective test data may not be very valid. If a description of personality is required in clinical practice the preliminary data we have suggests that statistical descriptions obtained by the cookbook method of Halbower or Marks and Seeman may be more valid. However, it is not clear if the effort involved in developing such descriptions is worthwhile from a purely practical point of view. The descriptions are validated against a criteria of therapist's judgments. Meehl (1966) points out that therapist's judgments about the personality characteristics of his patients crystalize rather rapidly. The clinician generally forms a coherent and complete impression of his patient in three or four hours of psychotherapy. Therefore to provide the therapist with a statistically derived description of a patient is, in effect, to give the therapist information which he will shortly obtain on his own. In view of these considerations it is hard to understand the extensive effort placed in the use of diagnostic testing in clinical settings.

When we turn from personality description to prediction of outcomes such as recidivism, success in college and response to therapy, statistical prediction would appear to have a clear and definite advantage. In addition to the fact that statistical procedures for combining data are superior to clinical procedures in accuracy of prediction they have the additional advantage of being cheap and of freeing the time of highly trained individuals for other constructive activities. Despite the findings reviewed by Meehl and Sawyer most predictions are made clinically. Why? There are a number of objections to statistical prediction. Individuals frequently express resentment at being treated as statistics. What is apparently involved here is the belief that no set of categories can exhaust their individuality and that the attempt to encapsulate an individual in terms of a limited number of categories is dehumanizing and may miss the significant features of the individual which may in fact make him an exception to the statistical regularities which hold for groups of individuals. This is a difficult objection to deal with. It is obviously true that no set of categories can properly encompass the complexity of any individual. However, the price to pay for allowing a clinician to deal with that complexity by permitting him to depart from statistical regularities would appear to be, in most cases, the addition of error. Also, Sarbin's findings suggest, paradoxically, that clinicians may in some cases rely more heavily on objective data than the statistical formula.

A second possible limitation to the use of statistical prediction comes from situations in which no adequate criterion information exists. In such cases, it is impossible to directly develop statistical predictions. Goldberg (1970) has dealt with such situations giving as an example the situation of a psychologist working in a suicide prevention clinic who attempts to predict whether or not a person will commit suicide on the basis of a telephone interview. There are certain cues which can be coded from such an interview, for example, sex, age, education, number of past attempts, etc. However, data indicating the relationship between such cues and the criterion (committing suicide) is not readily available. Without these data there is no way of directly developing a statistical formula for prediction. However, it is possible to develop a statistical model which will predict the clinician's predictions. And, this model of the clinician may be substituted for the clinician. At first glance it would appear that this might be an inadequate procedure. Unless the clinician's predictions were perfectly predictable the model of the clinician would appear to be an inadequate substitute for the clinician. However, this argument neglects an important consideration—namely, the unreliability of the clinician. The model is perfectly consistent always assigning the same identical weightings to the same cues. The clinician may differ in his weightings of the same cues thus introducing error into his predictions. This implies, in principal, that the model of the clinician may actually be superior to the clinician dependent upon the accuracy of the model's predictions of the clinician's judgments and the degree of unreliability of those judgments.

Goldberg has reported a comparison of the accuracy of clinician's and statistical models of clinician's judgments. The data used were those originally collected by Meehl (1959) and reanalyzed by Goldberg in his study comparing linear and nonlinear predictions of psychoses and neurosis from MMPI profiles. For each of the 29 judges who participated in the study, Goldberg developed a linear multiple regression formula to predict the judge's predictions. The mean of the correlation between the judge's predictions and the formulas predicting the judge's predictions was .77. Then Goldberg compared the validity of the judge's predictions of the criterion with the predictions of the criterion obtained by using the model of the judge's predictions as a basis for prediction. He found in 28 of 29 cases that the model of the judge's predictions was equal or superior to the predictions of the judges. The most accurate judge had a validity coefficient of .39 and the most accurate model of a judge had a validity coefficient of .43. The mean of the validities of the judges was .28 and the mean validity of the model of the judge's predictions was .31. Thus, the models of the judges predictions were superior to the judges predictions as a means of predicting the criterion. Although the situation dealt with by Goldberg is one in which criterion information is available it is apparent that the importance of these findings is their potential generalization to the situation in which criterion information is not available. As long as it is possible to predict the clinicians predictions from certain cues the potential for equivalent or superior prediction of the criterion exists—thereby permitting the replacement of the clinician by his model.

A third possible reason for not using statistical prediction of outcomes stems from the fact that the empirical tests of the efficacy of such predictions have dealt with criteria of low content validity. That is, the criteria have not been those which are of major concern to the individuals who are making decisions. For example, in selecting individuals for college, the admissions officer may only be partially concerned with the grade-point average the individual is likely to achieve. He may be more concerned about the extent to which college education may enrich the individual's life and the extent to which that individual will contribute in salutary ways to the college environment. Consider another example. A psychiatrist faced with a decision about the release of a patient may be concerned with a variety of criteria other than the probability that the patient will be able to function sufficiently well so as to avoid rehospitalization. These concerns might include the therapeutic benefits associated with being in the home or in the hospital, the dangers to society and to the patient's family associated with a relapse and the needs and desires of the patient's family. These examples suggest that the practical decisions which are to be made may include consideration of criteria other than those investigated in studies comparing clinical and statistical predictions and that, for this reason, decisions about persons cannot be made solely on the basis of statistical formulas.

There are a number of possible rejoinders that the advocate of statistical prediction might make to this argument. First, there are prediction situations where this argument simply does not apply. For example, Mischel (1965) compared statistical predictions from statistical data of judgments made in the field of overall competence of Peace Corps volunteers with clinical predictions of success as a Peace Corps volunteer. He found that predictions based on scores on paper and pencil tests of personality were superior to clinical predictions. In this prediction situation the measure of overall competence presumably included all of the criteria of interest.

Second, there are situations in which it should be possible to make statistical predictions where multiple criteria are involved. One could attempt to develop a statistical prediction of each of several criteria and then proceed to devise a formula for combining these components which expressed the appropriate weights to be assigned to the various criteria which enter into the decision. Although this might be difficult there are probably situations where this type of statistical decision making would be useful.

Third, the argument that the clinician is required in order to appropriately weight a variety of criteria has a disturbing aura of familiarity. It is, in fact, analogous to the argument that only the clinician can appropriately consider all of the data which are relevant to a prediction. We have already seen that this argument is apparently spurious. If the clinician cannot optimally combine data to predict a fixed criterion there is little reason to believe that he can optimally predict multiple criteria and then in turn develop an optimal weighting of scores on these criteria to make a decision. That is, the task of decision making involving multiple criteria is analogous to the task of prediction for a single criterion. The latter requires the former and in addition a procedure of combining values on each of the criteria to arrive at an optimal decision. In view of what we know about clinical prediction in the simpler task it would not be unreasonable to be skeptical of the adequacy of clinical decisions in the more difficult task. This seems to lead to dilemma. There are situations in which decisions must be made about persons where we may feel that clinical decisions are inadequate and statistical decision do not deal with relevant criteria. The case of selection for college admission provides a neat example of this situation. It appears to be quite reasonable to argue that in selecting individuals for college we are not solely interested in the probable grade point average of an individual. On the other hand, the criteria we are interested in, contribution to the individual's life and the individual's contribution to the college environment seem hopelessly vague and unpredictable. In fact they may be meaningless, or if meaningful, they may not be predictable by either the clinician or the statistician principally because we do not know how to measure or quantify such criteria. In practice, the clinicians (college admissions officers) rely on rather crude stereotypes to predict such criteria—for example, individuals who participate in extra-curricular activities are well rounded and individuals who are well rounded get more out of college. Or, individuals who have traveled have broadened their outlook on life and hence will be more open to new experiences at college and will therefore benefit more from college. Such rather crude generalizations give the illusion of predicting the unpredictable to the clinician, and would appear to violate humanistic concerns for the complexity and richness of persons. The great advantage of the reliance on statistical procedures for decisions about persons is that they do not attempt to deal with intangible elements in prediction in crude ways. In selecting individuals for college admission a statistical formula could be used to predict grade-point average. After accumulating a group of individuals who have acceptably low risks of failing at college, a random selection device could be used to make the actual decision. Random procedures have the virtue of not introducing systematic sources of bias into decision making situations.

The research we have reviewed has represented a triumph of what is sometimes called dust bowl empiricism over theoretical efforts in applied situations. The empiricist with his patient effort to ferret out and discover relationships between the past and future has been more successful than the clinician armed with the insights of psychoanalytic theory or the personality theorist working with the kinds of dimensions we have considered in Chapters 2 through 6. We can, however, anticipate some future time when the development of a systematic description of personality will permit the personality theorist to make precise predictions about how individuals will behave in a variety of situations of interest to the applied psychologist. Such predictions are likely to be contingent in form. That is, they will specify the kind of situation in which particular outcomes are to be expected for particular kinds of persons. Predictions of this type will enable the applied psychologist to simultaneously consider the characteristics of persons and situations. For example, predictions about the probability of rehospitalization for psychoses might specify the expected outcomes for different kinds of posthospital therapeutic interventions. Our ability to predict and control behavior is likely to be improved when we simultaneously consider the characteristics of the person and attempt to manipulate the environment in ways which are beneficial to the person.

# CHAPTER 9

# PRINCIPLES OF SOCIAL LEARNING

---

We have assumed that the task of personality theory is to discover dimensions which will order and describe individual differences. There, is however, an alternative approach to the understanding of personality. The personality psychologist may take as his task the explanation of the process by which individual differences arise. In such an approach personality psychology and general experimental psychology become integrated. The latter attempts to discover general laws which are valid for all men (or all organisms) and the former attempts to show how these laws may be used to explain individual differences. Consider an oversimplified example. According to the principle of reinforcement, responses which are followed by a reinforcer (reward) will be strengthened and, as a result, the probability of their occurrence will be increased. The principle is assumed to be valid for all organisms. However, individual differences may, in part, be due to the idiosyncrasies of each individual's reinforcement history. Individuals respond differently because they have experienced different patterns of reward and punishment.

In order to use general principles of behavior to explain individual differences, psychologists have emphasized principles of learning. As a result, personality is understood in terms of the cumulative effects of a series of learning experiences. In explicating this view we shall emphasize Bandura's social learning or sociobehavioristic approach (Bandura, 1969; Bandura & Walters, 1963).

## Background Assumptions of Social Learning Theory

Bandura's theory of personality represents a major departure from earlier attempts to understand personality from a learning theory point of view. Most of the earlier approaches, starting with an influential book written by Dollard, Doob, Miller, and Sears (1939), were neo-Hullian in approach. This approach was dominant through the nineteen fifties. The major book summarizing neo-Hullian personality theory was written by Dollard and Miller in 1950. In 1963 Bandura and Walters published a book called *Social Learning and Personality Development*, which represented a major departure from the neo-Hullian point of view. More recently, Bandura (1969) has published a book which deals extensively with the use of social learning principles as a basis for behavior modifications.

In what follows we shall try to outline the major concepts of Bandura's social learning theory and we shall indicate some of the respects in which it is different from the neo-Hullian personality theory of Dollard and Miller.

Perhaps the principal respect in which social learning theory is radically different from neo-Hullian personality theory is in its attitude toward psychoanalytic theory. Neo-Hullian theorists such as Dollard and Miller (1950) tried to develop a rapprochement between learning theory and psychoanalytic theory. They assumed that Freud had discovered the outlines of a complete theory of personality. They attempted to show how the fundamental insights of psychoanalytic theory could be given more precise expression and formulation by the use of learning theory. By contrast, Bandura and Walters are radically anti-Freudian. They do not accept the view that psychoanalytic theory is essentially correct and provides the basis for the science of personality. As we shall see, they attempt to develop explanations of phenomena which are at variance with traditional psychoanalytically derived explanations. They argue that their explanations of such phenomena are superior and more parsimonious than those given by reference to psychoanalytic principles.

Many of the earlier attempts to explain personality in learning theory terms involved extrapolations from research conducted with animals. The basic principles of learning theory were developed in laboratory studies, typically using rats as subjects, and then extrapolated to phenomena of interest to the personality psychologist.

Neo-Hullian personality theorists did do empirical work on topics of interest to the personality psychologist [for example, Whiting and Child's (1953) study of relationships between socialization practices and cultural practices]. However, the basic principles used in their studies almost invariably were based on laboratory work with animals.

By contrast, Bandura and Walters' theory is based on a program of laboratory work with children. Consequently, their extrapolation from laboratory to "real life" phenomena is less artificial.

Finally, Bandura and Walters' theory is distinguished from earlier theories by its emphasis on models and the importance of imitation. Their theory implies that individuals are affected not only by the rewards and punishments they receive but also by the rewards and punishments they observe other individuals receiving. Although Miller and Dollard did write a book dealing with social learning and imitation in 1941 (Miller and Dollard, 1941), their more systematic subsequent treatment of personality (Dollard and Miller, 1950) practically ignores the issue.

## Basic Principles of Social Learning

In this section we will attempt to present some of the basic principles of the theory developed by Bandura and Walters. Perhaps the most fundamental principle of social learning is the principle of reinforcement. This principle is used by them to explain the acquisition of many behaviors which are of interest to the personality theorist, for example, aggression, dependency, and sex. An experiment by Cowan and Walters (1963) provides an example of the application of principles of reinforcement to the increase of aggressive response tendencies. Children were given a large Bobo clown with a sign saying, "Hit me," painted on the clown and were reinforced by being given a marble for hitting the clown. The rates of responding were increased as a result of reinforcement.

One of the fundamental principles of reinforcement theory is that partial reinforcement leads to greater resistance to extinction than continuous reinforcement (Ferster and Skinner, 1957). This principle was investigated in the Cowan and Walters study. The children were reinforced on one of three schedules:

1. Continuous reinforcement in which a marble was dispensed for each hitting response.
2. Fixed ratio, 1:3, in which they were reinforced for every third hitting response.
3. Fixed ratio, 1:6, in which they were reinforced for every sixth response.

After 18 responses had been reinforced no more marbles were dispensed. Continuously reinforced subjects responded less frequently before stopping than the subjects who had experienced partial reinforcement (fixed ratio) schedules, that is, the latter subjects showed greater resistance to extinction.

The experiment discussed above involves the direct application of reinforcement principles to a response tendency of interest to the personality psychologist. Bandura and Walters tend to emphasize a somewhat different application of reinforcement principles involving an extension of the principle of reinforcement to situations in which a person observes the actions of another person (a model) who is reinforced or punished for these actions. Vicarious reinforcement refers to the modification of an observer's behavior by reinforcements administered to a model who is being observed. Bandura and his associates (see Bandura, 1962; Bandura, Ross, & Ross, 1961, 1963a) have performed a number of experiments which illustrate the effects of vicarious reinforcement. In these experiments nursery school children are exposed to films of adults, or live adults, behaving aggressively, physically and verbally, to a large plastic doll. They found that children exposed to models who behaved aggressively tended to behave toward the doll in the same way and exhibited a large number of precisely matching responses. Such responses rarely occurred for children who were not exposed to models behaving aggressively. These experiments indicate that children can acquire novel responses through vicarious reinforcement.

The process of learning through imitation is influenced by the nature of the reinforcement given to the model. Bandura, Ross, and Ross (1963b) did an experiment in which they compared the effects of rewards and punishments given to models for their actions. Children were exposed to a film showing an adult model behaving aggressively towards another adult. In one condition the aggressive model was punished for his actions and in another condition he was rewarded. Children who observed the film in which a model was rewarded for aggression tended to show more imitation of aggressive behavior than children exposed to the film of a model who was punished for aggression. The experiment indicates that rewards and punishments given to a model influence the tendency of observers to imitate the responses of the model.

Vicarious reinforcement not only can influence the acquisition of novel response tendencies but it can also lead to inhibitory and disinhibitory effects. For example, children in Bandura's studies who were exposed to aggressive models tended to exhibit aggressive responses which the models had not used. This finding suggests that the exposure served to disinhibit aggressive response tendencies. Similarly, exposure to inhibited models or models punished for aggression led to a decrease in aggressive responding— indicating an inhibiting effect. Walters, Bowen and Parke (as cited in Bandura & Walters, 1963) have investigated inhibitory and disinhibitory effects of models on a sexual observing response. College undergraduates were exposed to a movie film of pictures of male and female nudes. Subjects were told that a dot of light which moved across the surface of the pictures represented the actual eye movements of a previous subject. For half the Ss, the dot of light concentrated on the bodies of the nudes, particularly on the breast and genital regions. For the remaining Ss the dot of light concentrated on the background rather than the bodies of the nudes. The Ss were then given an opportunity to view slides of the pictures of the nudes. Their eye movements were recorded. Subjects who were exposed to the film in which the dot of light concentrated on sexually significant areas spent more time looking at these areas than subjects who were exposed to the film in which the dot of light avoided the body of the nudes. This study demonstrates that exposure to models can inhibit or disinhibit sexual response tendencies.

We have discussed studies which indicate that response tendencies are influenced by reinforcements given directly to a person or to a model who is observed by a person. However, many reinforcements, particularly for adults, are self-administered. Bandura and Kupers (1964) have reported a study indicating the influence of models on the development of standards for self reinforcement. In this experiment children played a bowling game with an adult or peer model who was a confederate of the experimenter. The model set relatively high (a score of 20 or more out of 30) or low (a score of 10 or more out of 30) standards for self-reinforcement. Models reinforced themselves verbally with self-approving statements and with candy when they were successful. Also, the models berated themselves and refused to take candy on trials in which they did not reach their standard for self-reinforcement. Subsequently, the children played the bowling game in the absence of the models. Figures 9.1 and 9.2 present the results of the experiment. Figures 9.1 and 9.2 indicate that the children tended to adopt standards for self-reinforcement which matched the standards of the models to which they had been exposed.

The Bandura and Kupers study attempts to show how internal standards are influenced by the exposure to external events which are under the control of the experimenter.

Bandura and Mischel (1965) have reported a study indicating the influence of models on the development of self-control as indicated by preference for delay of gratification with large rewards as opposed to immediate gratification with small rewards. The Ss were given a test consisting of a series of items in which they had to choose one of two alternatives involving a preference for immediate gratification with a small reward or delayed gratification with a large reward. Those children who scored in the top 25 percent and the bottom 25 percent of scores on this test were then exposed to live or symbolic adult models who exhibited a preference which was opposite from their own. In the symbolic model conditions, the children were given the choices of an adult and a statement of his philosophy which justified the choices, and in the live model conditions, the children observed the adult models making their choices and listened to him express his philosophy which justified the choices. The children were then given an opportunity to express their preferences for immediate or delayed gratification after the models left and four weeks later. Figures 9.3 and 9.4

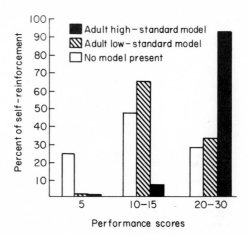

FIG. 9.1. The distribution of self-reinforcement as a function of performance level by control children and those exposed to adult models adopting high and low criteria for self-reinforcement. (From A. Bandura  & Carol J. Kupers, Transmission of patterns of self-reinforcement through modeling. *Journal of Abnormal and Social Psychology,* 1964, **69,** 1–9.)

indicate the changes in preference for children who preferred immediate gratification who were exposed to high-delay models and the high-delay children exposed to low-delay models.

The Bandura and Mischel study illustrates the influence of vicarious reinforcement on the development of self control. The study indicates a

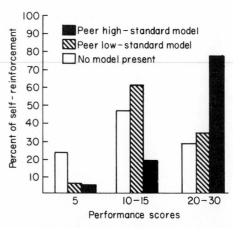

FIG. 9.2. The distribution of self-reinforcement as a function of performance level of control children and those exposed to peer models adopting high and low criteria for self-reinforcement. (From A. Bandura  & Carol J. Kupers, Transmission of patterns of self-reinforcement through modeling. *Journal of Abnormal and Social Psychology,* 1964, **69,** 1–9.)

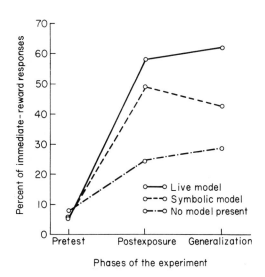

Fig. 9.3. Mean percentage of immediate-reward responses by high-delay children on each of three test periods for each of three experimental conditions. (From A. Bandura & W. Mischel, Modification of self-imposed delay of reward through exposure to live and symbolic models. *Journal of Personality and Social Psychology*, 1965, **2**, 698–705.)

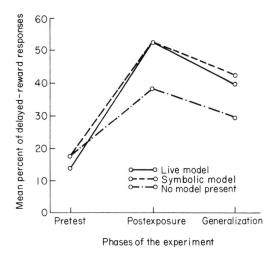

Fig. 9.4. Mean percentage of delayed-reward responses by low-delay children on each of three test periods for each of three experimental conditions. (From A. Bandura & W. Mischel, Modification of self-imposed delay of reward through exposure to live and symbolic models. *Journal of Personality and Social Psychology*, 1965, **2**, 698–705.)

contrast between the social learning approach to the development of self control and psychoanalytic theory which, briefly, asserts that the development of preference for delay of gratification is the result of complex intrapsychic events resulting from the dominance of ego over id.

Our discussion of principles of social learning has emphasized the role of positive reinforcements and rewards. We have not dealt extensively with the influence of punishment and aversive stimulation on behavior. Responses which are followed by the presentation of aversive stimuli tend to be suppressed or weakened. We have already seen the extension of this principle to vicarious reinforcement. Bandura *et al.* (1963b) found exposure to models who were punished for aggressive responses led to a decrease in aggressive responding. Personality psychologists have not emphasized the suppressing effect of punishment. Rather, they have been more interested in the classical conditioning of aversive stimulation. That is, neutral stimuli which are paired with aversive stimuli become aversive. More precisely, they develop the capacity to elicit an intrapsychic aversive state which may be called anxiety. A study by Campbell, Sanderson, and Lafferty (1964) illustrates this process. They used hospitalized chronic alcoholics as subjects. The subjects were given a single conditioning trial in which a tone (CS) was paired with an administration of the drug Scoline (UCS). Scoline creates an extremely aversive state involving complete paralysis for approximately two minutes with a feeling of suffocation. After this single conditioning trial subjects were exposed to the tone alone. As a result of this conditioning procedure the tone developed the capacity to elicit many of the autonomic nervous system changes associated with states of agitation and fear. After 100 unreinforced trials in which the CS was presented without the UCS three of the five Ss showed no indication of extinction. They continued to show a rise in GSR, and irregular breathing and heart rate in response to the tone. For two of the subjects the autonomic responses to the tone extinguished in ten trials but then exhibited spontaneous recovery such that the tone continued to elicit the autonomic nervous system changes characteristic of aversive states.

Not only do neutral stimuli acquire the capacity to elicit aversive states but organisms will learn various responses which will permit them to terminate or escape from the previously neutral stimuli, and, presumably, the aversive state which they elicit. Some of the principles involved in this type of learning are illustrated by a classic experiment with rats performed by Miller (1948a). Miller used the apparatus illustrated in Figure 9.5 in his experiments. Rats were exposed to electric shock while confined to the white compartment. They were permitted to escape from the shock by leaving the white compartment and entering the black compartment. On subsequent trials the shock was omitted. The rats placed in the white compartment showed obvious signs of fear such as urination and defecation.

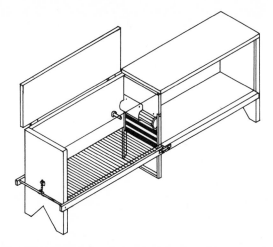

FIG. 9.5. Apparatus for studying fear as a learned drive. The left compartment is painted white, the right one black. In order to train the animals to fear the white compartment, a mild shock is administered through the floor of this compartment, which is a grid. During this training the experimenter, by pressing a button, causes the door between the compartments to drop open in front of the animal. In order to see whether the animal can learn a *new* habit when he is motivated by fear alone (without the primary drive of shock) the experimenter leaves the door closed and adjusts the apparatus so that the door drops when the animal performs the correct response, which is turning the wheel or pressing the bar as the case may be. An electric clock is automatically started when the animal is placed in the white compartment and stopped when the animal performs the correct response. (From J. Dollard & N. E. Miller, *Personality and psychotherapy.* New York: McGraw-Hill, 1950. Used with permission of McGraw-Hill Book Company.)

If given an opportunity to escape from the white compartment into the black, the rats would do so. Further, Miller showed that rats would learn responses which would permit them to escape from the white compartment. For example, rats were able to learn to turn a wheel if this response permitted them to escape from the white compartment.

Turner and Solomon (1962) have performed experiments on traumatic avoidance conditioning with humans. They showed that humans could learn to make avoidance responses to a neutral stimulus which had been paired with traumatic levels of shock.

Avoidance responses to conditioned stimuli which have acquired the capacity to elicit aversive states are extraordinarily resistant to extinction (Solomon & Wynne, 1954). Because of this, many psychologists have assumed that many responses which are made by neurotics which are inappropriate and ineffective have been acquired by a process of avoidance conditioning. Thus they are functionally analogous to the response of escaping from the white compartment acquired by the rats in Miller's experiment. Such responses enable the individual to terminate or avoid the aversive state which is elicited by stimuli which have been paired with aversive stimulation.

## Extensions of Social Learning Principles to Personality Phenomena

In what follows we shall discuss the extension of these principles to topics of interest to the personality psychologist. We shall also contrast the explanations developed by Bandura and Walters with more traditional psychodynamic explanations.

### CONFLICT AND DISPLACEMENT

Miller (1944, 1948b) has developed an analysis of conflict situations based on principles of learning. The conflict situation which has been most extensively studied is an approach–avoidance conflict situation in which an individual is in a situation in which he simultaneously has a desire to approach and avoid the same goal. Miller makes four assumptions about such conflicts. These are:

1.  The tendency to approach a goal is stronger the nearer the subject is to it. This is called a gradient of approach.
2.  The tendency to avoid a feared stimulus is stronger the nearer the subject is to it. This is called a gradient of avoidance.
3.  The strength of the avoidance tendency increases more rapidly with nearness than the strength of the approach tendency. Put another way, the avoidance gradient is steeper than the approach tendency.
4.  The strength of the tendencies to approach or avoid varies with the strength of the drive upon which they are based. An increase of the motivation raises the height of the entire gradient.

Figures 9.6, 9.7, and 9.8 present graphic illustrations of Miller's analysis of approach–avoidance conflicts.

The original research validating this theory was done with rats and frequently involved approach–avoidance conflicts based on hunger and fear. (See Miller, 1944.) Distance from the goal was actually defined in terms of physical distance. In agreement with the theory, rats would approach a goal and then stop before reaching it. The distance from the goal at which the rat stopped could be manipulated by operations designed to change the underlying motivation supporting the approach and avoidance gradients. Thus, rats could be made to come nearer a goal by increasing their hunger drive.

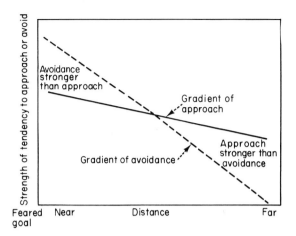

Fig. 9.6. Simple graphic representation of an approach-avoidance conflict. The tendency to approach is the stronger of the two tendencies far from the goal, while the tendency to avoid is the stronger of the two near to the goal. Therefore, when far from the goal, the subject should tend to approach part way and then stop; when near to it, he should tend to retreat part way and then stop. In short, he should tend to remain in the region where the two gradients intersect.

It is only for the sake of simplicity that the gradients are represented by straight lines in these diagrams. Similar deductions could be made on the basis of any curves that have a continuous negative slope is steeper for avoidance than for approach at each point above the abscissa. (From J. Dollard & N. E. Miller, *Personality and psychotherapy*, New York: McGraw-Hill, 1950. Used with permission of McGraw-Hill Book Company.)

When Miller's theory is applied to situations of interest to the personality psychologist the dimension of distance from the goal is defined in terms of stimulus similarity rather than geographic distance. This definition of distance permits an extension of the conflict model to deal with the psychoanalytic concept of displacement. Displacement occurs when an impulse cannot be directly expressed but is indirectly expressed by the substitution of a new goal object. In Miller's analysis, displacement occurs in an approach–avoidance conflict situation in which the avoidance gradient is stronger than the approach gradient for the goal of direct expression of an impulse. However, at some point distant from the goal, for a similar goal object, the avoidance gradient will be lower than the approach gradient since it falls off more steeply with distance from the goal, thus permitting the displacement of the original impulse to a new goal object.

The above analysis may be applied to the "scapegoat" theory of prejudice. According to this theory, prejudice towards minority groups represents the displacement of hostile and aggressive feelings whose original goal objects were different. Miller and Bugelski (1948) studied the

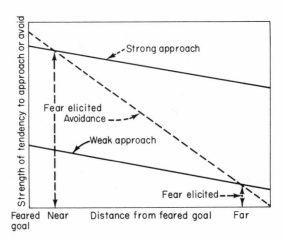

Fig. 9.7. How increasing the strength of approach in an approach-avoidance conflict increases the amount of fear and conflict elicited. The subject will be expected to advance or retreat to the point where the gradients intersect, that is, where the strengths of the competing tendencies are equal. Thus as the strength of approach is increased, he will move nearer the feared goal. When he is nearer the feared goal, the strength of both tendencies will be increased. Therefore, more fear and conflict will be elicited.

This deduction holds only for the range within which the two gradients intersect. If approach is increased until it is stronger than avoidance at the goal, the subject will advance to the goal. Then further increases in the strength of approach will not be expected to produce further increases in the amount of fear and conflict elicited. It is only for the sake of simplicity that the gradients are represented by straight lines in these diagrams. Similar deductions could be made on the basis of any curves that have a continuous negative sope that is steeper for avoidance than for approach at each point above the abscissa. (From J. Dollard & N. E. Miller, *Personality and psychotherapy.* New York: McGraw-Hill, 1950. Used with permission of McGraw-Hill Book Company.)

effects of frustration on prejudice. Their subjects were living in a camp for unemployed young men. One evening when they were expecting to go to a movie they were forced to take a series of dull and difficult tests. Miller and Bugelski found greater expression of hostility toward Mexicans and Japanese as a result of this frustrating experience. The results can be interpreted as an instance of the displacement of an aggressive impulse caused by the frustrating experience. The aggressive impulse was presumably directed against the frustrating agents and was then displaced onto the minority group.

Bandura and Walters (1959) found that highly aggressive adolescents tended to be punished more severely for aggression in the home than nonaggressive adolescents. This phenomenon may be explained as an instance of displacement. The tendency to be punished severely for aggression in the home may set up an approach–avoidance conflict in which the child develops a desire to express aggression against the punishing father but is at the same time deterred from this expression by an avoidance tendency based on the fear of the consequences of the expression of this aggressive tendency. Although the avoidance gradient may prohibit the direct expression of the aggressive impulse, Miller's analysis implies that the aggressive implulse may be expressed indirectly by being displaced onto other objects. The approach–avoidance conflict is "resolved" by the expression of aggression outside the home.

Bandura and Walters (1963) have several criticisms of this type of analysis. The principal difficulty with this type of analysis is that there is no precise way of defining and ordering the dimension of similarity to the goal object. Miller's analysis of conflict falls victim to the postdictive character

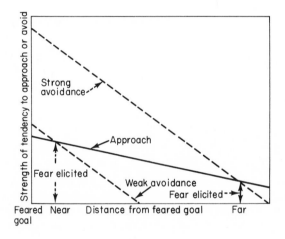

Fig. 9.8. How decreasing the strength of avoidance in an approach-avoidance conflict increases the amount of fear and conflict elicited. The subject will be expected to advance or retreat to the point where the gradients intersect, that is, where the strengths of the opposing tendencies are equal. Thus, with weak avoidance, he will approach nearer to the feared goal. When he is nearer to the feared goal, the strength of both tendencies will be increased. Therefore, more fear and conflict will be elicited.

This deduction holds only for the range within which the gradients of approach and avoidance intersect. If the gradient is weakened so much that it no longer intersects the gradient of approach, the subject will advance to the goal and further decreases in the gradient of avoidance will decrease the amount of fear and conflict. It is only for the sake of simplicity that the gradients are represented by straight lines in these diagrams. Similar deductions could be made on the basis of any curve that has a continuous negative slope that is steeper for avoidance than approach at each point above the abscissa. (From J. Dollard & N. E. Miller, *Personality and psychotherapy*. New York: McGraw-Hill, 1950. Used with permission of McGraw-Hill Book Company.)

of Freudian theory on which it is based. That is, Freudian theory is rarely predictive (see Rapoport, 1959). The theory may be used to explain phenomena postdictively. In the present case psychoanalytic theory does not endeavor to predict the specific form that displacement will take—or, indeed, if displacement would be the defense mechanism of choice here. However, if a particular target for the aggression was found, psychoanalytic theory might well construe the expression of aggression against the target as an instance of displacement of hostility (possibly of an unconscious hostility) felt against the father. Similarly, Miller's analysis implies that if the aggression against the father cannot be expressed directly it will always be expressed indirectly. However, Miller's analysis does not predict the particular target which will be selected for the expression of aggression.

Bandura and Walters (1963) prefer a more precise and parsimonious explanation which rests on an analysis of the reinforcement histories of aggressive boys. They point out that aggressive boys who were punished for aggression in the home were rewarded for aggression outside the home. As a result, the tendency to be aggressive outside the home is an instance of the acquisition of a discrimination based on the reinforcement history of these boys. The process by which such discriminative control is acquired over aggressive responses is assumed to be functionally analogous to the process by which a rat is trained to press a bar in a Skinner box when a light is on and not to press when the light is off. In such a case the light acquires discriminative control over the bar pressing response.

Although Bandura and Walters' explanation of the finding that aggressive boys are punished for aggression in the home is more parsimonious than an explanation based on displacement they point out that the explanation of displacement phenomena from social learning theory requires knowledge about a number of variables which are not dealt with in the analysis based on approach-avoidance conflicts. These include the influence of the punishing agent—in this case the parent—in administering positive reinforcements and the influence of parents and other socializing agents as models in the selection of appropriate targets for the expression of hostile and aggressive responses. Bandura and Walters would view the validity, if any, of the scapegoat theory of aggression as being due principally to the influence of direct or vicarious reinforcement for the expression of hostility toward minority groups. In summary, Miller's theory of displacement, like the psychoanalytic theory from which it derives, assumes that some form of indirect expression of an impulse will always occur if, as a result of an approach–avoidance conflict, the individual is prevented from a direct expression of the impulse. Bandura and Walters do not view such a displacement as inevitable. It may or may not occur. And, if it occurs, the precise target for the expression of the tendency is chosen as the result of a specific reinforcement history in which responses directed towards that target have been directly or vicariously reinforced.

## CONTINUITIES AND DISCONTINUITIES IN DEVELOPMENT

Psychoanalytic theory assumes that personality development is characterised by a universal sequence of partially discontinuous stages which are the result of the interaction of maturational changes and experiences. For example, according to Freudian theory psychosexual development involves a maturational shift from preoccupation with the mouth during the oral stage to preoccupation with activities centered around defecation during the anal stage. Stage theories assume that developmental changes occur as a result of intraorganismic changes which are not totally derivative of environmental events. Social learning theory attempts to account for behavior without postulating intraorganismic events whose occurrence is not derivable from the learning history of an organism. Consequently, it is not surprising to find that Bandura and Walters discount the importance of stage theories of development. Their criticism of stage theories extends to a critique of any theory of development which emphasizes that certain problems or conflicts are inevitable accompaniments of personality development. For example, Dollard and Miller, while not accepting the Freudian view of maturational changes in psychosexual development, do feel that the conflicts associated with the various stages of development discussed by Freud are universal and result as an inevitable consequence of the socialization of the child. As a result they would argue that children will inevitably develop conflicts centered around toilet training and the control of sexual attraction for the opposite sexed parent (Oedipus complex).

Bandura and Walters do not deal specifically with the theory of psychosexual development. However, they emphasize the view that there are marked differences between individuals in their reinforcement history. These differences are sufficient to render invalid any theory of universal conflicts or stages in development. They would argue that whether or not a child would develop a conflict surrounding sexual attraction for the opposite sexed parent would depend entirely on the specific nature of his learning experiences. Presumably, the development of an oedipal complex would depend on such variables as the frequency and nature of reinforcement of sexual responses of a child by a child's opposite sexed parent, the reaction of the same sexed parent to such reinforcements by the opposite sexed parent, the number and nature of sexual responses between the parents which a child had been permitted to observe, and the discriminative control, if any, acquired by the child with respect to sexual responses.

A study by Bandura and McDonald (1963) illustrates the social learning approach to the notion of developmental stages. The study dealt with a suggestion by Piaget (1948) that children's concepts of morality develop sequentially. A stage of objective morality in which the gravity of a deviant act is judged by the amount of damage it causes irrespective of the intentions of the person committing an act is assumed to be followed by a subjective stage of morality in which children judge the gravity of an act by the intent of the person who commits the act. Bandura and McDonald attempted to change the moral judgments of children who were predominantly objective or subjective in their moral judgments. The children were exposed to one of three experimental conditions. One group of children were exposed to an adult model who expressed moral judgments contrary to those of the dominant orientation of the child and rewarded the child for expressing judgments like the models. A second group of children were exposed to an adult model who expressed judgments contrary to theirs but did not reinforce the child for adopting new moral judgments. A third group of children were not exposed to models but were rewarded for expressing judgments counter to their dominant orientation. After this exposure the children's moral orientation was assessed in a new situation in the absence of the adults who modeled and/or reinforced the children's moral judgments. Figures 9.9 and 9.10 present the principal results of the study. Figures 9.9 and 9.10 indicate that children exposed to models who expressed moral judgments contrary to their dominant orientation tended to change the direction of their judgments in ways which were in agreement with the model. These results cast doubt on the notion of a universal sequence of stages of moral judgment and suggest that such judgments are, in part, the result of the reinforcement history of the children and the behavior of adult models observed by the children.

### IDENTIFICATION WITH THE AGGRESSOR

Since Bandura and Walters emphasize the importance of imitation it is necessary for them to specify the conditions under which a child will reproduce the actions of a model whose behavior he has observed. Psychoanalytic theory proposes a set of conditions which will create imitation of a model who behaves aggressively. Identification with the aggressor refers to the tendency of a person to imitate (and identify with) the behavior of a person whose real or imagined aggression against him he fears. Such an identification may involve imitation of the behavior of the person or of his personal characteristics. This identification is assumed to relieve fear by permitting a person to think of himself as an aggressor rather than the victim of aggression.

A frequently cited example of this type of identification is based on observations made by a psychoanalyst named Bettleheim (1943) while he was imprisoned in a German concentration camp during World War II.

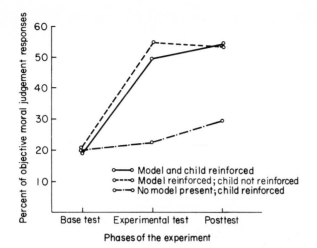

FIG. 9.9. Mean percentage of objective moral judgment responses produced by subjective children on each of the three test periods for each of three experimental conditions. (From A. Bandura & F. J. McDonald, Influence of social reinforcement and the behavior of models in shaping children's moral judgments. *Journal of Abnormal and Social Psychology*, 1963, **67,** 274–281.)

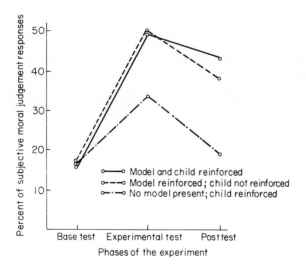

FIG. 9.10. Mean percentage of subjective moral judgment responses produced by objective children on each of three tests periods for each of three experimental conditions. (From A. Bandura & F. J. McDonald, Influence of social reinforcement and the behavior of models in shaping children's moral judgments. *Journal of Abnormal and Social Psychology*, 1963, **67,** 274–281.)

Bettleheim reported that prisoners who had been in the camp for a long period of time tended to imitate the behavior of the guards. This would include the tendency to treat new prisoners cruelly when they were placed in charge of them and enforcing prison regulations which had become obsolete. Also, some of the old prisoners would attempt to walk like the guards and to dress like the guards. Bettleheim assumed that these behaviors were indicative of identification with the aggressor.

Bandura and Walters discuss Bettleheim's results and state a number of reasons why they doubt that identification with the aggressor occurs. First, they note that prisoners were often given group punishments for infractions of the rules established by the guards. The enforcement of conformity to rules might have been a way of avoiding punishment. However, this explanation does not work for the tendency of prisoners to match the personal behavior of the guards with respect to such things as manner of dress. Bandura and Walters point out that, according to Bettleheim, prisoners were punished for this behavior. However, only a small number of prisoners actually adopted this behavior. Consequently, it is possible that this minority may have been exhibiting behavior tendencies which they had developed prior to their incarceration. Even if this is not the case the behavior may be explained by reference to the findings of an experiment by Bandura *et al.* (1963b). Bandura, Ross and Ross found that children tended to imitate the behavior of an adult model who controlled and dispensed reinforcements rather than an adult model who competed for reinforcements. Bandura and Walters note that children may identify with a person whom they dislike if his behavior is successful. They view fear of the aggressor as an irrelevant factor in the tendency to imitate an aggressor.

Bandura and Walters' discussion of identification with the aggressor again indicates their attempt to substitute for the series of intrapsychic events—for example, fear of the aggressor, conscious or unconscious fantasy identification, and subsequent reduction of fear—extrapsychic events or intrapsychic events which are derivative from extrapsychic events—in this case principally the rewards and punishments delivered to a model as a result of his actions.

## The Unconscious

Freud believed that many instances of deviant behavior as well as jokes, slips of the tongue, and dreams, were the results of indirect expressions of unconscious impulses. Some idea of the way in which such impulses allegedly influence behavior can be obtained from the following case history discussed by Mahl (see Janis, Mahl, Kagan, & Holt 1969).

## A Sexual Conflict: Ed

A young man, whom we shall call Ed, periodically attempted to find sexual satisfaction in masturbation and in premarital intercourse with his fiancee. However, in both circumstances he felt uneasy, tense and sweaty, and a vague sense of impending doom engulfed him afterward. Hence, Ed avoided both activities most of the time.

Conscious guilt and shame were very important causes of Ed's discomfort. He did not want anyone to know about his masturbation, and, despite a boastful attitude toward his premarital intercourse, he preferred that no one know about it. Mere discretion or a sense of privacy was not his only motivation; he felt that both acts were sinful and relieved evil urges on his part. He discovered a still more powerful and previously unknown source of his discomfort as he explored his behavior day after day in psychoanalysis: He feared that his genitals would be cut off if he engaged in these activities. This fear was unconscious; it manifested itself most clearly in frightening dreams that only occurred following an increase in either masturbation or intercourse. After one such upsurge in sexual activity, for example, Ed dreamed that he had a fatal illness and was in hospital. The doctors had removed an organ from his body and wrapped it up. It made a small, elongated package. As Ed told the dream to his analyst, the shape of the package reminded him of the shape of a penis.

Following another upsurge in sexual activity, Ed dreamed that one of his testicles was quite large owing to a tumor growing within it. A man, presumably a doctor, was going to cut it off. Ed's view of his sexuality as a fatal and evil cancerous process as well as his fear that he would be castrated were very thinly disguised in these dreams. While thinking about this dream, he remembered suddenly that he had dreamed something similar when he was about 7 years old: "A woman had cut off my penis and was starting to slice the end of it the way my mother sliced bananas for my cereal. This woman had cut the penises off all the little boys in the world. She looked like a witch."

The content of these nightmares, their close temporal correlation with active phases in his sexual life, and his associations to them strongly suggest that Ed's uneasiness, tension, sweating, and sense of doom associated with masturbation and intercourse were surface manifestations of an unconscious fear of castration, a fear present in his childhood and still operative in his adult life. It appears that sexual behavior activated this fear and that he avoided the danger of castration by inhibiting his sexual behavior.

A diagram of Ed's sexual conflict, including the known behavioral components and the inferred causal relations, is presented [Figure 9.11].

As a boy Ed had loved one of his sisters dearly. He had frequently played sexual games with this sister, and he had been terrified that his mother would cut off his penis if she ever found out. This was one reason he had castration dreams at the age of 7. His boyhood fear manifested itself in yet another way during this period of his incestuous play with his sister: Once when he was being examined by his doctor, he became so frightened that he doubled up his knees over his abdomen so that she would not be able to examine his scrotum and groin. It seemed that he was afraid that the doctor would be able to divine what had happened between him and his sister and would then tell his mother, whereupon the two would castrate him. This boyhood castration fantasy caused Ed to inhibit his sexual play with his sister and to repress his love for her. The fantasy was also recorded in Ed's memory just as though it were an objectively real experience, and the unconscious memory of this fantasy experience continued to affect his adult behavior. Its influence can be detected in Ed's castration dreams as an adult. There too, doctors were castrators.

Ed's early experiences with his sister had a significance transcending the arousal of castration anxiety. His erotically toned attachment to her served as a model for his relationships with women. Eventually... Ed "just happened" to marry a woman who resembled his childhood incestuous love object and substituted for her. There were several details—such as age, intellectual interest, and emotional attitudes—in which the two women resembled each other, but they were insignificant compared to one major attribute. The woman came from a cultural background that was despised by Ed's parents. His marriage to her was a tabooed act in their eyes, and to some extent in his own. It was in being a "tabooed female" that his wife most clearly resembled his sister.

There was a good deal of other evidence that his wife represented his sister. For example, once, when his sexual conflicts were prominent, Ed dreamed he saw a brother and a sister sitting in front of a television set and thought to himself that they were emotionally disturbed. Earlier that night he and his wife actually had sat in the front row of a theater watching a sensuous play. Ed had become sexually excited by the play and had felt guilty about it. When the analyst pointed out the similarity between the real scene with his wife and the dream scene, Ed realized that recently he had been thinking that living with his wife was like living with a sister. Later he commented that all his wife did when he was home in the evening was watch television. During other periods in his analysis, Ed found that for several days in a row his sister's name would come to the tip of his tongue in place of his wife's. And visits with his sister intensified his anxiety over his sexual intimacy with his wife. It is reasonable to conclude that his wife was a "generalized sister stimulus."

Making love with his wife, then, often made Ed feel tense, uneasy, and sweaty because it activated conflicting unconscious fantasies that resembled the conscious sexual conflict of his childhood. Sexual intimacy with a woman who resembled his sister stimulated repressed incestuous fantasies and, in turn, his unconscious castration fantasies. His adult conscious experience of anxiety was simply *the emotional component of these*

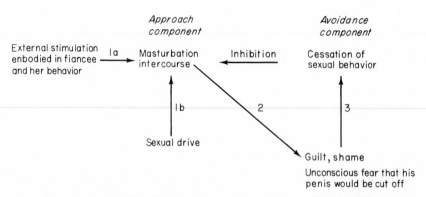

FIG. 9.11. Ed's approach-avoidance conflict. The combined effects of his fiancee and his sexual drive prompt Ed to engage in sexual behavior (1a and 1b). But such activity arouses conscious guilt and shame and unconscious castration anxiety (2), which in turn motivate Ed to stop engaging in sexual behavior (3). He does so by activity inhibiting the actions he wants to perform. As a result, he no longer experiences the guilt, shame, and fear. Thus, the inhibition has defended him from very unpleasant emotional experiences, but at the expense of his losing full sexual gratification. (Based on Janis *et al.*, 1969.)

*castration fantasies stripped of the castration thoughts themselves.* These he continued to repress, but they manifested themselves in his castration dreams... .

Ed's anxiety motivated him to avoid sexual intimacy with his wife until his own sexual needs, his wife's demands, or his "need to be masculine" became imperative.

(Janis *et al.*, 1969, pp. 226, 227, 310, 311)

This example illustrates the way in which overt behavior (choosing a wife, dreams, anxiety associated with sexual activity, etc.) are seen as derivatives of unconscious impulses in Freudian explanations.

Dollard and Miller also emphasize the role of the unconscious. They define the unconscious as that which is not verbally labeled. They assume that many conflicts which occur early in life, such as those surrounding early feeding experiences and toilet training, are unconscious because they occur prior to the development of language. In addition, Dollard and Miller assume that many thoughts are unconscious because they have been repressed. According to Dollard and Miller repression develops when certain internal stimuli—for example, thoughts involving sexual desire—are associated with traumatic events and, as a result, become capable of eliciting aversive states. The individual can remove the aversive state by not thinking the thoughts. The "stop thinking" responses are reinforced by the reduction in the aversive state. Repression is thus defined as the result of reinforcement of the stop thinking response.

The repression of certain thoughts and impulses is expected to generalize to other thoughts and impulses which are similar thus forming a gradient of avoidance. However, there may also be an approach gradient for repressed material caused by a tendency to appropriately label repressed thoughts and other similar thoughts. On the assumption that the gradient of avoidance is steeper than the gradient of approach, stimuli which are sufficiently dissimilar from the repressed stimulus will be appropriately labeled. Consequently, conscious thoughts may represent the resolution of unconscious conflicts. Dollard and Miller attempt to provide a rapprochement between learning theory and psychoanalytic theory by showing how behavior and thoughts can represent derivatives or displacements of unconscious impulses.

Bandura and Walters do not accept the dominant role assigned to the unconscious in psychoanalytic theory. Their views on this are contained in the following quotation dealing with deviant behavior.

Some clinicians who have adopted this medical model hold the view that the basic pathology is somatic in nature; the majority, however, regard the underlying disturbance as a psychologic, rather than neurologic, dysfunction. The latter employ symptom-underlying disease models in which the "disease" is a function of conscious or (more often) unconscious inner agents akin to the supernatural forces that once provided the

explanatory concepts of physics, biology, and (more recently) medicine. General medicine has progressed from the demonology that dominated it during the dark ages; as
scientific knowledge has increased, magical explanations have been replaced by scientific
ones. In contrast, theories of psychopathology, in which demons reappear in the guise
of "psychodynamic forces," still reflect the mystical thinking that once predominated
in science. These demonic agents are typically "ego-alien," buried under layers of personality, and held in check by counteragents or lines of defenses.

The psychodynamic "disease" model thus leads one to seek determinants of deviant
behavior in terms of relatively autonomous internal agents and processes in the form
of "unconscious psychic forces," "dammed-up energies," "cathexes," "counter-ca-
thexes," "defenses," "complexes," and other hypothetical conditions or states having
only a tenuous relationship to the social stimuli that precede them or even to the behavioral "symptoms" or "symbols" that they supposedly explain. In contrast, our
social-learning theory, instead of regarding internal processes as primary links in causal
sequences that generate deviant patterns of response, treats such processes as mediating
events, the nature of, and modifications in, which must be inferred from the conjunction
of certain manipulable stimulus conditions and observable response sequences. While
these inferred events may play an important role within an explanatory system that
generates predictions concerning behavioral change, they cannot be directly manipulated and consequently are of little importance in implementing programs for modifying
behavior. Moreover, they have predictive value only to the extent that they are systematically related to both the manipulable stimulus conditions and the observable
response variables, a condition that is rarely met in the cases of the constructs employed
in psychodynamic theories.

                                              (Bandura & Walters, 1963, pp. 30, 31)

In addition to the metatheoretical basis of their rejection of the unconscious, Bandura and Walters would probably disagree with the kind of
analysis given by Dollard and Miller on a substantive issue. Bandura and
Walters accept the view that verbal behavior can be inhibited. Further,
they would probably accept the view that thoughts as well as verbal
behavior may be inhibited (repressed?). However, it does *not* follow from
their theory that the generalization of approach tendencies for such thoughts
will be wider than the generalization of avoidance tendencies resulting in a
displaced expression of the originally repressed thought. Their objections to
such a displacement are identical to those we discussed earlier in connection
with the displacement of aggression.

Bandura has emphasized the difference between social learning and
psychoanalytic views of repressed and inhibited stimuli as follows:

Social-learning theory not only makes no appeal to prohibitive psychic agents in accounting for the inhibitory process, but it differs from psychodynamic approaches also
in the assumptions made about the nature of inhibited response tendencies. While
formerly punished responses may retain their capacity to generate emotional effects if
they are activated, it is not assumed that they lead a dynamic existence within an unconscious mind, that they possess a drive energy which must be reduced periodically,
that they press continuously for discharge in one guise or another, or that they require

unceasing restraint to confine them in the unconscious domain. Rather, it is assumed that inhibited behavior propensities remain inert unless activated by appropriate stimulation. Under circumstances where the incompatible controlling responses to the same stimuli are clearly dominant and therefore readily evoked the punished behavior is unlikely to reach even the incipient level.

(Bandura, 1969, p. 592)

## Therapy

Psychanalytic therapy attempts to deal with the unconscious causes of behavior problems. The therapy aims to give the patient insight into the causes of his difficulty. The patient is aided in this task by the creation of transference. As a result of transference the patient is able to represent the analyst as one of the persons involved in an earlier conflict. The person is, as a result, able to reexperience earlier conflicts and gain insight into the unconscious causes of his symptoms.

Dollard and Miller accept the essential outline of this theory of psychotherapy. According to their analysis, psychotherapy involves the gradual extinction of inappropriate responses. This comes about through the gradual lifting of repressions permitting the patient to gain insight, that is, to attach appropriate labels to previously repressed materials. The following passage from Dollard and Miller summarizes their view of this process:

### Adaptive Discriminations

One of the functions of verbal and other cue-producing responses is to make innately similar situations more distinctive and thus to cut down on the amount of primary stimulus generalization. This helps in the formation of adaptive discriminations, especially with respect to culturally emphasized differences. Such discriminations can reduce irrational fears. As was pointed out in the previous chapter, the removal of the repression that obscures the past helps the patient to discriminate by enabling him to contrast the childhood conditions responsible for establishing the fear with the quite different ones of his adult life. Even without recapturing past repressed memories, somewhat similar results can also be achieved by labeling the current situation accurately. Verbal labels and other cue-producing responses also help to cut down on the type of generalization responsible for displacement.

Effects of this type were evident in the case of Mrs. A. As the result of the cruel domination of her foster mother, who punished any form of independence or counteraggression, she was practically unable to express any form of anger. In fact she had learned to suppress her anger by protestations of love that would be described in analytic terms as a reaction formation. Since she could not label her foster mother as being to blame, her smoldering aggression generalized to other people who reminded her of her foster mother but did not frighten her so much. This generalized (i.e. displaced) aggression came out in sudden, inexplicable, murderous thoughts. For example, once when she was washing dishes with a girl friend, she was frightened by the thought: "What if I picked up this knife and killed her?"

The therapist pointed out the differences between the childhood conditions, when she was helpless in the face of the cruel domination of her foster mother, and the current conditions of her life as an adult. As he directed her attention toward and helped her to label these differences, she became able to bear the thought of being angry. Once the drive of anger was labeled, it was possible to help her to make another socially important discrimination. While our society taboos irrational and unjustifiable expressions of aggression, it does permit a certain amount of aggression in self-defense or in response to unfair treatment by others. After this difference was pointed out, Mrs. A. was able to get angry at the snubs that she received from her mother-in-law, who was from a higher social class, and to point out to her husband the unfair treatment that she was receiving.

With the source of the anger clearly labeled and the proper self-defense measures taken, one would expect the irrational murderous impulses against friends to drop out.

(From J. Dollard & N. E. Miller, *Personality and psychotherapy.* New York: McGraw-Hill, 1950. Used with permission of McGraw-Hill Book Company.)

For Dollard and Miller psychotherapy involves a slow process permitting the patient to deal with previously repressed materials.

The social learning approach to therapy is radically different. Since they accord no special relevance to the unconscious they do not believe that the goal of therapy is to permit the patient to gain insight into the unconscious causes of his behavior. Bandura and Walters have emphasized the use of models in producing behavior modification. A study by Bandura, Blanchard, and Ritter (1969) illustrates the kind of procedures of behavior modification which are consonant with social learning principles. The subjects in this study were severely snake phobic. The study compared the efficacy of three methods of treatment of the phobia. The first method of treatment involved the use of systematic desensitization (Wolpe, 1958, 1961). This method has three steps. First, there is training in muscular relaxation (see Jacobson, 1938). Second, the therapist attempts to identify the areas of anxiety of the patient and constructs a heirarchy of successively more anxiety-producing situations. Third, the relaxation responses are now paired with the least anxiety-arousing situations. The patient is instructed to imagine an anxiety-inducing situation while muscularly relaxed. This procedure continues until the patient has progressed through the hierarchy.

In addition to the use of systematic desensitization, Bandura *et al.* investigated two types of modeling approaches to behavior modification. One group of Ss was exposed to a symbolic model who engaged in various fear provoking behaviors with a snake without showing fear and while showing positive responses to the snake. A second group of Ss were exposed to a live model who exhibited positive responses to the snake. In addition, the live model guided the snake phobic Ss and helped them to make several responses to the snake.

After subjects were given their various treatments they were tested for their ability to perform various responses with the snake. Figure 9.12 presents the results of these tests. Figure 9.12 indicates that the most effective behavior modification occurred for those subjects exposed to the live model who assisted them to make responses.

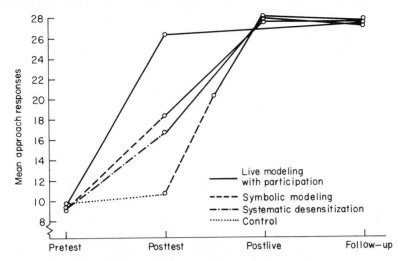

Fig. 9.12. Mean number of approach responses performed by subjects before and after receiving their respective treatments (posttest). (Control subjects subsequently received symbolic modeling without relaxation. The positive point combines the scores of subjects in each condition who required no additional treatment and those who were later given the supplementary treatment combining modeling with guided participation. The approach behavior in all four groups was measured again in the follow-up study conducted one month later.) (From A. Bandura, E. A. Blanchard, & Brunhilde Ritter, Relative efficiency of desensitization and modeling approaches for inducing behavioral changes. *Journal of Personality and Social Psychology*, 1969, **13**, 173–199.)

A number of other findings in the Bandura, Blanchard, and Ritter study support the efficacy of the live modeling procedure. The subjects exposed to this method of behavior modification were able to perform more approach behavior when presented with a different kind of snake. In addition, they were the only group to show a reduction in another fear—the fear of animals.

The three methods of behavior modification studied by Bandura *et al.* have a common theoretical foundation—namely the extinction of an aversive state. The phobic response is viewed as an avoidance response. If the aversive state which is elicited by the phobic stimulus is removed the internal stimulation which controls and motivates the phobic response is removed. The process by which the aversive state is eliminated by these procedures may involve counterconditioning. That is, the pairing of stimuli which elicit aversive states with muscular relaxation may cause the stimulus to elicit relaxation responses which are incompatible with the aversive states it previously elicited thereby resulting in the extinction of the capacity of the phobic stimulus to elicit an aversive state. (See Yates, 1970, especially pp. 67–72) The use of models has the additional advantage of providing vicarious positive reinforcement for approach responses.

There are several differences between the methods of behavior modification advocated by Bandura (1969) and more traditional views of therapy. Unlike traditional interview methods of therapy, behavior modification procedures do not attempt to help their clients achieve insight into the reasons for their behavior. Relatively little emphasis is placed on the development of an intensive interpersonal relationship between the therapist and client. The behavior therapist attempts to discover the specific stimuli or reinforcing events which are assumed to control the behavior which is to be modified. Once these have been discovered he attempts to alter their influence or introduce new events which will lead to behavior modification. The principal differences between traditional views of therapy and social learning theory derive from their views as to the underlying determinants of behavior problems. Bandura's view of this difference is given in the following passage:

Psychodynamic and social-learning approaches to psychotherapy are, therefore, equally concerned with modifying the "underlying" determinants of deviant response patterns; however, these theories differ, often radically, in what they regard these "causes" to be, a crucial difference which in turn influences the types of stimulus conditions favored in the respective treatments. To take a simple but telling example, in an effort to gain a better understanding of some of the factors governing deviant behavior likely to be labeled "symptomatic," Ayllon, Haughton, and Hughes (1965) induced and sustained for a time a bizarre broom-carrying response in an adult schizophrenic by periodic positive reinforcement of the behavior. A psychotherapist, who was unaware of the conditions which had established and maintained this response pattern, invoked the following underlying causes:

> Her constant and compulsive pacing, holding a broom in the manner she does, could be seen as a ritualistic procedure, a magical action.... Her broom would be then: (1) a child that gives her love and she gives him in return her devotion, (2) a phallic symbol, (3) the sceptre of an omnipotent queen... this is a magical procedure in which the patient carried out her wishes, expressed in a way that is far beyond our solid, rational and conventional way of thinking and acting [p. 3].

In treating the persistent display of bizarre and apparently purposeless behavior this therapist, on the basis of his causal explanation, would subject the woman to extended interpretive probing of her sexual conflicts and delusions of omnipotence. On the other hand, the behavioral therapist, viewing the rewarding outcomes as the major determinant of the so-called psychotic symptom, would alter the reinforcement contingency governing the behavior. Indeed, when the occasional rewards for carrying a broom were completely withdrawn the "symptom" promptly vanished and, according to a two-year follow-up study, never reappeared.

In light of the above considerations, it would be both more accurate and advantageous to redefine the causal versus symptomatic treatment controversy as being primarily concerned with the question of whether a particular form of therapy chooses to modify conditions that, in actuality, exercise *strong* or *weak* or *no significant control* over the behavior in question.

(Bandura, 1969, pp. 49, 50)

## Conclusions and the Problem of Comparison

We have sketched, in a rather general way, some of the principle differences between social learning theory and more traditional psychodynamic views of personality dynamics. As far as possible, evaluative comments and the question of adequacy of theoretical explanations have been avoided. The differences between these two approaches would appear to raise a fundamental issue in understanding personality dynamics. Therefore, it is necessary to try to come to some view as to which of these approaches provides the proper basis for the understanding of personality dynamics. We shall return to this question subsequent to a further discussion of therapy and the unconscious in Chapters 10 and 11.

CHAPTER **10**

# THE UNCONSCIOUS

An essential substantive respect in which psychoanalytic theory differs from social learning theory is in the role assigned to the unconscious. In this chapter we shall review research and theory which deals with the unconscious in an attempt to evaluate the adequacy of these competing approaches to personality dynamics.

## Definition of the Unconscious

In order to examine research on the unconscious it is necessary to have some definition of the unconscious and the kinds of data which permit the inference of its existence. Miller (1942) in a classic review of research on the unconscious listed 16 different definitions of the unconscious. For our purposes a phenomenon which provides evidence for the existence of the unconscious is one which demonstrates that an external stimulus or an internal state which is out of awareness, which could be in awareness, has an influence on behavior which is different from the influence it would have if it were in awareness. This definition can be split into four parts for purposes of explication.

1. *A stimulus is out of awareness*. This is the most fundamental meaning of the unconscious. The term 'awareness' may be clarified by making a distinction between awareness (or experience) and a response to this awareness which serves to classify, categorize, or identify the nature of the experience (Brody & Oppenheim, 1966, 1967). (As we shall see, this distinction can be most precisely defined by reference to signal detectability theory). One way of testing whether a stimulus is or is not out of awareness is by the use of discrimination procedures. A stimulus is out of awareness if its presence or absence cannot be discriminated with greater than chance

accuracy. An example may serve to make this abstract statement concrete. A *S* might be confronted with a screen on which a psychologist is able to flash a dim light for a brief duration. The psychologist gives a warning signal and then either proceeds to flash the light or to present a blank slide. The *S* is instructed to indicate on each trial whether or not a stimulus has been presented. The *S* may give a verbal or a motor response— for example, raise your right hand on those trials in which the light is present. If the *S*'s responses are lawfully related to the presence or absence of the light the *S* is able to discriminate the presence or absence of the stimulus with greater than chance accuracy. Under these conditions the stimulus may be said to be in awareness. Ability to discriminate would be indicated in this situation by significant differences in probabilities. For example, a significant difference between the conditional probability of the *S* indicating the stimulus is present when it is in fact present and the conditional probability of the *S* indicating that the stimulus is present when it is in fact not present.

2. *The stimulus or state could be in awareness.* Psychologists are inclined to explain behavior with reference to many hypothetical abstract entities. Many of these entities are not the sort of thing which a person is aware of in the normal course of events. For example, we have discussed evidence which indicates genotypes influence personality. We do not normally think of an individual as being capable of experiencing his genotype. If genotypes influence behavior and if they are not experiencable, then entities which are out of awareness influence behavior. This example apparently indicates that entities which are out of awareness can influence behavior. This proposition would probably be acceptable to most psychologists. When we discuss evidence for the existence of the unconscious, apparently a stronger criterion is required—namely, that the stimulus or state is the sort of thing which could be experienced. In experiments dealing with external stimuli, for example, lights and sound, they may be presented at intensities below "threshold." However, it is assumed that, at some higher intensity, they can be experienced. In studies dealing with internal states we shall be concerned with such states as anger which is assumed to be experiencable.

3. *The stimulus or state has an influence on behavior.* It is obvious that there are an infinite variety of stimuli which we could be aware of but which we are not aware of at a moment in time. This, in and of itself, is utterly noncontroversial. We have evidence for unconscious influences on behavior when stimuli which are out of awareness can be shown to have some effect on behavior.

4. *The influence of the stimulus or state is different from the influence it would have if it were in awareness.* This last aspect of the definition may be expendable. That is, it is a legitimate question whether any stimulus which is out of awareness which could be in awareness does in fact influence behavior. However, from at least two points of view, the fourth condition is crucial. First, Freud assumed that stimuli which were repressed and denied awareness would obey different laws and would have different effects than stimuli which were in awareness or accessible (not repressed) to consciousness. Second, if a stimulus in awareness has the same effects as a stimulus out of awareness, then the distinction is irrelevant for the explanation of behavior and may be disregarded. We are required to take account of the unconscious and to introduce a construct with that name only if it has some explanatory value.

## Empirical Research on the Unconscious

Studies on the unconscious may be crudely divided into three categories. First, these are studies which are assumed to be relevant to the unconscious which do not in fact deal with the unconscious, at least as the term is used here. Second, these are studies which attempt to provide evidence for the existence of the unconscious by deriving a prediction using psychoanalytic theory. The findings of the experiment are then explained by reference to hypothetical states which are assumed to be unconscious. However, such studies provide, at best, only indirect evidence for the existence of the unconscious, since their interpretation rests on the acceptance of what is taken to be controversial in this chapter, the existence of the unconscious. Third, there are studies which deal more or less directly with the unconscious as it is defined here.

Studies of interoceptive conditioning provide an example of the first type of study. There have been a number of studies purporting to demonstrate unconscious processes in classical conditioning situations. Razran (1961) has written a monograph dealing with current Russian conditioning studies which he claims provide insight into the unconscious. Razran discusses a number of studies dealing with interoceptive conditioning—a type of classical conditioning in which either the CS or the UCS or both are presented directly to the viscera. Razran cites an experiment by P. O. Makarov which illustrates the procedures and the kinds of findings obtained in interoceptive conditioning studies. In this study an inflatable gastric tube was used which permitted the experimenter to warm or cool the interior of the stomach. Four different conditioning procedures were used:

1. The CS was cold to the interior of the stomach followed by the application of a hot stimulus to the exterior of the stomach (UCS).
2. The CS was an internal hot stimulus followed by an external cold stimulus.
3. The CS was an external cold stimulus followed by an internal hot stimulus.
4. The CS was an external hot stimulus followed by an internal cold stimulus.

The response recorded to these various stimuli was the amount of vasoconstriction or vasodilation in the arm. The response to a cold stimulus (whether internal or external) is vasoconstriction and the response to a hot stimulus is vasodilation. Under conditions where the CS was external, conditioning occurred in such a way that the CS began to elicit the same kind of response as the UCS. Thus, under Condition 3 the external cold stimulus elicited the vasodilation response rather than the vasoconstriction response which it had elicited prior to being paired with the UCS. However, where the CS was an internal stimulus (Conditions 1 and 2) the effect was different. Under these conditions the CS suppressed the responses of vasodilation and vasoconstriction which had previously occurred in Conditions 1 and 2 in response to the UCS. The external UCS changes in the direction of the internal CS.

In another experiment cited by Razran an external stimulus acquired dominance over an internal stimulus. In this study a patient in a hospital had a pressure gauge (manometer) attached to his bladder. The patient was permitted to observe the manometer readings. This established a classical conditioning procedure in which high readings of the dial (CS) were associated with high bladder pressure (UCS) which elicited the UCR of desiring to urinate. After the conditioning procedure the experimenter presented a CS indicative of a high pressure in the bladder even though the subject's true bladder pressure was low. Under these conditions the $S$ experienced a desire to urinate. Similarly, when the dial of the manometer falsely indicated low pressure in the bladder the subject experienced a reduced urge to urinate.

Razran argues that results such as these help to illuminate Freudian psychodynamics and help to make the unconscious observable. For example these experiments, according to Razran, illuminate the process by which emotions such as anxiety and its accompanying physiological changes might act as conditioned stimuli which elicit such internal changes as rectal distension or its opposite leading to constipation. Conversely, changes in the rectal sphincter could act as a CS eliciting anxiety and its accompanying physiological changes.

The studies of interoceptive conditioning cited by Razran are intrinsically interesting. It is not clear however that they are relevant to understanding unconscious phenomena. Razan assumes that interoceptive stimuli are by their very nature unconscious. If one grants this, then it is easy to see how external stimuli can elicit internal changes which are, by definition, unconscious, or how internal states which are unconscious can through a conditioning process, elicit reactions which are different from those which they naturally elicit.

Razran assumes that the internal stimuli used in interoceptive conditioning studies are unconscious. There is little evidence that the stimuli are unconscious in the sense of being out of awareness. There is no reason to believe that individuals would not be able to discriminate the presence and absence of interoceptive stimuli which are used as the stimuli in these studies. Razran may be using the term "unconscious" to refer to that which is not verbalized rather than that which is out of awareness. However, there is no indication that $S$s in these experiments do not have a verbal description for interoceptive stimuli—although the description might use terms which are quite at variance with the terms used by the experimenter. Further, it should be possible to train a person to assign the same verbal description to an interoceptive stimulus as is used by the experimenter. This could be done by training the subject to recognize the sensation caused by the interoceptive stimulus and to assign to it the label used by the experimenter.

An alternative sense in which interoceptive conditioning might be unconscious is that the $S$ is believed to be unable to identify the contingency between CS and UCS. But there is no evidence of this. That is, $S$s may in fact verbalize the contingency of CS and UCS although it is not clear that such a verbalization would influence interoceptive conditioning. The process of interoceptive conditioning may not be subject to voluntary control. In any case, it appears clear that Razran presents no evidence that interoceptive conditioning is, in the sense in which the term is used here, indicative of unconscious influences on behavior.

Sarnoff and Corwin (1959) have reported a study of the second type. They assumed, in agreement with psychoanalytic theory, that some male $S$s were high in castration anxiety. Such individuals were assumed to develop unconscious fears of castration in response to sexual arousal. This repressed unconscious fear would influence conscious thoughts and behavior. In order to test this notion Sarnoff and Corwin gave a group of male undergraduates a card from the Blacky test (Blum, 1950), a projective test designed to measure psychoanalytic constructs. The card depicted a blindfolded dog and a large knife which appeared about to cut off the dog's tail. A second dog watched the first dog. The *S*s were presented with a series of statements describing the emotions of the second dog as he watched the first dog. Those *S*s who chose statements indicating that the dog was very upset by this experience were assumed to be high in castration anxiety. Subsequently, *S*s who were high or low in castration anxiety were exposed to a series of pictures of female nudes or fully clothed females. Sarnoff and Corwin found that the high-castration-anxiety *S*s showed a greater increase in fear of death as a result of looking at the female nudes than the low-castration-anxiety subjects. No differences in in fear of death were observed among high- and low-castration-anxiety *S*s who were exposed to the pictures of fully clothed females. Sarnoff and Corwin interpret these findings as indicating the influence of unconscious castration anxiety on fear of death.

The Sarnoff and Corwin study provides only indirect evidence for the existence of the unconscious. Even if we accept the view that the Blacky test does in fact measure castration anxiety we have little or no evidence that the castration anxiety is unconscious. This is not demonstrated in the experiment but is assumed as given by psychoanalytic theory.

In the review of experiments of the unconscious presented here we shall emphasize the third kind of study. Namely, studies which have attempted to gain relatively direct information about the unconscious by indicating that stimuli which have been empirically shown to be out of awareness do in fact influence behavior.

## Alleged Empirical Demonstrations of the Unconscious

In order to demonstrate that a stimulus which is out of awareness has influenced behavior it is necessary to establish that the stimulus is in fact out of awareness. The easiest way to demonstrate this is to ask the subject if he is in fact aware of the stimulus. However, we must be sure that the *S*'s report is veridical—that is, that the report may be taken as an adequate index of the state of the *S*'s awareness. We shall begin our discussion of empirical demonstrations of the unconscious with a review of three types of studies, verbal operant conditioning, unconscious generalization and hypnosis studies in which there is an alleged demonstration of the unconscious. In each case there is reason to be skeptical of the demonstration because of doubts about the adequacy of the verbal reports which are used to index awareness.

VERBAL OPERANT CONDITIONING

Verbal operant conditioning is an operant conditioning type of experiment in which the response which is reinforced is a class of verbal responses, for example, plural nouns. The reinforcer may be either a verbal response of the experimenter, for example, good, or a nonverbal reinforcer. Evidence of operant conditioning is obtained when the frequency of occurrence of the reinforced response class increases. The results of the first experiments on verbal operant conditioning indicated that the effect of the reinforcer was automatic and was not mediated by awareness. A verbal operant conditioning situation has three elements, a response, a reinforcer, and a contingent relationship between the response and the reinforcer. When it is asserted that conditioning occurs without awareness it is *not* assumed that the response is not in awareness. Presumably, a $S$ who utters a plural noun is clearly aware of the response he makes. Similarly, the $S$ is aware of the occurrence of the reinforcer. What is alleged is that the $S$ is not aware of, and forms no hypothesis about, the relationship between the reinforced response and the reinforcer. The basis for this assertion involved postexperimental questioning by the experimenter. On the basis of rather casual questioning, $S$s generally stated that they were not aware of the contingency between the response to be reinforced and the reinforcer (see Greenspoon, 1955). Subsequent studies used more extensive postexperimental interview procedures. These studies indicate that only $S$s who were judged to be aware of the contingency between reinforced response and reinforcer tended to condition (Spielberger and De Nike, 1966). These studies appeared to indicate that awareness of contingency was a necessary condition for the occurrence of verbal operant conditioning. However, there are a number of reasons why such results are not critical. Spielberger and De Nike (1966) list the following objections to the inference that verbal operant conditioning requires awareness of contingency on the basis of data showing that, as judged by a postexperimental interview, only $S$s who are aware condition:

1. The awareness is suggested by the questions and is not in fact present during the conditioning situation.

2. Conditioning may occur without awareness. The $S$ then notices his response and becomes aware of the relationship between the response and the reinforcer.

3. Awareness is itself an acquired operant response which is conditioned. However, the awareness has no influence on the acquisition of the critical response.

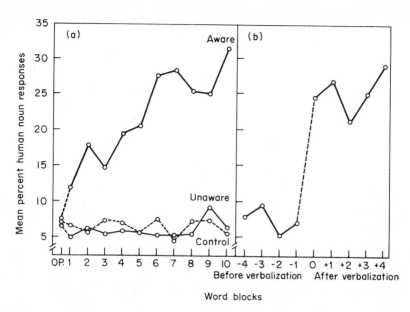

FIG. 10.1. Conditioning curves. (a) Mean percentage of human-noun responses given by the Aware, Unaware, and Control groups on the conditioning task. (b) Conditioning curve for the Aware group in which the data for preverbalization and postverbalization word blocks have been Vincentized. (From C. D. Spielberger & L. D. DeNike, Descriptive behaviorism versus cognitive theory in verbal operant conditioning. *Psychological Review*, 1966, **73**, 306–326.)

In order to circumvent the difficulties involved in assessing awareness from postexperimental interviews, a number of experimenters have attempted to assess awareness during the experiment (see Spielberger & De Nike, 1966). De Nike (1964) reinforced human noun responses by saying "mmm-hmm" in a word naming task. He asked his *S*s to write their "thoughts about the experiment" after each block of 24 response words. Four judges classified the *S*'s protocols into those indicating awareness or lack of awareness of the correct contingency. Figure 10.1 presents the results of the experiment. The left-hand side of Figure 10.1 indicates that only those *S*s who were judged to be aware at some trial block conditioned. The data presented on the right-hand side of Figure 10.1 presents an analysis of performance for aware *S*s as a function of trial block on which they were first judged to be aware. The "0" block represents the trial block of 25 responses in which the *S*s were first judged aware. The negative trial blocks are those prior to the "aware" trial block and the positive trial blocks are those subsequent to the aware block. The data clearly indicate that $S$s do not exhibit evidence of conditioning prior to the block on which they correctly verbalize the contingency. These results apparently indicate that awareness of contingency is a necessary condition for the occurrence of verbal operant conditioning. The results would be somewhat more conclusive if awareness was assessed on a trial-by-trial basis. It is still possible that awareness follows the occurrence of the reinforcer. However, this possibility is somewhat farfetched in that it would require that the reinforcer has no effect on behavior for several trial blocks and then a dramatic effect followed by the rapid occurrence of awareness. The most plausible interpretation of the results of the De Nike study is that no conditioning occurred prior to the development of awareness of the correct contingency.

There is one study which presents results which challenge the conclusion that awareness of contingency is necessary for verbal conditioning. Dixon and Oakes (1965) started with the hypothesis that in the typical verbal conditioning study, $S$s had time during the intertrial intervals to form hypotheses about the nature of the experiment. In order to prevent this activity they designed a study in which $S$s were required to perform a color-naming task during the intertrial intervals. They then assessed awareness postexperimentally. They found that $S$s who were assigned to the color-naming group conditioned as well as the other $S$s. Also, under color naming conditions the correlation between their measure of awareness and conditioning was .06. Under conditions without color naming the correlation between a measure of awareness of contingency and conditioning was $-.66$, indicating that $S$s who tended to be aware of the contingency tended to condition better than those who did not. The Dixon and Oakes study suggests that the relationship between awareness and verbal operant conditioning is not invariant and that, under some conditions, verbal operant conditioning can occur without awareness of the contingency between critical response and the reinforcer.

What do the verbal operant conditioning studies tell us about unconscious phenomena? First, there is a methodological point. Different procedures for assessing awareness will give rather different indications of a $S$'s awareness. A $S$'s response to a casual question about the purpose of an experiment may not elicit the full range of his awareness. Second, the studies do suggest that $S$s may not be aware of the rules which determine their responses even though the rules are capable of being experienced. However, in the Dixon and Oakes study for subjects in the color naming condition, awareness or its lack was unrelated to conditioning. Consequently, these findings do not fulfill the fourth criterion of an unconscious phenomenon—namely, that the stimulus which is out of awareness affects behavior *differently* than it does when in awareness.

Unconscious Generalization

Diven (1937) used a classical conditioning situation to study the process of unconscious generalization. Diven presented *S*s with a list of words including the word "barn." The subjects were asked to associate to the words for 12 sec. Whenever the subject had finished associating to the word "barn" he was given an electric shock. After this conditioning experience the subject's GSR responses to the stimuli were recorded. He found that subjects who were reportedly unaware of the contingency between barn and shock, exhibited GSR responses to the words which had rural connotations.

Chatterjee and Eriksen (1962) designed a study based on Diven's. Their study employed a more sensitive inquiry procedure to determine awareness. They found that the majority of *S*s in their study could not correctly verbalize the contingency between a critical word and the shocks which followed it. And, like Diven, the found that *S*s gave GSR response to words which were similar in meaning to the shock word. Chatterjee and Eriksen went on to ask their *S*s to rate each of the words in the experiment with respect to whether or not it was followed by shock. They found that the GSR response was larger to words which *S*s believed were followed by shock than to words which he believed were not followed by shock. The "unconscious generalization" which occurred in the Diven study was probably an artifact of the subject's inability to correctly verbalize the contingency. That is, *S*s who are uncertain of the critical stimulus may entertain a variety of hypotheses with respect to it. When a stimulus is presented which has an uncertain status the *S* has an emotional response indexed by the GSR.

Hypnosis

One of the empirical demonstrations of the unconscious accepted by Freud (1957) was the occurrence of posthypnotic phenomena in which a subject is assumed to carry out a posthypnotic suggestion without any awareness of having received the suggestion. The *S*s can be given instructions while under hypnosis to perform some action in response to a signal posthypnotically. In addition, *S*s may be given instructions to have complete amnesia for the posthypnotic suggestion. Under these conditions it is alleged that some *S*s perform posthypnotic responses without awareness of the reason for their response.

The claims for the occurrence of posthypnotic phenomena with amnesia, until recent years, rested on clinical demonstration rather than controlled investigation. In recent years there has been an upsurge of research on

hypnosis employing various control groups in order to evaluate the au-
thenticity of the various phenomena associated with hypnosis. In particular, there has been an emphasis on the attempt to duplicate the
phenomena associated with hypnosis without the induction of a hypnotic
state. One approach to this problem involves the use of Ss who are told
to simulate hypnosis (Orne, 1959). Such Ss are used to indicate the extent
to which responses in a hypnotic situation are the results of what Orne
calls the demand-characteristics of the experiment. A study by Orne and
Evans (1965) illustrates the use of this type of control group. Orne and
Evans were interested in the influence of hypnosis on the performance of
dangerous, harmful, or criminal actions. In their study Ss were asked to
pick up a venomous snake and to throw acid at the experimenter. The
snake and the experimenter were behind a plate of invisible glass. Six
subjects who were good hypnotic subjects were firmly instructed to perform these actions while they were under hypnosis. Five of the six hypnotic Ss performed these actions. Another group of six Ss who were poor
hypnotic subjects and allegedly incapable of entering a "trance" state
were instructed to simulate hypnosis. All six of the Ss in this group attempted to pick up the snake and to throw the acid. The Orne and Evans
study indicates that criminal and dangerous actions in an experimental
setting will be as readily performed by Ss in hypnosis as by subjects who
are not. Orne and Evans indicated that all of the Ss believed that they
would not be harmed because they were in an experiment conducted by
responsible individuals. The tendency to perform the dangerous actions
was thus apparently a result of the "demand characteristics" of the experimental situation and cannot be attributable to the special influence
of the hypnotic state.

Orne, Sheehan, and Evans (1968) used a simulating control group in
a study of posthypnotic phenomena. Two groups of Ss participated in
the experiment. One group consisted of 17 highly selected, excellent hypnotic subjects who had been given special training in hypnosis. The second
group consisted of 14 Ss who were low in susceptibility to hypnosis who
acted as hypnotic simulators. All Ss were given a trance induction and
were given the posthypnotic suggestion to touch their forehead with their
right hand for the next 48 hours whenever they heard the word, "experiment." In addition, the Ss were told that they would not be aware of
making the response. The subjects were given a number of different tests
for posthypnotic response. In addition to tests by the experimenter the
Ss were tested in a context which was removed from the experimental
setting. The Ss were asked by the secretary whether they had arrived for
Dr. Sheehan's *experiment*. On another occasion the Ss were asked by the
secretary if it would be all right to pay them for today's *experiment*.

TABLE 10.1

*Responses to Casual Tests of the Posthypnotic Suggestion*[a]

| Type of test | Hypnotized[b] (passed all), n = 6 | Hypnotized (failed some), n = 11 | Simulating (passed all) n = 6 | Simulating[c] (failed some), n = 7 |
|---|---|---|---|---|
| By secretary in waiting room | | | | |
| #1 (1st day) | 4 | 1 | 0 | 3 |
| #2 (1st day) | 3 | 2 | 0 | 0 |
| #3 (2nd day) | 3 | 2 | 0 | 0 |
| Both days #1 or #2, or both, and also #3 | 3 | 2 | 0 | 0 |
| By E | | | | |
| #4 (in corridor) | 6 | 4 | 6 | 6 |
| #5 (at conclusion) | 0 | 2 | 1 | 2 |

From M. T. Orne, P. W. Sheehan, & F. J. Evans, Occurrence of posthypnotic behavior outside the experimental setting. *Journal of Personality and Social Psychology*, 1968, **9,** 189–196.

[a] Each entry represents the number of subjects in the given category making a positive response.

[b] The Ss are separated on the basis of passing all, or failing at least one of the six criteria for good hypnotic performance. For specification of criteria, see text.

[c] One intended simulator was excluded from the results. Although he received simulating instructions, he spontaneously decided not to simulate during the experiment

Table 10.1 presents a summary of the principal results of this experiment. The most interesting finding in the study is the difference in response to the word "experiment" when the word was uttered by the secretary in a context which was removed from the experimental setting. Although the simulators responded to the critical word when it was uttered by the experimenter about as frequently as the true hypnotic subjects, not one simulator consistently responded to the word when it was uttered by the secretary. A number of true hypnotic subjects consistently responded to the critical word when it was uttered by the secretary.

In a subsequent discussion of the results of this experiment Sheehan and Orne (1968) indicate that the hypnotic subjects who responded consistently to the posthypnotic suggestion on all occasions when it was given reported amnesia for the suggestion. These results lead Sheehan and Orne to suggest that the hypnotist's posthypnotic suggestion acts as an unconscious motivational influence. In addition, the nature of the posthypnotic response is different when the suggestion is in awareness than when it is out of awareness. Simulators and the good hypnotic subjects who failed to respond consistently were allegedly aware of the suggestion. If the subject is aware of the suggestion it tends to be restricted in its occurrence to the experimental setting itself and is not likely to occur outside of this setting. The data of the Orne *et al.* study, if accepted at face value, appear to fulfill the general definition of unconscious phenomena given at the beginning of this chapter. That is, they indicate that a particular suggestion which is not in awareness which could be in awareness has an influence on behavior which is different from the influence it would have it it were in awareness.

The adequacy of this interpretation of the data of the Orne, Sheehan, and Evans experiment rests on the difference in response of the simulating subjects and the true hypnotic subjects. There are at least two reasons for being cautious in the interpretation of these results. First, the simulating *S*s are given instructions to deceive the experimenter. These instructions would appear to direct the *S*'s behavior particularly to the experimental situation and to set up a demand to be particularly vigilant in the presence of the experimenter and carry no instruction to be vigilant outside of the experimental context. If the bias implicit in the instructions to the simulators was not present, it is possible that the pattern of response of the simulators to the posthypnotic suggestions would have been similar to that of the true hypnotic *S*. Second, the simulators are drawn from a totally different population of *S*s who, in addition to the fact of not being capable of entering the "trance state," have not had the benefit of special training in hypnosis given to the hypnotic subjects prior to the critical experimental situation. It is possible that the differences in personal characteristics and the differences in preexperimental treatments might have been responsible for the different pattern of responses of the simulators and the true hypnotic subjects. For example, because of their history of longer involvement with the experimenter and perhaps because of qualities associated with being a good hypnotic *S*, they would be more motivated to report amnesia for the suggestions when this was part of their instructions. That is, a good hypnotic *S* is one who, *inter alia*, responds positively to suggestions. One such suggestion is to have amnesia. Consequently, the report that the *S* does in fact have amnesia is peculiarly subject to being biased.

Bowers (1966) has reported a study of response to posthypnotic suggestion which circumvents some, but not all, of the objections raised above to the Orne, Sheehan and Evans study. In his study Bowers used only *S*s who were susceptible to hypnosis and who were given equal training in hypnosis. The *S*s were randomly assigned to a hypnotic and a simulating group. The *S*s were given instructions to respond posthypnotically to a verbal operant conditioning task by using the responses, "he" and "they," although they would have no awareness of making this response or the reasons for making the response. The *S*s in the hypnotic group received these instructions while hypnotized. The *S*s in the simulating group were awakened before receiving these instructions and were then asked to act as if they were hypnotized. Then, a second experimenter administered the verbal operant conditioning task to both groups. Experimenter 1 returned and then asked the *S*s to talk to a third experimenter who was doing pilot research on verbal behavior. The *S*s were led to believe that the experiment on hypnosis was finished. Experimenter 3 then asked the *S*s a series of questions about their behavior in the verbal operant conditioning task.

There was no difference in the behavior of the hypnotic and simulating subjects in the verbal conditioning task. However, there was a dramatic difference in their response to the postexperimental interview conducted by experimenter 3. All 13 *S*s in the simulating group were judged to be aware of their use of "he" and "they", and presumably the reason for their use of "he" and "they". Of the 14 *S*s in the hypnotic group, 8 were judged to be unaware of their use of "he" and "they" and their reasons for using these words. Bowers points out that these results suggest that the basis for the identical behavior of simulators and hypnotic *S*s may be quite different. In particular, these results suggest that the hypnotic *S*s performed the posthypnotic behavior without awareness of the suggestion.

Barber (1969, see Footnote 1, pp. 28 and 29) has criticized Bowers' interpretation of his results. He points out that the differences in the behavior of the hypnotic and simulating *S*s may be attributable to the differences in the instructions they have received rather than the special properties of the hypnotic state. The simulating *S*s are told to act as if they were hypnotized, suggesting that they were not to forget the instructions but only that they were to act as if they had forgotten. Barber points out that the results of a study by Barber and Calverley (1966) suggest that hypnosis is not necessary to create posthypnotic amnesia. In their study, *S*s under hypnosis and control *S*s not under hypnosis were instructed to learn a list of six words. One fourth of the *S*s in each group were asked to try to forget the words they had learned. One fourth of the *S*s in each group were given peremptory suggestions that they would forget. Another fourth of the *S*s were instructed to act as if they had forgotten, and the remaining *S*s were given no special instructions with respect to the list of words. Barber and Calverley (1966) found that nonhypnotic *S*s showed more forgetting than hypnotic *S*s when given permissive motivational instructions to try to forget. The hypnotic and nonhypnotic *S*s showed approximately equal forgetting when they were given peremptory suggestions to forget and when they were told to act as if they had forgotten. These results suggest that hypnotic induction is not necessary to achieve amnesia, and that hypnotic induction contributes little or nothing to the efficacy of instructions to forget suggestions.

The amnesia obtained in the Barber and Calverley study is based on reported inability to recall the words which had been learned. Barber and Calverley found that *S*s who were unable to recall the words were able to recognize them by selecting them from a list containing these and other words. In other words, the subjects were able to discriminate the presence of the words and hence, by the most critical test of awareness, the subjects were aware although they stated they were not.

Blum (1961) instructed three good hypnotic subjects while under hypnosis to feel nervous and upset whenever a stimulus consisting of three dots in a horizontal line was presented tachistoscopically to the subject. In addition, the subject was instructed not to see the stimulus when it was flashed. Presumably, the *S* would be required to unconsciously recognize the stimulus and then block its access to consciousness. The *S*s reported that they were not aware of the presentation of the critical stimuli. Even though they reported lack of awareness, the *S*s were asked to guess which stimulus were presented to them. The *S*s exhibited GSR responses indicative of a strong emotional reaction only on those trials in which they guessed that the critical stimulus was present. If the critical stimulus was present but the *S*'s guess about it was wrong the GSR response was absent. Blum's experiment suggests that *S*s who report lack of awareness to a stimulus induced by hypnosis will not respond to that stimulus unless they are able to discriminate its presence. Put another way, the instructions given to the *S*s in the Blum experiment were contradictory. If the *S* was truly unaware of the stimulus then he could not respond with anxiety in its presence. In order to be anxious, the *S* must first know that the appropriate stimulus is present.

The findings of the recognition tests in the Barber and Calverley experiment and the findings of Blum's study suggest an alternative interpretation of the demonstration of response to posthypnotic suggestion without awareness. The suggestion for amnesia may bias the veridicality of the verbal reports about amnesia. This biasing may come about in a variety of ways. The *S*s may not wish to inform the experimenter that they have violated his instructions. Alternatively, *S*s may be unable to accurately reconstruct their own experiences if those experiences are counter to hypnotic or experimental suggestions. That is, the *S*'s report may represent a distortion of which he is unaware. The evidence we have reviewed on the veridicality of verbal reports about awareness in hypnosis research does not permit us to accept demonstrations of response to posthypnotic suggestion without awareness as supporting the influence of unconscious suggestions.

PERCEPTUAL DEFENSE AND SUBCEPTION: THE USE
OF CONCURRENT RESPONSE MEASUREMENT

The studies we shall review in this section attempt to overcome the difficulty of accepting the veridicality of verbal reports indicating lack of awareness by the presentation of stimuli below "threshold" values of awareness while indicating that the subject is capable of response in another response made to the stimuli which are below threshold.

McGinnies (1949) reported the first experiment of this type dealing with what he called perceptual defense. McGinnies experiment involved the presentation of "tabu" words, for example, "whore," "Kotex," and ordinary words, tachistoscopically to *S*s. The stimuli were presented at first very rapidly and then with increased duration until the *S* correctly identified the words presented to him. McGinnies recorded GSR responses during the stimulus presentation. McGinnies reported two principal findings. First, the threshold for correct identification of the tabu words was consistently higher than the threshold for correct identification of neutral words. Second, the GSR responses to tabu words *prior* to correct recognition were higher than the GSR responses to neutral words. McGinnies argued that these two results implied that the *S* was aware of the tabu words but by some defensive process blocked their access to consciousness. That is, the fact that the *S* gave GSR responses to the tabu words prior to their correct recognition indicated a process of discrimination without awareness.

Howes and Solomon (1950) criticized McGnnies' interpretation and suggested two difficulties in his interpretation. First, they pointed out that the threshold for words varies inversely as a function of the frequency of occurrence of the words in English. Words which occur frequently are recognized at lower levels of stimulus duration than words which occur infrequently. Their second, and more important, criticism dealt with the possibility that the *S*s were aware of the tabu words but withheld their verbal report to make sure that they were correct before uttering the socially tabu word in the presence of the phychologist.

Lazarus and McCleary (1951) designed a study to demonstrate discrimination without awareness that would circumvent some of the problems in the original perceptual defense study. They presented ten nonsense syllables to their *S*s. Five of the nonsense syllables, selected at random, were paired with shock in the initial stage of the experiment. Then, they presented the nonsense syllables tachistoscopically at ascending durations until the *S* correctly identified the syllable. They also obtained GSR responses to the stimulus. Their analysis centered on the GSR responses to neutral and shock stimuli on those trials in which the *S* did not correctly identify the stimulus. They found that the average GSR response to stimuli that were not correctly identified was larger when the stimulus which was presented was a shock syllable rather than a nonshock syllable. This difference defined the "subception effect"—which was taken as evidence of discrimination without awareness. This implies that the individual is able to emotionally respond to the stimuli at levels which are below conscious recognition.

Goldiamond (1958) and Eriksen (1957, 1958) both criticized the discrimination without awareness interpretation of the subception effect on methodological grounds. Eriksen has presented an empirical and theoretical analysis of subception which supports an alternative interpretation of the phenomenon. Eriksen's analysis starts with the observation that the subception effect is defined in terms of a discrepancy between two different response systems which are indices of the $S$'s perception. The GSR response system is a continuous one which permits the registration of a range of magnitudes of response to the stimulus. The verbal scoring system used in the Lazarus and McLeary study, by contrast, permits only a dichotomous response—correct recognition versus incorrect recognition. This difference raises the possibility that the verbal scoring system may artifically restrict the sensitivity of the verbal response. This possibility could plausibly arise in the following way: On a particular stimulus presentation the $S$ is uncertain whether or not the stimulus was one of two stimuli. His first response (and the only response permitted him in the Lazarus and McLeary study) might be a nonshock syllable which is incorrect. However, the second verbal response which would have been a shock syllable and the correct response is never given. The GSR on the other hand registers the $S$'s uncertainty and possible awareness of the presence of a shock syllable.

Eriksen designed a series of studies to explicate the relationship among various response indicators of perception. In one of these studies Eriksen presented $S$s with 11 different sized squares. Each square was assigned a number indicative of its size. The stimuli were presented tachistoscopically. Three different response systems were used as indicators of perception, a first verbal response, a second verbal response, and a motor response in which the $S$ adjusted a continuously varying lever to the point indicative of his judgment of the magnitude of the stimulus. Eriksen computed the correlation between each response and the stimulus. He found that the magnitude of the correlation of the first verbal response with the stimulus was higher than the correlation of the other responses with the stimulus. This finding supported earlier results in Eriksen's studies indicating that the verbal system is equal to, or more sensitive than, any other response indicator of perception including the GSR. For example, in a repeat of the Lazarus and MacLeary study, Eriksen found that the verbal response correctly identified the nonsense syllable presented on 45 percent of the trials. The GSR was able to discriminate the presence or absence of a shock syllable (Note: the GSR does not indicate which syllable was presented) on 60 percent of the trials. However, the probability of being correct by change is 50 percent in the GSR case (that is, on 50 percent of the trials a shock syllable will be presented)whereas the probability of being correct by change for the verbal response is 10 percent. If the verbal response is set the same task as the GSR, to discriminate the presence or absence of a shock syllable, a correction for chance responding can be obtained as follows: The verbal response is accurate on 45 percent of the trials. By change, the verbal response should be accurate on one-half the remaining trials. One-half of 55 percent is 27 $\frac{1}{2}$ percent, giving a corrected estimate of accuracy for the verbal response of 72.5 percent, which exceeds the obtained accuracy of the GSR. These results indicate that the verbal response system is a more accurate index of perception than the GSR and question the notion of the GSR as an index of unconscious perception.

Eriksen went on to compute a series of partial correlations to study the relationship between response systems and stimuli in the experiment involving the discimination of different sized squares. He found that the partial correlation between the second verbal response and the stimuli, holding constant the first verbal response, was significant. This finding indicates that the second verbal response gives information about the stimulus which is independent of that which is given by the first response. Put another way, this finding indicates that one would be more accurate in predicting the stimulus actually present on any given trial if one had information about both the first and second verbal response than if one had information about only one of these responses.

The partial correlation between the lever response and the stimuli holding constant the first verbal response was also significant. This indicates that the lever response contains information about the stimulus which is independent of that contained in the first verbal response. The partial correlation between the lever response and the stimulus with the first verbal response held constant is exactly analogous to the subception effect which may be defined as a significant partial correlation between the GSR and the stimuli with the first verbal response held constant. Eriksen's studies indicate that different response indicises of perception tend to be correlated imperfectly with each other and to have significant partial correlations with stimuli when one of the other response systems is held constant. The subception effect will occur for any pair of response indices which account for partially independent sources of variance in the stimuli. Such an interpretation of subception contradicts the view that it represents discrimination without awareness.

Bandura (1969), citing Eriksen's work, prefers to interpret "unconscious" phenomena in terms of the discrepancy between concurrent response systems. Bandura points out that the discrepancies between response systems may be a function of reinforcement. His views are given in the following quotation:

> Genuine disparities among different classes of behavior can be produced through the application of differential reinforcement. Thus, if hostile thoughts and verbalizations are approved or permissively accepted but overt aggressive actions are consistently punished, persons will readily verbalize aggressive feelings without exhibiting any of their motor equivalents. Similarly, by reversing the reinforcement contingencies one could effectively inhibit cognitive representations of behavioral manifestations. It should likewise be possible to produce other patterns of correlations by varying systematically the contingencies of reinforcement into which the responses enter.
>
> (Bandura, 1969, p. 590)

Bandura's views of the contrast between the concurrent response system and the Freudian view of the unconscious are given in the following quotation:

> Apart from its more secure empirical status, the concurrent response system model has many advantages over formulations which assume the existence of an unconscious mind. The former conceptualization does not lend itself to pseudo-explanations in which a descriptive label for response disparities is reified and assigned causal properties—for example, discrepancy between symbolic and motor or physiological responses to the same stimulus events is given the descriptive label of "unconscious," which is then converted into an internal agency that exercises powerful control over behavior. The multiple-response-systems interpretation of phenomena designated as unconscious also encourages systematic exploration of the variables which give rise to response disparity. Finally, the theory has important treatment implications. Given the existence of independent but partially correlated modes of response to significant stimuli, the psychotherapist can profitably concentrate his efforts on direct modification of the classes of response that the treatment is designed to alter, rather than embarking on a protracted search for unconscious causative agents that one can predict in advance will prove to be highly concordant with the therapist's particular theoretical predilections.
>
> (Bandura, 1969, p. 593)

In recent years, partly as a result of the critique discussed, research on perceptual defense has shifted away from the attempt to demonstrate discrimination without awareness by reference to a response discrepancy procedure. Brown (1961) and Minard (1965) define perceptual defense as a systematic relationship between the emotionality of a stimulus and the ease of its recognition. Minard (1965) has attempted to show that perceptual defense, as defined above, is not a function of some form of response bias but is rather a genuine perceptual phenomenon. In his study subjects were presented with neutral and emotional stimuli. The emotional stimuli were selected by means of an individually administered word associate test. The words were presented tachistoscopically. On half the trials the experimenter omitted the stimuli and presented blank slides. By noting the differences between the percentage of times a neutral word was given as a response when a blank stimulus was presented from the percentage of times an emotional word was given as a response when a blank stimulus was present it is possible to obtain a measure of response bias, that is, the tendency to choose neutral or emotional responses independent of the contribution of the stimulus on the perceptual process engendered by the stimulus. By comparing the differences in accuracy of responses of neutral and emotional words when the stimuli were present it is possible to obtain a measure of perceptual defense. If the magnitude of the perceptual defense effect is in excess of the magnitude of the response bias effect, then the differences in recognition may be attributable to the effects of the emotional stimuli on the process of recognition.

Minard found that male subjects had a slight nonsignificant tendency to choose emotional words more often in response to the blank stimuli than neutral words. The perceptual defense effect, however, was clear and present. Male *S*s were 19 percent less likely to accurately recognize an emotional stimulus than a neutral stimulus. The results were opposite for female *S*s who were 17 percent more likely to accurately recognize a neutral stimulus than an emotional stimulus. Minard's results indicate that the emotionality of a stimulus may be related to the ease of its recognition and that this tendency is not attributable to the tendency to utter a particular type of response in the absence of any stimulus information.

It is not clear what bearing, if any, Minard's results have on the issue of the possibility of discrimination without awareness. Since the experiment does not involve observation of discrepancies between concurrently observed response systems no direct evidence or claim is made for discrimination without awareness. Presumably, such a claim would be derivative of the attempt to develop a general theoretical explanation of the relationship between emotionality and recognition. One could argue that the relationship comes about through a partial recognition of the emotional content of the words which then sets up facilitating processes which aid awareness for females or inhibiting processes which block awareness for males. In any case, the implications of Minard's results for understanding the unconscious remains obscure pending the development of a theoretical explanation.

INDIRECT INFLUENCES OF STIMULI OUT OF AWARENESS

In this section we shall review research which attempts to directly test the notion that stimuli which are out of awareness will have different effects on behavior than those in awareness. Two types of studies will be discussed, studies of projection and studies dealing with the "restricting effects" of awareness.

In psychoanalytic theory projection is a mechanism of defense. Projection occurs when an individual attributes negative personal characteristics of his of which he is unaware to others. Holmes (1968) has recently reviewed research on projection. He points out that the term projection has been used to refer to four rather different types of psychological processes. The classical Freudian type of projection is called similarity projection by Holmes and is defined as the projection of a characteristic possessed by a person of which he is *not aware* to others. A person might project a characteristic which is opposite to one which he has of which he is not aware. Also, projection may refer to the tendency to project a trait or its opposite of which he is aware. Holmes is able to distinguish four types of projection dependent upon whether the person is aware or not aware of the characteristic assigned to others and whether or not the projected characteristic is the same or different from the characteristic which the person is assumed to possess. Table 10.2 illustrates this scheme for distinguishing types of projection.

Holmes' review of research on projection suggests that there is ample evidence for attributive and complementary projection— the two varieties of projection in which the $S$ is assumed to be aware of the characteristics which he projects. Murray (1933) demonstrated complementary projection in a study in which he found that young girls who evidently become

TABLE 10.2

*Dimensions and Types of Projection*

|  | Type of projection | |
|---|---|---|
| *S awareness* | *Same trait projected* | *Different trait projected* |
| $S$ not aware of the trait in self | Similarity | Panglossian–Cassandran |
| $S$ aware of the trait in self | Attributive | Complementary |

From D. Holmes, Dimensions of projection. *Psychological Bulletin*, 1968, **69**, 248–268.

frightened playing a game of murder were likely to see photographs as frightening. In this type of projection a person projects the complement of a characteristic of which he is aware as a way of justifying his own feelings.

Katz and Allport (1931) demonstrated attributive projection in a survey of attitudes of college students. They found that there was a positive relationship between a student's admitted frequency of cribbing and his assertion of the frequency of cribbing among others. In this type of projection the person attributes a personal characteristic of which he is aware to others.

Similarity projection would be an instance of an unconscious phenomenon. That is, if similarity projection occurred it would indicate that a personal characteristic of which a person is unaware of which he could be aware influenced behavior in a way which is different from the influence it would have if it were in awareness. Its influence being the attribution of the characteristic to others. Holmes indicates that there is no empirical evidence for similarity projection. (Nor is there evidence for the other type of projecton of a personal characteristic of which a person is not aware.)

Sears (1936) did a classic study which is frequently cited as indicating similarity projection. Sears took a group of individuals who were acquainted with each other and asked them to rate themselves and others on a series of traits. For each trait Sears selected a group of "noninsightful" *S*s. A noninsightful *S* was a person who rated himself lower than others on a trait but who was rated by others as relatively high on the trait. An "insightful" *S* was one who rated himself as having more of a trait than he rated others as having that trait and whom others rated as high on the trait. Sears found that noninsightful *S*s tended to attribute the trait more to others than insightful *S*s thus supporting the occurrence of similarity projection.

Sears' results are contaminated by a statistical artifact. Noninsightful *S*s who rate themselves lower on a trait relative to others must necessarily rate others high on the trait. When this artifact is eliminated evidence of similarity projection is no longer present. Campbell, Miller, Lubetsky, and O'Connell (1964) have reported a very thorough study of similarity projection. They took *S*s whose self-ratings on a trait fell in the lowest third of the distribution of self ratings on that trait. This group of *S*s was split into two groups—insightful and noninsightful. The former were those who were rated in the lowest third by them of the distribution of ratings of that trait by others. The latter were *S*s who were rated in the highest third of the distribution. Campbell *et al.* obtained data with respect to 112 traits. They found evidence of similarity projection—that is, the tendency for noninsightful *S*s to assign significantly higher trait scores to others than are assigned by insightful subjects in only one of the 112 comparisons. The Campbell *et al.* study thus provides no evidence of similarity projection.

Although classical similarity projection would provide evidence for the unconscious there is no evidence that it does in fact occur.

Spence (1964, 1966; Spence & Holland, 1962) has attempted to test the notion that awareness acts as a restricting influence on a stimulus. He assumes that the registration of a stimulus is independent of awareness of a stimulus. Further, a stimulus which is registered but out of awareness will have a different pattern of cognitive effects, than a stimulus which is in awareness.

A registered stimulus which is out of awareness will radiate and will influence a wider range of associated stimuli. In one test of this notion, Spence presented Ss serially with a list of 27 words which they were required to recall. Ten of the words were associates of the word "cheese" and ten of the words were unrelated words which were not associates of the word "cheese." The word "cheese" was included in the middle of the list. A number of findings were taken to indicate the restricting effects of awareness. Spence found that a significantly larger number of cheese associates than words which were not "cheese" associates were recalled *prior* to the recall of the word "cheese." *After* cheese was recalled there was no difference in the recall of cheese associates and other words. The difference was taken to support the notion that prior to entering awareness "cheese" freely influenced a large network of associates. After awareness (recall) the influence of cheese was inhibited.

Spence also found that subjects who recalled the word "cheese" early did not differ in the number of cheese associates and other words which they recalled. However, Ss who recalled the word "cheese" late tended to recall more "cheese" associates than other words. This finding was taken to support the view that the late recallers of the word "cheese" had more time for associative diffusion to operate. Spence also found that there was no difference in recall of "cheese" associates and other words for Ss who did not recall the word at all. This finding led Spence to suggest that where the stimulus was unconscious—that is, blocked or incapable of of entering awareness then the associative diffusion would not take place.

In summary, Spence proposed a rather intricate theoretical structure according to which stimuli which were unconscious would be restricted in their influence on their associates, stimuli which were preconscious—that is, capable of entering awareness—would exert a diffuse influence on a network of associates *prior to* entering awareness, and stimuli in awareness would be restricted in their influence.

A number of criticisms have been published of Spence's experiment and his interpretation of his data. Bruel, Ginsbeng, Lukomnik, and Schmeidler (1966) were unable to replicate his findings. Worrell and Worrell (1966) reported a series of studies in which data was obtained which was at variance with that reported by Spence and which supported an alternative theoretical formulation. Worrell and Worrell proposed an interpretation in terms of associative clustering. Spence argued that the ten "cheese" associates were unrelated to each other because when single word associates were given to each word there was little or no tendency for these words to be given as associates to any of the other words. Worrell and Worrell point out that when the associates are given as a group these words should have high interitem associative strength. When presented with a difficult recall problem the subject attempts to cluster the stimuli to facilitate recall. By virtue of their high interitem associative strength the ten associates of "cheese" ought to lend themselves to clustering. Accordingly there should be a tendency to recall them early and to recall them as a group whether or not the critical stimulus ("cheese" in Spence's experiment) is recalled early or late or not at all or is not even present in the stimulus list.

In order to test this associative clustering interpretation, Worrell and Worrell conducted four experiments which were similar in design to Spence's experiment. In the first study which was most closely related to Spence's, a list of words containing the critical word "anger" was presented to *S*s for subsequent recall. The list included ten associates of "anger" and ten unrelated words matched in frequency of occurrence in English to the "anger" associates and seven filler words. Study 2 involved the use of the same list with the sole exception of the substitution of "cheese" for "anger." Study 3 involved the same list Spence used with the substitution of the word "anger" for "cheese." Study 4 involved the same list as used in Study 3 with the substitution of the word "shirt" for "anger" in order to control for the emotional overtones of the word "anger." Table 10.3 presents data indicating the amount of recall of the anger associates and cheese associates in each of the four studies before recall of the critical word and after recall of the critical word. Note that in each study the words which are all associates of a common word are recalled more often than the control words before the critical word is recalled. After the critical word is recalled the tendency to recall associates is diminished. This finding holds irrespective of the relationship between the critical words and the list of ten associates. In Studies 2, 3, and 4 these results are obtained even though the critical word is totally unrelated to the associates. These results may be explained by appeal to the clustering hypothesis. The critical word is in each of these studies as well as in Spence's study, in the center of the list. Therefore, it is surrounded by many competing

TABLE 10.3

*Mean Recall of Three Classes of Words in Four Studies Before and After the Recall of the Critical Stimulus*

| | | Before | | | After | | |
|---|---|---|---|---|---|---|---|
| Study | N | Asso-ciates | Control | Buffer | Asso-ciates | Control | Buffer |
| 1. ANGER with | | | | | | | |
|    ANGER associates | 59 | 1.51 | 0.90 | 2.34 | 1.22 | 1.03 | 1.00 |
| 2. CHEESE with | | | | | | | |
|    ANGER associates | 30 | 1.63 | 0.63 | 2.73 | 1.13 | 0.83 | 0.97 |
| 3. ANGER with | | | | | | | |
|    CHEESE associates | 24 | 2.13 | 1.17 | 3.08 | 1.38 | 0.83 | 0.67 |
| 4. SHIRT with | | | | | | | |
|    CHEESE associates | 26 | 2.00 | 1.19 | 3.04 | 1.23 | 1.08 | 0.54 |

From L. Worrell & J. Worrell, An experimental and theoretical note on "conscious and preconscious influences on recall." *Journal of Personality and Social Psychology,* 1966, **3,** 119–123.

stimuli. This should result in a tendency to recall the critical stimulus late,[1] or at least not in the beginning of recall. On the other hand the ten associates of a common word should be recalled early because of their susceptibility to clustering. These two principles, taken together, imply (a) that there will be more recall of associates than control words prior to the recall of the critical word irrespective of the content of the critical word, and (b) that there will be a reduced tendency to recall more associates than control words after recall of the critical word.

Worrell and Worrell compared the recall of associates and control words among early late and nonrecallers of the critical word. Recall that Spence found it was the late recallers of the critical word who tended to recall more associates than control words. The associative clustering hypothesis predicts, by contrast, that the time of recall of the critical word is irrelevant to the tendency to recall associates more than control words. Table 10.4 presents data indicating the differences in recall of associates and control words as a function of the time of recall of the critical word in each of the four studies performed by Worrell and Worrell. Note that associates are recalled more than control words in each study irrespective of the time of recall of the critical word in each of the four studies performed by Worrell

---

[1] Note: This explanation of the results is slightly at variance with that given by Worrell and Worrell.

TABLE 10.4

*Mean Recall of Associates, Control, Buffer Words, and Intrusions for Early Recallers, Late Recallers, and Nonrecallers in Four Studies*

| | | Study 1 ANGER *with* ANGER *associates* | | | Study 2 CHEESE *with* ANGER *associates* | | |
|---|---|---|---|---|---|---|---|
| | | Recallers | | | Recallers | | |
| *Words* | | *Early* (*N* = 22) | *Late* (*N* = 37) | *Non* (*N* = 74) | *Early* (*N* = 10) | *Late* (*N* = 20) | *Non* (*N* = 49) |
| Associates | (10) | 3.09 | 2.46 | 2.26 | 3.40 | 2.45 | 2.63 |
| Control | (10) | 2.23 | 1.73 | 1.55 | 1.80 | 1.30 | 1.73 |
| Buffer | (6) | 3.55 | 3.24 | 3.36 | 3.30 | 4.00 | 4.00 |
| Total | (26) | 8.87 | 7.43 | 7.17 | 8.50 | 7.75 | 8.36 |
| Intrusions | | 1.64 | 1.68 | 1.49 | 1.30 | 1.15 | 1.24 |

| | | Study 3 ANGER *with* CHEESE *associates* | | | Study 4 SHIRT *with* CHEESE *associates* | | |
|---|---|---|---|---|---|---|---|
| | | *Early* | *Late* | *Non* | *Early* | *Late* | *Non* |
| | | (*N* = 5) | (*N* = 19) | (*N* = 88) | (*N* = 6) | (*N* = 20) | (*N* = 82) |
| Associates | (10) | 4.40 | 3.26 | 3.39 | 2.83 | 3.35 | 3.11 |
| Control | (10) | 2.00 | 2.11 | 2.09 | 2.67 | 2.15 | 2.13 |
| Buffer | (6) | 4.00 | 3.68 | 3.48 | 4.00 | 3.45 | 3.65 |
| Total | (26) | 11.40 | 9.05 | 8.96 | 9.50 | 8.95 | 8.89 |
| Intrusions | | 1.40 | 0.89 | 1.65 | 1.17 | 1.70 | 1.56 |

From L. Worrell & J. Worrell, An experimental and theoretical note on "conscious and preconscious influences on recall." *Journal of Personality and Social Psychology,* 1966, **3,** 119–123.

and Worrell. The findings of Study 1 (where the critical word is related to the associates) are at variance with Spence's findings on this point.

The findings of the four Worrell and Worrell studies support the view that Spence's findings are more plausible interpreted as the results of associative clustering rather than the preconscious influences of a stimulus which is not in awareness.

## Toward a "Response" Theory of the Unconscious

In what follows we shall suggest a way of thinking of unconscious phenomena which is different from the psychoanalytic approach and which is compatible with a social learning theory approach. This approach is based on signal detection theory and on Schachter's theory of emotion.

## SIGNAL DETECTION THEORY AND THE UNCONSCIOUS

Signal detection theory is a mathematical theory which deals with the application of statistical decision theory to perception. Its implications for the analysis of subception and perceptual defense have been dealt with by Goldiamond (1958) and by Swets, Tanner, and Birdsall (1961) in their general explication of the theory. In what follows we shall present a very brief and nontechnical presentation of the theory. In the simplest detection situation an individual is required to discriminate the presentation of a signal from a blank. An experimental situation which conforms to this might be one in which a S is presented with a flash of light or no flash on a series of trials. The S is instructed to indicate the trials on which he believes a stimulus was present. The theory assumes that sensory experience may be represented by a set of numbers which represent quantitative attributes of a sensory experience. On trials in which the stimulus (signal) is absent a quantity of sensory experience which varies randomly over time is invariably present. This quantity is called noise. The values of noise present on a series of trial form a noise distribution ($N$). The sensory experience which occurs on trials in which a signal is presented is represented by a distribution of values called the signal + noise ($S + N$) distribution. The distributions overlap. The $S + N$ distribution has a mean value which is invariably greater than the mean value of the $N$ distribution. Thus, the additions of a signal, in effect, adds a constant to the $N$ distribution. Figure 10.2 presents a graphical representation of these distributions.

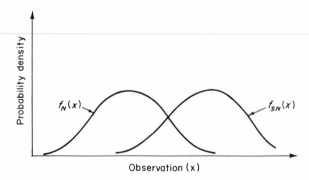

FIG. 10.2. The probability density functions of noise and signal + noise. (From J. A. Swets, W. P. Tunner, Jr., & T. G. Birdsall, Decision processes in perception. *Psychological Review*, 1961, **68**, 301–340.)

The $S$'s task on any given trial is to decide whether a particular observation (that is, a quantitative value of sensory experience) belongs to the $N$ or the $S + N$ distribution. For any given observation a likelihood ratio may be formed by dividing the probability that a particular observation belongs to the $S + N$ distribution by the probability that it belongs to the $N$ distribution. The $S$ is assumed to choose a criterion value which permits him to assign all values above the criterion to the $S + N$ distribution and all values below the criterion to the noise distribution. The $S$ can increase the number of hits he makes (that is, the correct assignment of a quantity to the $S + N$ distribution) by moving the criterion to the left. However, the consequences of this increase in hits will be an increase in false alarms (the assignment of a value belonging to the $N$ distribution to the $S + N$ distribution), that is, the assertion that a signal is present when in fact it is absent. Conversely, if the $S$ moves the criterion to the right he will decrease the number of hits and simultaneously decrease the number of false alarms. The criterion can be chosen to maximize a number of different values. If, for example, the $S$ is instructed to assert that a signal is present only when he is relatively certain (that is, that false alarms are to be avoided) the criterion will be shifted to the right.

Sensory detection theory implies that a $S$'s performance in the task we have described is a function of two parameters. First is the criterion which the subject sets. Second is a parameter representing a relatively pure sensory function called $d'$, which is the difference between the means of the $S$ and the $S + N$ distribution expressed in terms of their standard deviation. Different signal intensities will have different $d'$ values associated with them.

There are two interesting consequences of this theory. First, the theory permits one to obtain a measure of sensory function which is less biased than that obtained by conventional psychophysical functions.

Clark (1969) has reported a study which indicates the utility of these procedures. Clark presented subjects with a painful heat stimulus. Half the $S$s in his experiment were given a placebo—a pill which they were told would reduce pain. The $S$s given the placebo were less likely to report a particular stimulus was painful. However, a sensory detection analysis indicated that the $d'$ value for the placebo and the nonplacebo group was not significantly different. The placebo did not effect the sensory experience of pain but only the criterion, that is, the quantity of experience required for an $S$ to assert that a stimulus was painful. The Clark study provides a neat illustration of the way in which an $S$'s response tendencies in a detection situation may be manipulated without effecting estimates of sensory functioning.

The second implication which is suggested by the theory of sensory detection is that there is no lower limit of sensitivity. Or put another way, there is no threshold or value of sensory intensity above which there is always a positive response and below which responses are simply random.

This interpretation of signal detection theory suggests that the attempt to demonstrate unconscious phenomena by introducing stimuli at intensities or durations which are below "threshold" is wrong in principle. For any stimulus which can be .detected at some level of intensity there is no level of intensity for which the mean of the $S + N$ distribution does not exceed the mean of the $N$ distribution. However, the difference between the means of the two distributions may be sufficiently small as to render the attempt to demonstrate better than chance discrimination in a limited number of trials impossible. This implies that every such stimulus enters awareness (that is, $d' > 0$).

Signal detection theory contains a precise distinction between an experience and the response of an individual to that experience. It is plausible within the context of this theory to view emotional and motivational influences on perception as principally affecting the response an individual makes to his experience rather than the experience *per se*. Broadbent (1967) has presented a signal detection theory analysis of the recognition of words which differ in their frequency of occurrence in English. Broadbent's analysis indicates that there is no difference in perceptual sensitivity to words whose frequency of occurrence is low or high. However, individuals set a lower criterion for the response of a high frequency word than a low frequency word. In this sense the perceptual system is biased towards the detection of high frequency words.

Broadbent's analysis provides a convenient way to think of motivational and emotional influences in perception. For example, it is possible that the influences of hunger and thirst on perception may occur because of a change in response criterion such that hunger may shift the criterion for food related perception to the left, resulting in a greater number of correct identifications of food related stimuli and a greater number of false alarms—the assignment of a nonfood-related stimulus to the food related category. Similarly, individual differences in the case of recognition of emotional words may be due to differences in the decision criterion set for words differing in emotionality. Certain individuals may tend to be particularly vigilant and to have relatively low decision criterion for the detection of emotional stimuli, leading to the tendency to correctly and incorrectly identify many stimuli as emotional. Other individuals may be defensive and may require more evidence (that is, they set a higher criterion) for the decision to identify a stimulus as emotional. Such individuals will be less likely to correctly identify emotional stimuli, and will be less likely to perceive a nonemotional stimulus as emotional.

In summary, signal detection theory implies that there are no external stimuli which are observed which are out of awareness. However, the theory permits a distinction between awareness and response to that awareness. Individuals may differ in the criterion they set for assigning experiences to various response categories.

It is instructive to compare this type of theory with Spence's hypothesis, derived from psychoanalytic theory, of registration without awareness. The signal detection theory analysis would suggest that a stimulus may be experienced but not responded to correctly. For example, a tabu word may be called a nontabu word. Presumably, Spence would consider such a stimulus registered but out of awareness. This theory implies that such a stimulus would exert a relatively unrestricted effect and would appear indirectly in fantasy or would lead to an increased tendency to be aware of stimuli which belong to a network or its associates. By contrast, signal detection theory assigns no special dynamic properties to such an incorrectly perceived stimulus.

## Unconscious Internal States

We have argued that external stimuli which are observed cannot be out of awareness. This still leaves open the question of the possible influences on behavior of internal states which are out of awareness—for example, love, hate, fear, hunger, etc.[2]

Can emotions or other internal states which are out of awareness exert an influence on behavior which is different from the influence they would exert if they were in awareness? Schachter and Singer (1962) have presented a theory of emotion which suggests a way of dealing with this question. According to Schachter and Singer, an emotional state has two components:

1. a state of physiological arousal, and
2. a cognition which labels and defines the state.

According to this theory, the state of physiological arousal which accompanies an emotion is not sufficient to indicate the kind of emotion it is. The individual is dependent on cues present in the immediate situation which permit him to interpret and appropriately label his physiological state. Conn and Crowne (1964) attempted to extend the Schachter and Singer theory to deal with ego defenses. They attempted to test the hy-

---

[2] Freud (1957) believes that emotions were, by definition, conscious states. Thus the phrase "unconscious fear" would be considered a misnomer by him.

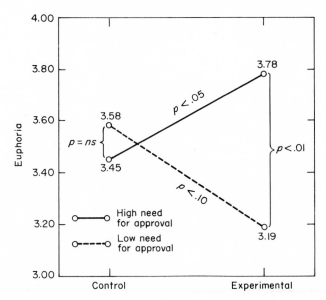

Fig. 10.3. Mean amount of euphoria of high- and low-need-for-approval groups in the experimental and control conditions. (From D. P. Crowne & D. Marlowe, *The approval motive.* New York: Wiley, 1964. Reprinted by permission of John Wiley & Sons, Inc.)

pothesis that individuals who scored high on the Marlowe–Crowne scale (see Chapter 2) and who are assumed to be high in the need for approval, tend to repress anger. Conn and Crowe exposed their *S*s to an anger-arousal situation. This was accomplished with the aid of an accomplice of the experimenter who acted as a *S*. The accomplice and the true *S*s were required to play a game. The accomplice suggested a way of playing the game to the *S* which would permit them both to win money. After the accomplice secured the agreement of the *S* he violated the agreement in a way which permitted him to win money and the true *S* to win no money.

After this attempt to arouse anger, the subjects were asked to wait in a room with the accomplice who proceeded to go through an elaborate sequence of 17 euphoric activities. The *S*'s behavior was rated by observers through a one-way mirror. A control group of *S*s were exposed to the euphoric sequence without the previous anger arousal procedure.

Figure 10.3 presents the principal results of the Conn and Crowne study. Figure 10.3 indicates that there was very little difference in the amount of euphoria of the *S*s high and low in need for approval in the control group. However, in the experimental group the *S*s high in need for approval were rated as responding more euphorically than the low-need-for-approval *S*s.

Conn and Crowne interpret their results as follows: The high-need-for-approval *S*s initially are aware of anger and the physiological arousal which accompanies it. However, these *S*s have a tendency to repress anger. Conn and Crowne assume that the repression is effective in removing the label "anger" associated with the state but not the physiological arousal which accompanies it. The *S* is then faced with a state of high physiological arousal without an appropriate label or set of explanatory cognitions for the state. The accomplices euphoric behavior provides the *S* with an opportunity to assign an alternative label to his state of physiological arousal.

If we accept this interpretation then the Conn and Crowne study provides evidence for the unconscious. According to this interpretation, the *S*s who are high in need for approval repress anger and hence are not aware of it. The repression of anger combined with the presence of the state of physiological arousal leads these *S*s to reinterpret their state of physiological arousal as one of euphoria. Thus a state which is out of awareness has had an effect on behavior which is different from the effect it would have if it were in awareness—it has led to euphoria. The difficulty with accepting this interpretation as evidence for the unconscious is that we have no information at all about the sequence of events which precede the occurrence of the euphoric state. Apparently, this sequence was suggested by an analogy to Schachter and Singer's experiment in which *S*s who were not informed, or who were misinformed about the physiological effects of a drug which produced physiological arousal, tended to react more euphorically to the antics of an accomplice than *S*s who were given the drug and provided with information about its physiological effects. In the Schachter and Singer study we have reasons to assume a state of physiological arousal unaccompanied by an appropriate explanation. In the Conn and Crowne study we simply assume a complex sequence of events which culminates in a state of physiological arousal without an adequate explanation. There is one respect in which this sequence may not be completely plausible. If the *S*s high in need for approval repress anger then one would expect that they would never experience the emotion or the accompanying state of physiological arousal in the first place. An alternative sequence which is at least as plausible is the following. The *S*s high in need for approval in the experimental condition experienced the state of anger up to the point where they were provided with the opportunity to embrace an alternative interpretation of their state—euphoria. It might be argued that in this case the *S*s would not embrace euphoria as an explanation of their state since they already had acceptable explanation—anger. However, the anger label might not be congenial and when given a preferred alternative which was not present previously, the *S*s might well choose it.

On this latter interpretation the Conn and Crowne study does not provide evidence for the unconscious. The euphoric behavior of the high-need-approval subjects on this interpretation would not be caused by the consequences of the repressed anger state—that is, physiological arousal without a label. Rather, the experiment would indicate that a $S$ might reinterpret his physiological state in a new way when the cues available in the environment change. This interpretation is analogous to the response criterion interpretation of motivational and emotional influences on perception. Individuals may have different criteria for the labeling of their internal states. Differences in the interpretation of internal states—for example, hunger, anger, may not be due to differences in awareness but rather in the kinds of experiences and cues required for an individual to label his internal state in a particular way. However, according to Schachter's theory the emotional state is not present until the $S$ has in fact labeled it in a particular way. Thus, an individual may have a tendency not to label an internal state as anger or to substitute an alternative label for the state if it is available. However, Schachter's theory makes no assumption that a state which has not been labeled in the usual or appropriate fashion is in any sense present as a latent dynamic force which exerts an indirect influence on behavior. Further, Schachter's theory implies that a state which has been idiosyncratically labeled has in all respects the properties of its idiosyncratic label. Similarly, the state whose label has been changed does not have the properties of its previous label but only of its new label. The lack of indirect influence of the "unlabeled" or the "mislabeled" state differentiates the Schachter interpretation from psychoanalytic theory which implies that the "repressed" state will exert indirect influences on behavior. The Conn and Crowne study does not permit us to choose between these interpretations. If it could be shown that the $S$s high in need for approval who behaved euphorically also behaved in ways which indicated the indirect influence of the "latent" anger state then we would have clear evidence for the existence of the unconscious.

In summary, both signal detection theory and the Schachter and Singer theory of emotion imply that the perception of external stimuli or internal states requires a response which labels or categorizes the experience of an individual. Individuals may differ in the criterion set for the assignment of an experience to various response categories. Experiences which have been idiosyncratically labeled or incorrectly labeled are not assumed to have dynamic properties which lead to indirect influences on behavior.

## Conclusion

In this chapter we have reviewed theory and research relating to the unconscious. We have presented theoretical views which permit us to emphasize the role of response parameters in explaining research dealing with the unconscious.

Our review of research dealing with the unconscious indicates that these are no unequivocal demonstrations of unconscious phenomena. Research conducted under controlled conditions does not provide evidence for the kind of explanatory role assigned to the unconscious in traditional psychodynamic theories. Consequently, the research dealing with the unconscious available at this time is compatible with the sociobehavioristic position of Bandura.

CHAPTER **11**

# BEHAVIOR THERAPY AND PSYCHOTHERAPY

---

In this chapter we shall review research dealing with the effectiveness of traditional interview methods of psychotherapy and the methods of behavior modification that are compatible with social learning theory. This research will be reviewed in order to see what implications, if any, can be drawn with respect to the validity of social learning theory and more traditional theories dealing with personality dynamics. In drawing these implications it is necessary to distinguish between methods of therapy and the theoretical position of individuals who use these various methods of therapy. The methods may or may not be compatible with the theory from which they are allegedly derived. Further, the methods may be effective or ineffective for reasons which are unrelated to their theoretical *raison d'être*. Despite these cautions a review of the efficacy of these methods of inducing personality change is warranted, for no other reason than the historical relationship between theories of personality and methods of effecting personality change. Psychoanalytic theory is, of course, derived from psychoanalytic therapy. Bandura's latest book-length presentation of his theory occurs in the context of a discussion of behavior modification (Bandura, 1969). Consequently, evidence for the efficacy of various therapy procedures is important in conditioning one's attitude toward different approaches to personality dynamics.

## Studies of the Effectiveness of Psychotherapy

The studies we shall review in this section deal with the effectiveness of psychotherapy. Some psychologists (for example, Kiesler, 1966) would argue that the question is meaningless, and can only be made meaningful if it is qualified and made more precise. In particular, the term "psychotherapy" can be used to cover a great diversity of activities of varying durations administered by individuals of varying degrees of professional competence for varying periods of time. Psychotherapy may encompass anything from one session of nondirective therapy by a first-year graduate student to ten years of orthodox psychoanalysis. Also, the characteristics of patients or clients may differ greatly. And the characteristics of therapists may differ greatly. In addition to differences in patients, therapists and methods of therapy, the answer to the question of the effectiveness of therapy may depend on the criteria one uses to define effectiveness. Consequently, our general question might be more precisely defined as follows: What methods of therapy administered by what kinds of therapists are effective by what criteria for what patients?

Studies of the effectiveness of any therapeutic procedure ideally should fulfill four requirements (see Meehl, 1955):

1. Some sort of control group should be used to establish a base rate of change on the criteria which are investigated for individuals who have not received the therapy which is being investigated. The value of the control group depends on the degree to which it is comparable to the therapy group. Ideally, it should be composed of individuals who are randomly assigned from the same pool to the control or therapy group or it should be composed of individuals who are comparable in as many relevant aspects as possible to the therapy group. The control group should be assessed on the same measures as the therapy group.

2. Unbiased and/or multiple criteria of effectiveness should be used. Evidence for the effectiveness of therapy depends on the validity of the criteria used. The problem of the criterion in outcome research is a most vexing one. No single criterion will be satisfactory to all therapists. However, certain criteria are more likely to be valid than others. For example, criteria of demonstrably low reliability are obviously invalid. Judgments of success by the therapist himself are obviously suspect inasmuch as the therapist has a vested interest in the effectiveness of the treatment. In view of the evidence of extensive method variance in measures of therapy change (see the discussion of the Cartwright *et al.* (1963) study in Chapter 2), it would seem that the use of multiple criteria including objective measurement of behavior changes, personality ratings by therapist, patient, family, and friends, and various personality test measures is warranted. We can be confident of the effectiveness of a method of therapy when its effects are sufficiently powerful to transcend the method variance associated with different criterion measures.

3. A measure of behavior outside the therapeutic situation should be included among the criteria. Many of the studies of therapy which use multiple criteria rely on therapist judgments and a variety of tests given to the patients. The possibility exists that therapy may bias the patient's report or may lead the subject to change his response to various tests without significantly changing the patient's behavior. There are at least two studies in which this sort of discrepancy has occurred.

Powers and Witmer (1951) studied 650 underprivileged boys, 6–10-years old, in the Cambridge–Somerville area. The sample was obtained from welfare workers who were asked to supply names of boys who were likely to become delinquent. Pairs of boys were matched on such variables as age, intelligence, school grade, delinquency rating, ethnic, and socioeconomic background. Each member of a matched pair was randomly assigned to a treatment or a control group. The Ss in the treatment group were given a variety of individual forms of psychotherapy. Powers and Witmer obtained records of the delinquency of the 650 boys in the study, of which 96 boys in the treatment group and 92 boys in the control group had court appearances. The total number of offenses for the control group was 218 and the total number of offenses for the treatment group was 264. However, there was a slightly greater (but nonsignificant) incidence of serious offenses in the control group. One other finding of some interest was obtained in this study. The therapists were asked to list all boys who substantially benefited from the therapy. Approximately two-thirds of the boys were listed by the therapists as having substantially benefited. Also, more than half the boys believed that they had been clearly helped by the treatment they had received. Despite the belief that therapy was effective on the part of both therapists and patients, the results clearly contradicted this belief with respect to the criterion of a reduction in delinquency.

Rogers and Dymond (1954) have reported the results of several investigations of the effectiveness of client-centered therapy using a variety of different procedures. The most relevant control group used was an "own control." A number of clients were asked to wait 60 days before beginning therapy. The difference between scores on various measures at the first contact and after sixty days provides a base line of changes associated with the passage of time itself. Then, measures taken after therapy provide an indication of changes attributable to therapy. If the changes attributable to therapy are larger than the changes attributable to the passage of time (waiting) then there is evidence for the effectiveness of therapy.

The Rogers and Dymond report contains the results of a number of different investigations with many complex analyses carried out within the framework of the same samples. Rather than attempt to reproduce all of the results we shall emphasize some of the more salient findings. Rogers and

Dymond report a number of findings which indicate changes in the clients' self-perception as a function of therapy. In one study Butler and Haigh (1954) obtained an index of the discrepancy between actual self- and ideal self-ratings. Presumably, the smaller the discrepancy (as indexed by high correlations between self and ideal), the better the adjustment of an individual. The mean correlation for 25 Ss in their therapy group prior to counseling was −.01. Following counseling the mean correlation was .36 and, at a follow-up 6–12 months later, the mean correlation was .32. Of these subjects, 15 served as their own controls. Their mean self-ideal correlation was −.01 at the beginning of their contact and 60 days later the mean correlation was again −.01. This study indicates that client-centered therapy produces smaller discrepancy between self and ideal concepts.

In another study of changes in self-concepts, Dymond (1954) took a series of self-concepts and had clinical psychologists indicate which ones were indicative of good and bad adjustment. The Ss were asked to sort checks with these self-concepts, indicating the extent to which they were descriptive of themselves. "Adjustment scores" were derived from these sorts. Dymond found that the adjustment score of 11 control Ss changed from 29.54 in the initial testing to 30.18 after the waiting period. The 25 Ss in the therapy group (including the 11 in the wait group) did show a significant increase in adjustment scores as a result of therapy. The scores changed from 29.80 to 39.80. On follow-up the adjustment scores in the therapy group remained high with a mean of 38.36. Dymond's study indicates that changes in self-concept as a result of client-centered therapy indicative of better adjustment are greater than those which occur as a function of the passage of time.

In the final study we shall cite this series, Rogers (1954) obtained measures of behavior based on the rating of the client by two people who knew him well as well as by the client himself. Rogers found that therapy did not lead to a significant change in the rated maturity of an individual's behavior for observer ratings either at the close of therapy or after a follow-up period. However, for self-ratings of maturity, there was a significantly larger increase from the beginning of therapy to the end of therapy than from the initial test period to the beginning of therapy. We can, therefore, conclude that client-centered therapy tends to lead to an increase in an individual's self-rating of maturity which is greater than the increase which occurs as a result of the passage of time. However, this increase is not accompanied by increases in the maturity of one's behavior as rated by observers who know the client well. This finding indicates the importance of including measures of behavior in the assessment of therapy. Evidently changes in self-report measures of change can occur as a result of therapy, which are not related to observed changes in behavior.

4.  The research design should permit follow-up measures. The effects of therapy should be long lasting and some effort should be made to indicate that the changes persist over time after the termination of therapy. There are a number of excellent treatments available dealing with methodological problems of outcome research in therapy (e.g. Goldstein, Heller, and Sechrest, 1966; and Volsky, Magoon, Norman, & Hoyt, 1965). Rather than attempt to review these extensively we shall discuss the methodological problems in connection with the various studies which shall be reviewed.

## The Eysenck Critique

Much of the concern about the efficacy of psychotherapy stems from a controversial article written by Eysenck in 1952. In this article Eysenck summarized data which failed to indicate that therapy was effective. Eysenck attempted to establish a base rate of change among neurotics who were not given psychotherapy. One of the studies used to determine the base rate was reported by Denker (as cited in Eysenck, 1952). Denker obtained data on 500 consecutive disability cases from the files of an insurance company. The cases studied were neurotics who were unable to work for at least three months. The patients were treated by general practitioners who gave only the most superficial type of psychotherapy. Denker followed the cases for at least a five-year period. Recovery from neurosis was defined as (a) return to work and ability to carry on well in economic adjustments for at least five years, (b) no major complaints in making successful social adjustments. Denker found that 45 percent of the patients recovered after one year and 27 percent after two years. After five years, 90 percent of the patients had recovered.

Eysenck used the Denker and other studies to arrive at an estimate of a "spontaneous recovery" rate from neurosis of 72.5 percent. Eysenck then surveyed reports of the effectiveness of therapy made by therapists. Eysenck summarized these studies and found that psychoanalysts had reported cure or much improvement in 44 percent of the cases treated. Eclectic therapists had reported success in 64 percent of 7293 cases treated.

Eysenck concluded that the comparison of the spontaneous recovery rate with the recovery rate achieved by psychotherapy indicated that therapy failed to lead to greater recovery than that which would be obtained without it. This implied that therapy was not effective or, at a minimum, that the efficacy of psychotherapy was not established by the reported claims for its effectiveness.

Eysenck's paper proved to be highly controversial (see De Charms, Levy, & Wertheimer, 1954; Rosenzweig, 1954). There are a number of reasons why the data cited by Eysenck are inconclusive. There is no indication that the groups used in the different comparisons are comparable. More critically, the criteria of improvement or cure are entirely subjective and unsubstantiated. It is possible that the individuals rated as much improved by Denker would not be considered improved at all by the subjective criteria used by the various therapists. However, it should be noted that Eysenck was well aware of the limitations of this sort of comparison and indicated the need for more systematic study of the outcome problem.

Eysenck has reviewed research on outcome problems in psychotherapy several times (see Eysenck 1960, 1965). Each time he has concluded, on the basis of his review of the literature, including several studies with adequate controls, that psychotherapy has not been demonstrated to be effective.

## MELTZOFF AND KORNREICH'S REVIEW

The most important challenge to Eysenck's review and conclusion that the effectiveness of psychotherapy has not been demonstrated is contained in a very comprehensive review of research on psychotherapy reported by Meltzoff and Kornreich (1970). Their principal criticism of Eysenck's reviews is that they deal with an extremely limited number of the available studies on the outcome of psychotherapy. In addition, according to Meltzoff and Kornreich, the studies which are dealt with represent a biased sample of the available literature. They were able to find 101 studies dealing with the outcome of some form of psychotherapy in which some type of control group was included which permitted some comparison of a therapy treatment with its absence. Of these, 81 studies reported positive results and 20 studies reported null effects (no significant differences) or negative effects as a result of treatment. However, Meltzoff and Kornreich indicate that, in their opinion, 44 of the 101 studies they reviewed had some sort of design flaw which vitiated the conclusions drawn. This still leaves 57 adequately designed studies, evaluating the effectiveness of therapy. Of this latter group, 48 studies indicated positive results and 9 studies reported no significant differences or negative effects of psychotherapy. Meltzoff and Kornreich make one further distinction among the 57 adequate studies. 54 percent of these studies reported results which Meltzoff and Kornreich consider major (this category includes findings indicating multiple or central benefits of therapy) and 30 percent of the studies reported minor benefits of therapy.

Even if we discount inadequately designed studies and those indicating only minor benefits of therapy, we are still left with 22 studies which, according to Meltzoff and Kornreich, provide evidence for the effectiveness of therapy. Meltzoff and Kornreich note that they are the first responsible authors who have reviewed outcome research on therapy, and concluded that this research enables one to reject the null hypothesis that therapy produces no beneficial changes compared to the changes which occur in suitably chosen control groups. They attribute the discrepancies in the conclusions drawn about the effectiveness of therapy to the fact that they have somewhat more rigorous standards of evaluation of research which leads them to reject many studies indicating therapy was not effective on the grounds that the studies were inadequately designed and, most importantly, to the fact that their review is by far the most comprehensive and considers more of the available research than any other published survey. The Meltzoff and Kornreich review is extremely important since it argues against a belief held by many psychologists (including partisans and critics of psychotherapy) that research has failed to demonstrate that therapy is effective.

For a number of reasons I found the Meltzoff and Kornreich review unconvincing. First, the review includes classes of therapy which I would prefer to exclude for the purposes of this chapter. These include studies of various kinds of behavior therapy which we shall consider separately, studies of therapeutic consequences of hypnosis, and studies dealing with the beneficial effects of brief encounters (for example, breifly exchanging conversations with patients). Of the 22 studies cited by Meltzoff and Kornreich 8 or 9 thus do not really deal with the effectiveness of psychotherapy if psychotherapy is to be understood as the attempt to achieve beneficial changes in individuals by the discussion and exploration of their emotional problems.

A second respect in which the conclusions of Meltzoff and Kornreich are subject to challenge concerns the criteria by which therapy is evaluated. A number of studies which they cite as indicating benefits of therapy do not include follow-up data. Also, some studies in the category including major benefits do not include measures of the behavior of the subjects outside the therapeutic situation. Such studies may include a variety of measures including self-reports, projective test data, rating scales of behavior in the therapy situation, and the like. However, for the reasons cited earlier I believe that any study of the effectiveness of therapy which does not include measures of behavior outside the therapy situation is suspect. If we exclude such studies from consideration we are left with six studies demonstrating the effectiveness of psychotherapy, including evidence that therapy leads to change in behavior outside of the therapy situation. Of these, I have reservations about four and find two acceptable. The six studies discussed by Meltzoff and Kornreich which include behavioral measures and follow-up data and indicate that therapy is successful are reviewed below.

Grace, Pinsky, and Wolff (1954) studied the effectiveness of "superficial" psychotherapy designed to alleviate stress in the treatment of ulcerative colitis. A first group contained 34 patients who were assigned to the psychotherapy group. A second group was composed of 34 other patients who were matched for age, sex, severity, and duration of illness, and X-ray data. The matches for severity of illness and X-ray data were made by physicians not associated with the study and may be assumed to be unbiased. In addition, there was another group of 109 patients with ulcerative colitis who were studied. This third group was in no way matched to the first two groups. Patients in the latter two groups received the usual treatment for their condition including diet and medication.

Grace, Pinsky, and Wolff followed their patients for a two-year period and reported that patients in the first group showed more improvement than patients in the second and third group. They judged 65 percent of the patients in Group I as improved as against 32 percent of the patients in Group II. Three patients in Group I died, versus six in Group II. Three patients in Group I were given operations for their condition versus ten patients in Group II. They concluded that psychotherapy was more effective in the treatment of ulcerative colitis than the traditional medical forms of treatment.

There are a number of shortcomings in the report of the Grace, Pinsky, and Wolff study which makes it rather difficult to evaluate. First, and most critically, they do not indicate whether or not the patients were randomly assigned to the treatment groups. Although *S*s were matched for severity of illness, if they were not randomly assigned, then the possibility exists that the decision of the subject to choose or accept psychotherapy might be related to other variables which determine the outcome of their illness. Second, it is not clear from the report whether patients in Group I were given diet and medication as well as psychotherapy. If they were, the possibility exists that the effectiveness of psychotherapy might be due to a tendency of subjects given therapy to follow their medical regimen more rigorously. Also, it is possible that the physician who treated his patients predominantly by psychotherapy might have been a more skilled medical clinician than the other physicians. Of course, this latter argument is not valid if the patients in Group I received no treatment other than psychotherapy. Third, it is not clear if the evaluations of improvement were made by unbiased physicians who were not aware of the treatment received by the patients. Of course, the occurrence of death is an unbiased event. However, the difference in frequency of death is not statistically significant.

Because of the inadequacies of the report of their study it is difficult to be certain that Grace, Pinsky, and Wolff have unambiguously demonstrated

TABLE 11.1

*Improvements among Alcoholics in Various Therapy Groups in the Ends and Page Study*

| | Group | | | |
| --- | --- | --- | --- | --- |
| *Rating* | *Learning theory* | *Client centered* | *Analytic* | *Control* |
| Greatly improved | 1 | 7 | 6 | 3 |
| Possibly improved | 1 | 1 | 0 | 1 |
| No change | 5 | 1 | 4 | 4 |
| Rehospitalized | 7 | 3 | 5 | 9 |
| Not located | 2 | 3 | 0 | 0 |

Based on Ends & Page, 1957.

$X^2$ test for client centered and analytic versus control (leaving out not located category: $X^2 = 4.3$, d.f. $= 3$, p. $> 05$).

the superior effectiveness of psychotherapy in the treatment of ulcerative colitis.

Ends and Page (1957) studied the effectiveness of group therapy with alcoholics. Their study attempted to compare three different methods of group therapy, client-centered or Rogerian therapy, psychoanalytically oriented therapy, and a form of psychotherapy based on a learning theory approach.[1] In addition, a control group was used which met for social discussion purposes. The same therapists acted as therapists in each of the four conditions. Ends and Page included an 18-month follow-up of the drinking behavior of the alcoholics in their study. They found that the learning theory therapy had little or no beneficial effects. However, they report that alcoholics given client-centered therapy or psychoanalytically oriented therapy are more likely to be rated as greatly improved and are less likely to be rehospitalized. Table 11.1 presents the results of their follow-up. The data in Table 11.1 indicate a slight superiority in the behavior of patients in two of the group therapy conditions. A statistical test of the differences between the two therapy groups and the control group indicates that the differences are not statistically significant (see Table 11.1). Hence, on the most critical follow-up data the Ends and Page study fails to find support for the effectiveness of group therapy.

Arbuckle and Boy (1961) tested the effectiveness of client-centered therapy in the treatment of junior high school students with behavior

[1] Ends and Page do not describe the learning theory approach in any detail. It was probably not a form of behavior therapy.

problems. Three groups of twelve matched pupils were formed. One group received psychotherapy, another group was put on detention, and a third group was released from detention. The therapy extended for a twelve-week period. On a variety of measures, the therapy group showed significant improvement in comparison to the other groups. Significant changes occurred in $Q$-sort measures and in behavior ratings by teachers. On a six-week follow-up it was found that the therapy students tended to have fewer referrals for discipline problems than students in the other two groups. However, during the follow-up period therapy was available to the students in the therapy group on a voluntary basis and eleven of the twelve students continued in therapy. Consequently, this study really does not include a posttherapy follow-up and as a result the demonstration of the effectiveness of therapy, strictly speaking, does not fulfill all the criteria used to evaluate such studies in this chapter.

Massimo and Shore (1963) studied the effectiveness of vocationally oriented psychotherapy in the treatment of adolescent delinquent boys who had long-standing histories of antisocial behavior. Twenty boys were randomly assigned either to a therapy or a control group. The boys in the therapy group received extensive therapy including an involvement by their therapists in all phases of their life. Therapists helped the boys find jobs and acted as "father surrogates."

A very extensive battery of measures was used to evaluate the effectiveness of therapy. The treated boys showed significant improvement on tests of academic achievement. Perhaps the most critical data evaluating the effects of therapy in this study is the result of a two- to three-year follow-up reported by Shore and Massimo (1966). In addition to a continued superiority in academic achievement, there was some indication that the overt behavior and social adjustment of the boys had been affected by therapy. Five of the ten boys in the therapy group were still in school, compared to two of the ten boys in the control group. The untreated boys had a pattern of more serious difficulties with the law. Six of the ten untreated boys had been arrested for offenses ranging from disorderly conduct to manslaughter. Only two of the ten treated boys had been arrested and these two boys had been arrested for traffic violations. The overall picture was one of significant improvement for the treated boys.

The principal difficulty in accepting the dramatic findings in the Shore and Massimo study stems from the very small number of cases included in their study. On many of their most critical measures (number of boys in school, frequency of arrests, etc.), the percentage differences are large but the small number of cases does not permit one to establish that the differences are statistically significant. If the study had dealt with a larger number of adolescents (perhaps 40 rather than 20) and obtained the differences of the magnitude reported, it would have constituted an exemplary and powerful study of the effectiveness of this form of therapy. However, because of the size of the sample, the study should properly be considered as an exploratory one which supports the effectiveness of this type of therapy but does not clearly establish that effectiveness.

Persons (1966, 1967) studied the effectiveness of group and individual psychotherapy in the treatment of institutionalized delinquent boys aged 15–19, 82 of whom who were matched on such variables as I.Q., race, and nature of criminal offense were randomly assigned to a therapy group and a no-therapy control group. Each of the 41 boys in the therapy group received 40 hours of group therapy and 20 hours of individual therapy over a 40-week period. At the end of therapy a number of significant differences between the groups existed. The group receiving psychotherapy had profiles on the MMPI test which were indicative of lower delinquency and less pathology. Also, the boys in the therapy group had significantly fewer disciplinary reports submitted for them, indicating superior institutional adjustment. Persons went on to study the community adjustment of the two groups in their study. Table 11.2 presents a summary of these data. Table 11.2 indicates that the boys who received psychotherapy in the institution were clearly superior to their matched controls on such variables as rate of reinstitutionalization, employment, and frequency of parole violations. The Persons study is an exemplary one, indicating clear cut improvement resulting from psychotherapy.

Truax, Wargo, and Silber (1966) studied the effectiveness of group therapy on a sample of incarcerated female delinquents. The girls were

TABLE 11.2

*Community Adjustment of Therapy and Control Groups*

|  | Therapy (N = 41) | Control (N = 41) |
|---|---|---|
| Subjects staying in community | 28 | 16 |
| Subjects reinstitutionalized | 13 | 25 |
| $\bar{X}$ offenses by returnees | 1.94 | 3.07 |
| Number of parole violators | 20 | 32 |
| $\bar{X}$ parole violations | 1.75 | 3.91 |
| Successes employed | 20 | 6 |
| Returnees employed | 4 | 5 |
| Successes $\bar{X}$ time employed | 6.2 months | 3.2 months |
| Returnees $\bar{X}$ time employed | 2.3 months | 1.9 months |

From R. W. Persons, Relationships between psychotherapy with institutionalized boys and subsequent community adjustment. *Journal of Consulting Psychology,* 1967, **31,** 137–141.

randomly assigned to a therapy or a control group. Two therapists were used who, in previous research studies, had been rated as high on "accurate empathy" and "nonpossessive warmth." The 40 girls in the therapy groups received 24 sessions of therapy over a three-month period. In addition to changes in self-image as measured by *Q* sorts, the amount of time spent out of the institution for the 344 days following the beginning of group therapy was noted. This measure reflects both the time from the initiation of therapy to initial release from the institution and the time spent out of the institution subsequent to an initial release. It was found that the girls given group therapy tended to be released earlier from the institution and tended to stay out of the institution for longer periods of time subsequent to their release. The Truax, Wargo, and Silber study supports the findings of the Persons study in indicating that group therapy for institutionalized delinquents can improve their adjustment to the community.

## CONCLUSION: IS PSYCHOTHERAPY EFFECTIVE?

What can we conclude about the effectiveness of psychotherapy on the basis of the studies we have reviewed? Perhaps the most cautious assessment that can be given is that there does not exist a body of research which would permit one to assert that psychotherapy in one or more of its several forms has been adequately shown to be effective—at least according to the criteria developed at the beginning of the chapter. The only studies which provide clear-cut support for the effectiveness of therapy (the studies of Persons and Truax, Wargo, and Silber) are both studies of the effectiveness of therapy with groups, which paradoxically are assumed by clinicians to be incapable of response to psychotherapy, male and female incarcerated delinquents.[2] Whether psychotherapy is or is not effective when given to other types of individual in other contexts is simply not established.

## Studies of the Effectiveness of Various Kinds of Behavior Therapy

### SYSTEMATIC DESENSITIZATION

The method of behavior therapy whose effects have been most extensively studied in controlled investigations is systematic desensitization. We shall review two types of studies—those which are designed to test the effectiveness of systematic desensitization against a nontreatment control group and those which are designed to compare various types of therapy including

---

[2] It is perhaps worth noting that Massimo and Shore also reported success with a program of therapy for deliquent-prone adolescents—although the size of the sample precluded any firm assessment of the effectiveness of therapy.

TABLE 11.3

*Mean Pre- to Posttreatment Change Scores for All Fear Measures*

| Group | Avoidance test | Fear thermometer | FSS number 38 | Fear survey |
|---|---|---|---|---|
| Combined control ($N = 21$) | −.03 | 1.14 | .48 | 12.14 |
| Pseudotherapy ($N = 10$) | .14 | 1.30 | .40 | 12.50 |
| No treatment ($N = 11$) | −.19 | 1.00 | .54 | 11.82 |
| Desensitization ($N = 23$)[a] | .27 | 2.43 | 1.41 | 18.64 |
| (hierarchy items completed) | | | | |
| 15 or more ($N = 13$) | .47 | 3.58 | 2.31 | 23.77 |
| Less than 15 ($N = 10$) | .01 | .89 | .11 | 7.33 |

From A. D. Lang, A. D. Lazovik, & D. J. Reynolds, Desensitization, suggestibility, and pseudotherapy. *Journal of Abnormal Psychology*, 1965, **70,** 395–402.

Note: The avoidance test score is the percentage change statistic previously described. All other change scores were simply the difference between pre- and posttests. The correlations between initial performance and fear change for all measures were insignificant and inconsistent in direction.

[a] Data were incomplete for three *S*s. The fear thermometer and FSS *N*s are 22 and 21, respectively.

different procedures for using systematic desensitization and conventional therapies.

Lang, Lazovik, and Reynolds (1965) attempted to remove snake phobias in "normal" college students who were severely snake phobic. Three different groups were used. One group received systematic desensitization. One group was an untreated control group and a third group was a pseudotherapy control who, like the subjects in the systematic desensitization group, received training in relaxation followed by discussion of aspects of the person's life which were unrelated to the snake phobia. This pseudotherapy group acts as a control for the effects of being in therapy including periodic meetings with a therapist and the effects of relaxation training itself. The outcome of treatment was assessed in terms of ability to perform a variety of graded behavioral tasks involving progressively more intensive interactions involving snakes. Table 11.3 presents the principal results of the study. Table 11.3 indicates that only the *S*s who received the systematic desensitization training made significant progress in eliminating their phobia. Lang, Lazovik, and Reynolds note that this progress was limited to those *S*s who were desensitized to 15 or more out of 20 items in the standardized heirarchy of snake phobia stimuli. If the treatment had extended beyond 11 desensitization sessions, it is likely that more subjects would have been able to advance further in the desensitization hierarchy leading to better outcomes for this treatment.

Davison (1965) has also studied systematic desensitization for male phobic *S*s. Davison had four groups of *S*s in his study: A systematic desensitization group, a group given relaxation training followed by the pairing of relaxation with snake irrelevant stimuli, a group exposed hierarchically to the same set of stimuli used for the desensitization group without pairing the stimuli with relaxation, and a nontreatment control group. The *S*s were assigned to these groups who were matched on their behavioral avoidance of snake responses and by their self-report of anxiety. Behavioral outcome measures were used. The results indicated that only the *S*s who underwent desensitization showed significant changes in their ability to interact with snakes. The Davison study indicates that the separate components of the desensitization treatment—visualization of a hierarchy of stimuli related to snakes, and relaxation training itself are not sufficient to remove phobic responses. It is only when there is a pairing of these two components that the phobia is reduced.

Nawas, Welsch, and Fishman (1970) have also studied systematic desensitization with snake phobic subjects. They used five different treatment groups:

1. a no-treatment group,
2. a pseudotherapy control group,
3. a systematic desensitization group,
4. a group in which graded aversive stimuli were imagined and paired with such neutral tasks as adding numbers, and
5. a group in which imagined aversive stimuli were paired with muscular tension responses.

Behavioral outcome measures were used. The pseudotherapy and the no-treatment control group had change scores of 1.5 and 1.4 respectively, indicating little change in their ability to perform snake relevant responses. Groups 4 and 5 who had the pairing of aversive stimuli with nonrelaxation responses had change scores of 6.4 and 6.7 respectively. The group given systematic desensitization had a change score of 9.1. These data indicate that muscular relaxation is not essential to remove snake phobias. Evidently, the pairing of aversive imaginal stimuli with any antagonistic response will reduce the phobia. However, the relaxation response appears to be more effective than the other responses used. (See also Lazarus, 1965; and Rachman, 1968.)

Mealiea (as cited in Bandura, 1969) has also compared systematic desensitization treatment with other treatments. Snake phobic *S*s were administered either taped desensitization, implosive therapy which involves the repeated imaginal presentation of extremely aversive stimuli (see Stampfl & Levis, 1967), a modified desensitization procedure in which

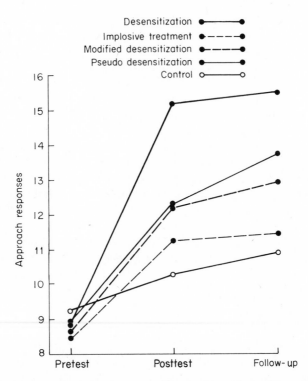

Fɪɢ. 11.1. Mean number of snake-approach responses performed by subjects in each of five conditions before treatment, immediately after treatment, and nine months later. (Plotted from data of Mealiea, 1967 as reported in Bandura, 1969.)

relaxation was paired with scenes taken from the implosive treatment, a pseudotherapy control group in which relaxations were paired with pleasant stimuli, and a no-treatment control group. Behavioral outcome measures were used. Figure 11.1 presents the results of the study. Figure 11.1 indicates that the systematic desensitization treatment was superior to all others on a posttest and after a one-month follow-up.

The study of the effectiveness of systematic desensitization has not been restricted to snake phobic Ss. Moore (1965) used systematic desensitization in the treatment of asthma. Asthmatics who had proved unresponsive to treatment were given relaxation treatment alone, relaxation combined with suggestions that they would show improvement, or they received systematic desensitization in which relaxation was paired with imaginal representations of situations likely to induce asthmatic attacks. Each patient received two of the treatments in a design which presented each possible pair of treatments in each possible order. Three outcome measures were used—self-

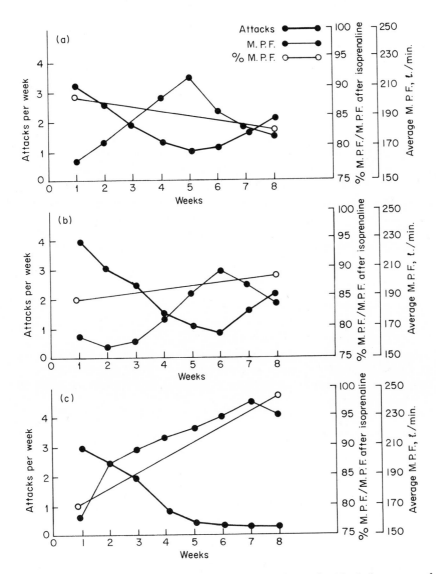

FIG. 11.2. Changes in reported asthmatic attacks, and two physiological measures of respiratory function associated with each of three treatment conditions: (a) Relaxation alone; (b) relaxation with suggestion; and (c) relaxation with reciprocal inhibition. (Based on Moore, 1965.)

reports of improvement and two physiological measures of respiratory function. Figure 11.2 represents the results of the study. Figure 11.2 indicates that all treatment conditions led to some improvement in self-report measures of frequency of asthmatic attacks. However, the best and most consistent improvement in this measure of outcome was obtained for patients given systematic desensitization (labeled relaxation with reciprocal inhibition in Figure 11.2). Only the patients given systematic desensitization treatment showed clear and consistent improvement of the two physiological measures of respiratory function. Moore's study indicates that systematic desensitization is effective in the treatment of asthma.

Paul (1966) has reported the use of systematic desensitization in the treatment of stage fright in what is probably the best study of the effectiveness of different forms of therapy which has been reported. Paul selected his $S$s from a pool of 710 $S$s on the basis of their scores on a variety of measures of anxiety and measures of social extroversion and a self-report measure of confidence as a speaker. Paul selected 96 $S$s who seemed high in anxiety who were required to give a speech to an audience of psychologists who assessed their anxiety. The $S$s were randomly assigned to different treatment conditions on the basis of their scores on the various anxiety tests as well as their behavior in the stress speech condition. Five different groups were used in the experiment:

1. Systematic desensitization using hierarchies related to public speaking.

2. Insight oriented psychotherapy.

3. Attention–placebo—a group given an inert pill which they were told was a tranquillizer and given, in addition, support and attention.

4. A no treatment classroom control in which $S$s were required to make two speeches in class and given a promise of future treatment.

5. A noncontact classroom group who were not contacted between pre- and postassessments.

Five experienced psychotherapists gave all three treatments. Each $S$ in the treatment groups received five sessions of treatment over a six-week period. Following completion of the treatments the $S$'s degree of physiological arousal, rated behavior, and self-reported distress was measured in a stress speech situation in which a $S$ had to give a speech to a number of psychologists. Bandura (1969) has summarized Paul's data in the graph presented in Figure 11.3, which indicates the percentage of $S$s in each group who exhibited reductions above a certain magnitude on each of the measures of performance in the stress situation. (Note: the two nontreatment groups are considered as one group.) Figure 11.3 indicates that the groups given insight psychotherapy and attention placebo were somewhat

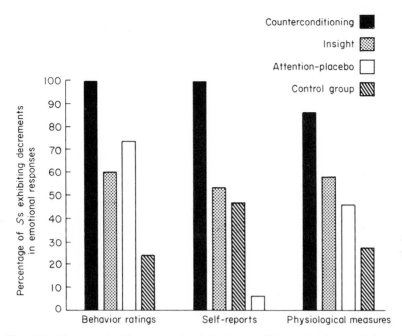

Fig. 11.3. Percent of subjects in each of the four conditions who displayed decreases in anxiety as measured by behavior ratings, self-reports of emotional disturbance and measure of physiological arousal. Drawn from data of Paul, 1966. (Based on Bandura, 1969.)

improved over the nontreatment control groups. However, the group given systematic desensitization was clearly superior to all other groups on all three types of measures.

In addition, the Ss were given a follow-up battery after six weeks and after two years. (See Paul, 1967.) The battery included the following self report measures: Anxiety differential, IPAT Anxiety scale, Pittsburgh Social Extroversion and Emotionality scales, and a modified version of a stimulus–response inventory of anxiety designed to obtain information about anxiety in an interview, exam, and contest situation. In addition a composite measure of anxiety in a speech situation was obtained. Figure 11.4 presents the results of these follow-ups. Figure 11.4 indicates that the group given desensitization treatment was superior or extended its improvement over the other groups over a two-year period on all measures except the tendency to become anxious in a contest situation which was relatively removed from the focus of desensitization. After two years, the desensitization group is less anxious in a speech situation, reports less anxiety in an

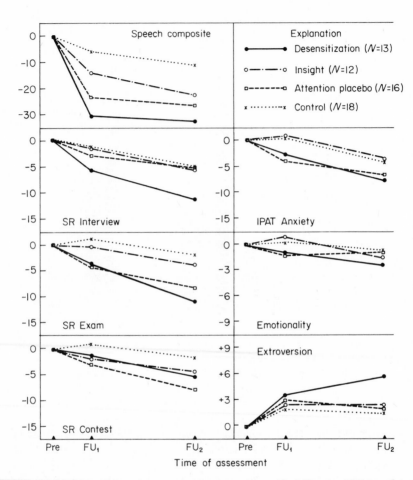

Fig. 11.4. Mean change from pretreatment to six-week follow-up (FU₁) and two-year follow-up (FU₂) for *S*s retained at FU₂. (From G. L. Paul, Insight versus desensitization in psychotherapy two years after termination. *Journal of Consulting Psychology*, 1967, **31**, 333–348.)

interview and exam situation, reports slightly lower general anxiety, reports lower emotionality, and a rather clear-cut gain in extroversion.

Paul and Shannon (1966; Paul, 1968) have reported equally good results using a group procedure for the administration of systematic desensitization.

Paul's study clearly indicates that systematic desensitization is effective in treating anxiety associated with public speaking. What is particularly impressive in this study is the clear cut gains on large variety of measures over an extended period of time following a relatively brief set of treatments.

Also, the study clearly establishes that systematic desensitization is more effective than an equally brief form of insight oriented psychotherapy in the treatment of anxieties surrounding public speaking.

A number of other studies have attempted to compare systematic desensitization procedures with psychotherapy. Lazarus (1961) used a group desensitization procedure with individuals with different types of phobias (for example, claustrophobia, acrophobia) and with individuals who were impotent. The patients were matched on age and type of phobia and were randomly assigned to homogeneous group therapy or group desensitization treatments administered by the same therapist. A mean of 22 sessions was used for each of the treatment groups. Most of the phobic $S$s were given behavioral tests. The $S$s who were impotent were asked to give self-reports about their progress. The phobic behavior was judged to be completely removed in 13 of the 18 patients given systematic desensitization treatment and in only 2 of the 12 patients given group therapy. Although this study does not employ as vigorous an assessment of behavioral change, it does indicate that systematic desensitization is more effective in eliminating a variety of phobic behaviors than conventional group therapy. (See also Gelder, Marks, & Wolff, 1967.)

## THE USE OF MODELING PROCEDURES IN THE TREATMENT OF PHOBIAS

Despite the generally favorable evidence that has been obtained of the effectiveness of systematic desensitization in the treatment of phobias, there is evidence that it is not the most effective behavior modification procedure available. In Chapter 9 we briefly discussed a study by Bandura *et al.* (1969) which indicated that snake-phobic $S$s who were exposed to live models who assisted them in the performance of various responses related to snakes had a greater reduction in phobic behavior than $S$s who were given systematic desensitization. Bandura (1969) has noted that clients given systematic desensitization training are usually improved but are not usually totally rid of their phobia. Depending on the nature of the criteria used, usually only 30–50 percent of the $S$s are able to engage in the terminal activities of the behavioral tests used to assess the effectiveness of therapy. By contrast, Bandura, Blanchard and Ritter report that 96 percent of the subjects in their study who had been exposed to live models who assisted them were able to perform terminal activities with a live snake. This figure includes $S$s in other conditions who were not completely relieved of their phobia who were then given the live modeling treatment. In addition 70 percent of the subjects were able to perform terminal activities with a different kind of snake. Also, these levels of approach were maintained in a one- or two-month follow-up. One further point is worth noting about these dramatic results. The average duration of treatment in the live modeling group was 2 hours and 20 min. The Bandura, Blanchard, and Ritter study suggests that phobias are almost completely eliminated with very brief treatments.

Ritter (1968) has shown that live modeling with models assisting can be used to eliminate snake phobias in children aged five to eleven years. She used two 35-min. group sessions in which children watched fearless peers play with a snake and were then asked to play with the snake and assist other children in the group to play with the snake; 80 percent of the children were able to perform terminal behaviors with the snake.

Ritter (1969) used live models who demonstrated activities and then assisted clients to perform them while holding them in the removal of acrophobias (fear of height). A 135-min. treatment session was held on a roof. Three different treatments were compared—systematic desensitization, the vicarious observation of live models, and contact desensitization—the use of live models to hold and assist the $S$s to engage in activities which they would be unable to perform on their own. Behavioral outcome measures were used. The mean change scored for the live modeling group was 3.4, for systematic desensitization 9.0, and for contact desensitization 13.6. These data again indicate that the use of live models to assist $S$s to perform activities related to their phobias is more effective than systematic desensitization in removing phobias.

Various types of behavior therapy have been used to deal with a variety of other conditions. In what follows we shall briefly review research related to enuresis, the use of aversive counterconditioning, and the control of severely psychotic patients.

ENURESIS

Mowrer and Mowrer (1938) are generally credited with the discovery of a behavior therapy method for the treatment of enuresis. The procedure involves the use of a pad placed in the bed of an enuretic child. The pad is connected to a battery and will lead to the ringing of a bell when the child urinates. The bell awakens the child or summons the parents to awaken the child. It will continue to ring until it is turned off. Lovibond (1964) has presented a theoretical analysis, which is at variance with the original theory given by Mowrer and Mowrer, which explains the basis for the treatment. According to Lovibond, the detrusor contraction and sphincter relaxation which follow urination are conditioned stimuli which precede the occurrence of a noxious stimulus—the bell—which disturbs the sleep of the child. The kinesthetic stimuli associated with sphincter relaxation come to act as conditioned aversive stimuli—eliciting an aversive state. The aversive state is avoided by the induction of an antagonistic response—

sphincter contraction which prohibits urination. Through generalization the process moves backward in time, leading to an earlier occurrence of the sphincter contraction.

A number of studies have indicated the effectiveness of this type of procedure. De Leon and Mandell (1966) compared this treatment with psychotherapy. Using an initial criterion of 13 successive dry nights, they achieved 86 percent success among 51 children treated by the conditioning method. Only 18 percent of 13 children treated by psychotherapy achieved this criterion.

Baker (1967) tested the effectiveness of the Mowrer and Mowrer treatment for enuresis in a well-controlled study. He used three groups of matched *S*s. One group was assigned to the Mowrer and Mowrer conditioning apparatus, one group had a wake-up treatment and one group was a waiting list control who received no treatment. Of the 14 *S*s, 11 who were given the conditioning treatment attained a criterion of 14 consecutive dry nights in a mean of 14.7 weeks and 26.5 reinforcements (ringing of the bell). Of the 14 *S*s in the other groups only 2 attained this criterion.

Yates (1970) has summarized studies dealing with the effectiveness of the Mowrer and Mowrer procedure for treating enuretics. Table 11.4 presents his summary of these data. Table 11.4 indicates that a number of investigators, using a variety of criteria, have reported success rates for this treatment varying between 21.4 and 100 percent. It is clear from the data reported in Table 11.4 that the Mowrer and Mowrer apparatus is effective in the treatment of enuresis.

AVERSIVE COUNTERCONDITIONING

Aversive counterconditioning refers to procedures which are used to eliminate behaviors which produce positive reinforcement but are socially disapproved or socially deviant by associating these positively valenced behaviors with aversive stimulation. The behavior, by a conditioning process, should come to elicit the aversive state which has been associated with them, thus leading to a reduction in the tendency to engage in such behavior. This type of treatment has been used in the treatment of drug addiction, sexual deviance, and alcoholism.

A number of different kinds of aversive stimulation have been used in the treatment of alcoholism over the last 35 years. The usual procedure involves the association of the sight, taste and smell of alcohol with drugs which produce nausea and regurgitation, or electric shock, or hypnotically induced feelings of nausea and vomiting created by the reexperience of the patient's worst hangover. Bandura (1969) has summarized the outcome of aversion therapy treatment of confirmed alcoholics. The criterion of success

## TABLE 11.4

Results of CR Treatment of Enuresis

| Study | N M | N F | Age range | Percentage achieving initial criterion | Relapse rate (%) No retraining | Relapse rate (%) After retraining | Follow-up period (months) | Success rate (% dry at follow-up including those retrained) | Posttreatment adjustment (+: improvement; 0: no change; −: deterioration) | Symptom substitution |
|---|---|---|---|---|---|---|---|---|---|---|
| Baller and Schalock (1956) | 43 | 12 | 5–26 | 98 | 23 | 0 | 24–40 | 70 | + | No |
| Behrle et al. (1956) | 12 | 8 | 5–14 | Not stated | 15 | 5 | 18–40 | 75 | 0 | No |
| Crosby (1950) | 17 | 12 | 3½–10½ | Not stated | 3.5 | — | Not stated | 96.5 | Not stated | Not stated |
| | 5 | 1 | 3½–10½ | | 20.0 | — | | 80.0 | | |
| | 15 | 8 | 11–38 | | 13.0 | — | | 87.0 | | |
| Davidson and Douglass (1950) | 17 | 3 | 5–30 | Not stated | — | 0 | 1–13 | 100 | + | No |
| De Leon and Mandell (1966) | 42 | 14 | 5½–14 | 86 | 79.6[a] | — | 1–22 | 21.4 | Not stated | Not stated |
| Forrester et al. (1964) | 7 | 9 | 8–14 | Not stated | Not stated | — | 6 | 62 | Not stated | Not stated |

| Study | | | | | | | | | | |
|---|---|---|---|---|---|---|---|---|---|---|
| Freyman (1959, 1963) | 47 | 24 | 5–15+ | 72 | 35 | 20 | 10 | 80 | Not stated | No |
| Geppert (1953) | 30 | 12 (approx.) | 5–10+ | 90 | — | 20 | Not stated | 90(?) | + | Not stated |
| Gillison and Skinner (1958) | 64 | 36 | 3½–21 | Not stated | — | 0 | No systematic follow-up | 90(?) | + | No |
| Martin and Kubly (1955) | (79)[b] | (35) | 3½–18 | Not stated | 26 | — | 14 (average) | 74 | Not stated | Not stated |
| Mowrer and Mowrer (1938) | | 30 | 3–13 | 100 | — | — | Up to 30 | 100 | + | No |
| Seiger (1952) | 73 | 33 | 2½–29 | — | 11 | — | 2–many years | 89 | Not stated | Not stated |
| Taylor (1963) | 62 | 38 | 5–15 | 64 | 16 | — | 6+ | 53 | Not stated | Not stated |
| Wickes (1958)[c] | 81 | 19 | 5–17 | Not stated | 26 | — | Not stated | 74 | + | Not stated |
| Young and Turner (1965) | 105 | | 4–15 | 65(93)[d] | 13 | — | 12 | 53(81)[d] | + | No |

Based on Yates, 1970.

[a] The relapse criterion was very severe—a single wet night.

[b] In four cases sex was unknown (study was carried out by questionnaire on commercial users).

[c] Wickes (1963) reported a success rate of 74% (dry) in a series of 445 cases; but insufficient details are given to justify inclusion in the table.

[d] 93% rate if cases where treatment was discontinued are excluded; 65% if they are included. Same comments apply to success rate.

TABLE 11.5

*Abstinence Rates Obtained by Aversion Therapy*

| Investigator | Number of cases | Aversive stimulus | Complete abstinence (%) | Duration of follow-up |
|---|---|---|---|---|
| Edlin, Johnson, Hletko, & Heilbrunn (1945) | 63 | Emetine | 30 | 3–10 months |
| Kant (1945) | 31 | Emetine | 80 | Unspecified |
| Lemere & Voegtlin (1950) | 4096 | Emetine | 51 | 1–10 years |
| Miller, Dvorak, & Turner (1960) | 10 | Emetine | 80 | 8 months |
| Shanahan & Hornick (1946) | 24 | Emetine | 70 | 9 months |
| Thimann (1949) | 275 | Emetine | 51 | 3–7 years |
| Wallace (1949) | 31 | Emetine | 42 | 4–17 months |
| DeMorsier & Feldmann (1950) | 150 | Apomorphine | 46 | 8–31 months |
| Mestrallet & Lang (1959) | 183 | Apomorphine | 41 | |
| Ruck (1956) | | Apomorphine | 50 | 1.5 years |
| Kantorovich (1934) | 20 | Electric shock | 82 | 3 weeks–20 months |
| Black (1967) | 25 | Electric shock | 23 | 12 months |
| | 37 | Electric shock with relaxation training | 48 | 12 months |
| Miller (1959) | 24 | Verbally induced aversion | 83 | 9 months |
| Anant (1967) | 26 | Verbally induced aversion | 96 | 8–15 months |
| Ashem & Donner (1968) | 15 | Verbally induced aversion | 40 | 6 months |

Based on Bandura, 1969.

in therapy is *complete* abstinence. Table 11.5 presents Bandura's summary of these investigations. Table 11.5 indicates that complete abstinence has been obtained in anywhere from 30 to 96 percent of the cases studied by various investigators with follow-up procedures of various durations. The data indicates aversion treatment is an effective method of treating alcoholism.

Bandura (1969) indicates that aversive treatment of alcoholism may need to be supplemented by a variety of other procedures to give alcoholics additional competence in coping with the culture. Aversion treatment has been supplemented by operant conditioning training to acquire job related skills and systematic desensitization of stress provoking situations.

More recently, aversion therapies have been used to treat various kinds of sexual deviance. Unfortunately, these treatments have only come into use recently and there are few adequately controlled outcome studies of the effectiveness of these methods. Feldman (1966; Feldman & MacCulloch, 1964; Feldman, MacCulloch, Mellor, & Pinsch of 1966) used electric shock in the treatment of homosexuality. Feldman's procedure involves the association of pictures of male nudes with electric shock which is presented on a variable interval/variable ratio schedule. He reports that 18 of 26 severely homosexual males, with Kinsey ratings of 3 or over, were improved as a result of this treatment. Improvement was defined as engaging in heterosexual activities or as having heterosexual fantasies.

Freund (1960) has used emetic mixtures injected subcutaneously in the treatment of homosexuality. When the emetic mixture became effective, slides of dressed and undressed male nudes were shown to the patients. In a second phase of the treatment, the *S*s received an injection of *testosteronum propionicim* and seven hours later were shown movies of nude and seminude females. Table 11.6 presents the results of three-year follow-up of these patients. Table 11.6 indicates that heterosexual adaptation occurred in only 25.5 percent of the cases. However, some improvement was obtained among a majority of patients who voluntarily presented themselves for

TABLE 11.6

*Results in Treatment of Homosexuals*

|  | Sent by police, magistrates etc.[a] | Unrequited homo- sexual love | Sent by relatives | No obvious external pressure | Total | Pro- portion (%) |
|---|---|---|---|---|---|---|
| No improvement | 17 | 7 | 5 | 12 | 24 | 51.1 |
| Short-term hetero- sexual adaptation | 3 | 2 | 0 | 5 | 7 | 14.9 |
| Adaptation lasting for several years | 0 | 0 | 1 | 11 | 12 | 25.5 |
| Outcome not suffi- ciently doc- umented | 0 | 0 | 1 | 3 | 4 | 8.5 |
| Total: | 20 | 9 | 7 | 31 | 47 | 100 |

Based on Freund, 1960.

[a] Not included in calculations in last column.

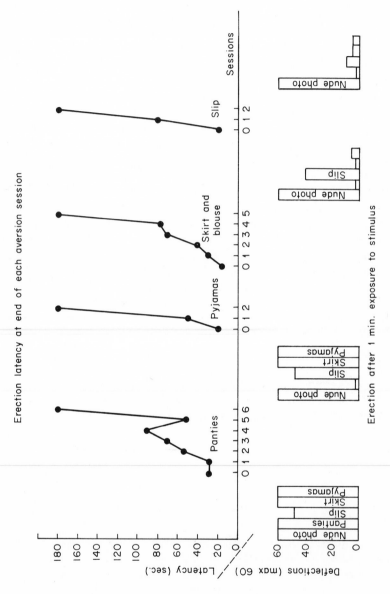

FIG. 11.5. Specificity of autonomic changes (Patient B). (Based on Marks & Gelder, 1967.)

treatment, whereas almost total lack of improvement was obtained for patients who were sent for treatment by police magistrates. Even in the cases where successful heterosexual adjustment is claimed, the treatment is only partially successful since all of these patients report that they still have preponderantly homosexual erotic attractions. Freund's treatments appear to have had limited effectiveness.

One difficulty with outcome studies such as Freund's is that they are based on verbal reports of success. In recent years a number of ingenious procedures have been developed to index sexual responses physiologically and to use these indices as evidence of the outcome of various treatment procedures. Marks and Gelder (1967) used shock as a conditioned aversive stimulus in the treatment of sexual perversions (fetishism and transvestism) in five patients. Shocks were administered to these patients while they carried out their deviant activities or imagined themselves engaging in this activity. They used a variety of outcome measures including the measurement of latency and amplitude of penile erections in response to relevant stimuli. Figure 11.5 presents data indicating changes in the amplitude and latency of penile erection responses as a function of treatment for a transvestite. Figure 11.5 indicates that the latency of penile erection responses to female clothes progressively increased as a function of treatment. Also, the amplitude of penile erection responses to female items of clothing progressively decreased. The changes were accompanied by changes in attitude and reported changes in fantasy activity which were elicited by the stimuli. The physiological changes apparently provide sensitive objective indices of relatively widespread changes.

Although there has been no comprehensive assessment of the use of aversion therapy in the modification of sexual disorders, preliminary indications are that this form of therapy is useful. However, its usefulness remains to be demonstrated in more systematic research.

## OPERANT CONDITIONING TREATMENT FOR PSYCHOTICS

There have been a large number of attempts to use the principles of reinforcement developed in research with animals to modify the behavior of severely disturbed and psychotic individuals. Working with such individuals who, on superficial examination, appear to be totally unresponsive and removed from ordinary social influence and control, represents a particularly rigorous test of the application of principles of reinforcement. The principle of reinforcement emphasizes that behavior is controlled by the consequences of responses. Therefore, in order to modify behavior it is necessary to create a "responsive" environment which will provide desirable rewards for actions which are in the intended direction. We shall discuss one such attempt to create a responsive environment in order to illustrate the possibilities of this form of treatment. Ayllon and Azrin (1968) attempted to set up a responsive environment for the treatment of chronic female psychotics. Patients were obtained for treatment in a ward of a state hospital by asking supervisors of other wards to name patients that they would like to have transferred from their wards. By this procedure patients were obtained who might be old, who were not performing useful work, who were not verbal, or, if verbal, were abusive. The patients selected had a median age of 50 and had been in a mental hospital for a median number of 16 years. They were almost all poorly educated, some were incontinent, and others were described as vegetative.

Ayllon and Azrin attempted to create an environment in which these patients could function productively. In order to accomplish this they first defined, in behavioral terms, a large number of jobs which could be performed on and off the ward. The jobs included such things as working in the kitchen, cleaning, performing various kinds of personal behaviors relevant to grooming and personal hygiene, etc. Performance of each activity was immediately rewarded by the ward attendants with a number of tokens. The number of tokens given for the satisfactory completion of an activity was dependent principally upon the time involved to do the activity. Having specified a series of useful behavior which could be accomplished by the patients, Ayllon and Azrin attempted to define the kinds of rewards which would be of interest to the patient. By observing patients' preferred activities and by systematically asking patients to state the kinds of things they wanted, they were able to construct a list of rewards. Any available reward could be obtained by exchanging a specified number of tokens. Table 11.7 presents the list of reinforcers available for tokens.

The program was quite effective in getting patients to engage in the various activities. It is also clear that the reinforcers was effective. This was demonstrated by an experiment in which the reinforcement was made not contingent on job activity. The job activity dropped sharply and was restored when reinforcement was made contingent on performance of job activities. Figure 11.6 presents the results of this experiment.

Ayllon and Azrin also used shaping procedures in which behaviors were reinforced which approximated or were a component of the target behavior to assist patients to participate in the program. In one experiment a group of five patients who had not participated in any off-ward jobs were trained to work in the hospital laundry. The procedure involved giving tokens for various behaviors which are successive approximations of the target behavior. Table 11.8 presents the sequence of behavior and the rewards assigned to each. Although none of these five patients had held any off-ward job for the past three years, all of them were able to work in the laundry for six hours after this training.

Ayllon and Azrin indicate that many of the more bizarre psychotic behaviors of the patients in the ward decreased or were eliminated after the responsive environment was operative. The institution of such an environ-

TABLE 11.7

*List of Reinforcers Available for Tokens*

| Item | No. of tokens daily | Item | Tokens |
|---|---|---|---|
| I. *Privacy* | | IV. *Devotional opportunities* | |
| Selection of room 1 | 0 | Extra religious services on ward | 1 |
| Selection of room 2 | 4 | Extra religious services off ward | 10 |
| Selection of room 3 | 8 | | |
| Selection of room 4 | 15 | | |
| Selection of room 5 | 30 | V. *Recreational opportunities* | |
| Personal chair | 1 | Movie on ward | 1 |
| Choice of eating group | 1 | Opportunity to listen to a live band | 1 |
| Screen (room divider) | 1 | Exclusive use of a radio | 1 |
| Choice of bedspreads | 1 | Television (choice of program) | 3 |
| Coat rack | 1 | | |
| Personal cabinet | 1 | | |
| Placebo | 1–2 | VI. *Commissary items* | |
| | | Consumable items such as candy, milk, cigarettes, coffee, and sandwich | 1–5 |
| II. *Leave from the ward* | | | |
| 20-min. walk on hospital grounds (with escort) | 2 | Toilet articles such as Kleenex, toothpaste, comb, lipstick, and talcum powder | 1–10 |
| 30-min. grounds pass (3 tokens for each additional 30 min.) | 10 | | |
| Trip to town (with escort) | 100 | | |
| | | Clothing and accessories such as gloves, headscarf, house slippers, handbag, and skirt | 12–400 |
| III. *Social interaction with staff* | | | |
| Private audience with chaplain, nurse | 5 min. free | Reading and writing materials such as stationery, pen, greeting card, newspaper, and magazine | 2–5 |
| Private audience with ward staff, ward physician (for additional time—1 token per min.) | 5 min. free | | |
| Private audience with ward psychologist | 20 | Miscellaneous items such as ashtray, throw rug, potted plant, picture holder, and stuffed animal | 1–50 |
| Private audience with social worker | 100 | | |

Based on Ayllon & Azrin, 1968.

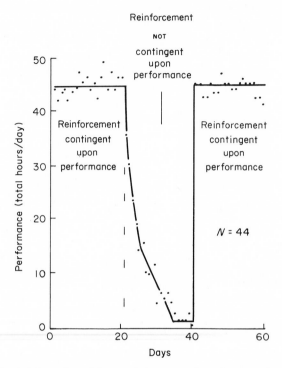

FIG. 11.6. The total number of hours of the on-ward performance by a group of 44 patients. (Based on Ayllon & Azrin, 1968.)

ment is not a "cure" for psychosis. However, it helps to maintain many of the behaviors required to function effectively in the nonhospital environment. Finally, the Ayllon and Azrin study indicates that the principles of reinforcement may be used to influence the behavior of chronic psychotic patients.

This brief review of outcome studies of behavior therapy has indicated some of the procedures used and the kinds of results obtained in modifying behavior with these procedures. It would be beyond the scope of this book to deal extensively with all the variety of procedures which have been used. Fortunately, there are two excellent recent systematic treatments of behavior therapy available (Bandura, 1969; Yates, 1970). The data indicates that these procedures have proved effective in a variety of circumstances. In many cases the effectiveness of the procedures has yet to be demonstrated in large-scale controlled outcome studies. However, the amount of evidence which is already available is encouraging. Also, there is some evidence in controlled investigations that behavior therapy procedures are more effective than brief psychotherapy in the treatment of certain relatively circumscribed problems, for example, enuresis, phobias, etc. On the negative side, it should be noted that the well-controlled outcome studies demonstrating the effectiveness of behavior therapy have dealt with problems which are well-focused and can be defined relatively easily, for example, enuresis, phobias, alcoholism, etc. It is not clear whether or not behavior therapy would be equally valuable and effective in the treatment of more diffuse forms of psychopathology in which a variety of behavior patterns must be changed. Finally, considering the relatively brief time in which behavior therapy has been in widespread use, the evidence of its effectiveness appears far more substantial than the evidence for the effectiveness of psychotherapy which has been in widespread use for over 50 years.

## Conclusions and Implications

What can be concluded about the paradigm clash we are considering as a result of the studies we have reviewed? It appears that the evidence supporting the effectiveness of behavior therapy and the relative lack of evidence for the effectiveness of psychotherapy would tend to favor the acceptance of a social-learning position over a more traditional psychodynamic one. However, to infer that evidence for the effectiveness of a procedure of therapy supports or fails to support some theoretical position, it is necessary to show that the procedure does in fact follow from a particular theory or does in fact contradict what would be expected on the basis of some other theory. These issues have been under heated discussion in connection with behavior therapy (see Yates, 1970, especially Chapter 19).

One issue which has been the focus of attention concerns the question of symptom substitution. Psychoanalytically oriented writers have frequently argued that procedures which involve relatively direct manipulation and change of behavior without considering the underlying psychological matrix will inevitably lead to the substitution of one symptom by another which may even be more dangerous. Thus, for example, enuresis may be considered a symptom of some complex, typically an unconscious complex. The removal of enuretic behavior without a consideration of the underlying psychodynamic influences would, as a result, be of little value and would only lead to the substitution of a new maladaptive "symptom" for enuresis. The view of behavior therapists is somewhat different. Symptom substitution is by no means assumed to be an automatic occurrence. There are a number of variables which should govern the

TABLE 11.8

*Prompting–Shaping of Work Assignments for Five Patients*

| Behavioral step | Day behavioral step was achieved by each patient | | | | | Verbal prompt associated with the behavioral step | No. of tokens given for each behavioral step |
| --- | --- | --- | --- | --- | --- | --- | --- |
| | M.D.[a] | M.W. | F.C. | W.S. | C.N. | | |
| 1. Walked with attendant on ward | 1 | | 1 | 1 | | Come with me | 10 |
| 2. Walked with attendant outside ward | 1 | | 3 | | | Come with me outside | 10 |
| 3. Walked with attendant to laundry | 2 | | 4 | 2 | 1 | Come with me to the laundry | 10 |
| 4. Worked for 5 min. in laundry (attendant present) | 7 | | | | | Patient instructed to do whatever specific job needed | 10 |
| 5. Worked for 15 min. in laundry (attendant present) | 9 | | | | | Patient instructed to do whatever specific job needed | 10 |
| 6. Worked for 30 min. in laundry (attendant present) | 10 | | | 2 | | Patient instructed to do whatever specific job needed | 10 |

320

| Behavior | | | | | Prompt | Percentage |
|---|---|---|---|---|---|---|
| 7. Worked for 45 min. in laundry (attendant present) | 11 | | | | Patient instructed to do whatever specific job needed | 10 |
| 8. Worked for 1 hour in laundry (attendant present) | 11 | | 16 | 1 | Patient instructed to do whatever specific job needed | 20 |
| 9. Worked for 3 hours in laundry (attendant occasionally absent) | 12 | | 17 | 8 | Patient instructed to do whatever specific job needed | 40 |
| 10. Worked for 6 hours in laundry (attendant occasionally absent) | 18 | 1 | 22 | 12 | Would you like to work 6 hours a day at the laundry? | 80 |
| 11. Worked for 6 hours in laundry (attendant absent) | 20 | | | | Would you like to work 6 hours a day at the laundry? | 80 |
| 12. Worked for 6 hours without being prompted individually (attendant absent) | 21 | 2 | 23 | 13 | No prompt | 80 |

Based on Ayllon & Azrin, 1968.

[a] Initials of patients.

consequences of removal of a maladaptive response. Behavior therapists working in England have been influenced by Eysenck's dimensional analysis. From such a perspective, individuals who are high in neuroticism would be more likely to acquire new maladaptive responses than individuals who are low in neuroticism. However, the acquisition of a new maladaptive response would be functionally independent of the previous response, being related to it only in the sense that certain individuals have genetically determined predisposition to develop maladaptive responses. Bandura (1969) has emphasized a number of conditions which will lead to behavior suggestive of symptom substitution (see also Cahoon, 1968). For example, if behavior is modified without removing internal aversive states (anxiety) which provide the controlling stimuli for the behavior, some new type of unadaptive response may occur. If an individual has acquired several maladaptive responses which are hierarchically arranged, the elimination of the dominant response will lead to its substitution by a new response. In certain cases removal of a maladaptive form of response may still leave an individual incapable of functioning. For example, a homosexual of long standing may not have acquired various interpersonal skills to use in heterosexual contexts. Consequently, the removal of his homosexual behavior may leave him unadjusted. Of course, in such a case therapy might include various kinds of heterosexual training procedures. Also, in cases where deviant behavior is reinforced by deviant subcultures (skid row, delinquent groups), removal of behavior in an institutional setting may be ineffective if the individual is returned to the reinforcement contingencies operative in the deviant subculture. Although there are a number of factors which might make the change of a particular maladaptive response ineffective in producing better adjustment, these failures are, for the most part, understandable in terms of the failure of the behavior therapist to modify or obtain control over relevant variables. In no case is there the assumption of automatic symptom substitution in the psychoanalytic sense. In fact, in many cases, the elimination of maladaptive behavior may carry with it various kinds of "secondary gains." An individual may benefit from an increased sense of competence from such changes. Also, the elimination of certain behaviors may permit the individual to engage in new activities and gain new competencies which were previously unattainable. In summary, it can be argued that the occurrence of symptom substitution provides a test of the differences between two orientations. Psychoanalytic theory, on the one hand, predicting the inevitable occurrence of such behaviors, and behavior therapy predicting it, will not automatically occur and, if therapy has been properly managed, one should obtain secondary gains.

The evidence on the question of symptom substitution is relatively clear-cut. It does not occur. Several investigators have searched for symptom substitution in follow-up investigations of behavior therapy and have uniformly reported negative results. For example, Baker (1967) used a number of posttherapeutic measures in his study of the treatment of enuresis and reported no evidence that successfully-treated children had new symptoms or an increase in maladjustment. Paul (1966; 1968) found positive changes on general measures of anxiety and extroversion as a result of the successful treatment of anxiety about public speaking. Bandura *et al.* (1969) also found a number of positive changes associated with the removal of snake phobias. The data available indicate that the expectation of automatic symptom substitution is unwarranted.

The fact that symptom substitution does not occur would seem to indicate that the psychoanalytic conception of the meaning of symptoms is incorrect. However, Weitzman (1967) has argued that psychoanalytic theory does not necessarily predict symptom substitution. Weitzman argues that the failure of symptom substitution to occur in systematic desensitization treatment is perfectly compatible with psychoanalytic theory. Weitzman presents several arguments in support of his position. First, psychoanalytic theory is not a predictive theory but can only be used postdictively. Consequently, the theory makes no prediction about the necessity of symptom substitution. Second, Weitzman indicates that Freud entertained the hypothesis in his published writings that a particular impulse might exist only in its symptomatic expression. Third, in psychoanalytic theory a symptom is meaningfully related to an underlying process of which it is a symptom. Therefore to treat the symptom is, in effect, to treat, at a distance, the underlying complex of which it is a manifestation. Because of the relationship between the symptom and the underlying complex, it is technically incorrect from the point of view of psychoanalytic theory to assert that a treatment has dealt only with a symptom.

Weitzman attempts to develop a psychoanalytic explanation of the effectiveness of systematic desensitization. Weitzman asserts that systematic desensitization permits an individual to become aware of impulses which generate anxiety which is normally defended against by the symptoms. If the individual can deal with these impulses without the presence of anxiety, there would be, in terms of psychoanalytic theory, reality oriented binding of cathexes. Weitzman points out that clients who are asked to visualize an image during desensitization report that the image is followed by a flow of images and fantasy material which permits the individual to understand the underlying meaning of his symptom. In short, systematic desensitization is viewed as a procedure for telescoping the therapeutic procedures which are used in psychoanalytic theory.

Weitzman not only presents a psychoanalytic theory to explain the effectiveness of systematic desensitization, but he criticizes the usual behavioristic interpretation of systematic desensitization. His principal criticism centers on the almost allegorical use of the terms "stimulus" and "response" in connection with this method of therapy. The stimulus is an image followed by a flow of fantasy. The response is a complex internal state including instructions to attend to internal feelings. (See also Breger and McGaugh, 1966.) In view of the rather strained analogy between stimulus and response the relevance of principles of learning to this situation is questionable.

In summary, Weitzman argues that systematic desensitization is an effective method of therapy which is best explained in terms of psycho-analytic theory rather than in terms of vague reference to learning theory principles. Weitzman's critique raises the question of the relationship of the procedures of behavior therapy to various principles of learning from which they allegedly derive. This relationship varies with different procedures. For example, the use of aversive conditioning in the treatment of alcoholism represents a rather direct application of principles of learning to behavior modification. Similarly, Ayllon and Azrin's development of a responsive environment for psychotics is closely based on principles of reinforcement. On the other hand, a theoretical analysis, in learning theory terms, of the Mowrer and Mowrer procedure for the treatment of enuresis poses great difficulty (see Yates, 1970). With respect to systematic desensitization, perhaps an effective rejoinder which could be made to Weitzman by a social-learning theorist would involve reference to the study of Bandura *et al.* (1969). Recall that they found that the use of live models who assisted snake-phobic subjects to make various responses was a more effective procedure than systematic desensitization. In this procedure, the definitions of stimuli and responses is relatively straightforward and poses no difficulty. A stimulus is a snake. A response is any of a series of hierarchically arranged activities which can be performed. The finding that the modeling procedure is more effective than systematic desensitization is relatively easy to explain in social learning theory terms. Systematic desensitization requires that responses which are desensitized in imagery must generalize to the actual situations. By the use of an *in vivo* procedure, desensitization by modeling enables the client to practice the actual responses which form the target of therapy. Further, the fear is eliminated toward actual rather than symbolic threats. However, the superiority of the modeling procedures would appear to pose some difficulty for Weitzman's psychoanalytic explanations of desensitization. This procedure does not actively encourage the subject to visualize and engage in fantasy activities, nor does it train him to pay attention to internal sensations in connection with relaxation training. Consequently, some of the features of systematic desensitization which Weitzman considers incompatible with a behavioristic analysis and compatible with various psychoanalytic theories, are not present in this form of treatment. Consequently, its superiority would appear to pose some difficulties for Weitzman's psychoanalytic explanation of systematic desensitization.

The studies we have reviewed would seem to indicate that procedures which attempt to gain control over the events which control behavior for purposes of behavior modification would appear to be effective for a variety of purposes. Although there may be some question of the proper theoretical interpretation of the reasons for their effectiveness, on balance the data available are not inconsistent with a social learning approach to personality dynamics. In addition, the evidence supporting the effectiveness of psychotherapy is too fragmentary to support either the view that (a) the traditional psychodynamic theories of personality are supported by the effectiveness of psychotherapy, or (b) that social learning theory approaches to personality dynamics are contraindicated by what is known about the effectiveness of psychotherapy.

CHAPTER **12**

# CONCLUSION

---

In the second part of this book we have considered some of the empirical foundations of the approach to the understanding of personality dynamics which is based on clinical procedures. This approach involves the acceptance of a set of propositions which are interrelated, and mutually supporting. These include the following:

1. Personality is to be described in terms of genotypical characteristics.
2. These characteristics may be validly ascribed to individuals on the basis of clinical interview procedures which frequently include projective tests.
3. The genotypical characteristics which form the basis of personality and which explain its phenotypical characteristics are largely unconscious.
4. Fundamental changes in personality can occur through the use of psychotherapy which (at least in its psychoanalytic version) aims to have the individual become aware of and deal with aspects of his personality which were previously repressed and out of awareness.

The research we have reviewed fails to support these propositions and, as a result, questions their utility as a basis for the understanding of personality dynamics. That is, the research reviewed in Chapter 8 suggests that genotypical characteristics ascribed to an individual by clinical procedures are unlikely to be valid personality descriptions. The research we have reviewed in Chapter 10 suggests that there is a lack of persuasive evidence which would support the role assigned to the unconscious in psychoanalytic theory. And, the research reviewed in Chapter 11 suggests that the ability of psychotherapeutic procedures to create fundamental beneficial changes in personality remains to be persuasively demonstrated. These considerations mitigate against our premature acceptance of traditional psychodynamic theory either as a basis for clinical practice or for the understanding of fundamental characteristics of personality.

## An Evaluation of Social Learning Theory

Does Bandura's social learning theory approach provide a more adequate basis for the understanding of personality dynamics than traditional psychodynamic theories? One way of reconciling such conflicts is to appeal to a fashionable notion based on a work in the history of science written by Kuhn (1962) of a "paradigm clash." Paradigm clashes have occurred in the history of science. They involve situations in which there are two coherent and competing systems of explanation which are irreconcilable. Each provides a sufficient basis for ordering and rendering coherent a large body of empirical work. Eventually, one of the paradigms is able to super-cede the other. The notion of paradigm clash may be used as a basis for a kind of theoretical defeatism in which it is argued that each approach is legitimate and valid and consequently there is no reason to choose between them. (See Katahn and Koplin, 1968, for a discussion of such a paradigm clash between, *inter alia*, social learning and traditional views of psycho-therapy.) It is sometimes argued that certain approaches are superior for certain kinds of data and problems. However, such a tolerant view is defeatist in that it tends to blunt critical issues and fails to encourage work which may help to resolve such paradigm clashes by indicating which of the approaches is superior. It is this latter type of approach which we will attempt.

Social learning theory attempts to explain phenotypical behaviors by reference to the direct or vicarious learning experiences of an individual. If it could be shown that important behaviors of an individual are displaced derivatives of other experiences rather than the direct or vicarious experiences of an individual, we would have evidence which would suggest that a theory such as Bandura's may not be completely valid.

A series of studies by Epstein and Fenz deal with this issue and provide data which poses difficulties for a social learning theory explanation (Epstein, 1962, 1967; Epstein & Fenz, 1962, 1965; Fenz, 1964; Fenz & Epstein, 1967).

Epstein and Fenz have investigated the reactions of sport parachutists to the approach–avoidance conflict engendered by a forthcoming jump. The situation provides an opportunity to study an intense, real-life conflict situation. Several lines of evidence indicate that novice parachutists are very fearful as they approach the jump situation. As the time of the jump nears, the novice parachutist is likely to become more physiologically aroused to cues indicative of parachute jumping. Epstein and Fenz (1962) measured the GSR response to stimulus words which had different degrees of relevance to parachuting two weeks from the the jump and at the day of the jump. Figure 12.1 presents the results of this study. Note that words

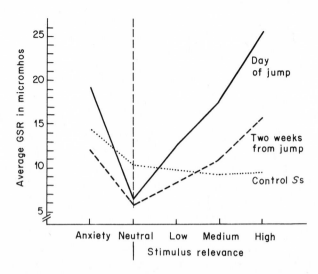

FIG. 12.1. Average GRS of novice parachutists and control *S*s for a stimulus dimension and for anxiety words in a word-association test. (Based on Epstein, 1967.)

which are indicative of parachuting elicit strong GSR responses on the day of a jump for novice parachutists.

In a subsequent study Fenz and Epstein (1967) obtained GSR, heart rate, and respiration measures for parachutists at 14 different times approaching and following a jump. Figures 12.2, 12.3, and 12.4 present the results of this study. Note that novice parachutists show increased amounts of physiological reactivity as the jump approaches on all three measures. (Disregard the data for the experienced parachutists. We will discuss these data subsequently.)

A number of other observations and findings in these studies indicate the novice parachutists' response to this fear-provoking experience. Epstein (1967) points out that the novice parachutist must learn to control and inhibit his fear if he is to perform successfully. Various defenses are used by the parachutists in this effort. For example, some parachutists simply deny the fear. When asked to write TAT stories to pictures relevant to parachuting, they write stories indicating only approach themes—for example, he will have a wonderful jump. Also, some novice parachutists exhibit drive displacement by interpreting their states of arousal as anger rather than fear. These types of defenses are indicative of an attempt to inhibit fear.

Experienced parachutists respond differently to the jump situation than novice parachutists. The data we have presented in Figures 12.2, 12.3, and

12.4 indicate that physiological reactivity and the rated fear of experienced parachutists peak at points which are relatively distant from the actual time of jump. Not only do experienced parachutists exhibit more intense responses at times which are temporally remote from the jump but they seem to respond most intensely to stimuli which are low rather than high in relevance to parachuting. Epstein (1962) found that experienced para-

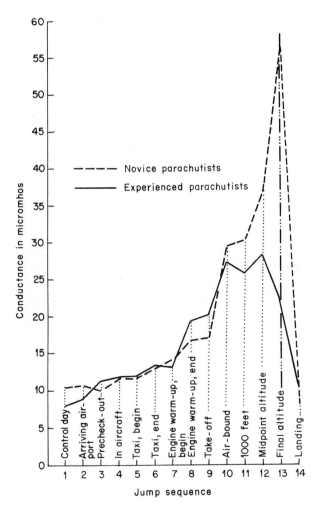

Fig. 12.2. Basal conductance of experienced and novice parachutists as a function of the sequence of events leading up to and following a jump. (Based on Epstein, 1967.)

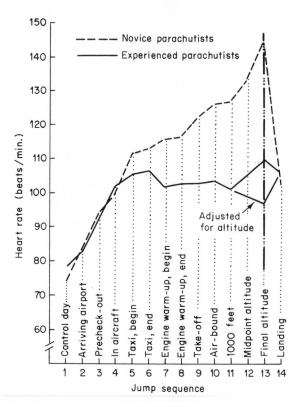

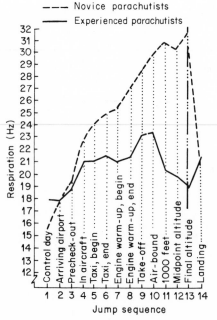

FIG. 12.3. (*above*) Heart rate of experienced and novice parachutists as a function of the sequence of events leading up to and following a jump. (Based on Epstein, 1967.)

FIG. 12.4. Respiration rate of experienced and novice parachutists as a function of the sequence of events leading up to and following a jump. (Based on Epstein, 1967.)

*330*

TABLE 12.1

*Form of GSR Curves as a Function of Experience*

| Level of experience | Monotonic gradient | Inverted V, peaking 1 step back | Inverted V, peaking 2 steps back | Total subjects |
|---|---|---|---|---|
| Group 1 (1 jump) | 6 | 0 | 0 | 6 |
| Group 2 (5–8 jumps) | 3 | 2 | 1 | 6 |
| Group 3 (25–50 jumps) | 1 | 2 | 3 | 6 |
| Group 4 ( >100 jumps) | 0 | 1 | 5 | 6 |

Based on Epstein, 1967.

chutists tended to produce monotonic gradients of increasing GSR responses to words of different degrees of relevance to parachuting on days other than the day of the jump. In this respect their responses are similar to those of novice parachutists. However, on the day of a jump the experienced parachutists show inverted V-shape gradients with the maximal GSR response occuring to stimuli of low or medium relevance to parachuting. Table 12.1 indicates the shape of the gradients of GSR response on the day of a jump to stimuli of increasing relevance to parachuting for $S$s with different degrees of experience in sporting parachuting. Table 12.1 indicates a very orderly development of a tendency to exhibit monotonic gradients to a tendency to exhibit inverted V-shaped gradients in which the most intense GSR responses are given to stimuli which are not most relevant to parachuting. Epstein (1967) explains this phenomenon by postulating the existence of a gradient of inhibition of fear which is steeper than the gradient of avoidance which it inhibits which increases in height and steepness as a function of experience in the fear producing situation. As a result of these two processes fear is displaced to dissimilar and temporally remote cues as a result of experience. Figure 12.5 presents a graphic representation of these theoretical assumptions.

Epstein argues that the two processes of generalization of fear and learned inhibition of fear are of benefit to an individual in mastering stressful situations. His views are summarized in the following quotation:

As a result of the expanding gradient of anxiety and its inhibition an increasingly early and efficient warning signal is provided at increasingly low levels of arousal until, if the process were not stabilized or reversed by perception of real danger, the anxiety would be displaced out of existence. Given a continued awareness of danger, the process stabilizes at some point less than complete displacement, but in arriving there has forced discrimination of relevant cues and the development of an ability to inhibit anxiety—producing responses at many levels, providing for a modulated system for the control of anxiety. It is proposed that this is the normal process by which anxiety is mastered.

(Epstein, 1967)

We have discussed the research of Epstein and Fenz at some length because of the challenge it poses to social learning theory. This research provides evidence of a lawful and orderly development of displacement as a function of experience such that fear is expressed to more and more remote cues. The processes by which this displacement occur are apparently

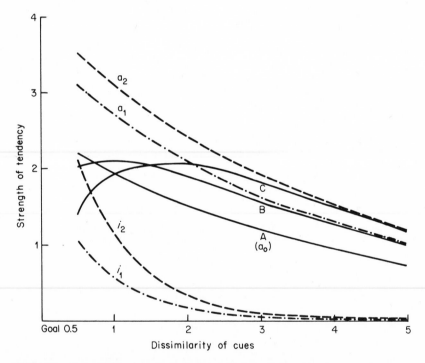

FIG. 12.5. Theoretical curves for the development of inverted V-shaped curves that peak increasingly earlier with experience. Curve A represents the initial generalization gradient of activation before inhibition has developed. The upper two broken-line curves, $a_1$ and $a_2$, represent successive levels in the buildup of conditioned activation. The lower two broken-line curves, $i_1$ and $i_2$, represent successive levels in the buildup of inhibition of activation (or of activation-producing responses). Curve B represents net activation as obtained by subtracting $i_1$ from $a_1$. Curve C represents net activation at a further level of development obtained by subtracting $i_2$ from $a_2$. (Based on Epstein, 1967.)

intrapsychic in nature and develop in a manner which appears relatively autonomous. That is, independent of the influence of extrapsychic direct or vicarious reinforcement. The intense GSR responses given by experienced parachutists to words which were of low relevance to parachuting indicates evidence of displacement. However, the displaced responses to such stimuli are not, at least in an obvious way, reinforced directly or vicariously. Consequently, these data do not appear to be amenable to an analysis in social learning terms. Further, these data appear to support a basic assumption of psychoanalytic theory—namely, the assumption that phenotypical behaviors can only be understood in terms of an interpretation which assumes that they are indirect expressions or displacements of other impulses. These data do not, however, indicate the generality of this phenomenon. It may be the case that some phenomenon are best understood in terms of social learning theory and others in terms of a more traditional psychodynamic approach.

There is another type of criticism which can be directed against Bandura's social learning theory. Bandura's theory is both an antitrait and an antigenetic approach to personality. Social learning theory replaces the notion of traits conceived as consistencies of behavior across situations with the notion of an analysis of the particular learning history which leads an individual to behave in a particular way in a particular situation. Such an approach emphasizes the importance of each particular situation in eliciting a particular behavior pattern for a particular individual. In addition, social learning theory makes no allowance for genotypical influences. Genotypical influences are influences which exist prior to and apart from the social learning process. Bandura's theory is based on an attempt to minimize or ignore any intraorganismic determinant of behavior which cannot be derived from a knowledge of an individual's social learning history. Where intra-organismic influences on behavior are postulated by Bandura, as for example in his discussion of standards of self-reinforcement, the intra-organismic characteristics are themselves the product of an individual's social learning history (see the discussion of the experiment by Bandura & Kupers, 1964, in Chapter 9).

The material we have presented in the first section would appear to contradict social learning theory on these two critical points. That is, we concluded at the end of the first part of this book that there was evidence for, at the most general level, the existence of the traits of neuroticism and introversion–extraversion and that position with respect to these traits was determined, in part, by an individual's genotype. This conclusion suggests that social learning theory should be modified and expanded to include a consideration of such influences on personality. Put another way, this conclusion suggests that it might be fruitful to attempt to integrate

Bandura's theory with Eysenck's theory. There are a number of respects in which these two theories share comparable ideological presuppositions. For example, both are antipsychoanalytic, both are behavioristic, both are in favor of the use of behavior modification procedures rather than psychotherapy, and both theories have roots in research on learning processes. Of course the theories differ most fundamentally on the role assigned to genotypical influences on personality. And, where they differ our analysis suggests that Eysenck is more nearly correct than Bandura. An integration of these two theories would lead one to consider the impact of particular social learning histories on individuals with different genotypes. Such a theory would provide for general traits (at the genotypical level) and detailed social behavior by consideration of the interaction of particular social learning histories and particular genotypes.

How might such an integration be effectual and what sort of problems would it deal with? At this stage it is only possible to speculate about these questions. Such an attempted integration might direct one to think about the influence of genotypical characteristics on the learning process itself. A consideration of the relationship between arousal level and vicarious conditioning provides an example of this sort of integration. Bandura and Rosenthal (1966) have suggested that vicarious conditioning is an inverted U function of arousal level. This principle implies that vicarious conditioning will most readily occur under conditions of intermediate arousal. Low arousal levels and high arousal levels are likely to impede vicarious conditioning. Eysenck's theory assumes that individuals who are introverted inherit nervous systems which are chronically high in arousal level. Claridge's research (see Chapter 3) suggests that a high arousal level is particularly characteristic of individuals who are both neurotic and introverted. Also, individuals who are extraverted and nonneurotic are, low in arousal level according to Claridge's results. Combining these principles, we get the suggestion that individuals who are at either extreme of the arousal dimension (that is, individuals who are either extraverted and nonneurotic or introverted and neurotic) are less likely to be subject to vicarious conditioning.

I do not wish to suggest that this hypothesis is correct. It is put forward only as an illustration of the kinds of hypotheses with which an integration of Bandura's theory with Eysenck's might deal. There are a number of other issues in personality with which such an approach might deal. For example, one might postulate genotypical influences on such sex-linked characteristics as masculine and feminine interest patterns or aggressive tendencies. Such genotypes might interact with and influence the outcome of various social learning histories dealing with the development of appropriate masculine and feminine interests and aggressive tendencies.

At the present stage of our knowledge we can only point to a future direction for research. The principles permitting the integration of a theory based on genotypes with one emphasizing social learning principles do not at present exist. However, I believe, that such principles provide the best direction for our future understanding of personality.

# REFERENCES

Ackner, B., & Pampiglione, G. An evaluation of the sedation threshold test. *Journal of Psychosomatic Research*, 1959, **3**, 271–281.

Adorno, T. W., Frenkel-Brunswick, Else, Levinson, D. J., & Sanford, R. N. *The authoritarian personality*. New York: Harper and Row, 1950.

Allport, G. W. *Pattern and growth in personality*. New York: Holt, Rinehart, and Winston, 1961.

Allport, G. W., & Odbert, H. S. Trait-names: A psycho-lexical study. *Psychological Monographs*, 1936, **47** (Whole No. 211).

Allport, G. W., Vernon, P. E., & Lindzey, G. *Study of values (Revised Edition). Manual of directions*. Boston, Massachusetts: Houghton-Miflin, 1951.

Altus, W. D. Birth order and its sequelae. *Science*, 1966, **151**, 44–49.

Arbuckle, D. S., & Boy, A. V. Client-centered therapy in counseling students with behavior problems. *Journal of Counseling Psychology*, 1961, **8**, 136–139.

Aronson, E. The need for achievement as measured by graphic expression. In J. W. Atkinson (Ed.), *Motives in fantasy, action, and society*. Princeton, New Jersey: Van Nostrand–Reinhold, 1958.

Atkinson, J. W. Studies in projective measurement of achievement motivation. Unpublished doctoral dissertation, University of Michigan, 1950.

Atkinson, J. W. Motivational determinants of risk-taking behavior, *Psychological Review*, 1957, **64**, 359–372.

Atkinson, J. W. (Ed.), *Motives in fantasy, action, and society*. Princeton, New Jersey: Van Nostrand–Reinhold, 1958.

Atkinson, J. W. An introduction to motivation. Princeton, New Jersey: Van Nostrand-Reinhold, 1964.

Atkinson, J. W., & Feather, N. T. Review and appraisal. In J. W. Atkinson and N. T. Feather (Eds.), *A theory of achievement motivation*. New York: Wiley, 1966.

Atkinson, J. W., & Litwin, G. H. Achievement motive and test anxiety conceived as motive to approach success and motive to avoid failure. *Journal of Abnormal and Social Psychology*, 1960, **60**, 52–63.

Ayllon, T., & Azrin, N. *The token economy. A motivational system for therapy and rehabilitation*. New York: Appleton-Century-Crofts, 1968.

Ayllon, T., Haughton, E., & Hughes, H. B. Interpretation of symtoms: Fact or fiction. *Behaviour Research and Therapy*, 1965, **3**, 1–7.

Bakan, P., Belton, J. A., & Toth, J. C. Extraversion-introversion and decrements in an auditory vigilance task. In D. N. Buckner and J. J. McGrath (Eds.), *Vigilance: A symposium*. New York: McGraw-Hill, 1963.

Baker, B. L. Symptom treatment and symptom substitution. Unpublished doctoral dissertation. Yale University, 1967.

Bandura, A. Social learning through imitation. In M. R. Jones (Ed.), *Nebraska symposium on motivation*. Lincoln, Nebraska: University of Nebraska Press, 1962.

Bandura, A. *Principles of behavior modification.* New York: Holt, Rinehart, and Winston, 1969.

Bandura, A., Blanchard, E. A., & Ritter, Brunhilde. Relative efficacy of desensitization and modeling approaches for inducing behavioral, affective, and attitudinal changes. *Journal of Personality and Social Psychology,* 1969, **13,** 173–199.

Bandura, A., & Kupers, Carol J. Transmission of patterns of self reinforcement through modeling. *Journal of Abnormal and Social Psychology,* 1964, **69,** 1–9.

Bandura, A., & McDonald, F. J. The influence of social reinforcement and the behavior of models in shaping children's moral judgments. *Journal of Abnormal and Social Psychology,* 1963, **67,** 274–281.

Bandura, A., & Mischel, W. Modification of self-imposed delay of reward through exposure to live and symbolic models. *Journal of Personality and Social Psychology,* 1965, **2,** 698–705.

Bandura, A., & Rosenthal, T. L. Vicarious classical conditioning as a function of arousal. *Journal of Personality and Social Psychology,* 1966, **3,** 54–62.

Bandura, A., Ross, Dorothea, & Ross, Sheila A. Transmission of aggression through imitation of aggressive models. *Journal of Abnormal and Social Psychology,* 1961, **63,** 575–582.

Bandura, A., Ross, Dorothea, & Ross, Sheila A. Imitation of film-mediated aggressive models. *Journal of Abnormal and Social Psychology,* 1963, **66,** 3–11. (a)

Bandura, A., Ross, Dorothea, & Ross, Sheila A. A comparative test of the status envy, social power, and the secondary reinforcement theories of identificatory learning. *Journal of Abnormal and Social Psychology,* 1963, **67,** 527–534. (b)

Bandura, A., & Walters, R. H. *Adolescent aggression.* New York: Ronald, 1959.

Bandura, A., & Walters, R. H. *Social learning and personality development.* New York: Holt, Rinehart and Winston, 1963.

Barber, T. X. *Hypnosis. A scientific approach.* Princeton, New Jersey: Van Nostrand–Reinhold, 1969.

Barber, T. X., & Calverley, D. S. Toward a theory of "hypnotic behavior": Experimental analyses of suggested amnesia. *Journal of Abnormal Psychology,* 1966, **71,** 95–107.

Barron, F. *Creativity and psychological health.* Princeton, New Jersey: Van Nostrand–Reinhold, 1963.

Bartholomew, A. A. Extraversion, introversion, and neuroticism. *British Journal of Delinquency,* 1959, **10,** 120–129.

Becker, W. C. The matching of behavior rating and questionnaire factors. *Psychological Bulletin,* 1960, **57,** 201–212.

Bell, R. Q. A reinterpretation of the direction of effects in studies of socialization. *Psychological Review,* 1968, **75,** 81–95.

Berman, Phyliss W., Walsman, H. A., & Graham, F. K. Intelligence in treated phenylketonuric children. A developmental study. *Child development,* 1966, **37,** 731–747.

Bettleheim, B. Individual and mass behavior in extreme situations. *Journal of Abnormal and Social Psychology,* 1943, **38,** 417–452.

Beyers, E. Atkinson's model of risk-taking. A test of probability of success and performance implications for achievement motivation. Unpublished doctoral dissertation. Graduate Faculty, New School for Social Research, 1968.

Bieri, J., Atkins, A. L., Briar, S., Leaman, Robin L., Miller, H., & Tripodi, T. *Clinical and social judgment: The discrimination of behavioral information.* New York: Wiley, 1966.

Bieri, J., Bradburn, Wendy M., & Galinsky, M. D. Sex differences in perceptual behavior. *Journal of Personality*, 1958, **26,** 1–12.

Bindra, D., Paterson, A. L., & Strzelecki, Joanna. On the relation between anxiety and conditioning. *Canadian Journal of Psychology*, 1955, **9,** 1–6.

Block, J. *The challenge of response sets.* New York: Appleton-Century-Crofts, 1965.

Blum, G. S. *The Blacky Pictures: A technique for the exploration of personality dynamics.* Ann Arbor, Michigan: Psychodynamic Instruments, 1950.

Blum, G. S. *Psychoanalytic theories of personality.* New York: McGraw-Hill, 1953.

Blum, G. S. *A model of the mind.* New York: Wiley, 1961.

Boudreau, D. Evaluation of the sedation threshold test. *Archives of Neurology and Psychiatry*, 1958, **80,** 771–775.

Bowers, K. Hypnotic behavior: The differentiation of trance and demand characteristic variables. *Journal of Abnormal Psychology*, 1966, **71,** 42–51.

Bradley, R. W. Birth order and school related behavior. A heuristic review. *Psychological Bulletin*, 1968, **70,** 45–51.

Breger, L., & McGaugh, J. L. Critique and reformulation of "learning-theory" approaches to psychotherapy and neurosis. *Psychological Bulletin*, 1966, **65,** 170–173.

Broadbent, D. E. Word-frequency effect and response bias. *Psychological Review*, 1967, **74,** 1–15.

Brody, N. Need achievement, test anxiety, and subjective probability of success in risk-taking behavior. *Journal of Abnormal and Social Psychology*, 1963, **66,** 413–318.

Brody, N., & Oppenheim, P. Tensions in psychology between the methods of behaviorism and phenomenology. *Psychological Review*, 1966, **73,** 295–305.

Brody, N., & Oppenheim, P. Methodological differences between behaviorism and phenomenology in psychology. *Psychological Review*, 1967, **74,** 330–334.

Bronfenbrenner, U. Socialization and social class through time and space. In Eleanor E. Maccoby, T. M. Newcomb, and E. L. Hartley (Eds.), *Readings in social psychology.* New York: Holt, Rinehart, and Winston, 1958.

Brown, Anne M., Stafford, R. E., & Vandenberg, S. G. Twins: Behavioral differences. *Child Development*, 1967, **38,** 1055–1067.

Brown, W. P. Conceptions of perceptual defense. *British Journal of Psychology, Monograph Supplements*, 1961, No. 35.

Bruel, Iris, Ginsberg, S., Lukomnik, Mary, & Schmeidler, Gertrude R. An unsuccessful attempt to replicate Spence's experiment on the restricting effects of awareness. *Journal of Personality and Social Psychology*, 1966, **3,** 128–130.

Buss, A. H., Wiener, M., Durkee, A., & Baer, M. The measurement of anxiety in clinical situations. *Journal of Consulting Psychology*, 1955, **19,** 125–129.

Butler, J. M., & Haigh, G. V. Changes in the relation between self-concepts and ideal concepts consequent upon client-centered counseling. In C. R. Rogers and Rosalind F. Dymond (Eds.), *Psychotherapy and personality change.* Chicago, Illinois: The University of Chicago Press, 1954.

Cahoon, D. D. Symptom substitution and the behavior therapies: A reappraisal. *Psychological Bulletin*, 1968, **69,** 149–156.

Campbell, D., Sanderson, R. E., & Laverty, S. G. Characteristics of conditioned response in human subjects during extinction trials following a single traumatic conditioning trial. *Journal of Abnormal and Social Psychology*, 1964, **68,** 627–639.

Campbell, D. T., & Fiske, D. W. Convergent and discriminant validation by the multitrait-multimethod matrix. *Psychological Bulletin*, 1959, **56,** 81–105.

Campbell, D. T., Miller, N., Lubetsky, J., & O'Connell, E. Varieties of projection in trait attribution. *Psychological Monographs*, 1964, **78** (Whole No. 592).

Campbell, D. T., Siegman, Carole R., & Rees, Matilda B. Direction-of-wording effects in the relationships between scales. *Psychological Bulletin*, 1967, **68**, 293–303.

Cartwright, D. S., Kirtner, W. L., & Fiske, D. W. Method factors in changes associated with psychotherapy. *Journal of Abnormal and Social Psychology*, 1963, **66**, 164–175.

Cassirer, E. *Substance and function and Einstein's theory of relativity*. New York: Dover, 1953.

Cattell, Psyche. *The measurement of intelligence of infants and young children*. New York: The Psychological Corporation, 1940.

Cattell, R. B. *Factor analysis*. New York: Harper, 1952.

Cattell, R. B. *Personality and motivation structure and measurement*. Yonkers, New York: World Book, 1957.

Cattell, R. B. The personality and motivation of the researcher from measurements of contemporaries and from biography. In C. W. Taylor and F. Barron (Eds.), *Scientific creativity. Its recognition and development*. New York: Wiley, 1963. (a)

Cattell, R. B. The theory of fluid and crystallized intelligence. A critical experiment. *Journal of Educational Psychology*, 1963, **54**, 1–22. (b)

Cattell, R. B. *The scientific analysis of personality*. Chicago, Illinois: Aldine, 1965.

Cattell, R. B., & Coan, R. W. Child personality structure as revealed by teachers' behavior ratings. *Journal of Clinical Psychology*, 1957, **13**, 315–327.

Cattell, R. B., & Drevdahl, J. E. A comparison of the personality profile (16PF) of eminent researchers with that of eminent teachers and administrators and of the general population. *British Journal of Psychology*, 1955, **46**, 248–261.

Chatterjee, B. B., & Eriksen, C. W. Conditioning and generalization of G S R as a function of awareness. *Journal of Abnormal and Social Psychology*, 1960, **60**, 396–403.

Child, I. L. Personality. *Annual Review of Psychology*, 1954, **2**, 149–170.

Christie, R., Havel, Joan, & Seidenberg, B. Is the F scale irreversible? *Journal of Abnormal and Social Psychology*, 1958, **56**, 143–159.

Churchill, J. A. The relation between intelligence and birth weight in twins. *Neurology*, 1965, **15**, 341–347.

Claridge, G. S. *Personality and arousal*. Oxford: Pergamon Press, 1967.

Claridge, G. W., & Herrington, R. N. Sedation threshold, personality and the theory of neurosis. *Journal of Mental Science*, 1960, **106**, 1568–1583.

Clark, C. *The conditions of economic progress*, 3rd ed. London: Macmillan, 1957.

Clark, W. C. Sensory-decision theory analysis of the placebo effect on the criterion for pain and thermal sensitivity ($d'$). *Journal of Abnormal Psychology*, 1969, **74**, 363–371.

Cohen, J. The factorial structure of the WISC at ages 7–6, 10–6, and 13–6. *Journal of Consulting Psychology*, 1959, **23**, 285–299.

Cohen, J. Multiple regression as a general data analytic system. *Psychological Bulletin*, 1968, **70**, 426–443.

Conn, L. K., & Crowne, D. P. Instigation to aggression, emotional arousal, and defensive emulation. *Journal of Personality*, 1964, **32**, 163–179.

Cooley, W., & Lohnes, P. R. *Multivariate procedures for the behavioral sciences*. New York: Wiley, 1962.

Cowan, P. A., & Walters, R. H. Studies of reinforcement of aggression. I. Effects of scheduling. *Child Development*, 1963, **34**, 543–552.

Crockett, H. J., Jr. The achievement motive and differential occupational mobility in the United States. *American Sociological Review*, 1962, **27**, 191–204.

Crockett, H. J., Jr., Social class, education, and motive to achieve in differential occupational mobility. *The Sociological Quarterly*, 1964, **5**, 231–242.

Cronbach, L. J. The two disciplines of scientific psychology. *American Psychologist*, 1957, **12**, 671–684.

Cronbach, L. J. Intelligence? Creativity? A parsimonious reinterpretation of the Wallach-Kogan data. *American Educational Research Journal*, 1968, **5**, 491–511.

Cropley, A. J. Creativity and intelligence. *The British Journal of Educational Psychology*, 1966, **36**, 259–266.

Crowne, D. P., & Marlowe, D. *The approval motive.* New York: Wiley, 1964.

Davison, G. C. The influence of systematic desensitization, relaxation, and graded exposure to imaginal aversive stimuli on the modification of phobic behavior. Unpublished Ph.D. dissertation, Stanford University, 1965.

De Charms, R., Levy, J., & Wertheimer, M. A note on attempted evaluations of psychotherapy. *Journal of Clinical Psychology*, 1954, **10**, 223–235.

De Leon, G., & Mandell, W. A comparison of conditioning and psychotherapy in the treatment of functional neurosis. *Journal of Clinical Psychology*, 1966, **22**, 326–330.

De Nike, L. D. The temporal relationship between awareness and performance in verbal conditioning. *Journal of Experimental Psychology*, 1964, **68**, 521–529.

Diven, K. Certain determinants in the conditioning of anxiety reactions. *Journal of Psychology*, 1937, **3**, 291–308.

Dixon, P. W., & Oakes, W. F. Effect of intertrial activity on the relationship between awareness and verbal operant conditioning. *Journal of Experimental Psychology*, 1965, **69**, 152–157.

Dohrenwend, Barbara S., & Dohrenwend, B. P. Field studies of social factors in relation to three types of psychological disorder. *Journal of Abnormal Psychology*, 1967, **72**, 369–378.

Dollard, J., Doob, L. W., Miller, N. E., Mowrer, O. H., & Sears, R. R. *Frustration and aggression.* New Haven, Connecticut: Yale University Press, 1939.

Dollard, J., & Miller, N. E. *Personality and psychotherapy.* New York: McGraw-Hill, 1950.

Drevdahl, J. E., & Cattell, R. B. Personality and creativity in artists and writers. *Journal of Clinical Psychology*, 1958, **14**, 107–111.

Dymond, Rosalind F. Adjustment changes over therapy from self-sorts. In C. R. Rogers and Rosalind F. Dymond (Eds.), *Psychotherapy and Personality Change.* Chicago, Illinois: The University of Chicago Press, 1954.

Edwards, A. L. The relationship between the judged desirability of a trait and the probability that the trait will be endorsed. *Journal of Applied Psychology*, 1953, **37**, 90–93.

Edwards, A. L. *The social desirability variable in personality assessment and research.* New York: Dryden, 1957.

Elkes, J. Drugs influencing affect and behavior: Possible neural correlates in relation to mode of behavior. In A. Simon, C. C. Herbert, and R. Straus (Eds.), *The physiology of the emotion.* Springfield, Illinois: Thomas, 1961.

Ends, E. J., & Page, C. W. A study of three types of group psychotherapy with hospitalized male inebriates. *Quarterly Journal of Studies on Alcoholism*, 1957, **18**, 263–277.

Endler, N. S., & Hunt, J. McV. Sources of behavioral variance as measured by the S—R inventory of anxiousness. *Psychological Bulletin*, 1966, **65**, 336–346.

Endler, N. S., Hunt, J. McV., & Rosenstein, A. J. An S—R inventory of anxiousness. *Psychological Monographs*, 1962, **76** (Whole No. 536).

Epstein, S. The measurement of drive and conflict in humans: Theory and experiment.

In M. R. Jones (Ed.), *Nebraska symposium on motivation,* **1962.** Lincoln, Nebraska: University of Nebraska Press, 1962.

Epstein, S. Toward a unified theory of anxiety. In B. A. Maher (Ed.), *Progress in personality research.* Vol. 4. New York: Academic Press, 1967.

Epstein, S., & Fenz, W. D. Theory and experiment on the measurement of approach-avoidance conflict. *Journal of Abnormal and Social Psychology,* 1962, **64,** 97–112.

Epstein, S., & Fenz, W. D. Steepness of approach and avoidance gradients in humans as a function of experience: Theory and experiment. *Journal of Experimental Psychology,* 1965, **70,** 1–12.

Eriksen, C. W. Prediction from and interaction among multiple concurrent discriminative responses. *Journal of Experimental Psychology,* 1957, **53,** 353–359.

Eriksen, C. W. Unconscious processes. In M. R. Jones (Ed.), *Nebraska symposium on motivation.* Lincoln, Nebraska: University of Nebraska Press, 1958.

Eysenck, H. J. The effects of psychotherapy: An evaluation. *Journal of Consulting Psychology,* 1952, **16,** 319–324.

Eysenck, H. J. *The psychology of politics.* London: Routledge & Kegan Paul, 1954.

Eysenck, H. J. The inheritance of extraversion-introversion. *Acta Psychologica,* 1956, **12,** 95–110.

Eysenck, H. J. *The dynamics of anxiety and hysteria.* London: Routledge and Kegan Paul, 1957.

Eysenck, H. J. Hysterics and dysthymics as criterion groups in the measure of introversion-extraversion: A reply. *Journal of Abnormal and Social Psychology.* 1958, **57,** 250–252.

Eysenck, H. J. *Manual of the Maudsley personality inventory.* London: University of London Press, 1959.

Eysenck, H. J. The effects of psychotherapy. In H. J. Eysenck (Ed.), *Handbook of abnormal psychology.* London: Pitman Medical Publishing Co., 1960.

Eysenck, H. J. Extraversion and the acquisition of eyeblink and GSR conditioned responses. *Psychological Bulletin,* 1965, **63,** 258–270.

Eysenck, H. J. Conditioning introversion-extraversion and the strength of the nervous system. *Proceedings of the International Congress of Psychology,* 1966, **18,** Symposium 9, 33–43.

Eysenck, H. J. *The biological basis of personality.* Springfield, Illinois: Thomas, 1967.

Eysenck, H. J., & Eysenck, S. B. G. *The manual to the Eysenck personality inventory.* San Diego, California: Educational and Industrial Testing Service, 1968.

Eysenck, H. J., & Eysenck, S. B. G. *Personality structure and measurement.* London: Routledge and Kegan Paul, 1969.

Eysenck, H. J., & Prell, D. B. The inheritance of neuroticism: An experimental study. *The Journal of Mental Science,* 1951, **97,** 441–463.

Feather, N. T. Subjective probability and decision under uncertainty. *Psychological Review,* 1959, **66,** 150–164.

Feather, N. T. The relationship of persistence at a task to expectation of success and achievement related motives. *Journal of Abnormal and Social Psychology,* 1961, **63,** 552–561.

Feld, Sheila. Longitudinal study of the origins of achievement strivings. *Journal of Personality and Social Psychology,* 1967, **7,** 408–414.

Feldman, M. P. Aversion therapy for sexual deviations: A critical review. *Psychological Bulletin,* 1966, **65,** 65–79.

Feldman, M. P., & MacCulloch, M. J. A systematic approach to the treatment of homosexuality by conditioned aversion: Preliminary report. *American Journal of Psychiatry*, 1964, **121**, 167–171.

Feldman, M. P., MacCulloch, M. J., Mellor, V., & Pinschof, J. M. The application of anticipatory avoidance learning to the treatment of homosexuality: III. The sexual orientation method. *Behaviour Research and Therapy*, 1966, **4**, 289–299.

Fenz, W. D. Conflict and stress as related to physiological activation and sensory, perceptual, and cognitive functioning. *Psychological Monographs*, 1964, **78** (Whole No. 585).

Fenz, W. D. & Epstein, S. Gradients of physiological arousal of experienced and novice parachutists as a function of an approaching jump. *Psychosomatic Medicine*, 1967, **29**, 33–51.

Ferguson, L. W. The stability of the primary social attitudes: I. Religionism and humanitarianism. *Journal of Psychology*, 1941, **12**, 283–288.

Ferster, C. B., & Skinner, B. F. *Schedules of reinforcement.* New York: Appleton-Century-Crofts, 1957.

Franks, C. M. Conditioning and personality: A study of normal and neurotic subjects. *Journal of Abnormal and Social Psychology*, 1956, **52**, 143–150.

Franks, C. M. Effects of food, drink, and tobacco deprivation on the conditioning of the eyeblink response. *Journal of Experimental Psychology*, 1957, **53**, 117–120. (a)

Franks, C. M. Personality factors and the rate of conditioning. *British Journal of Psychology*, 1957, **48**, 119–126. (b)

Franks, C. M. Personality and eyeblink conditioning seven years later. *Acta Psychologica*, 1963, **21**, 295–312.

Freud, S. The relation of the poet to daydreaming. In S. Freud, *Collected Papers.* Vol. 4 (Translated by J. Riviere). London: Hogarth Press, 1948.

Freud, S. The unconscious. In S. Freud, *The Standard edition of the complete psychological works of Sigmund Freud. Volume XIV.* London: Hogarth, Press, 1957.

Freund, K. Some problems in the treatment of homosexuality. In H. S. Eysenck (Ed.), *Behaviour therapy and the neurosis.* Oxford: Pergamon Press, 1960.

Friberg, L., Kaij, L., Dencker, S. J., & Jonsson, E. Smoking habits of monozygotic and dyzygotic twins. *British Medical Journal*, April 25, 1959, 1090–1092.

Fruchter, B. *Introduction to factor analysis.* Princeton, New Jersey: Van Nostrand–Reinhold, 1954.

Fuller, J. L., and Thompson, W. R. *Behavior genetics.* New York: Wiley, 1960.

Gardner, R. W. Cognitive controls in adaptation: Research and measurement. In S. Messick and J. Ross (Eds.), *Measurement in personality and cognition.* New York: Wiley, 1962.

Gardner, R. W., Holzman, P. S., Klein, G. S., Linton, Harriet B., & Spence, D. P. Cognitive control: A study of individual consistencies in cognitive behavior. *Psychological Issues*, 1959, **1** (No. 4).

Gelder, M. G., Marks, I. M., & Wolff, H. H. Desensitization and psychotherapy in the treatment of phobic states: A controlled inquiry. *British Journal of Psychiatry*, 1967, **113**, 53–73.

Getzels, J. W., & Jackson, P. W. *Creativity and intelligence.* New York: Wiley, 1962.

Gleitman, H., Nachmias, J., & Neisser, U. The S—R reinforcement theory of extinction. *Psychological Review*, 1954, **61**, 23–33.

Goldberg, E. M., & Morrison, S. Schizophrenia and social class. *British Journal of Psychology*, 1965, **109**, 785.

Goldberg, L. R. The effectiveness of clinicians' judgments: The diagnosis of organic brain damage from the Bender–Gestalt test. *Journal of Consulting Psychology*, 1959, **23,** 25–33.

Goldberg, L. R. Diagnosticians vs. diagnostic signs: The diagnosis of psychosis and neurosis from the MMPI. *Psychological Monographs*, 1965, **79** (Whole No. 602).

Goldberg, L. R. Man vs. model of man: A rationale, plus some evidence, for a method of improving on clinical inferences. *Psychological Bulletin*, 1970, **73,** 422–432.

Goldberg, L. R., & Werts, C. E. The reliability of clinician's judgments. *Journal of Consulting Psychology*, 1966, **30,** 199–200.

Goldiamond, I. Indicators of perception: I. Subliminal perception, subception, unconscious perception: An analysis in terms of psychophysical indicator methodology. *Psychological Bulletin*, 1958, **55,** 373–411.

Goldstein, A. P., Heller, K., & Sechrest, L. B. *Psychotherapy and the psychology of behavior change.* New York: Wiley, 1966.

Goodenough, Florence, L. *Measurement of intelligence by drawings.* Yonkers, New York: World Book, 1926.

Gottesman, I. I. Differential inheritance of the psychoneurosis. *Eugenics Quarterly*, 1962, **9,** 223–228.

Gottesman, I. I. Heritability of personality: A demonstration. *Psychological Monographs*, 1963, **77** (Whole No. 572).

Gottesman, I. I. Genetic variance in adaptive personality traits. *Journal of Child Psychology and Psychiatry*, 1966, **7,** 191–208.

Gottesman, I. I., & Shields, J. Contributions of twin studies to perspectives on schizophrenia. In B. Maher (Ed.), *Progress in experimental personality research.* Vol. 3. New York: Academic Press, 1966.

Goulet, L. R. Anxiety (Drive) and verbal learning: Implication for research and some methodological considerations. *Psychological Bulletin*, 1968, **69,** 235–247.

Grace, W. J., Pinsky, Ruth H., & Wolff, H. G. The treatment of ulcerative colitis: II. *Gastroenterology*, 1954, **26,** 462–468.

Gray, J. A. *Pavlov's typology.* Oxford: Pergamon Press, 1965.

Green, B. F. Description and explanation: A comment on papers by Hoffman and Edwards. In B. Kleinmuntz (Ed.), *Formal representation of human judgment.* New York: Wiley, 1968.

Greenspoon, J. The reinforcing effect of two spoken words on the frequency of two responses. *American Journal of Psychology*, 1955, **68,** 409–416.

Guilford, J. P. Creative abilities in the arts. *Psychological Review*, 1957, **64,** 110–118.

Guilford, J. P. Tests of creativity. In H. Anderson (Ed.), *Creativity and its cultivation.* New York: Harper, 1959.

Haber, R. N., & Alpert, R. The role of situation and picture cues in projective measurement of the achievement motive. In J. W. Atkinson (Ed.), *Motives in fantasy, action, and society.* Princeton, New Jersey: Van Nostrand–Reinhold, 1958.

Hammond, K. R., & Summers, D. A. Cognitive dependence on linear and nonlinear cues. *Psychological Review*, 1965, **72,** 215–224.

Hampson, J. L. Determinants of psychosexual orientation. In F. A. Beach (Ed.), *Sex and behavior.* New York: Wiley, 1965.

Harman, H. H. *Modern factor analysis.* Chicago, Illinois: University of Chicago Press, 1960.

Harvey, O. J., Hunt, D. E., & Schroder, H. M. *Conceptual systems and personality organization.* New York: Wiley, 1961.

Hassan, P., & Butcher, H. J. Creativity and intelligence: A partial replication with

Scottish children of the Getzels and Jackson study. *British Journal of Psychology*, 1966, **57**, 129–135.

Hebb, D. O. Drives and the c.n.s. (conceptual nervous system). *Psychological Review*, 1955, **62**, 243–254.

Heston, L. L. Psychiatric disorders in foster home reared children of schizophrenic mothers. *British Journal of Psychiatry*, 1966, **112**, 819–825.

Hilgard, E. R., Jones, L. V., & Kaplan, S. J. Conditioned discrimination as related to anxiety. *Journal of Experimental Psychology*, 1951, **42**, 94–99.

Hoffman, P. J. Cue-consistency and configurality in human judgment. In B. Kleinmuntz (Ed.), *Formal representation of human judgment*. New York: Wiley, 1968.

Hoffman, P. J., Slovic, P., & Rorer, L. G. An analysis-of-variance model for the assessment of configural cue utilization in clinical judgment. *Psychological Bulletin*, 1968, **69**, 338–349.

Holmes, D. S. Dimensions of projection. *Psychological Bulletin*, 1968, **69**, 248–268.

Holt, R. R. Clinical and statistical prediction: A reformulation and some new data. *Journal of Abnormal and Social Psychology*, 1958, **56**, 1–12.

Holt, R. R., and Luborsky, L. *Personality patterns of psychiatrists*. Vol. 1. New York: Basic Books, 1958.

Holt, R. R., and Luborsky, L. *Personality patterns of psychiatrists: Supplementary and supporting data*. Vol. II. Topeka, Kansas: The Menninger Foundation, 1958.

Honzik, Marjorie P. Developmental studies of parent-child resemblance in intelligence. *Child Development*, 1957, **28**, 215–228.

Horn, L. J., & Cattell, R. B. Refinement and test of the theory of fluid and crystallized general intelligence. *Journal of Educational Psychology*, 1966, **57**, 253–270.

Howes, D. H., & Solomon, R. L. A Note on McGinnes' "Emotionality and Perceptual Defense." *Psychological Review*, 1950, **57**, 229–240.

Hull, C. L. *Principles of behavior*. New York: Appleton-Century-Crofts, 1943.

Hundleby, J. D., Pawlik, K., & Cattell, R. B. *Personality factors in objective test devices: A critical integration of a quarter of a century's research*. San Diego, California: Robert R. Knapp, 1965.

Jacobson, E. *Progressive relaxation*. Chicago, Illinois: University of Chicago Press, 1938.

Jackson, D. N., & Messick, S. J. Acquiescence and desirability as response determinants on the MMPI. *Educational and Psychological Measurement*, 1961, **21**, 771–790.

James, W. *Pragmatism*. New York: Longmans, Green, 1907.

Janis, I., Mahl, G., Kagan, J., & Holt, R. R. *Personality: Dynamics, development, and assessment*. New York: Harcourt, Brace, Jovanovich, 1969.

Jessor, R., Young, H. B., Young, Elizabeth B., & Tesi, G. Perceived opportunity, alienation, and drinking behavior among Italian and American youth. *Journal of Personality and Social Psychology*, 1970, **15**, 215–222.

Jung, C. *Psychological types*. New York: Harcourt, Brace, and Jovanovich, 1923.

Kagan, J., & Kagan, N. Individual variation in cognitive processes. In P. H. Mussen (Ed.), *Carmichael's Manual of child psychology*. New York: Wiley, 1970.

Kaij, L. *Alcoholism in twins*. Stockholm: Almquist and Widsell, 1960.

Kallmann, F. J. Comparative twin studies in the genetic aspects of male homosexuality. *Journal of Nervous and Mental Disease*, 1952, **115**, 283–298.

Kallmann, F. J. Genetic principles in manic-depressive psychosis. In P. H. Hoch and J. Zubin (Eds.), *Depression*. New York: Grune and Stratton, 1954.

Kallmann, F. J., Deporte, J., Deporte, E., & Feingold, L. Suicide in twins and only children. *American Journal of Human Genetics*, 1949, **1**, 113–126.

Kamin, L. J., & Fedorchak, Olga. The Taylor scale, hunger and verbal learning. *Canadian Journal of Psychology*, 1957, **11**, 212–218.

Karp, S. A. Field dependence and overcoming embeddedness. *Journal of Consulting Psychology*, 1963, **27**, 294–302.

Katahn, M., & Koplin, J. H. Paradigm clash: Comment on "Some recent criticisms of behaviorism and learning theory with special reference to Breger and McGaugh and to Chomsky." *Psychological Bulletin*, 1968, **69**, 147–148.

Katz, D., & Allport, F. *Students' attitudes*. Syracuse, New York: Craftsman Press, 1931.

Kausler, D. H., & Trapp, E. P. Methodological considerations in the construct validation of drive-oriented scales. *Psychological Bulletin*, 1959, **56**, 152–157.

Kelly, G. A. *The psychology of personal constructs*. New York: Norton, 1955.

Kiesler, D. J. Some myths of psychotherapy research and the search for a paradigm. *Psychological Bulletin*, 1966, **65**, 110–136.

Kimble, G. A. *Hilgard and Marquis' Conditioning and learning. Second Edition*. New York: Appleton-Century-Crofts, 1961.

Kinsey, A. G., Pomeroy, W. B., & Martin, C. E. *Sexual behavior in the human male*. Philadelphia, Pennsylvania: Saunders, 1948.

Klein, G. S. Need and regulation. In M. R. Jones (Ed.), *Nebraska symposium on motivation*. Lincoln, Nebraska: University of Nebraska Press, 1954.

Klein, G. S. Cognitive control and motivation. In G. Lindzey (Ed.), *Assessment of human motives*. New York: Holt, Rinehart, and Winston, 1958.

Kleinmuntz, B. MMPI decision rules for the identification of college maladjustment. A digital computer approach. *Psychological Monographs*, 1963, **77** (Whole No. 577).

Kleinmuntz, B. Sign and seer: Another example. *Journal of Abnormal Psychology*, 1967, **72**, 163–165.

Kleinmuntz, B. The processing of information by man and machine. In B. Kleinmuntz (Ed.), *Formal representation of Human Judgment*. New York: Wiley, 1968.

Kogan, N., & Wallach, M. A. *Risk taking: A study in personality and cognition*. New York: Holt, Rinehart, and Winston, 1964.

Kolb, D. A. Achievement motivation training for underachieving high school boys. *Journal of Personality and Social Psychology*, 1965, **2**, 763–792.

Kranz, H. *Lebensschicksale Kriminellen Zwillinge*. Berlin: Springer, 1936.

Kris, E. Psychoanalysis and the study of creative imagination. *Bulletin of the New York Academy of Medicine*, 1953, **29**, 354–351.

Kuhn, T. S. *The structure of scientific revolutions*. Chicago, Illinois: Chicago University Press, 1962.

Lang, P. J., Lazovik, A. D., & Reynolds, D. J. Desensitization, suggestibility, and pseudotherapy. *Journal of Abnormal Psychology*, 1965, **70**, 395–402.

Lazarus, A. A. Group therapy of phobic disorder by systematic desensitization. *Journal of Abnormal and Social Psychology*, 1961, **63**, 504–510.

Lazarus, A. A. A preliminary report on the use of directed muscular activity in counterconditioning. *Behaviour Research and Therapy*, 1965, **2**, 301–303.

Lazarus, R. S. A substitutive defensive conception of apperceptive fantasy. In J. Kagan and G. Lesser (Eds.), *Contemporary issues in thematic apperceptive methods*. Springfield, Illinois: Thomas, 1961.

Lazarus, R. S., & McCleary, R. A. Autonomic discrimination without awareness: A study of subception. *Psychological Review*, 1951, **58**, 113–122.

Lewin, K. *A dynamic theory of personality*. New York: McGraw-Hill, 1935.

Lewin, K. *Field theory in social science*. New York: Harper and Row, 1951.

Lewin, K., Dembo, Tamara, Festinger, L., & Sears, Pauline S. Level of aspiration. In J. McV. Hunt (Ed.), *Personality and the behavior disorders*. New York: Ronald, 1944.

Lewinsohn, P. M., Nichols, R. C., Pulos, L., Lamont, J. F., Nickel, H. J., & Siskind, G. The reliability and validity of quantified judgments from psychological tests. *Journal of Clinical Psychology*, 1963, **19**, 64–73.

Lindzey, G. Seer versus sign: The first good example. *Journal of Experimental Research in Personality*, 1965, **1**, 27–32.

Littig, L. W., & Yeracaris, C. A. Achievement motivation and intergenerational occupational mobility. *Journal of Personality and Social Psychology*, 1965, **1**, 386–389.

Loeb, M., Hawkes, G. R., Evans, W. O., & Alluisi, E. A. The influence of d-amphetamine, benectyzine, and chlorpromazine on performance in an auditory vigilance task. *Psychonomic Science*, 1965, **3**, 29–30.

Lovaas, O. I. The relationship of anxiety level and shock on a paired-associate verbal task. *Journal of Experimental Psychology*, 1960, **59**, 145–152.

Lovibond, S. H. *Conditioning and enuresis*. Oxford: Pergamon Press, 1964.

Lowell, E. L. A methodological study of projectively measured achievement, motivation. Unpublished master's thesis. Wesleyan University, 1950.

Lowell, E. L. The effect of need for achievement on learning and speed of performance. *Journal of Psychology*, 1952, **33**, 31–40.

Lystad, Mary. Social mobility among selected groups of schizophrenic patients. *American Sociological Review*, 1957, **22**, 288–292.

McArthur, C. C. Clinical versus actuarial prediction. In Anne Anastasi (Ed.), *Testing problems in perspective*. Washington, D. C.: American Council on Education, 1966.

McClelland, D. C. Risk taking in children with high and low need for achievement. In J. W. Atkinson (Ed.), *Motives in fantasy, action, and society*. Princeton, New Jersey: Van Nostrand–Reinhold, 1958.

McClelland, D. C. *The achieving society*. Princeton, New Jersey: Van Nostrand–Reinhold, 1961.

McClelland, D. C. Toward a theory of motive acquisition. *American Psychologist*, 1965, **20**, 321–333.

McClelland, D. C., Atkinson, J. W., Clark, R. W., & Lowell, E. L. *The achievement motive*. New York: Appleton-Century-Crofts, 1953.

McClelland, D. C., & Winter, D. G. *Motivating economic achievement*. New York: The Free Press, 1969.

Maccoby, Eleanor E. Sex differences in intellectual functioning. In Eleanor E. Maccoby (Ed.), *The development of sex differences*. Stanford, California: Stanford University Press, 1966.

McGinnes, E. Emotionality and perceptual defense. *Psychological Review*, 1949, **56**, 244–251.

McGuire, R. J., Mowbray, R. M., & Vallance, R. C. The Maudsley Personality Inventory used with psychiatric inpatients. *British Journal of Psychology*, 1963, **54**, 157–166.

Machover, Karen. *Personality projection in the drawing of the human figure*. Springfield, Illinois: Thomas, 1949.

MacKinnon, D. W. The personality correlates of creativity: A study of American architects. In C. S. Nielsen (Ed.), *Proceedings of the XIV International Congress of Applied Psychology*. Copenhagen: Munksgaard, 1962.

MacKinnon, D. W. Creativity of architects. In C. W. Taylor (Ed.), *Widening horizons in creativity*. New York: Wiley, 1964.

Mackworth, H. N. Researches on the measurement of human performance. In H. W. Sinaiko (Ed.), *Selected papers on human factors in the design and use of control systems.* New York: Dover, 1961.

Mackworth, Jane F. The effect of amphetamine on the detectability of signals in a vigilance task. *Canadian Journal of Psychology,* 1965, **19,** 104–110.

Mackworth, Jane F. Vigilance, arousal, and habituation. *Psychological Review,* 1968, **75,** 308–322.

Magoun, H. *The waking brain.* Springfield, Illinois: Thomas, 1963.

Mahone, C. H. Fear of failure and unrealistic vocational aspiration. *Journal of Abnormal and Social Psychology,* 1960, **60,** 253–261.

Malmo, R. B. Activation: A neurophysiological dimension. *Psychological Review,* 1959, **66,** 367–386.

Mandler, G., & Sarason, S. B. A study of anxiety and learning. *Journal of Abnormal and Social Psychology,* 1952, **47,** 166–173.

Marks, I. M., & Gelder, M. G. Transvestism and fetishism: Clinical and psychological changes during faradic aversion. *British Journal of Psychiatry,* 1967, **163,** 711–729.

Marks, P. A. An assessment of the diagnostic process in a child guidance setting. *Psychological Monographs,* 1961, **75** (Whloe No. 507).

Marks, P. A., & Seeman, W. *The actuarial description of abnormal personality.* Baltimore, Maryland. Williams and Wilkins, 1963.

Massimo, J. L., & Shore, M. F. The effectiveness of a comprehensive vocationally oriented psychotherapeutic program for adolescent delinquent boys. *American Journal of Orthopsychiatry,* 1963, **33,** 634–642.

Mednick, Martha T. Mediated generalization and the incubation effect as a function of manifest anxiety. *Journal of Abnormal and Social Psychology,* 1957, **55,** 315–321.

Mednick, Martha T., Mednick, S. A., & Jung, C. C. Continual association as a function of level of creativity and type of verbal stimulus. *Journal of Abnormal and Social Psychology,* 1964, **69,** 511–515.

Mednick, S. A. The associative basis of the creative process. *Psychological Review,* 1962, **69,** 220–232.

Mednick, S. A., & McNeil, T. F. Current methodology in research on the etiology of schizophrenia: serious difficulties which suggest the high-risk-method. *Psychological Bulletin,* 1968, **70,** 681–693.

Meehl, P. E. *Clinical vs. statistical prediction.* Minneapolis, Minnesota: University of Minnesota Press, 1954.

Meehl, P. E. Psychotherapy. *Annual Review of Psychology,* 1955, **6,** 357–378.

Meehl, P. E. Wanted—a good cookbook. *American Psychologist,* 1956, **11,** 263–272.

Meehl, P. E. A comparison of clinician's with five statistical methods of identifying MMPI profiles. *Journal of Counseling Psychology,* 1959, **6,** 107–109.

Meehl, P. E. Seer over sign: The first good example. *Journal of Experimental Research in Personality,* 1965, **1,** 27–37.

Meehl, P. E. Some ruminations on the validation of clinical procedures. In E. I. Megargee (Ed.), *Research in clinical assessment.* New York: Harper and Row, 1966.

Meehl, P. E., & Dahlstrom, W. G. Objective configural rules for discriminating psychotic from neurotic MMPI profiles. *Journal of Counseling Psychology,* 1959. **6.** 102–109.

Meltzoff, J., & Kornreich, M. *Research in psychotherapy.* New York: Atherton Press, 1970.

Miller, J. G. *Unconsciousness.* New York: Wiley, 1942.

Miller, N. E. Experimental studies of conflict. In J. McV. Hunt (Ed.), *Personality and the behavior disorders*. New York: Ronald, 1944.

Miller, N. E. Studies of fear as an acquirable drive: I. Fear as motivation and fear-reduction as reinforcement in the learning of new responses. *Journal of Experimental Psychology*, 1948, **38**, 87–101. (a)

Miller, N. E. Theory and experiment relating psychoanalytic displacement to stimulus-response generalization. *Journal of Abnormal and Social Psychology*, 1948, **43**, 155–178. (b)

Miller, N. E., & Bugelski, R. Minor studies of aggression, 2: The influence of frustrations imposed by the in-group on attitudes expressed towards out-groups. *Journal of Psychology*, 1948, **25**, 437–442.

Miller, N. E., & Dollard, J. *Social learning and imitation*. New Haven, Connecticut: Yale University Press, 1941.

Minard, J. G. Response-bias interpretation of "perceptual defense." A selective review and an evaluation of recent research. *Psychological Review*, 1965, **72**, 74–88.

Minard, J. G., & Mooney, W. Psychological differentiation and perceptual defence: Studies of the separation of perception from emotion. *Journal of Abnormal Psychology*, 1969, **74**, 131–139.

Mischel, W. Predicting the success of peace corps volunteers in Nigeria. *Journal of Personality and Social Psychology*, 1965, **1**, 510–517.

Mischel, W. *Personality and assessment*. New York: Wiley, 1968.

Moore, N. Behaviour therapy in bronchial asthma: a controlled study. *Journal of Psychosomatic Research*, 1965, **9**, 257–276.

Moulton, R. W. Effects of success and failure on level of aspiration as related to achievement motives. *Journal of Personality and Social Psychology*, 1965, **1**, 399–406.

Mowrer, O. H. *Learning theory and personality dynamics*. New York: Ronald, 1950.

Mowrer, O. H., & Mowrer, W. A. Enuresis: A method for its study and treatment. *American Journal of Orthopsychiatry*, 1938, **8**, 436–447.

Murray, H. A. The effect of fear upon estimates of the maliciousness of other personalities. *Journal of Social Psychology*, 1933, **4**, 310–339.

Murray, H. A. Techniques for a systematic investigation of fantasy. *Journal of Psychology*, 1936, **3**, 115–143.

Nawas, N. M., Welsch, W. V., & Fishman, S. T. The comparative effectiveness of pairing aversive imagery with relaxation, neutral tasks and muscular tension in reducing snake phobia. *Behaviour Research and Therapy*, 1970, **6**, 63–68.

O'Connor, J. P., Lorr, M., & Stafford, J. W. Some patterns of manifest anxiety. *Journal of Clinical Psychology*, 1956, **12**, 160–163.

O'Conner, Patricia, Atkinson, J. W., & Horner, Matina. Motivational implications of ability grouping in the schools. In J. W. Atkinson and N. T. Feather (Eds.), *A theory of achievement motivation*. New York: Wiley, 1966.

Ominsky, M., & Kimble, F. A. Anxiety and eyelid conditioning. *Journal of Experimental Psychology*, 1966, **71**, 471–472.

Orne, M. T. The nature of hypnosis: Artifact and essence. *Journal of Abnormal and Social Psychology*, 1959, **58**, 277–299.

Orne, M. T., & Evans, F. J. Social control in the psychological experiment: Antisocial behavior and hypnosis. *Journal of personality and social psychology*, 1965, **1**, 189–200.

Orne, M. T., Sheehan, P. W., & Evans, F. J. Occurrence of posthypnotic behavior outside the experimental setting. *Journal of personality and social psychology*, 1968, **9**, 189–196.

Parsons, T. The school class as a social system—some of its functions in American society. *Howard Educational Review*, 1959, **29**, 297–316.

Passey, G. E. The influence of intensity of unconditioned stimulus upon acquisition of a conditioned response. *Journal of Experimental Psychology*, 1948, **38**, 420–428.

Paul, G. L. *Insight vs. desensitization in psychotherapy: An experiment in anxiety reduction.* Stanford, California: Stanford University Press, 1966.

Paul, G. L. Insight vs. desensitization in psychotherapy two years after termination. *Journal of Consulting Psychology*, 1967, **31**, 333–348.

Paul, G. L. Two-year follow-up of systematic desensitization in therapy groups. *Journal of Abnormal Psychology*, 1968, **73**, 119–130.

Paul, G. L., & Shannon, D. T. Treatment of anxiety through systematic desensitization in therapy groups. *Journal of Abnormal Psychology*, 1966, **71**, 124–135.

Pavlov, I. P. *Conditioned reflexes.* London: Oxford University Press, 1927.

Persons, R. W. Psychological and behavioral change in delinquents following psychotherapy. *Journal of Clinical Psychology*, 1966, **22**, 337–340.

Persons, R. W. Relationship between psychotherapy with institutionalized boys and subsequent community development. *Journal of Consulting Psychology*, 1967, **31**, 137–141.

Peterson, D. R. Scope and generality of verbally defined personality factors. *Psychological Review*, 1965, **72**, 48–59.

Piaget, J. *The moral judgment of the child.* New York: Free Press, 1948.

Podell, J. E., & Phillips, L. A developmental analysis of cognition as observed in dimensions of Rorschach and objective test performance. *Journal of Personality*, 1959, **27**, 439–463.

Powers, E., & Witmer, H. *An experiment in the prevention of delinquency.* New York: Columbia University Press, 1951.

Price, B. Primary biases in twin studies. *American Journal of Human Genetics*, 1950, **2**, 293–352.

Rachman, S. The role of muscular relaxation in desensitization therapy. *Behaviour Research and Therapy*, 1968, **6**, 159–166.

Rapoport, D. The structure of psychoanalytic theory: A systematizing attempt. In S. Koch (Ed.), *Psychology: A study of a science.* Vol. 3. New York: McGraw-Hill, 1959.

Raphelson, A. C. The relationships among imaginative, direct verbal, and physiological measures of anxiety in an achievement situation. *Journal of Abnormal and Social Psychology*, 1957, **54**, 13–18.

Razran, G. The observable unconscious and the inferable conscious in current Soviet psychophysiology: Introceptive conditioning, semantic conditioning, and the orienting reflex. *Psychological Review*, 1961, **68**, 81–147.

Ritter, Brunhilde. The group desensitization of children's snake phobias using vicarious and contact desensitization procedures. *Behaviour Research and Therapy*, 1968, **6**, 1–6.

Ritter, Brunhilde. The use of contact desensitization, demonstration-plus-participation and demonstration-alone in the treatment of acrophobia. *Behaviour Research and Therapy*, 1969, **7**, 157–164.

Roe, Anne. Children of alcoholic parentage raised in foster homes. In *Alcohol, science, and society.* Quarterly *Journal of Studies on Alcohol*, 1945.

Roe, Anne. A psychological study of eminent biologists. *Psychological Monographs*, 1951, **64** (Whole No. 331). (a)

Roe, Anne. A psychological study of eminent physical scientists. *Genetic Psychology Monographs*, 1951, **43**, 121–239. (b)

Roe, Anne. A psychological study of eminent psychologists and anthropologists, and a comparison with biological and physical scientists. *Psychological Monographs General and Applied*, 1953, **67** (Whole No. 352).

Rogers, C. R. Changes in the maturity of behavior as related to therapy. In C. R. Rogers & Rosaline F. Dymond (Eds.), *Psychotherapy and personality change*. Chicago, Illinois: The University of Chicago Press, 1954.

Rogers, C. R., & Dymond, Rosalind F. *Psychotherapy and personality change*. Chicago, Illinois: The University of Chicago Press, 1954.

Rokeach, M. *The open and closed mind. Investigations into the nature of belief systems and personality systems*. New York: Basic Books, 1960.

Rorer, L. G. The great response-style myth. *Psychological Bulletin*, 1965, **63**, 129–156.

Rosenthal, D. *Genetic theory and abnormal behavior*. New York: McGraw-Hill, 1970.

Rosenzweig, S. A transvaluation of psychotherapy: A reply to Hans Eysenck. *Journal of Abnormal and Social Psychology*, 1954, **49**, 298–304.

Saltz, E. Manifest anxiety: Have we misread the data? *Psychological Review*, 1970, **77**, 568–573.

Sampson, E. E. The study of ordinal position: Antecedents and outcomes. In B. Maher (Ed.), *Progress in experimental personality research*. Vol. 2. New York: Academic Press, 1965.

Sarbin, T. R. A contribution to the study of actuarial and individual methods of prediction. *American Journal of Sociology*, 1942, **48**, 593–602.

Sarbin, T. R., Taft, R., & Bailey, D. E. *Clinical inference and cognitive theory*. New York: Holt, Rinehart, and Winston, 1960.

Sarnoff, I., & Corwin, S. M. Castration anxiety and the fear of death. *Journal of Personality*, 1959, **27**, 374–385.

Sawyer, J. Measurement and prediction, clinical and statistical. *Psychological Bulletin*, 1966, **66**, 178–200.

Scarr, Sandra. Genetic factors in activity motivation. *Child Development*, 1966, **37**, 663–673.

Scarr, Sandra. Social introversion-extraversion as a heritable response. *Child Development*, 1969, **40**, 823–832.

Schachter, S. *The psychology of affiliation*. London: Tavistock Publications, 1961.

Schachter, S. Birth order, eminence, and higher education. *American Sociological Review*, 1963, **28**, 757–767.

Schachter, S., & Singer, J. E. Cognitive, social and physiological determinants of emotional state. *Psychological Review*, 1962, **69**, 379–399.

Schafer, H. R. Activity level as a constitutional determinant of infantile reaction to deprivation. *Child Development*, 1966, **37**, 595–602.

Schafer, R. Regression in the service of the ego: The relevance of a psychoanalytic concept for personality assessment. In G. Lindzey (Ed.), *Assessment of human motives*. New York: Rinehart, 1958.

Schroder, H. M., Driver, M. J., & Streufert, S. *Human information processing*. New York: Holt, Rinehart and Winston, 1967.

Sears, R. R. Experimental studies of projection: I. Attribution of traits. *Journal of Social Psychology*, 1936, **7**, 151–163.

Shagass, C. Sedation threshold. *Psychosomatic Medicine*, 1956, **18**, 410–419.

Shagass, C., & Jones, A. L. A neurophysiological test for psychiatric diagnosis. Results in 730 patients. *American Journal of Psychiatry*, 1958, **114**, 1002–1009.

Shagass, C., & Kerenyi, A. B. Neurophysiologic studies of personality. *Journal of Nervous and Mental Disease*, 1958, **126**, 141–147.

Shagass, C., & Naiman, J. The sedation threshold, manifest anxiety, and some aspects of eye function. *American Medical Association Archives of Neurology and Psychiatry,* 1955, **74,** 397–406.

Sheehan, P. W., & Orne, M. T. Some comments on the nature of posthypnotic behavior. *Journal of Nervous and Mental Disease,* 1968, **146,** 209–220.

Shields, J. Personality differences and neurotic traits in normal twin school children. A study in psychiatric genetics. *Eugenics Review,* 1954, **45,** 213–246.

Shields, J. *Monozygotic twins brought up apart and brought up together.* London: Oxford University Press, 1962.

Shore, M. F., & Massimo, J. L. Comprehensive vocationally oriented psychotherapy for adolescent delinquent boys: a follow-up study. *American Journal of Orthopsychiatry,* 1966, **36,** 213–217.

Sigal, J. J., Star, K. H., & Franks, C. M. Hysterics and dysthymics as criterion groups in the study of introversion-extraversion. *Journal of Abnormal and Social Psychology,* 1958, **57,** 143–148. (a)

Sigal, J. J., Star, K. H., & Franks, C. M. Hysterics and dysthymics as criterion groups in the measure of introversion-extraversion: A rejoinder to Eysenck's reply. *Journal of Abnormal and Social Psychology,* 1958, **57,** 381–382. (b)

Silverman, L. H. A Q-sort Study of the validity of evaluations made from projective techniques. *Psychological Monographs,* 1959, **73** (Whole No. 477).

Sines, J. O. Actuarial methods in personality assessment. In B. Maher (Ed.), *Progress in experimental personality research.* Vol. 3. New York: Academic Press, 1966.

Sinnott, E. W. *The biology of the spirit.* New York: Viking, 1955.

Slovic, P. Cue-consistency and cue-utilization in judgment. *American Journal of Psychology,* 1966, **79,** 427–434.

Smith, C. P., and Feld, Sheila. How to learn the method of content analysis for *n* Achievement, *n* Affiliation, and *n* Power. In J. W. Atkinson (Ed.), *Motives in fantasy, action, and society.* New York: Van Nostrand–Reinhold, 1958.

Smith, R. T. A comparison of socioenvironmental factors in monozygotic and dyzogotic twins, testing an assumption. In S. G. Vanderberg (Ed.), *Methods and goals in human behavior. Genetics.* New York: Academic Press, 1965.

Sokolov, E. N. *Perception and the conditioned reflex.* Oxford: Pergamon Press, 1963.

Solomon, R. L., & Wynne, L. C. Traumatic avoidance learning: The principles of anxiety conservation and partial irreversibility. *Psychological Review,* 1954, **61,** 353–385.

Spearman, C. *The abilities of man.* London: Macmillan, 1927.

Spence, D. P. Conscious and preconscious influences on recall: Another example of the restricting effects of awareness. *Journal of Abnormal and Social Psychology,* 1966, **3,** 131–132.

Spence, D. P. How restricted are the restricting effects? A reply: *Journal of Personality and Social Psychology,* 1966, **3,** 131–132.

Spence, D. P., & Holland, B. The restricting effects of awareness: A paradox and an explanation. *Journal of Abnormal and Social Psychology,* 1962, **64,** 163–174.

Spence, Janet T., and Spence, K. W. The motivational components of manifest anxiety: Drive and drive stimuli. In C. D. Spielberger (Ed.), *Anxiety and behavior.* New York: Academic Press, 1966.

Spence, Janet T., Underwood, B. J., Duncan, C. P., & Cotton, J. W. *Elementary statistics. 2nd ed.* New York: Appleton-Century-Crofts, 1968.

Spence, K. W. *Behavior theory and conditioning.* New Haven, Connecticut: Yale University Press, 1956.

Spence, K. W. A theory of emotionally based drive (D) and its relation to performance in simple learning situations. *American Psychologist*, 1958, **13**, 131–141.

Spence, K. W. Anxiety (drive) level and performance in eyelid conditioning. *Psychological Bulletin*, 1964, **61**, 124–139.

Spence, K. W., & Spence, Janet T. Relation of eyelid conditioning, manifest anxiety, extraversion, and rigidity. *Journal of Abnormal and Social Psychology*, 1964, **68**, 144–149.

Spence, K. W., Farber, I. E., & McFann, H. H. The relation of anxiety (drive) level to performance on competitional and noncompetitional paired-associates learning. *Journal of Experimental Psychology*, 1956, **52**, 296–305.

Spence, K. W., Taylor, Janet A., & Ketchel, Rhoda. Anxiety (drive) level and degree of competition in paired-associates learning. *Journal of Experimental Psychology*, 1956, **52**, 306–310.

Spielberger, C. D., & De Nike, L. D. Descriptive behaviorism versus cognitive theory in verbal operant conditioning. *Psychological Review*, 1966, **73**, 306–326.

Spielberger, C. D., & Smith, L. H. Anxiety (drive), stress, and serial-position effects in serial-verbal learning. *Journal of Experimental Psychology*, 1966, **72**, 589–595.

Stampfl, T. G., & Levis, D. J. Essentials of implosive theory: A learning theory based psychodynamic behavioral therapy. *Journal of Abnormal Psychology*, 1967, **72**, 496–503.

Standish, R. R., & Champion, R. A. Task difficulty and drive in verbal learning. *Journal of Experimental Psychology*, 1960, **59**, 361–365.

Strong, E. K., Jr. *Vocational interests of men and women*. Stanford, California: Stanford University Press, 1943.

Sweetbaum, H. A. Comparison of the effects of introversion-extraversion and anxiety on conditioning. *Journal of Abnormal and Social Psychology*, 1963, **66**, 249–254.

Swets, J. A., Tanner, W. P., Jr., & Birdsall, T. G. Decision processes in perception. *Psychological Review*, 1961, **68**, 301–340.

Taylor, C. W., & Ellison, R. L. Predicting creative performances from multiple measures. In C. W. Taylor (Ed.), *Widening Horizons in creativity*. New York: Wiley, 1964.

Taylor, Janet A. The relationship of anxiety to the conditioned eyelid response. *Journal of Experimental Psychology*, 1951, **41**, 81–92.

Taylor, Janet A. A personality scale of manifest anxiety. *Journal of Abnormal and Social Psychology*, 1953, **48**, 285–290.

Taylor, Janet A. The effects of anxiety level and psychological stress on verbal learning. *Journal of Abnormal and Social Psychology*, 1958, **57**, 55–60.

Taylor, Janet A., & Chapman, Jean P. Anxiety and the learning of paired associates. *American Journal of Psychology*, 1955, **68**, 671.

Terman, L. (Ed.). *Mental and Physical traits of a thousand gifted children: Genetic studies of genius*. Stanford: Stanford University Press, 1925.

Thomas, A., Chess, Stella, & Birch, H. G. *Temperament and behavior disorders in children*. New York: New York University Press, 1968.

Thomas, A., Chess, Stella, Birch, H. G., Hertzig, M. E., & Korn, S. *Behavioral individuality in early childhood*. New York: New York University Press, 1963.

Tienari, P. On intrapair differences in male twins with special reference to dominance-submissiveness. *Acta Psychiatrica Scandinavica Supplementum*, 1966, **42**, No. 188.

Tolman, E. C. Principles of performance. *Psychological Review*, 1955, **62**, 315–326.

Torrance, E. P. *Guiding creative talent*. Engelwood Cliffs, New Jersey: Prentice-Hall, 1962.

Torrance, E. P. *Torrance tests of creative thinking: Norms—technical manual, research edition.* Princeton, New Jersey: Personnel Press, 1966.

Trouton, D. S., & Maxwell, A. E. The relation between neurosis and psychosis. *Journal of Mental Science,* 1956, **102,** 1–21.

Truax, C. B., Wargo, D. G., & Silber, L. D. Effects of group psychotherapy with high accurate empathy and nonpossessive warmth upon female institutionalized delinquents. *Journal of Abnormal Psychology,* 1966, **71,** 267–274.

Turner, Lucille H., & Solomon, R. L. Human traumatic avoidance learning. Theory and experiments on the operant respondent distinction and failures to learn. *Psychological Monographs,* 1962, **76** (Whole No. 559).

Turner, D. R. Predictive efficiency as a function of amount of information and level of professional experience. *Journal of Projective Techniques and Personality Assessment,* 1966, **30,** 4–11.

Tyler, Leona E. *The psychology of human differences.* 3rd ed. New York: Appleton-Century-Crofts, 1965.

Underwood, B. J., & Schulz, R. W. *Meaningfulness and verbal learning.* Philadelphia, Pennsylvania: Lippincott, 1960.

Volsky, T., Jr., Magoon, T. M., Norman, W. T., & Hoyt, D. P. *The outcomes of counseling and psychotherapy. Theory and research.* Minneapolis, Minnesota: University of Minnesota Press, 1965.

Vandenburg, S. G. The hereditary abilities study. Hereditary components in a psychological test battery. *American Journal of Human Genetics,* 1962, **14,** 220–237.

Waldrop, Mary F., Pedersen, F. A., & Bell, R. Q. Minor physical anomalies and behavior in pre-school children. *Child Development,* 1968, **39,** 391–400.

Wallach, M. A., & Kogan, N. *Modes of thinking in young children.* New York: Holt, Rinehart, and Winston, 1965.

Wallach, M. A., & Wing, C. W., Jr. *The talented student.* New York: Holt, Rinehart, and Winston, 1969.

Weber, M. *The Protestant ethic and the spirit of capitalism.* 1904. (Transl. by T. Parsons) New York: Scribner, 1930.

Weisberg, P. S., & Springer, K. J. Environmental factors in creative function. *Archives of Genetic Psychiatry,* 1961, **5,** 554–564.

Weitzman, B. Behavior therapy and psychotherapy. *Psychological Review,* 1967, **74,** 300–317.

Weller, G. M., & Bell, R. Q. Basal skin conductance and neonatal state. *Child Development,* 1965, **36,** 647–657.

Werner, H. *Comparative psychology of mental development.* Rev. ed. Chicago, Illinois: Follett, 1948.

Whiting, J. W. M., & Child, I. L. *Child training and personality. A cross-cultural study.* New Haven, Connecticut: Yale University Press, 1953.

Wilde, G. J. S. Inheritance of personality traits. An investigation into the hereditary determination of neurotic instability, extraversion, and other personality traits by means of a questionnaire administered to twins. *Acta Psychologica,* 1964, **22,** 37–51.

Willerman, L., & Churchill, J. A. Intelligence and birth weight in identical twins. *Child Development,* 1967, **38,** 623–629.

Winer, B. J. *Statistical principles in experimental design.* New York: McGraw-Hill, 1962.

Winterbottom, Marian R. The relation of need for achievement to learning experiences in independence and mastery. In J. W. Atkinson, (Ed.), *Motives in fantasy, action, and society.* Princeton, New Jersey: Van Nostrand-Reinhold, 1958.

Witkin, H. A., Dyk, Ruth B., Fatterson, Hanna F., Goodenough, D. R., & Karp, S. A. *Psychological differentiation*. New York: Wiley, 1962.

Wolpe, J. *Psychotherapy by reciprocal inhibition*. Stanford: Stanford University Press, 1958.

Wolpe, J. The systematic desensitization and treatment of neuroses. *Journal of Nervous and Mental Disease*, 1961, **132,** 199–203.

Worrell, L., & Worrell, Judith. An experimental and theoretical note on "conscious and preconscious influences on recall." *Journal of Personality and Social Psychology*, 1966, **3,** 119–123.

Yamomoto, K. Effects of restriction of range and test unreliability on correlation between measures of intelligence and creative thinking. *British Journal of Educational Psychology*, 1965, **35,** 300–305.

Yamomoto, K., & Chimbidis, Maria E. Achievement, intelligence, and creative thinking in fifth grade children: A correlational study. *Merrill-Palmer—Quarterly*, 1966, **13,** 233–241.

Yates, A. J. *Behavior therapy*. New York: Wiley, 1970.

Yerkes, R. M., & Dodson, J. D. The relation of strength of stimulus to rapidity of habit formation. *Journal of Comparative and Neurological Psychology*, 1908, **18,** 459–482.

Zigler, E. A measure in search of a theory. *Contemporary Psychology*, 1963, **8,** 133–135. (a)

Zigler, E. Zigler stands firm. *Contemporary Psychology*, 1963, **8,** 459–460. (b)

# AUTHOR INDEX

Numbers in italics refer to the pages on which the complete references are listed.

## A

Ackner, B., 62, *336*
Adorno, T. W., 32, 152, *336*
Allport, F., 275, *345*
Allport, G. W., 7, 13, 14, 146, *336*
Alluisi, E. A., 64, *346*
Alpert, R., 88, *343*
Altus, W. D., 181, *336*
Arbuckle, D. S., 296, *336*
Aronson, E., 101, *336*
Atkins, A. L., 111, *337*
Atkinson, J. W., 86, 88, 94, 98, 100, 101, 103, 106, *336*, *347*, *348*
Ayllon, T., 252, 316, 317, 318, 321, *336*
Azrin, N., 316, 317, 318, 321, *336*

## B

Baer, M., 73, *338*
Bailey, D. E., 210, *350*
Bakan, P., 65, 66, *336*
Baker, B. L., 309, 323, *336*
Bandura, A., 227, 228, 230, 231, 232, 233, 234, 238, 239, 240, 241, 243, 244, 248, 249, 250, 251, 252, 272, 288, 301, 302, 304, 305, 307, 309, 312, 318, 322, 323, 324, 333, 334, *336*, *337*
Barber, T. X., 267, *337*
Barron, F., 144, *337*
Bartholomew, A. A., 47, *337*
Becker, W. C., 20, *337*
Bell, R. Q., 178, 182, 183, 184, *337*, *353*
Belton, J. A., 65, 66, *336*
Berman, Phyliss W., 155, *337*
Bettleheim, B., 242, *337*
Beyers, E., 108, 109, *337*
Bieri, J., 111, 119, *337*, *338*
Bindra, D., 75, *338*
Birch, H. G., 179, *352*
Birdsall, T. G., 280, *352*

## B (continued)

Blanchard, E. A., 250, 251, 307, 323, 324, *337*
Block, J., 34, *338*
Blum, G. S., 258, 268, *338*
Boudreau, D., 62, *338*
Bowers, K., 266, *338*
Boy, A. V., 296, *336*
Bradburn, Wendy M., 119, *338*
Bradley, R. W., 181, *338*
Breger, L., 324, *338*
Briar, S., 111, *337*
Broadbent, D. E., 282, *338*
Brody, N., 103, 104, 254, *338*
Bronfenbrenner, U., 178, *338*
Brown, Anne M., 159, *338*
Brown, W. P., 272, *338*
Bruel, Iris, 277, *338*
Bugelski, R., 237, *348*
Buss, A. H., 73, *338*
Butcher, H. J., 130, *343*
Butler, J. M., 291, *338*

## C

Cahoon, D. D., 322, *338*
Calverley, D. S., 267, *337*
Campbell, D., 234, *338*
Campbell, D. T., 34, 35, 207, 275, *338*, *339*
Cartwright, D. S., 31, 289, *339*
Cassirer, E., 38, 39, *339*
Cattell, Psyche, 179, *339*
Cattell, R. B., 8, 11, 16, 18, 19, 20, 22, 23, 27, 119, 147, *339*, *340*, *344*
Champion, R. A., 80, *352*
Chapman, Jean P., 78, *352*
Chatterjee, B. B., 263, *339*
Chess, Stella, 179, *352*
Child, I. L., 81, 228, *339*, *353*
Chimbidis, Maria E., 144, *354*

# SUBJECT INDEX

## A

Achievement motivation, 86–97
  economic development and, 90–97
  measurement of, 86–88
  occupational mobility and, 89–90
Acquiescence, 32–35
  item reversal studies, 32–33
Aggression, *see* Social learning theory
Alcoholism, *see* Heredity
Approval motive, *see* Social desirability
Aristotelian mode of thought, 38–39
Aspiration, level of *see* Atkinson's theory
  of achievement motivation, risk
  taking model
Atkinson's theory of achievement motivation, 86–109
  risk-taking model, 97–109
Attitudes, tender vs. tough minded, 67–69
Aversive counterconditioning, *see* Behavior therapy

## B

Bandura's theory of personality, *see*
  Social learning theory
Behavior therapy, 250–252, 299–319
  aversive counterconditioning, 309, 312–315
  contrasted with psychotherapy, 252
  enuresis and, 308–310
  modeling, 250–252, 307–308
  operant conditioning treatment of psychotics, 315–319
Birth order, 181–184
Body adjustment test, 113–114

## C

Cattell's theory of personality, 11–39, *see also* Factor analysis, Traits
Clinical and statistical description, 206–215

clinical descriptions validated by therapists judgments, 209–210
  reliability of clinical description, 207–208
  rule of clinical experience, 210–211
  statistical description, 211–215
Clinical and statistical prediction, 196–206
  contrast of process of prediction, 198–199
  computer simulation of clinical prediction, 219–220
  configural vs. linear prediction, 215–219
  definition of, 196–198
  objections to use of statistical predictions, 222–225
  of socially relevant criteria, 199–206
Cognitive styles, 112–152, *see also*
  Creativity, Differentiation
  invariance over situations, 149–152
Conflict and displacement, 236–242, 332–333
Contact desensitization, *see* Behavior therapy, modeling
Correlation, 8–9
  matrix among tests, 9
Creativity, 126–149
  convergent thinking as basis of, 141–145
  divergent thinking as basis of, 126–140
  personality correlates of, 145–149
  Remote Associates Test, 141–144
Criminality, *see* Heredity

## D

Development, Stages in, *see* Social learning theory, continuities and discontinuities in development
Differentiation, 115–126
  intelligence and, 118–126
  personality and, 115–118
Displacement, *see* Conflict and displacement
Divergent thinking, *see* Creativity